Sorcière de gré, pucelle de force

Sorcière de gré, pucelle de force

UNE TABLE DES MATIÈRES

Table of Contents

Chapter 9
The War-Loathing Witch

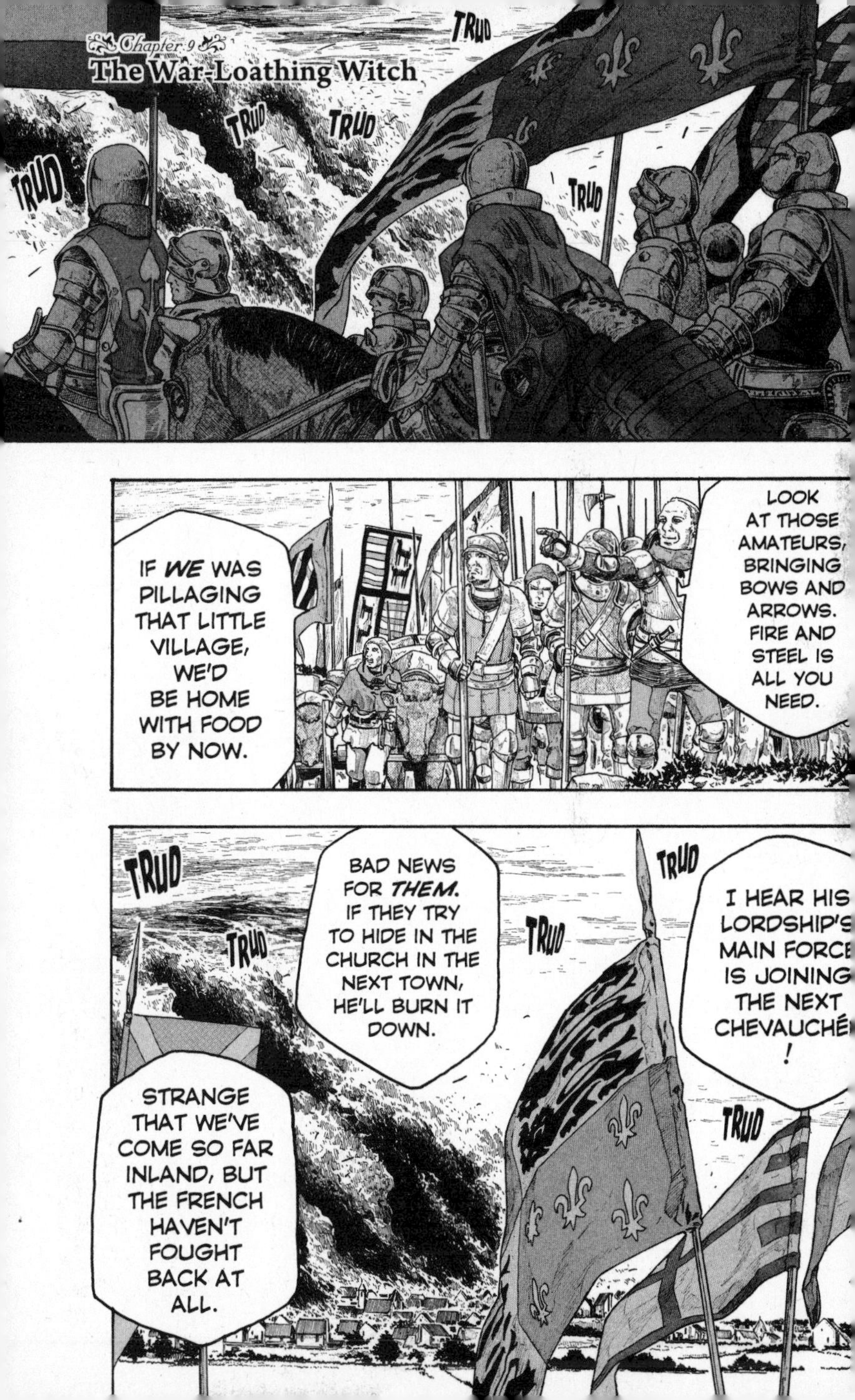
TRUD
TRUD
TRUD
TRUD
TRUD
LOOK AT THOSE AMATEURS, BRINGING BOWS AND ARROWS. FIRE AND STEEL IS ALL YOU NEED.
IF *WE* WAS PILLAGING THAT LITTLE VILLAGE, WE'D BE HOME WITH FOOD BY NOW.
TRUD
I HEAR HIS LORDSHIP'S MAIN FORCE IS JOINING THE NEXT CHEVAUCHÉE!
TRUD
BAD NEWS FOR *THEM*. IF THEY TRY TO HIDE IN THE CHURCH IN THE NEXT TOWN, HE'LL BURN IT DOWN.
TRUD
TRUD
TRUD
STRANGE THAT WE'VE COME SO FAR INLAND, BUT THE FRENCH HAVEN'T FOUGHT BACK AT ALL.

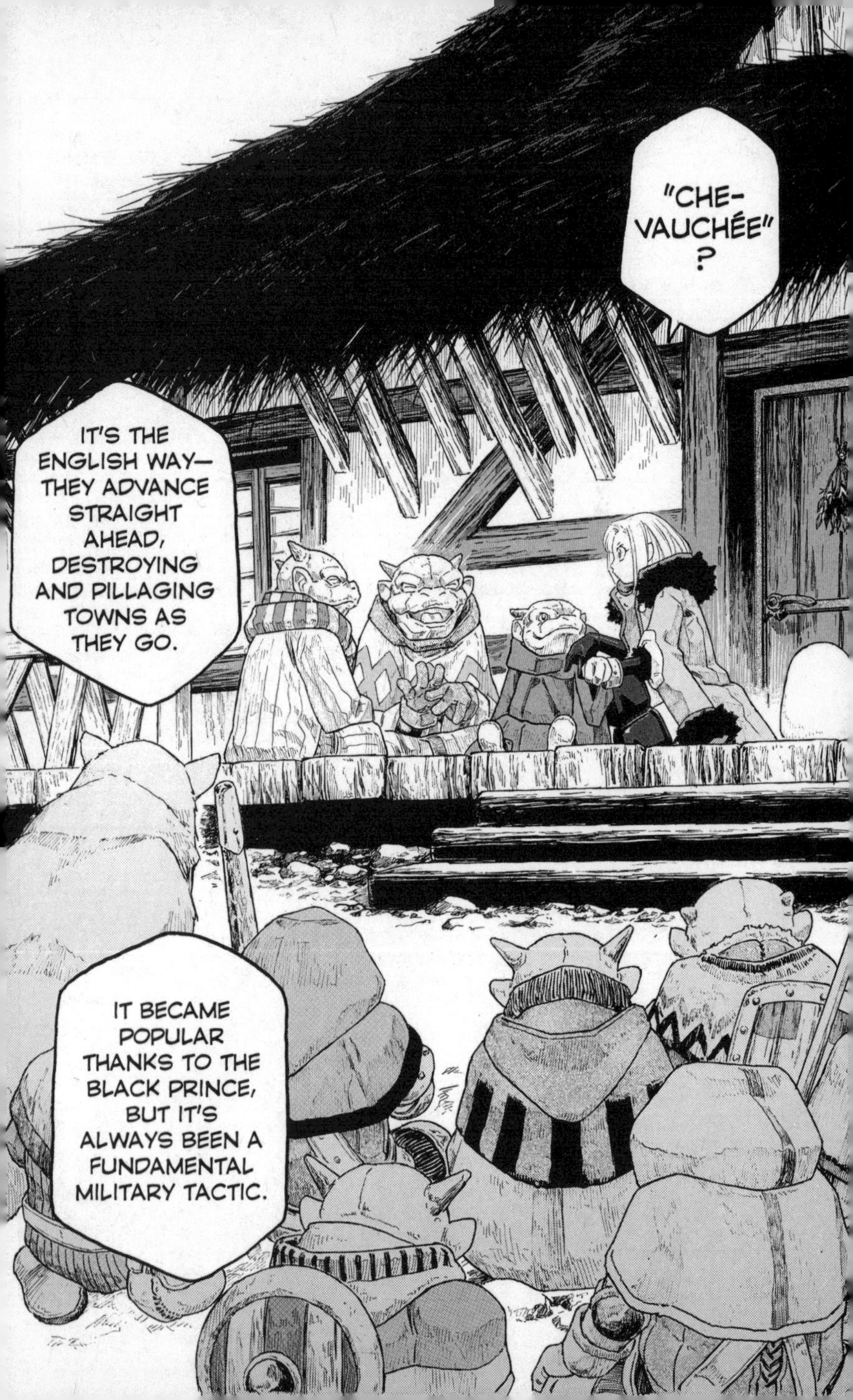
"CHE-VAUCHÉE"?
IT'S THE ENGLISH WAY—THEY ADVANCE STRAIGHT AHEAD, DESTROYING AND PILLAGING TOWNS AS THEY GO.
IT BECAME POPULAR THANKS TO THE BLACK PRINCE, BUT IT'S ALWAYS BEEN A FUNDAMENTAL MILITARY TACTIC.

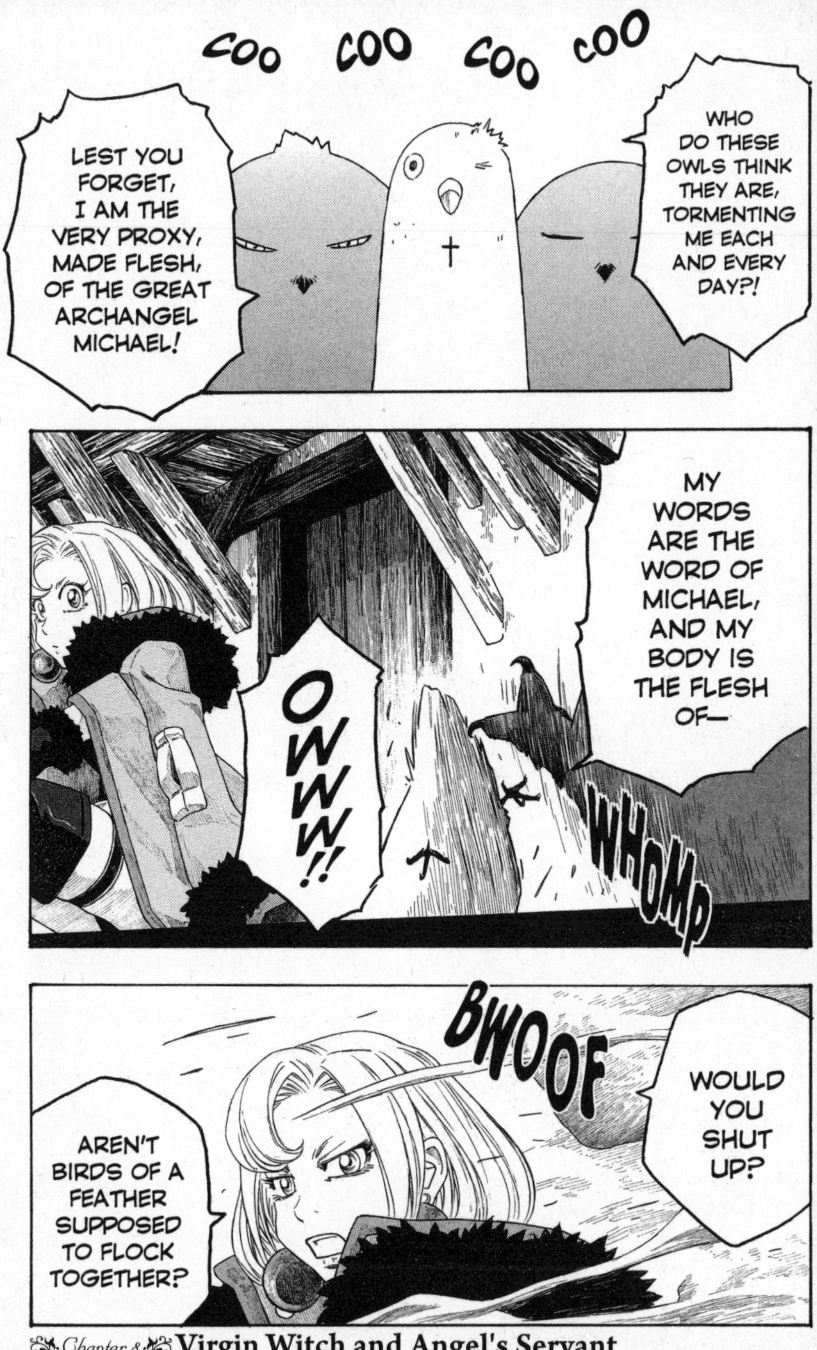
COO COO COO COO
WHO DO THESE OWLS THINK THEY ARE, TORMENTING ME EACH AND EVERY DAY?!
LEST YOU FORGET, I AM THE VERY PROXY, MADE FLESH, OF THE GREAT ARCHANGEL MICHAEL!
MY WORDS ARE THE WORD OF MICHAEL, AND MY BODY IS THE FLESH OF—
WHOMP
OWWW!!
BWOOF
WOULD YOU SHUT UP?
AREN'T BIRDS OF A FEATHER SUPPOSED TO FLOCK TOGETHER?

Chapter 8 Virgin Witch and Angel's Servant

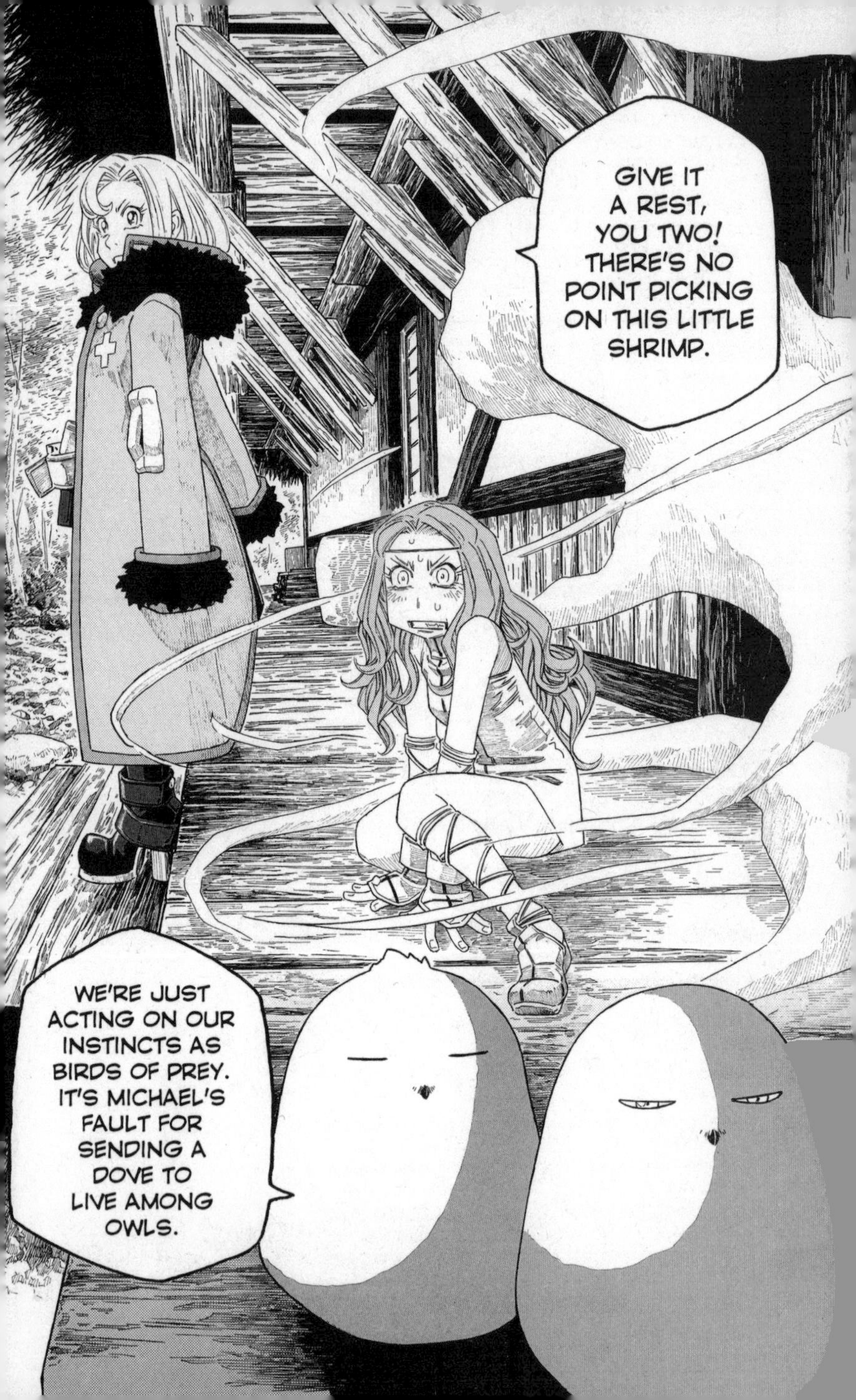
GIVE IT A REST, YOU TWO! THERE'S NO POINT PICKING ON THIS LITTLE SHRIMP.
WE'RE JUST ACTING ON OUR INSTINCTS AS BIRDS OF PREY. IT'S MICHAEL'S FAULT FOR SENDING A DOVE TO LIVE AMONG OWLS.

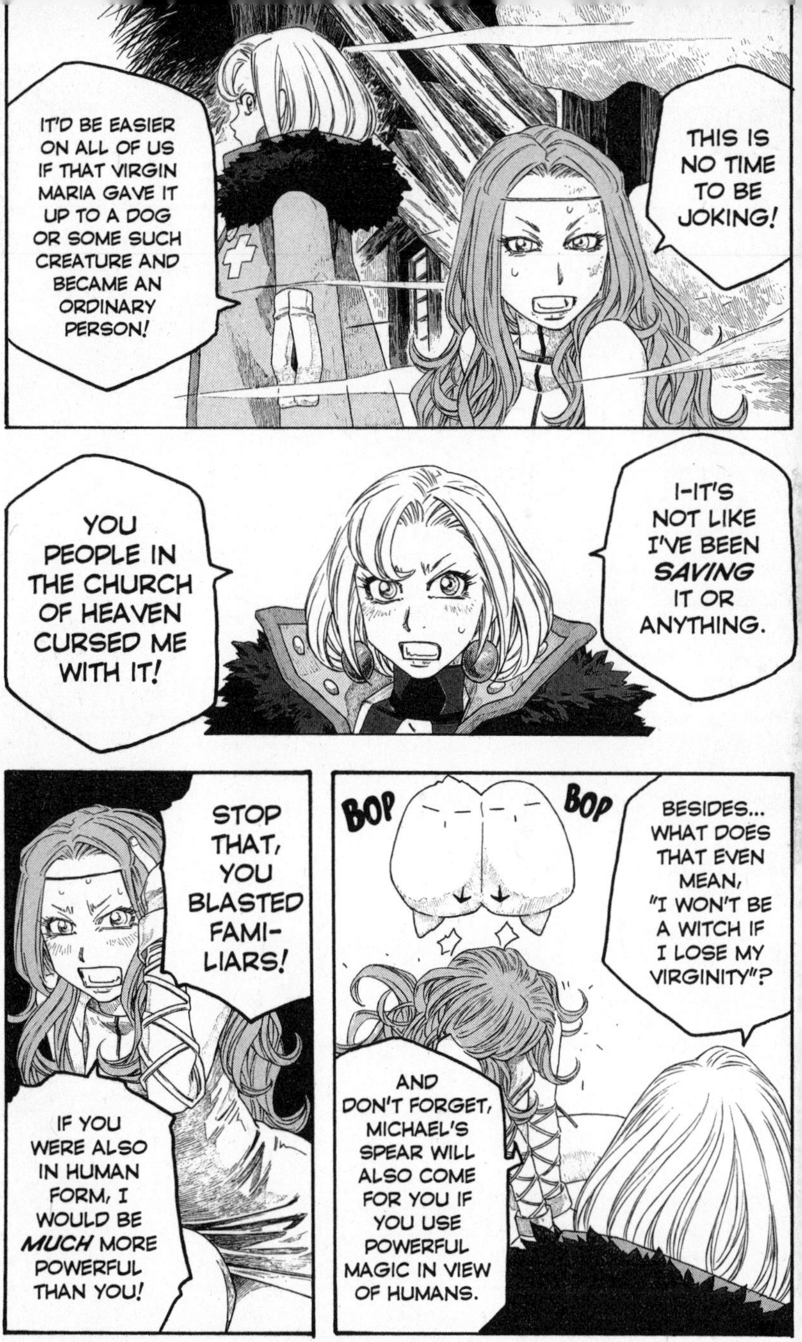
THIS IS NO TIME TO BE JOKING!
IT'D BE EASIER ON ALL OF US IF THAT VIRGIN MARIA GAVE IT UP TO A DOG OR SOME SUCH CREATURE AND BECAME AN ORDINARY PERSON!
I-IT'S NOT LIKE I'VE BEEN *SAVING* IT OR ANYTHING.
YOU PEOPLE IN THE CHURCH OF HEAVEN CURSED ME WITH IT!
BOP BOP
BESIDES... WHAT DOES THAT EVEN MEAN, "I WON'T BE A WITCH IF I LOSE MY VIRGINITY"?
AND DON'T FORGET, MICHAEL'S SPEAR WILL ALSO COME FOR YOU IF YOU USE POWERFUL MAGIC IN VIEW OF HUMANS.
STOP THAT, YOU BLASTED FAMI-LIARS!
IF YOU WERE ALSO IN HUMAN FORM, I WOULD BE *MUCH* MORE POWERFUL THAN YOU!

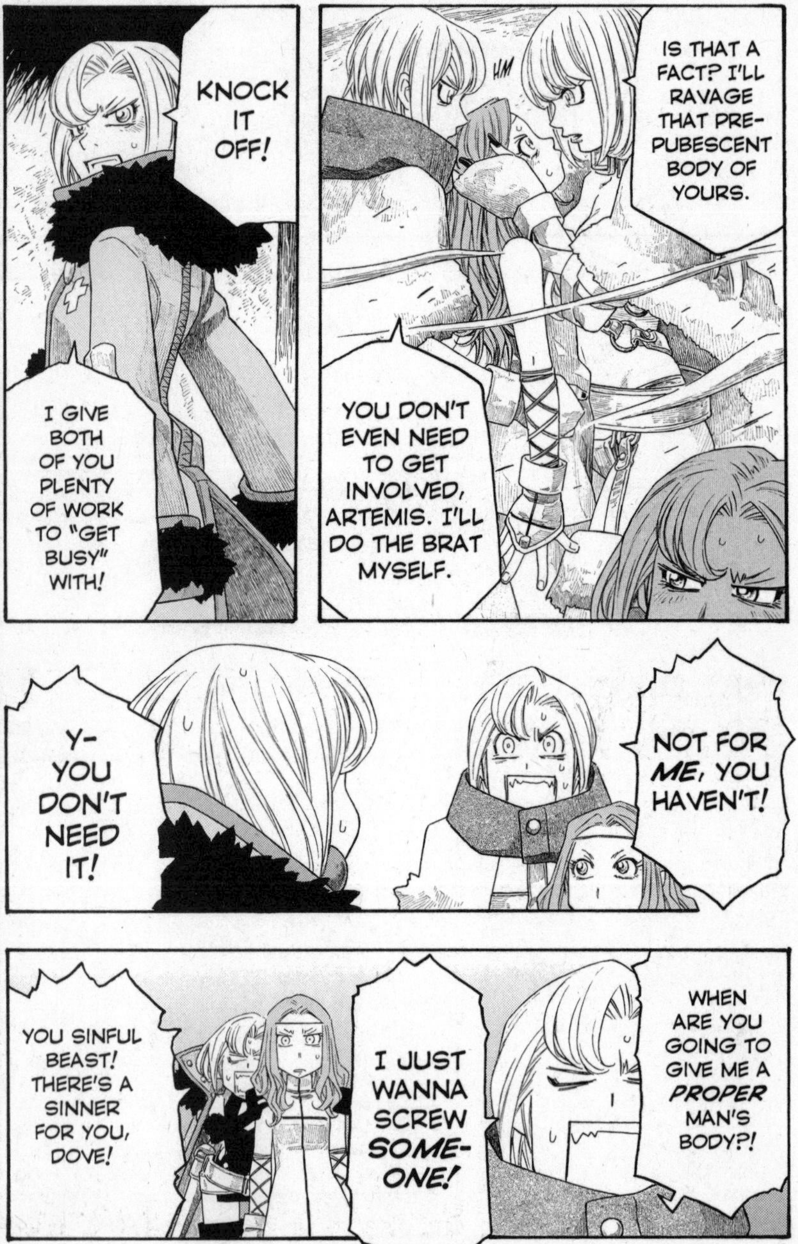
IS THAT A FACT? I'LL RAVAGE THAT PRE-PUBESCENT BODY OF YOURS.
HM
YOU DON'T EVEN NEED TO GET INVOLVED, ARTEMIS. I'LL DO THE BRAT MYSELF.
KNOCK IT OFF!
I GIVE BOTH OF YOU PLENTY OF WORK TO "GET BUSY" WITH!
NOT FOR *ME*, YOU HAVEN'T!
Y-YOU DON'T NEED IT!
WHEN ARE YOU GOING TO GIVE ME A *PROPER* MAN'S BODY?!
I JUST WANNA SCREW *SOMEONE!*
YOU SINFUL BEAST! THERE'S A SINNER FOR YOU, DOVE!

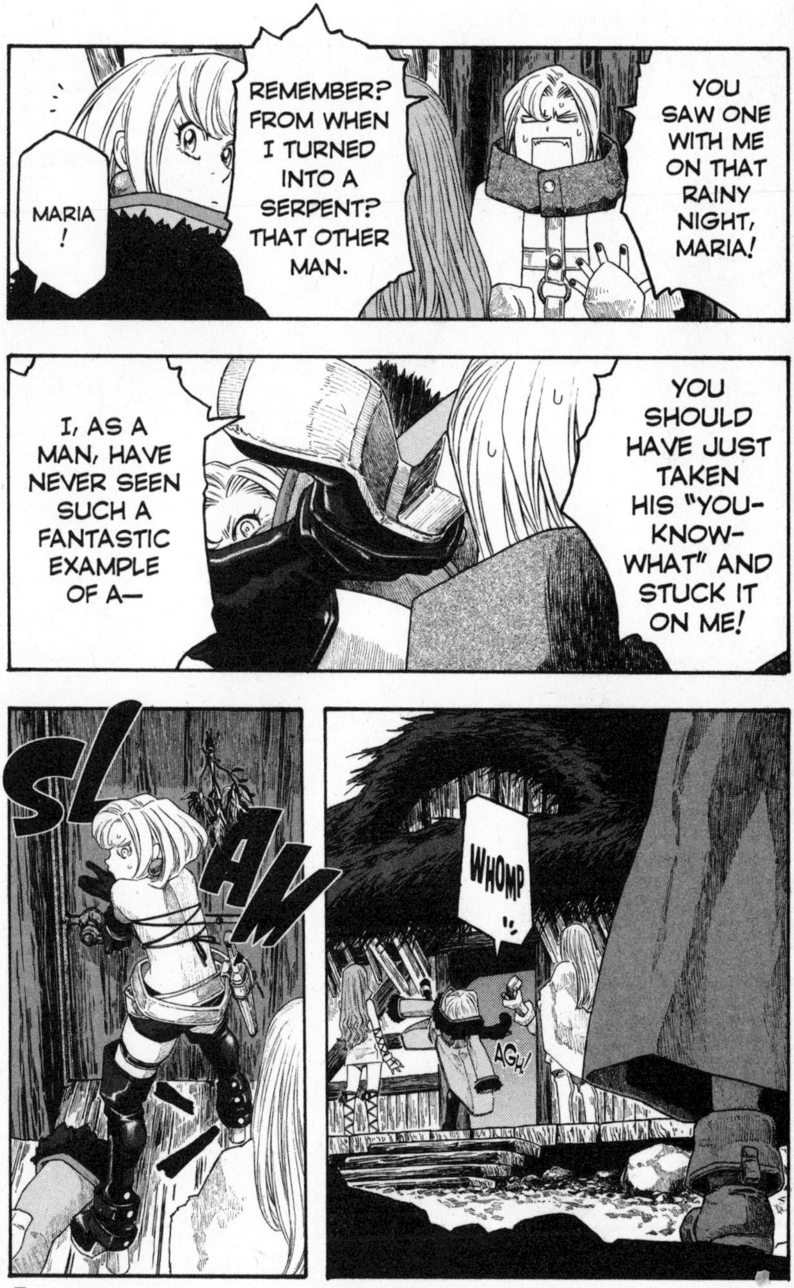
YOU SAW ONE WITH ME ON THAT RAINY NIGHT, MARIA!
REMEMBER? FROM WHEN I TURNED INTO A SERPENT? THAT OTHER MAN.
MARIA!
YOU SHOULD HAVE JUST TAKEN HIS "YOU-KNOW-WHAT" AND STUCK IT ON ME!
I, AS A MAN, HAVE NEVER SEEN SUCH A FANTASTIC EXAMPLE OF A—
WHOMP
AGH!
SLAM

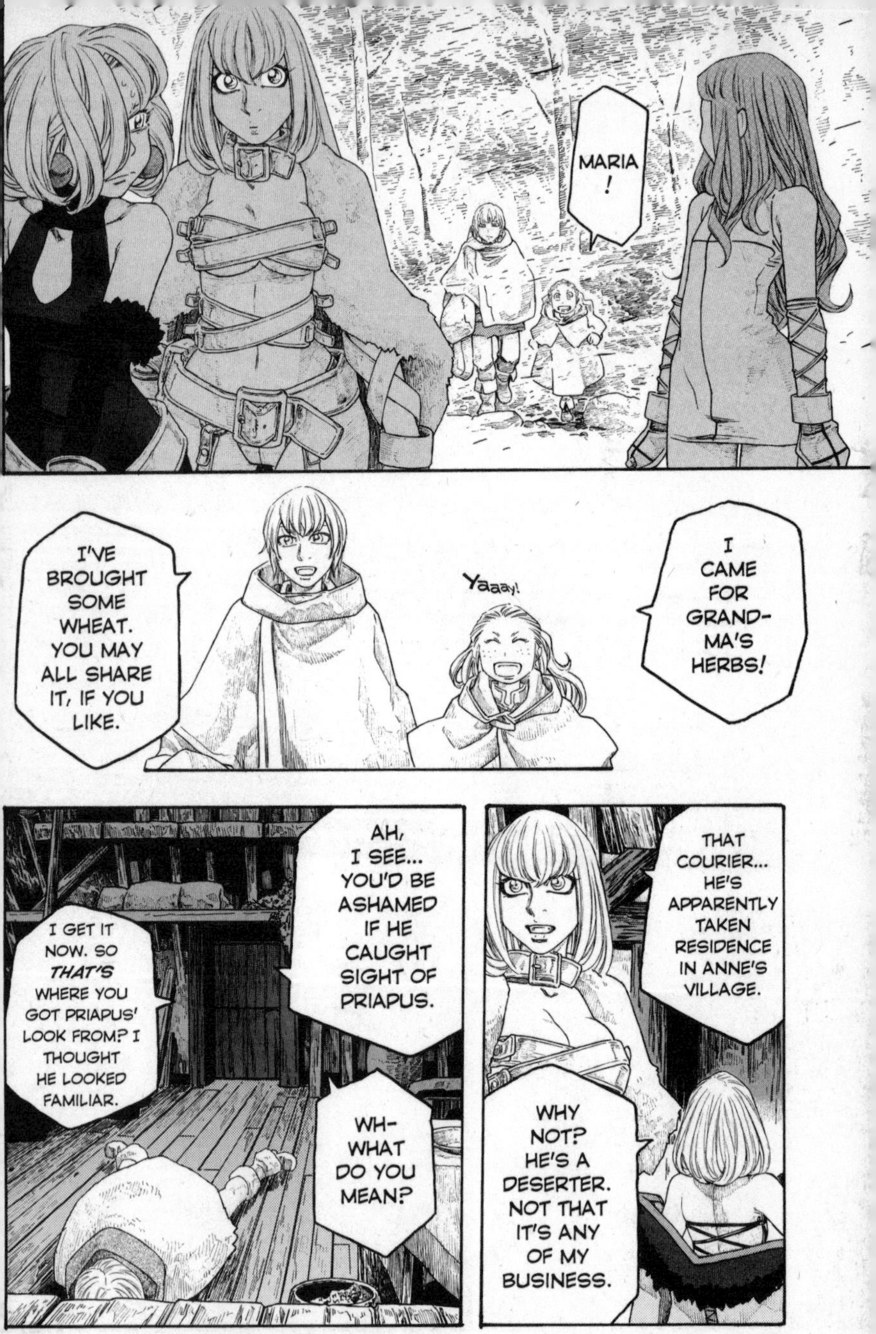
MARIA!
I CAME FOR GRAND-MA'S HERBS!
Yaaay!
I'VE BROUGHT SOME WHEAT. YOU MAY ALL SHARE IT, IF YOU LIKE.
THAT COURIER... HE'S APPARENTLY TAKEN RESIDENCE IN ANNE'S VILLAGE.
WHY NOT? HE'S A DESERTER. NOT THAT IT'S ANY OF MY BUSINESS.
AH, I SEE... YOU'D BE ASHAMED IF HE CAUGHT SIGHT OF PRIAPUS.
WH-WHAT DO YOU MEAN?
I GET IT NOW. SO *THAT'S* WHERE YOU GOT PRIAPUS' LOOK FROM? I THOUGHT HE LOOKED FAMILIAR.

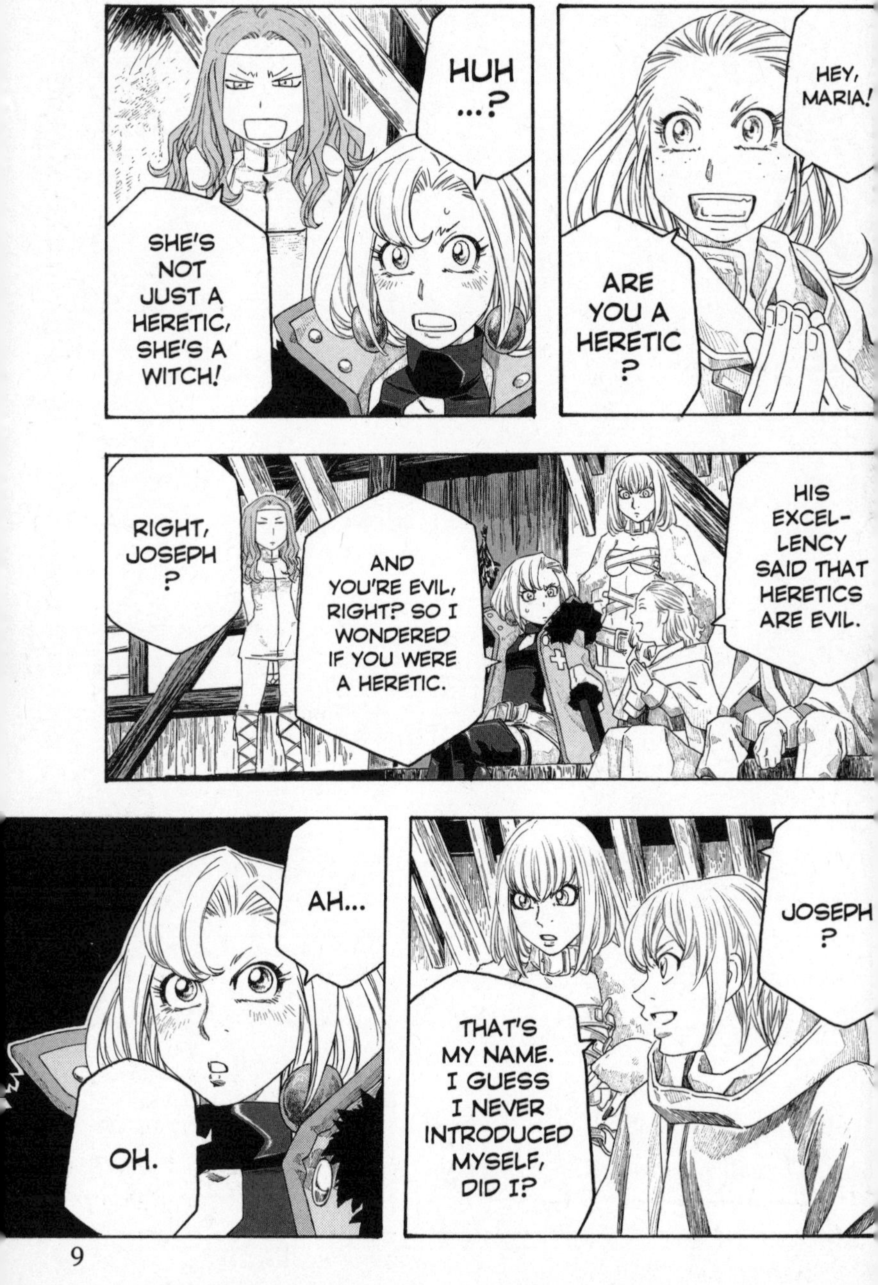
HEY, MARIA!
ARE YOU A HERETIC?
HUH ...?
SHE'S NOT JUST A HERETIC, SHE'S A WITCH!
HIS EXCEL-LENCY SAID THAT HERETICS ARE EVIL.
AND YOU'RE EVIL, RIGHT? SO I WONDERED IF YOU WERE A HERETIC.
RIGHT, JOSEPH?
JOSEPH?
THAT'S MY NAME. I GUESS I NEVER INTRODUCED MYSELF, DID I?
AH...
OH.

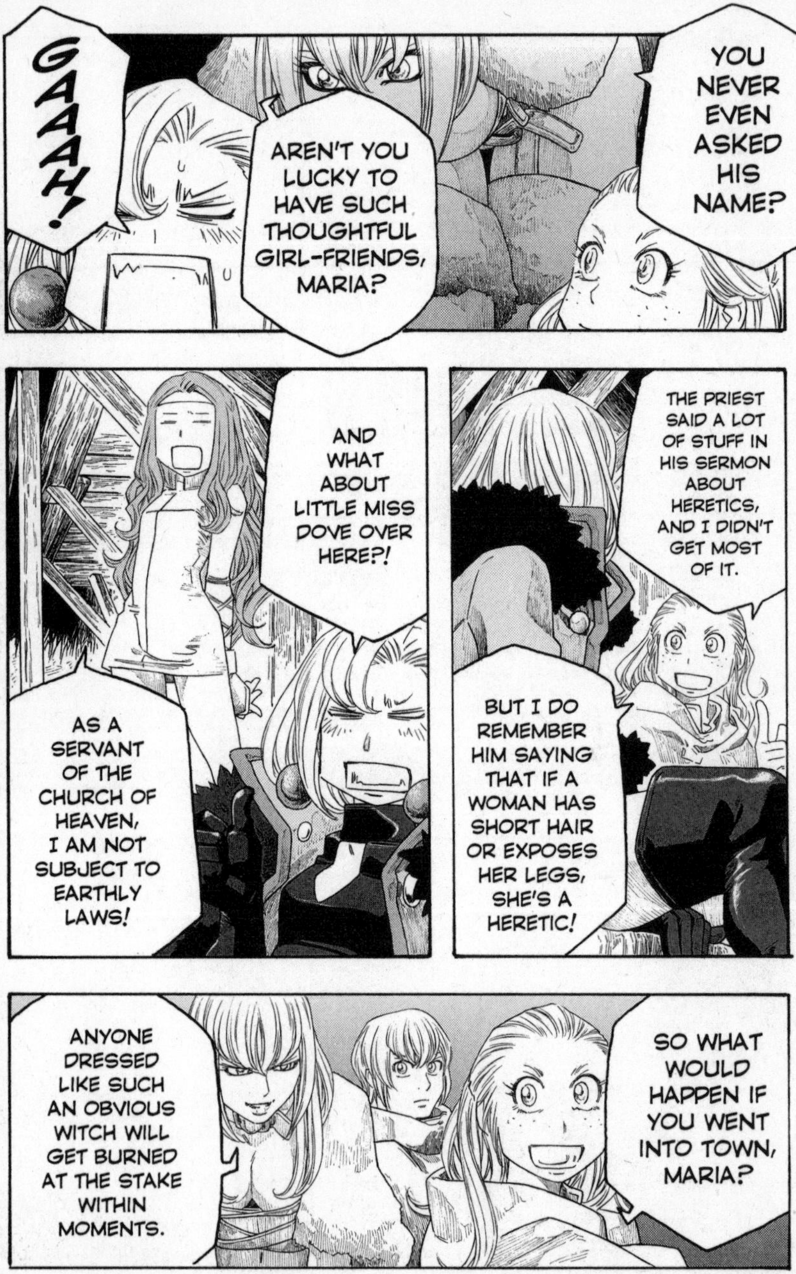
YOU NEVER EVEN ASKED HIS NAME?
AREN'T YOU LUCKY TO HAVE SUCH THOUGHTFUL GIRL-FRIENDS, MARIA?
GAAAH!
THE PRIEST SAID A LOT OF STUFF IN HIS SERMON ABOUT HERETICS, AND I DIDN'T GET MOST OF IT.
BUT I DO REMEMBER HIM SAYING THAT IF A WOMAN HAS SHORT HAIR OR EXPOSES HER LEGS, SHE'S A HERETIC!
AND WHAT ABOUT LITTLE MISS DOVE OVER HERE?!
AS A SERVANT OF THE CHURCH OF HEAVEN, I AM NOT SUBJECT TO EARTHLY LAWS!
SO WHAT WOULD HAPPEN IF YOU WENT INTO TOWN, MARIA?
ANYONE DRESSED LIKE SUCH AN OBVIOUS WITCH WILL GET BURNED AT THE STAKE WITHIN MOMENTS.

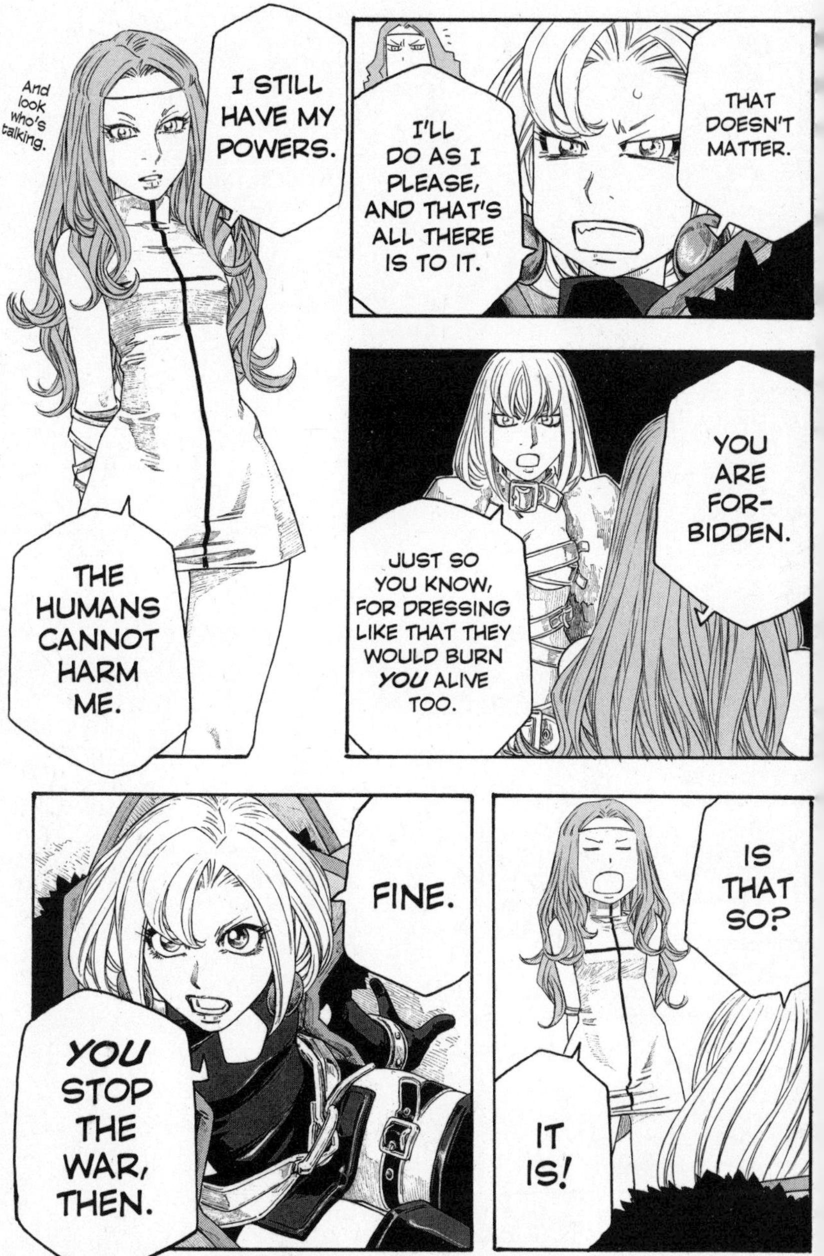
THAT DOESN'T MATTER.
I'LL DO AS I PLEASE, AND THAT'S ALL THERE IS TO IT.
YOU ARE FOR-BIDDEN.
JUST SO YOU KNOW, FOR DRESSING LIKE THAT THEY WOULD BURN *YOU* ALIVE TOO.
I STILL HAVE MY POWERS.
And look who's talking.
THE HUMANS CANNOT HARM ME.
IS THAT SO?
IT IS!
FINE.
YOU STOP THE WAR, THEN.

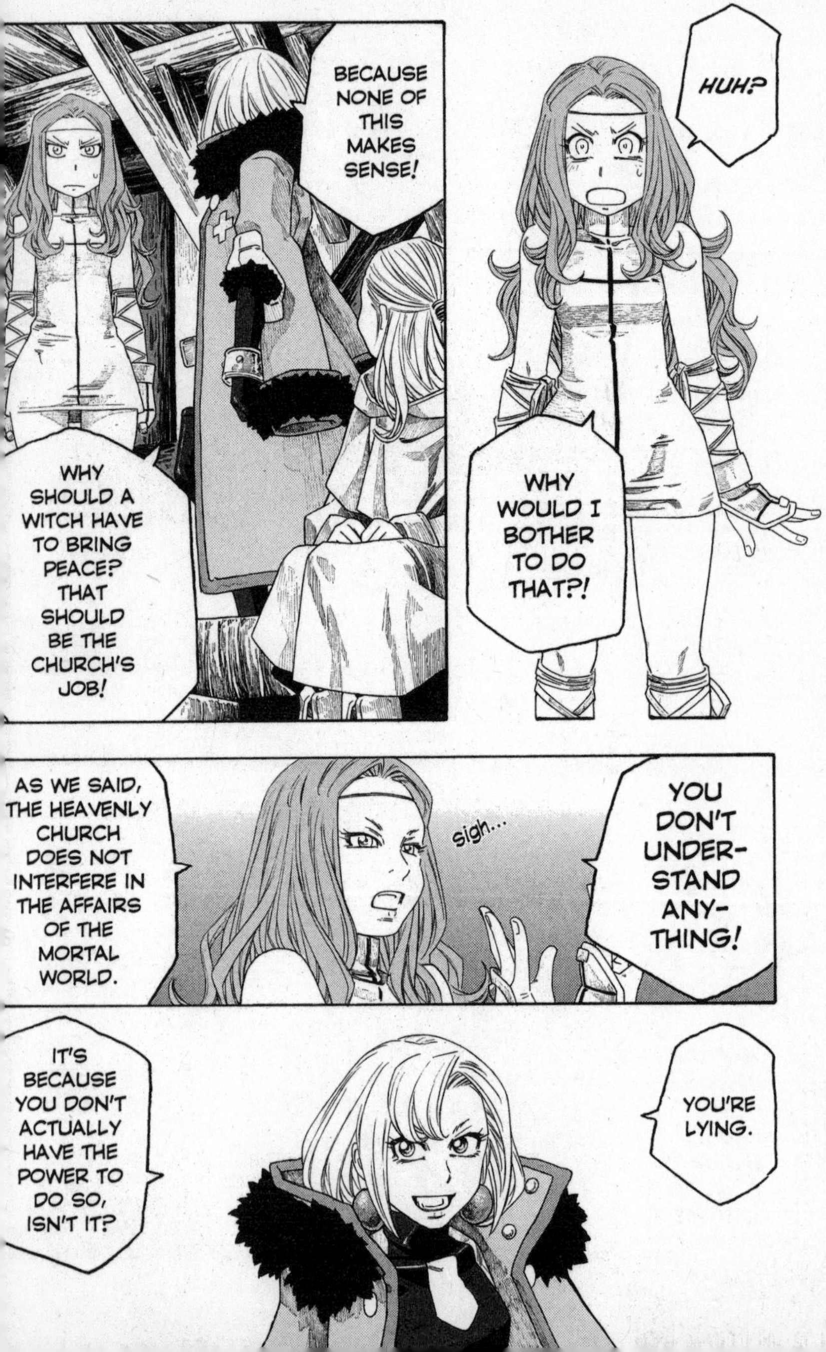
HUH?
WHY WOULD I BOTHER TO DO THAT?!
BECAUSE NONE OF THIS MAKES SENSE!
WHY SHOULD A WITCH HAVE TO BRING PEACE? THAT SHOULD BE THE CHURCH'S JOB!
YOU DON'T UNDER-STAND ANY-THING!
sigh...
AS WE SAID, THE HEAVENLY CHURCH DOES NOT INTERFERE IN THE AFFAIRS OF THE MORTAL WORLD.
YOU'RE LYING.
IT'S BECAUSE YOU DON'T ACTUALLY HAVE THE POWER TO DO SO, ISN'T IT?

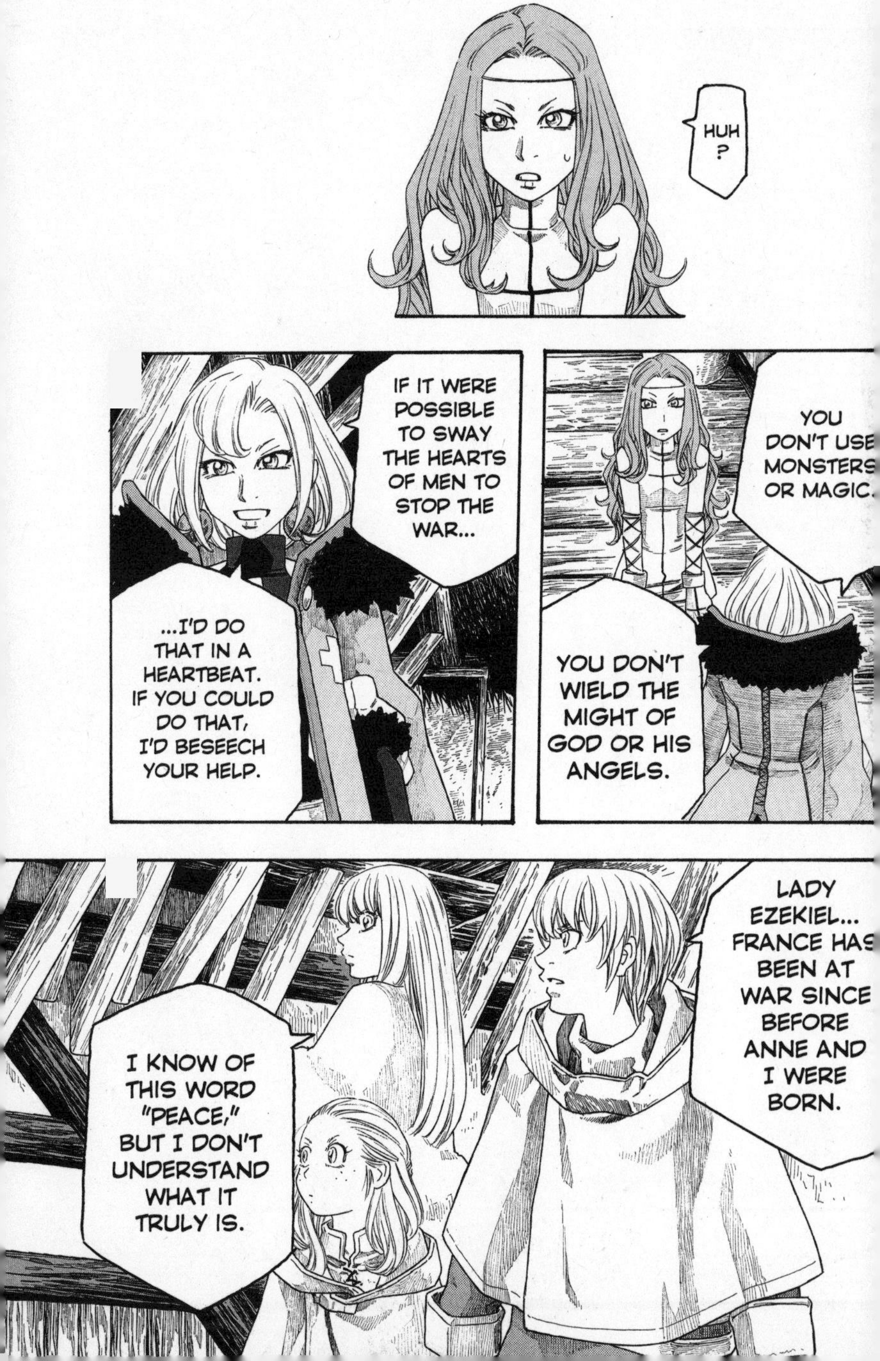
HUH?
YOU DON'T USE MONSTERS OR MAGIC.
YOU DON'T WIELD THE MIGHT OF GOD OR HIS ANGELS.
IF IT WERE POSSIBLE TO SWAY THE HEARTS OF MEN TO STOP THE WAR...
...I'D DO THAT IN A HEARTBEAT. IF YOU COULD DO THAT, I'D BESEECH YOUR HELP.
LADY EZEKIEL... FRANCE HAS BEEN AT WAR SINCE BEFORE ANNE AND I WERE BORN.
I KNOW OF THIS WORD "PEACE," BUT I DON'T UNDERSTAND WHAT IT TRULY IS.

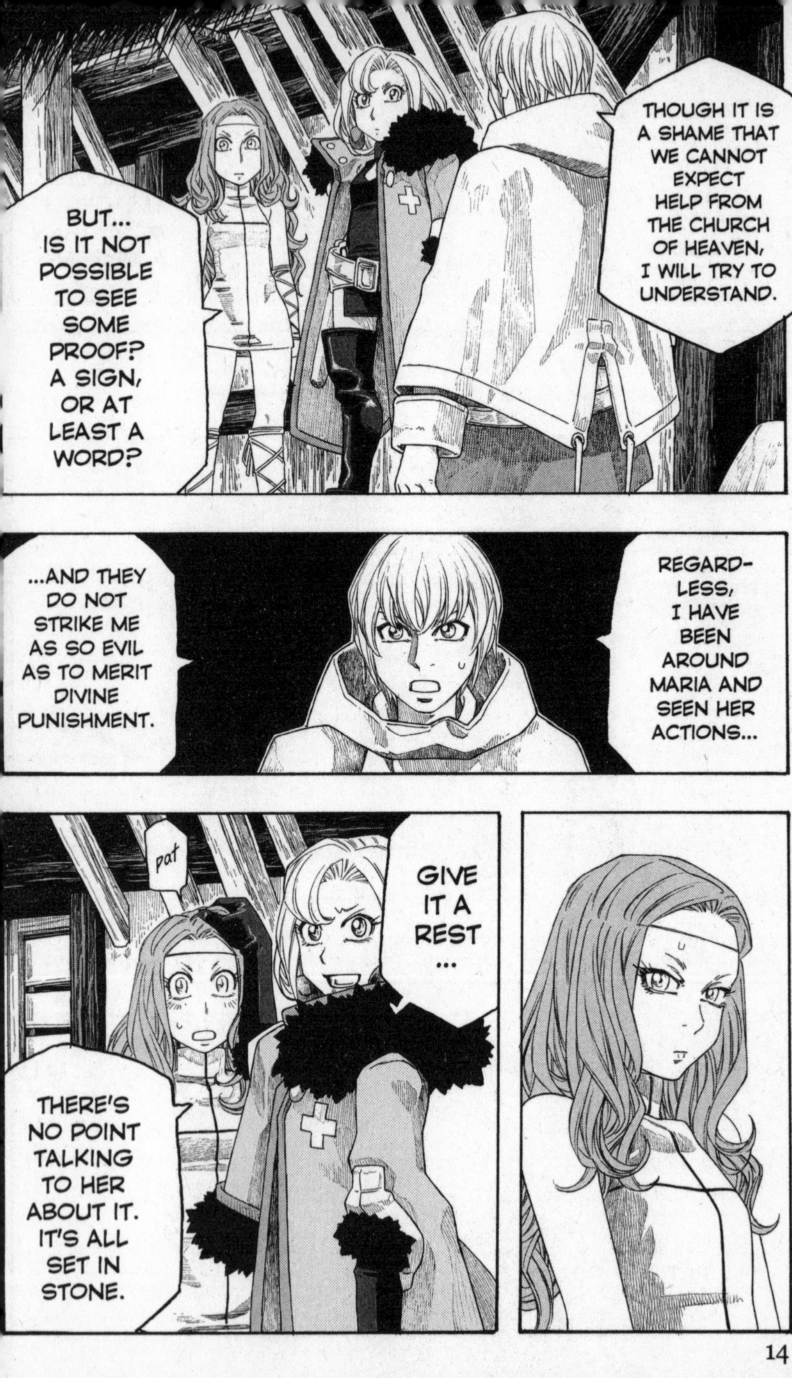
THOUGH IT IS A SHAME THAT WE CANNOT EXPECT HELP FROM THE CHURCH OF HEAVEN, I WILL TRY TO UNDERSTAND.
BUT... IS IT NOT POSSIBLE TO SEE SOME PROOF? A SIGN, OR AT LEAST A WORD?
REGARDLESS, I HAVE BEEN AROUND MARIA AND SEEN HER ACTIONS...
...AND THEY DO NOT STRIKE ME AS SO EVIL AS TO MERIT DIVINE PUNISHMENT.
GIVE IT A REST ...
pat
THERE'S NO POINT TALKING TO HER ABOUT IT. IT'S ALL SET IN STONE.

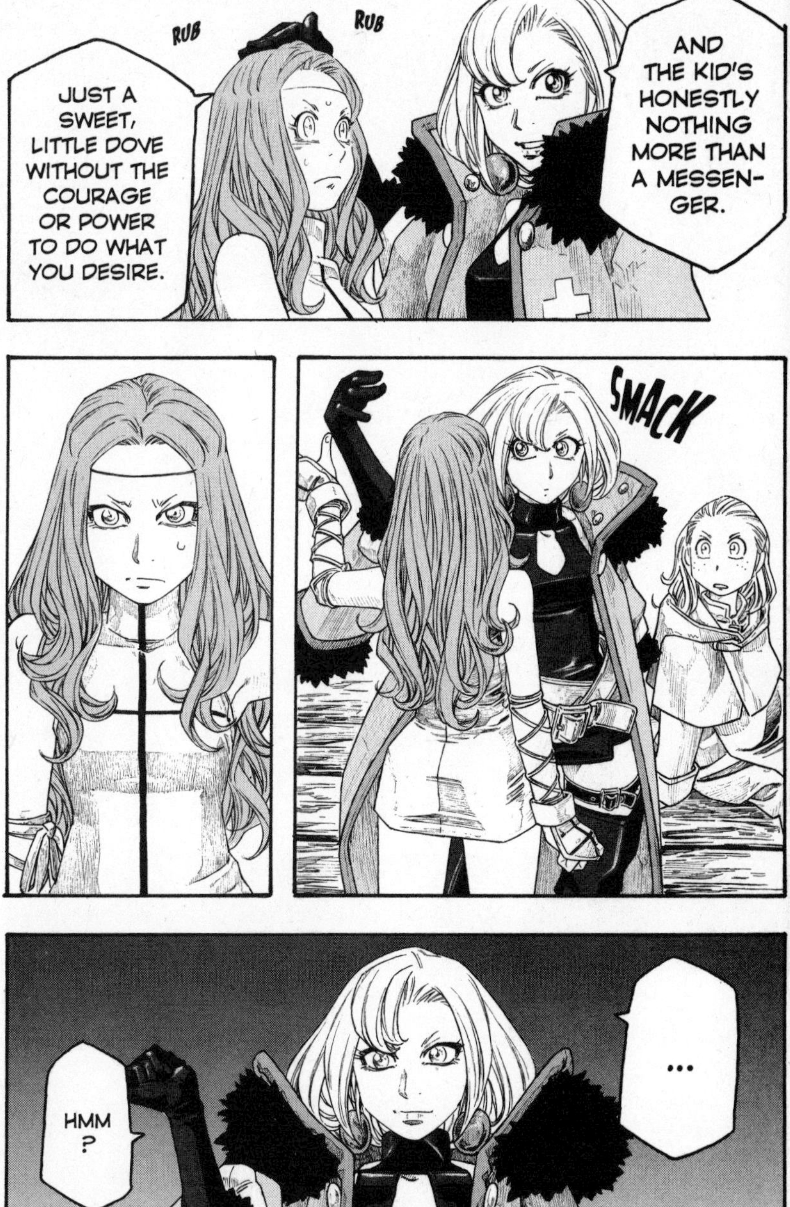
AND THE KID'S HONESTLY NOTHING MORE THAN A MESSEN-GER.
RUB
RUB
JUST A SWEET, LITTLE DOVE WITHOUT THE COURAGE OR POWER TO DO WHAT YOU DESIRE.
SMACK
...
HMM ?

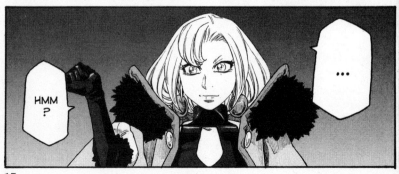

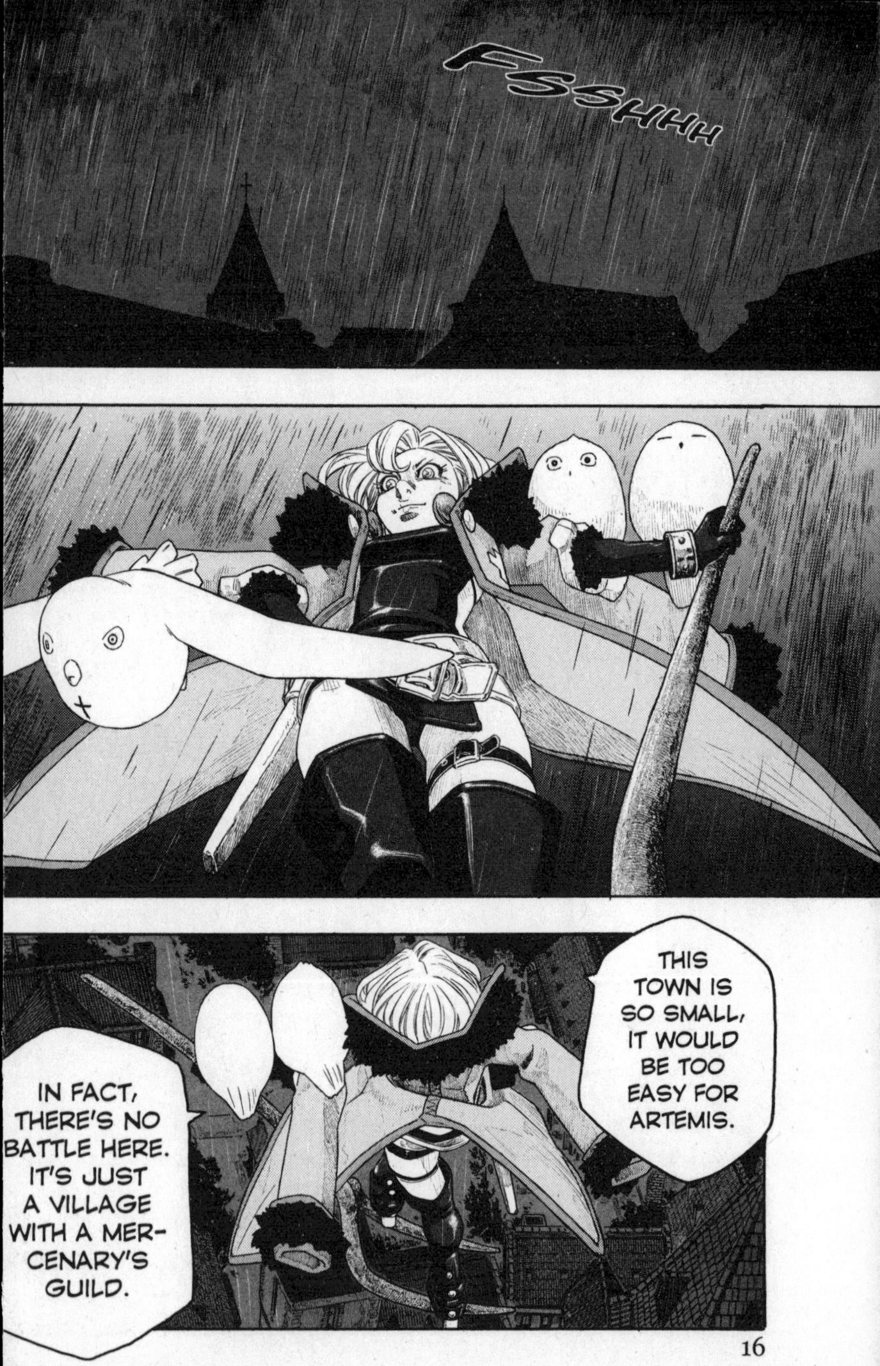
FSSHHH
THIS TOWN IS SO SMALL, IT WOULD BE TOO EASY FOR ARTEMIS.
IN FACT, THERE'S NO BATTLE HERE. IT'S JUST A VILLAGE WITH A MERCENARY'S GUILD.

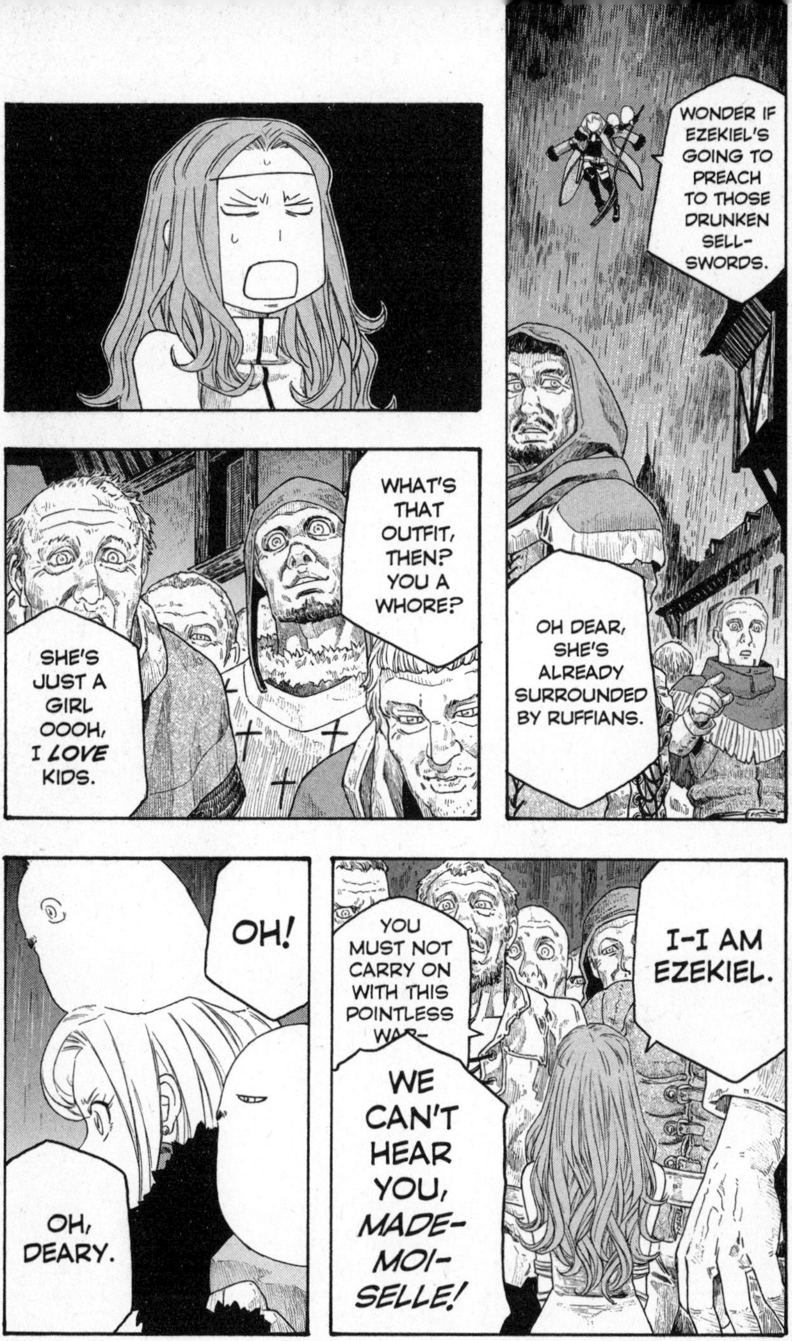
WONDER IF EZEKIEL'S GOING TO PREACH TO THOSE DRUNKEN SELL-SWORDS.
OH DEAR, SHE'S ALREADY SURROUNDED BY RUFFIANS.
WHAT'S THAT OUTFIT, THEN? YOU A WHORE?
SHE'S JUST A GIRL OOOH, I *LOVE* KIDS.
I-I AM EZEKIEL.
YOU MUST NOT CARRY ON WITH THIS POINTLESS WAR-
WE CAN'T HEAR YOU, *MADE-MOI-SELLE!*
OH!
OH, DEARY.

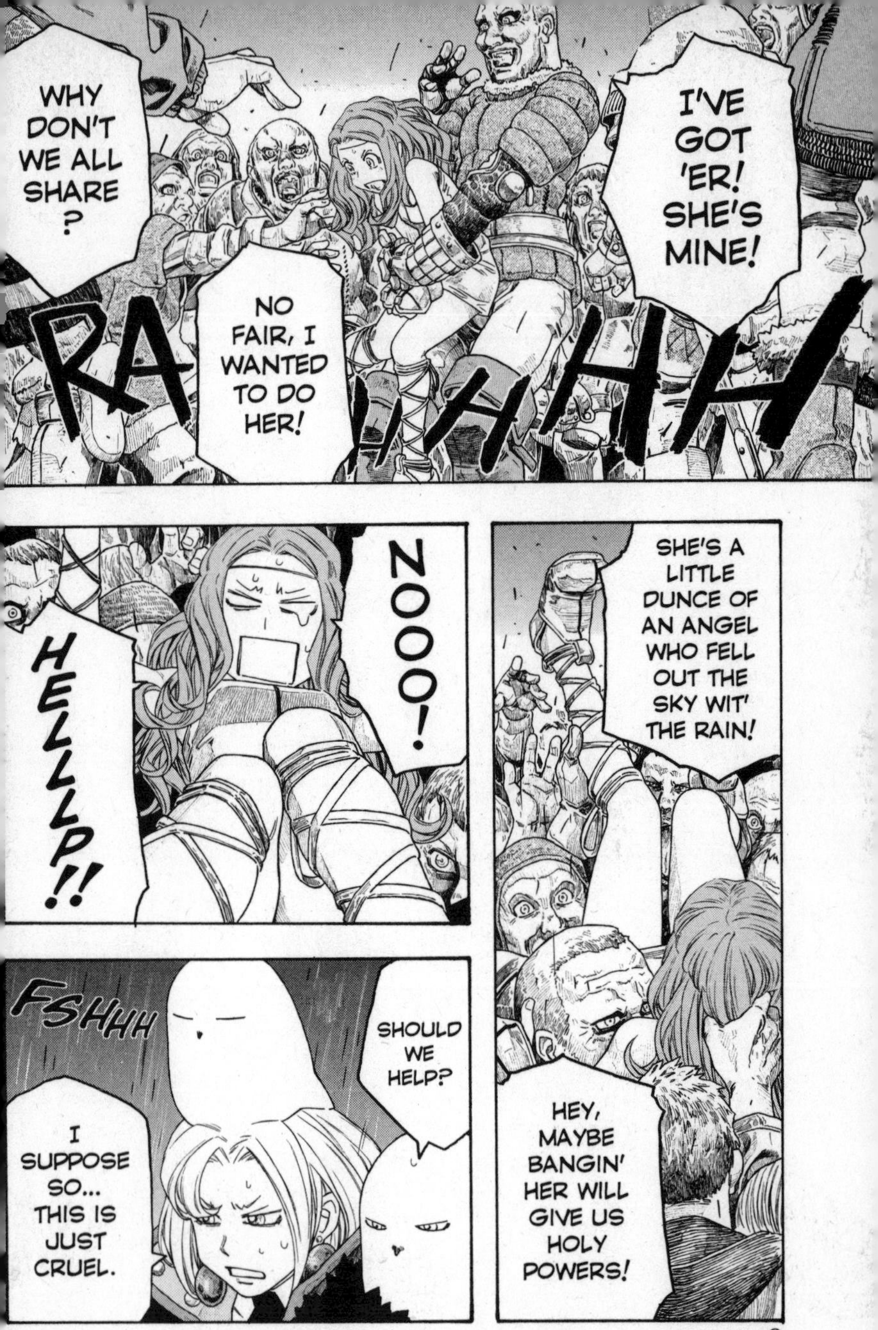
I'VE GOT 'ER! SHE'S MINE!
WHY DON'T WE ALL SHARE?
NO FAIR, I WANTED TO DO HER!
RAHHHH
SHE'S A LITTLE DUNCE OF AN ANGEL WHO FELL OUT THE SKY WIT' THE RAIN!
HEY, MAYBE BANGIN' HER WILL GIVE US HOLY POWERS!
NOOOO!
HELLLP!!
SHOULD WE HELP?
FSHHH
I SUPPOSE SO... THIS IS JUST CRUEL.

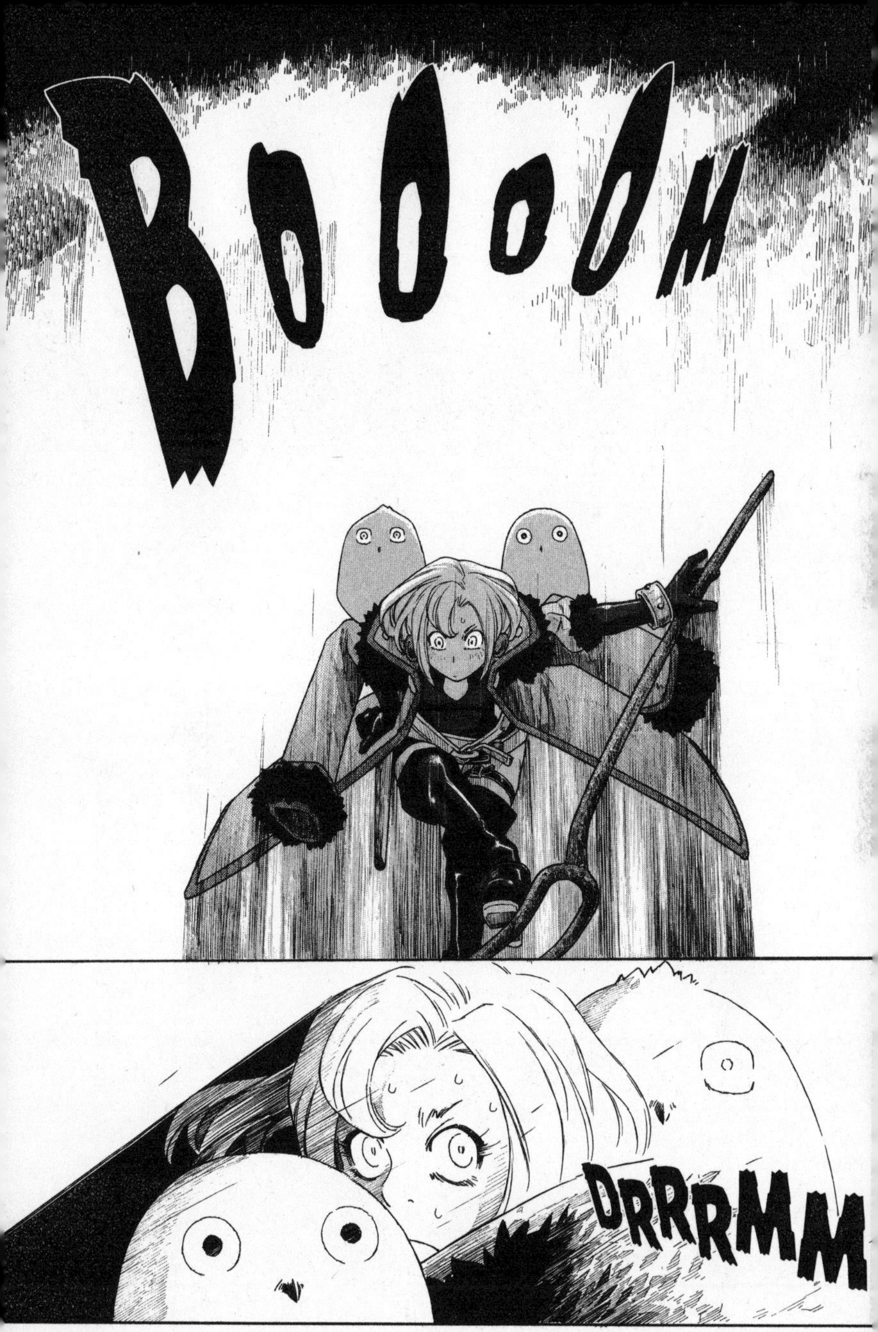
BOOOOM
DRRRMM

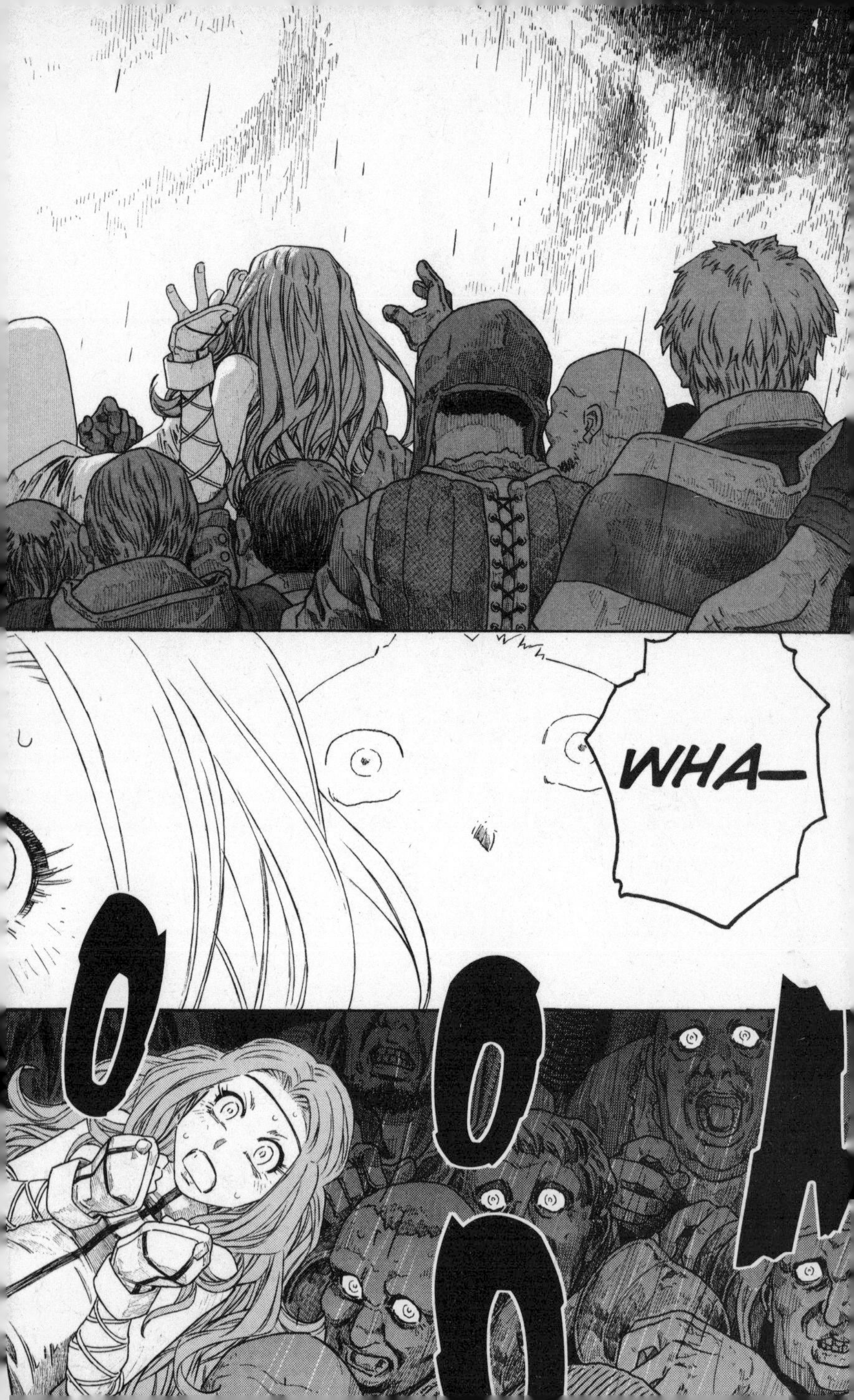
WHA—
OOOO

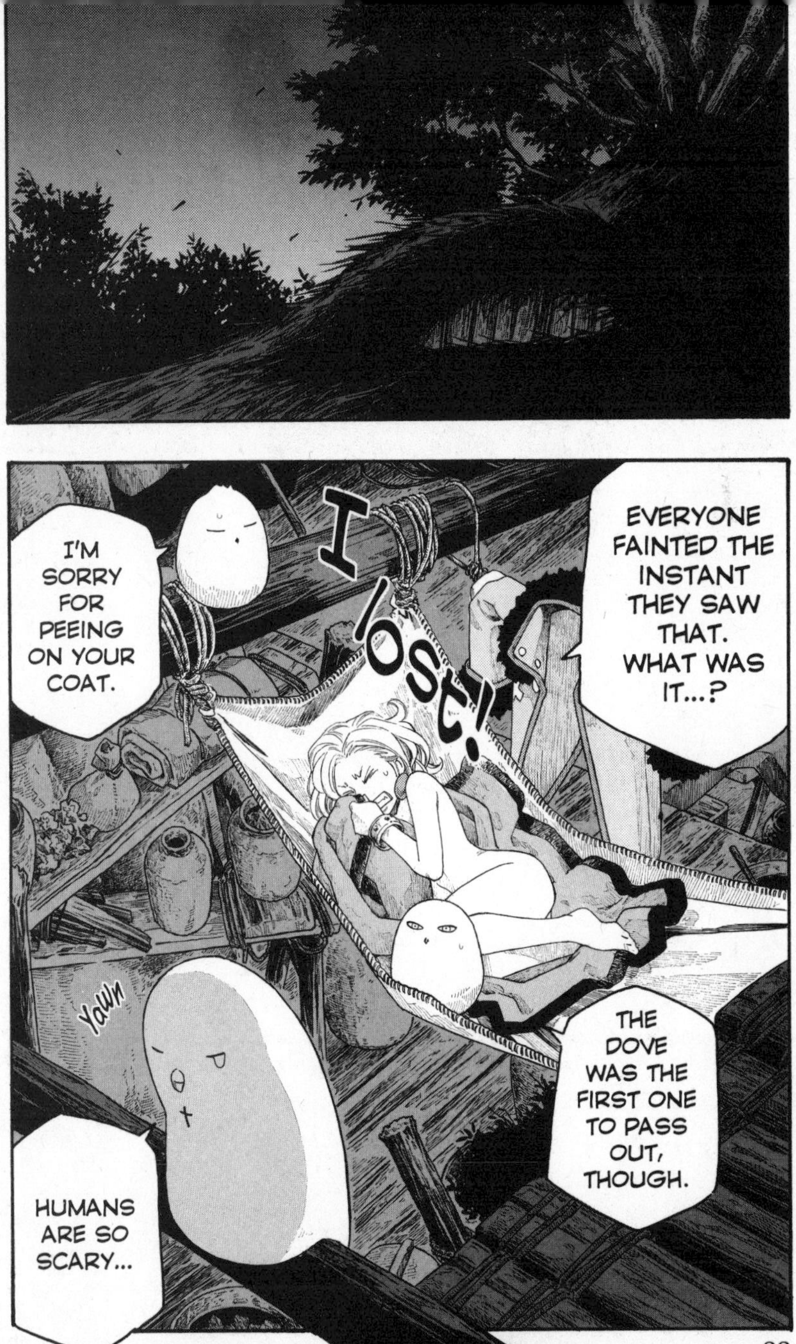
EVERYONE FAINTED THE INSTANT THEY SAW THAT. WHAT WAS IT...?
I lost!
I'M SORRY FOR PEEING ON YOUR COAT.
THE DOVE WAS THE FIRST ONE TO PASS OUT, THOUGH.
Yawn
HUMANS ARE SO SCARY...

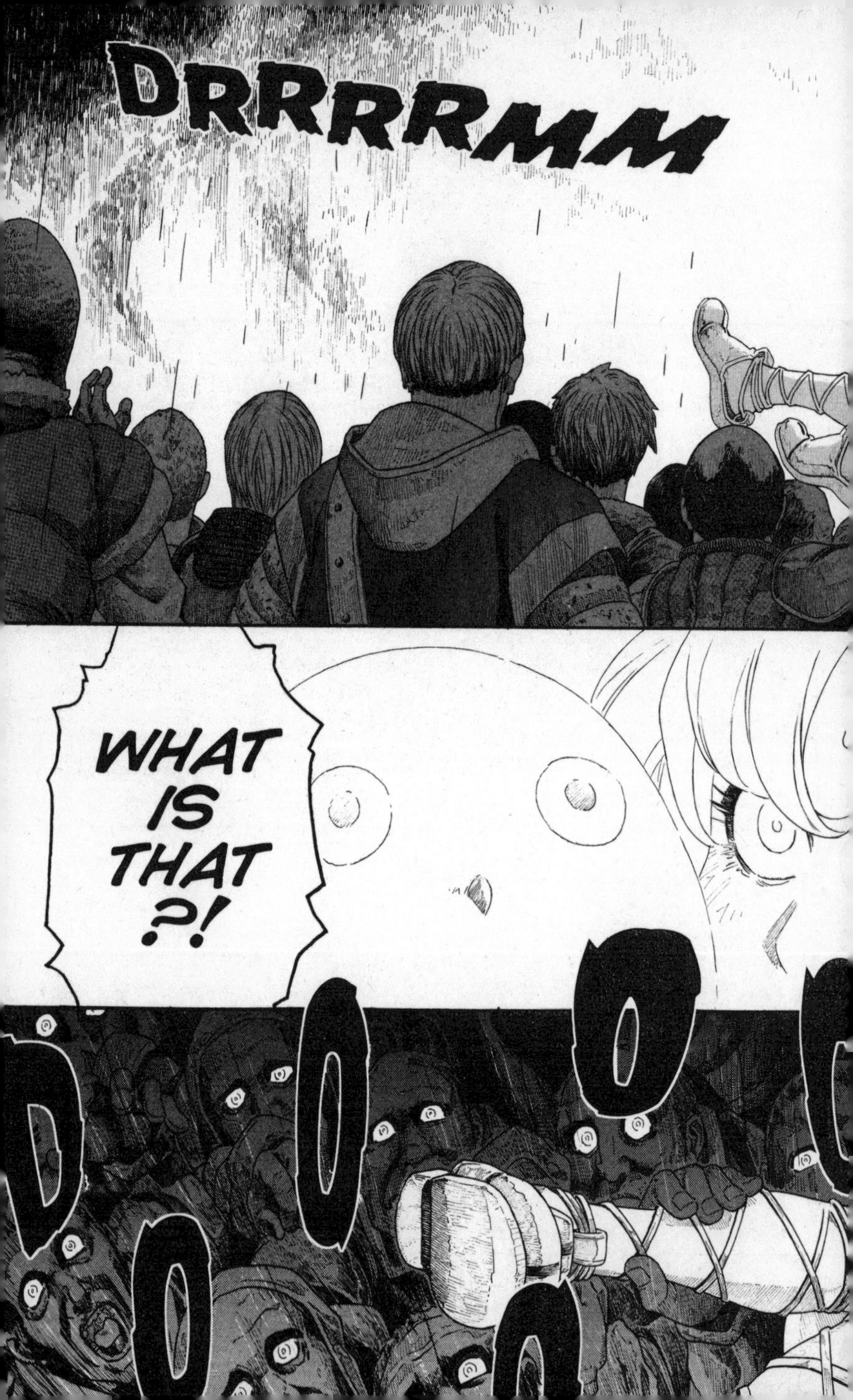
DRRRRRMM
WHAT IS THAT ?!

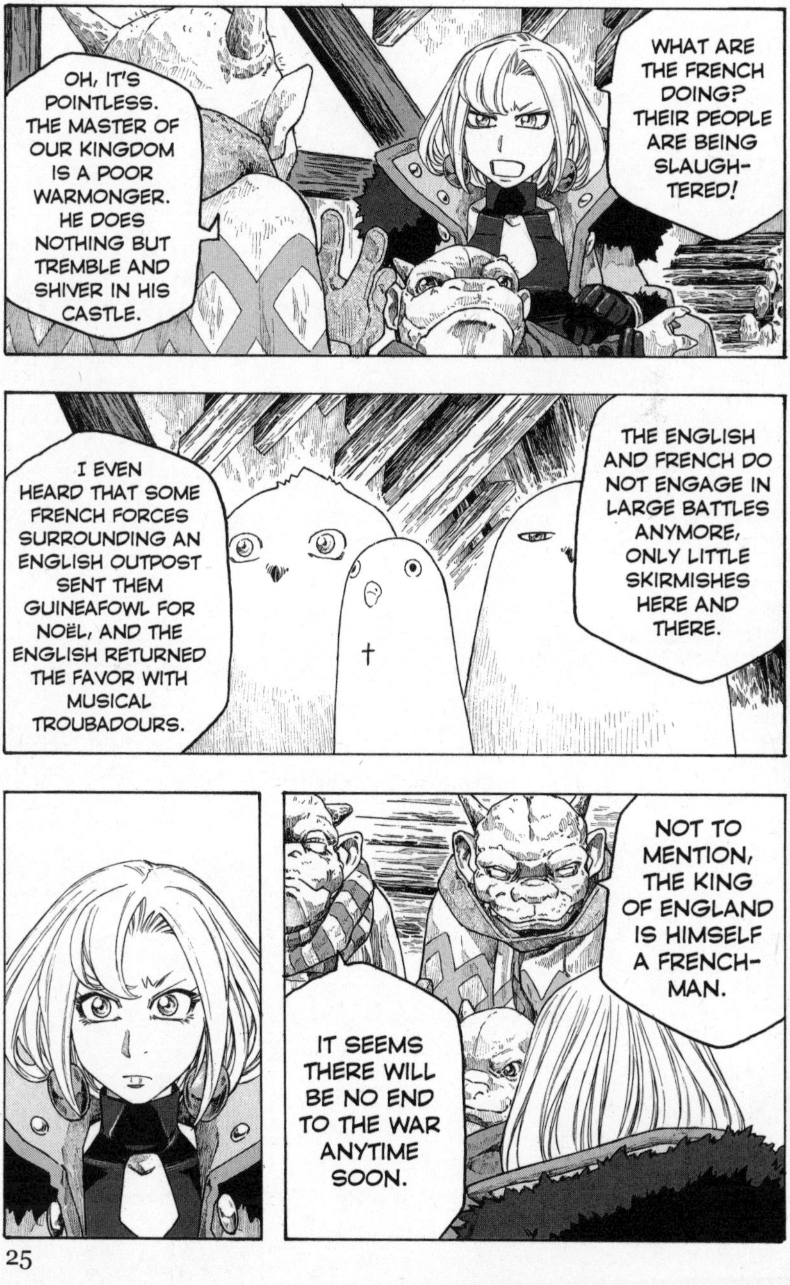
WHAT ARE THE FRENCH DOING? THEIR PEOPLE ARE BEING SLAUGH-TERED!
OH, IT'S POINTLESS. THE MASTER OF OUR KINGDOM IS A POOR WARMONGER. HE DOES NOTHING BUT TREMBLE AND SHIVER IN HIS CASTLE.
THE ENGLISH AND FRENCH DO NOT ENGAGE IN LARGE BATTLES ANYMORE, ONLY LITTLE SKIRMISHES HERE AND THERE.
I EVEN HEARD THAT SOME FRENCH FORCES SURROUNDING AN ENGLISH OUTPOST SENT THEM GUINEAFOWL FOR NOËL, AND THE ENGLISH RETURNED THE FAVOR WITH MUSICAL TROUBADOURS.
NOT TO MENTION, THE KING OF ENGLAND IS HIMSELF A FRENCH-MAN.
IT SEEMS THERE WILL BE NO END TO THE WAR ANYTIME SOON.

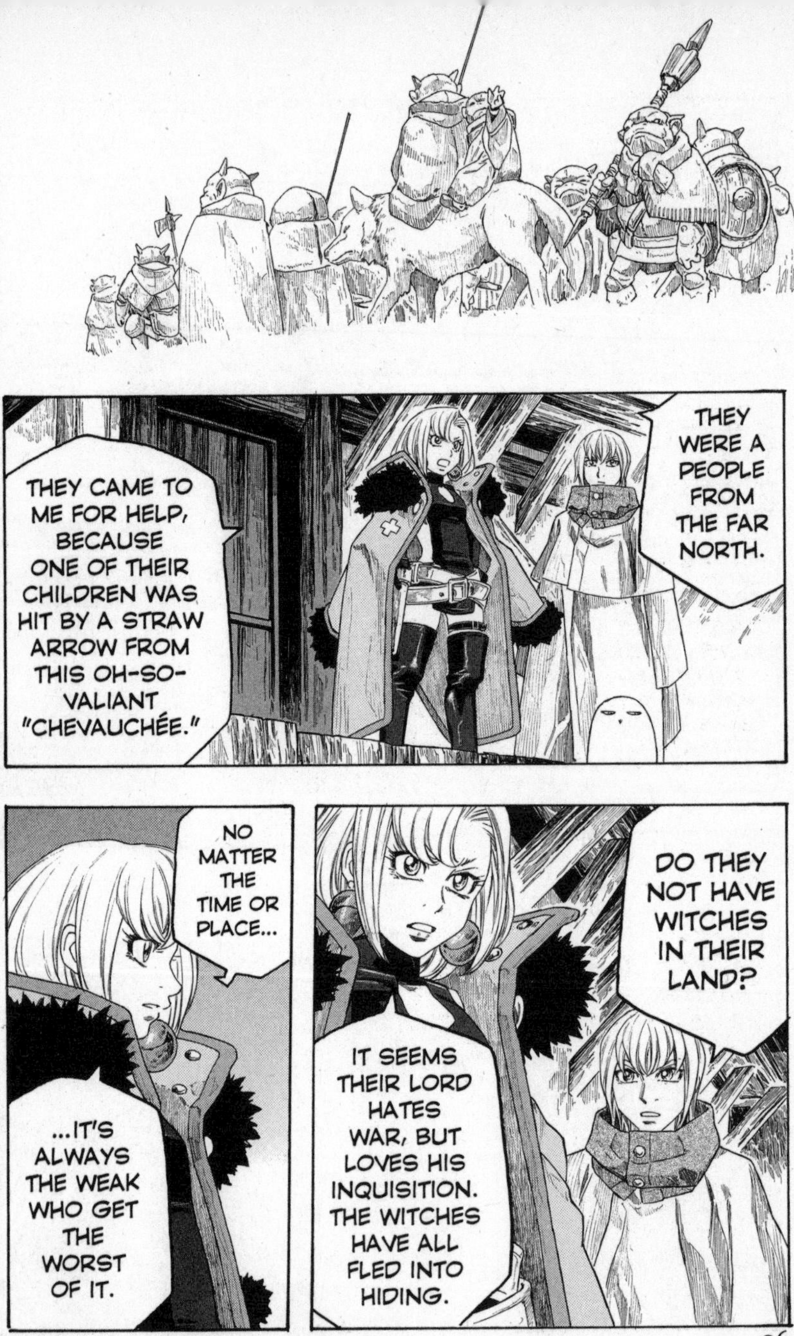
THEY WERE A PEOPLE FROM THE FAR NORTH.
THEY CAME TO ME FOR HELP, BECAUSE ONE OF THEIR CHILDREN WAS HIT BY A STRAW ARROW FROM THIS OH-SO-VALIANT "CHEVAUCHÉE."
DO THEY NOT HAVE WITCHES IN THEIR LAND?
IT SEEMS THEIR LORD HATES WAR, BUT LOVES HIS INQUISITION. THE WITCHES HAVE ALL FLED INTO HIDING.
NO MATTER THE TIME OR PLACE...
...IT'S ALWAYS THE WEAK WHO GET THE WORST OF IT.

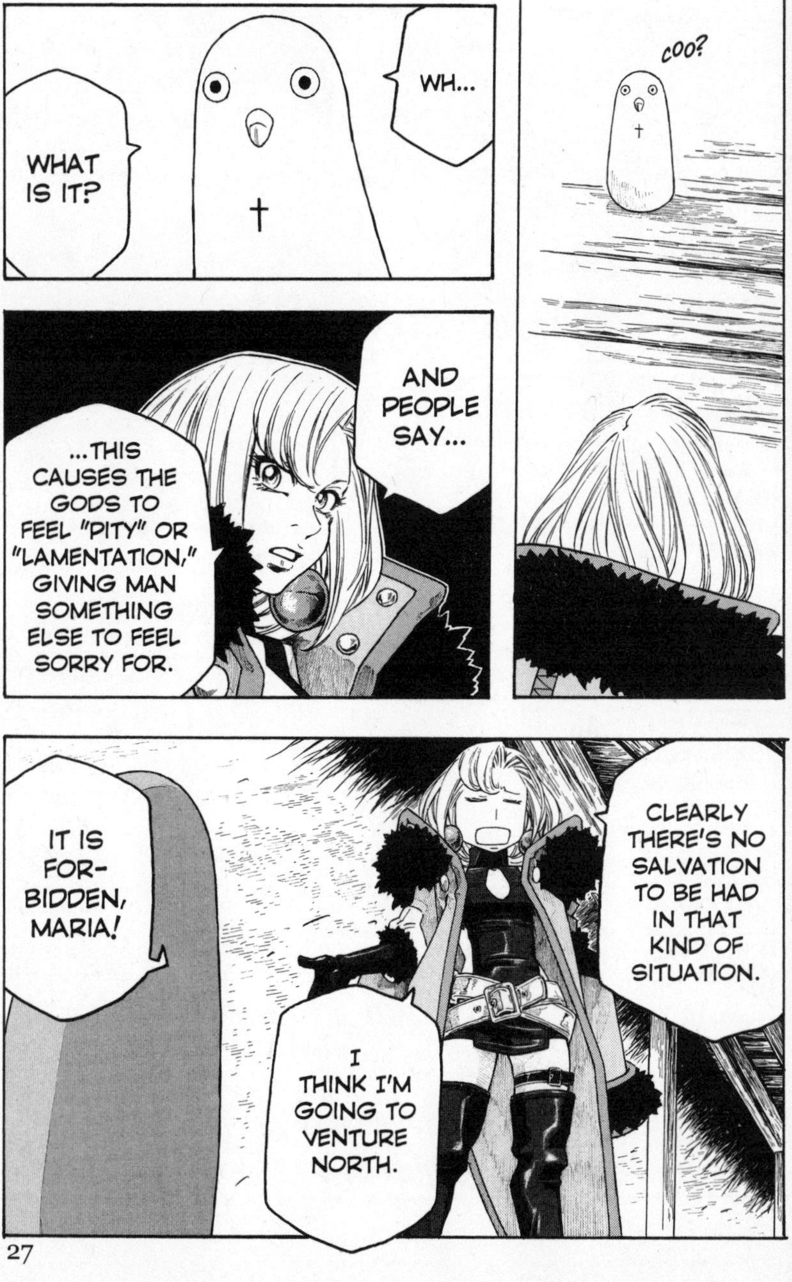
COO?
WH...
WHAT IS IT?
AND PEOPLE SAY...
...THIS CAUSES THE GODS TO FEEL "PITY" OR "LAMENTATION," GIVING MAN SOMETHING ELSE TO FEEL SORRY FOR.
CLEARLY THERE'S NO SALVATION TO BE HAD IN THAT KIND OF SITUATION.
I THINK I'M GOING TO VENTURE NORTH.
IT IS FOR-BIDDEN, MARIA!

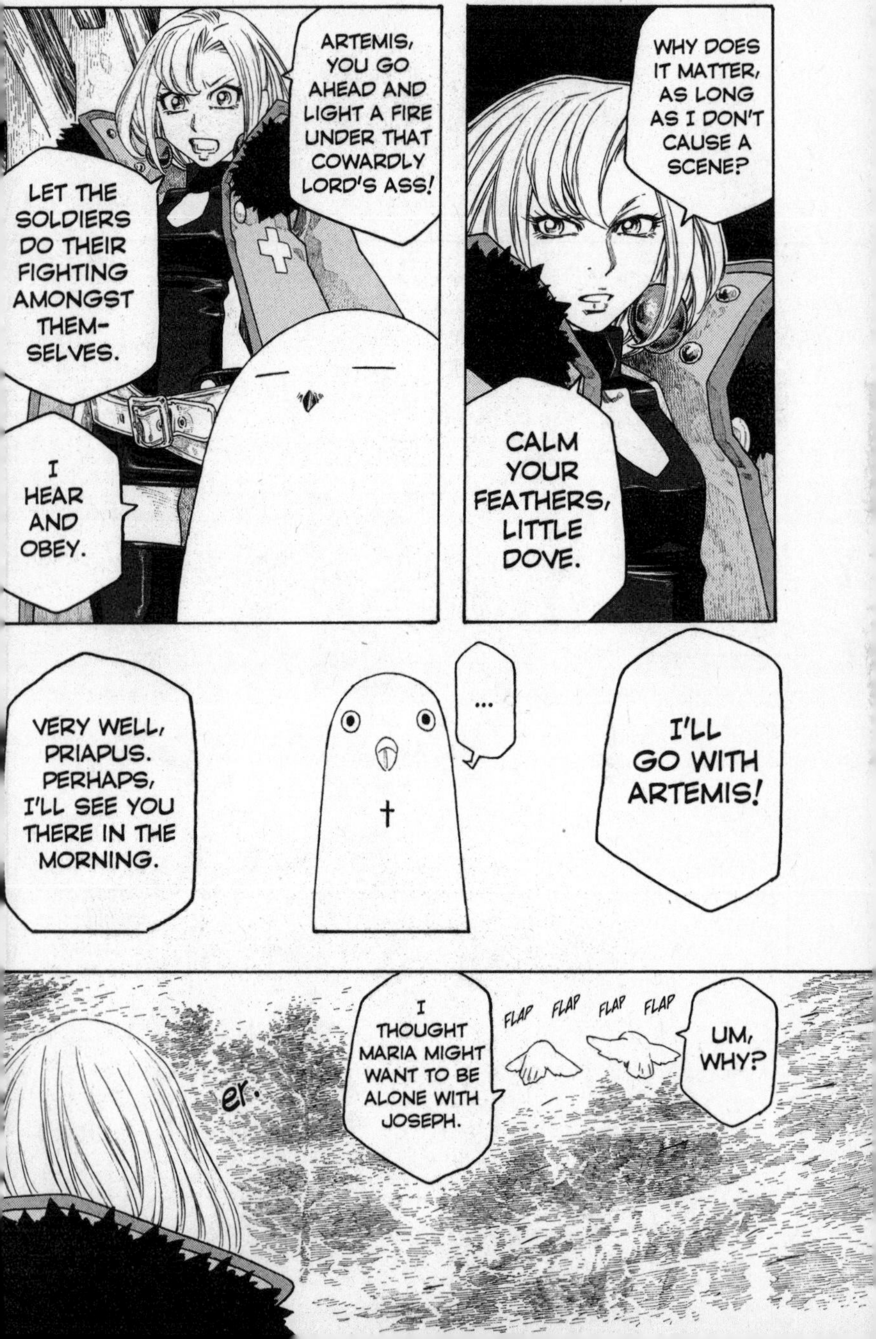
WHY DOES IT MATTER, AS LONG AS I DON'T CAUSE A SCENE?
CALM YOUR FEATHERS, LITTLE DOVE.
ARTEMIS, YOU GO AHEAD AND LIGHT A FIRE UNDER THAT COWARDLY LORD'S ASS!
LET THE SOLDIERS DO THEIR FIGHTING AMONGST THEM-SELVES.
I HEAR AND OBEY.
I'LL GO WITH ARTEMIS!
...
VERY WELL, PRIAPUS. PERHAPS, I'LL SEE YOU THERE IN THE MORNING.
UM, WHY?
FLAP FLAP FLAP FLAP
I THOUGHT MARIA MIGHT WANT TO BE ALONE WITH JOSEPH.
er.

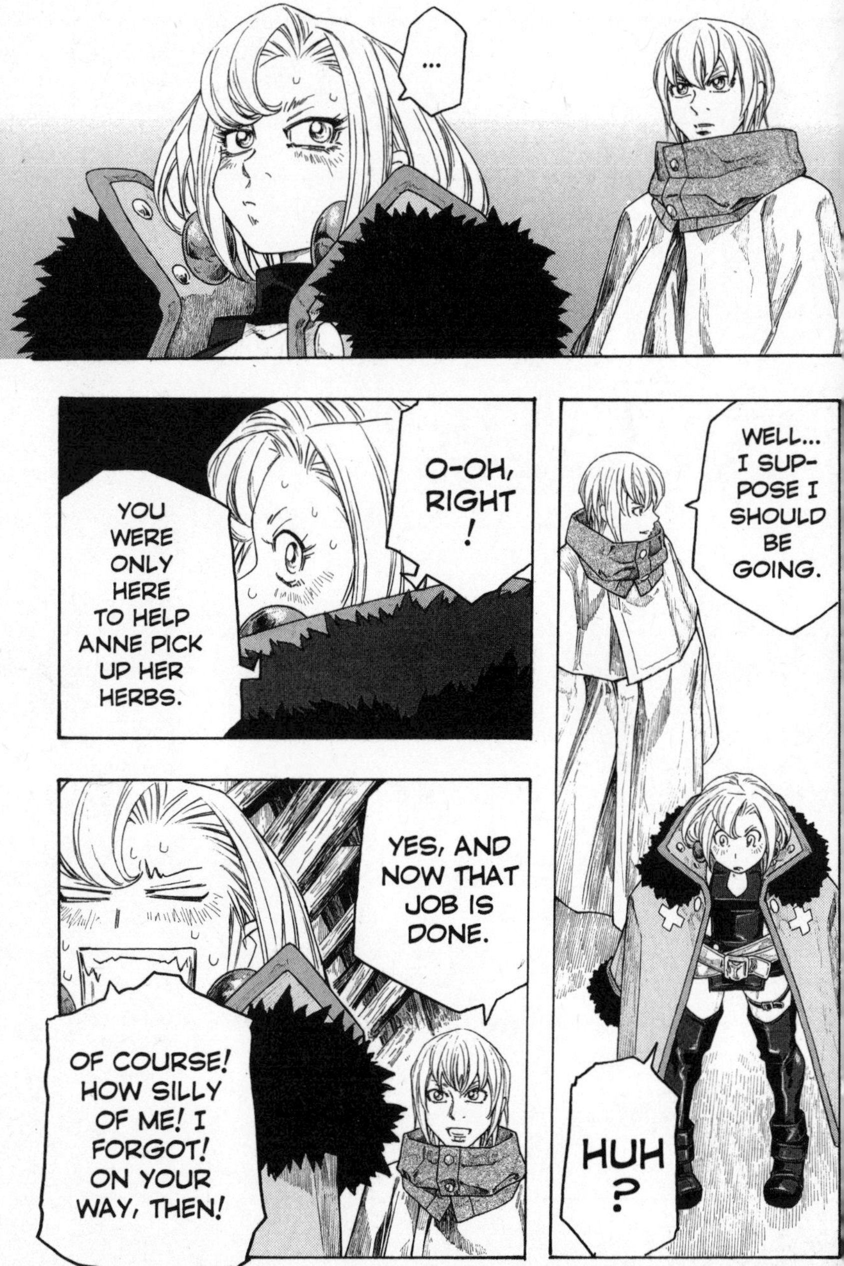
...
WELL... I SUPPOSE I SHOULD BE GOING.
HUH?
O-OH, RIGHT!
YOU WERE ONLY HERE TO HELP ANNE PICK UP HER HERBS.
YES, AND NOW THAT JOB IS DONE.
OF COURSE! HOW SILLY OF ME! I FORGOT! ON YOUR WAY, THEN!

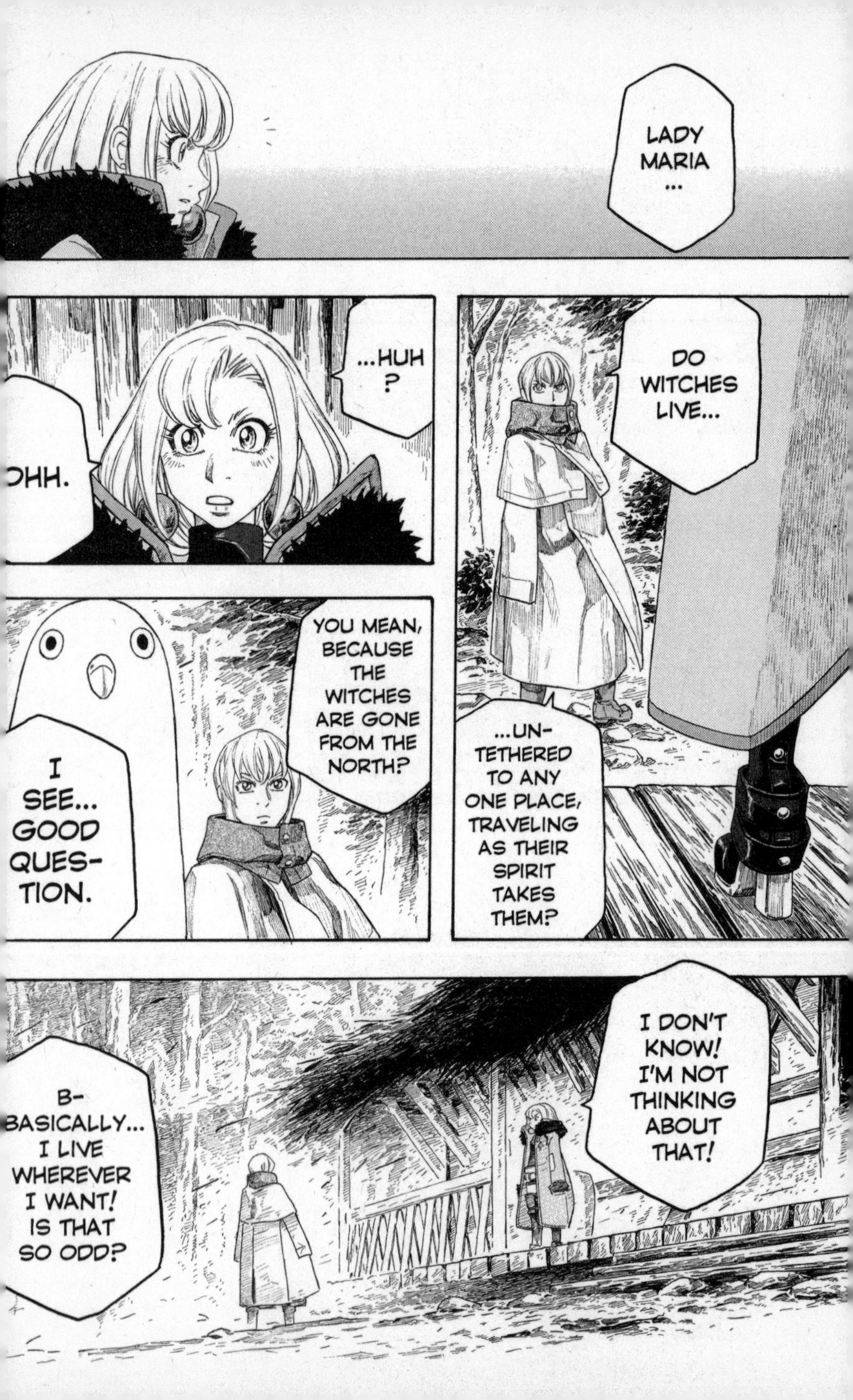
LADY MARIA ...
DO WITCHES LIVE...
...UN-TETHERED TO ANY ONE PLACE, TRAVELING AS THEIR SPIRIT TAKES THEM?
...HUH ?
OHH.
YOU MEAN, BECAUSE THE WITCHES ARE GONE FROM THE NORTH?
I SEE... GOOD QUES-TION.
I DON'T KNOW! I'M NOT THINKING ABOUT THAT!
B-BASICALLY... I LIVE WHEREVER I WANT! IS THAT SO ODD?

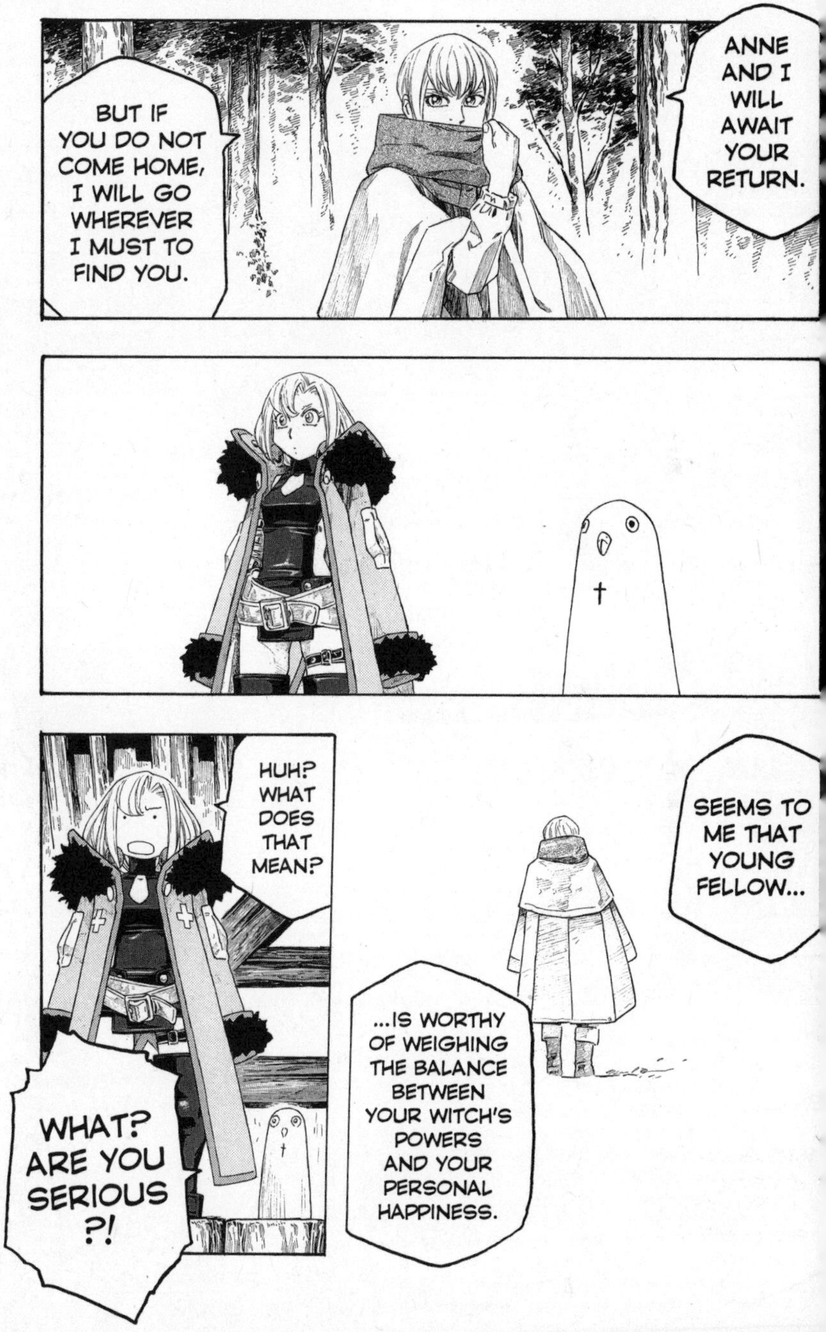
ANNE AND I WILL AWAIT YOUR RETURN.
BUT IF YOU DO NOT COME HOME, I WILL GO WHEREVER I MUST TO FIND YOU.
SEEMS TO ME THAT YOUNG FELLOW...
...IS WORTHY OF WEIGHING THE BALANCE BETWEEN YOUR WITCH'S POWERS AND YOUR PERSONAL HAPPINESS.
HUH? WHAT DOES THAT MEAN?
WHAT? ARE YOU SERIOUS ?!

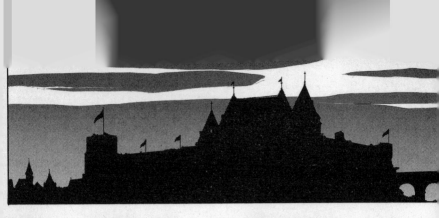

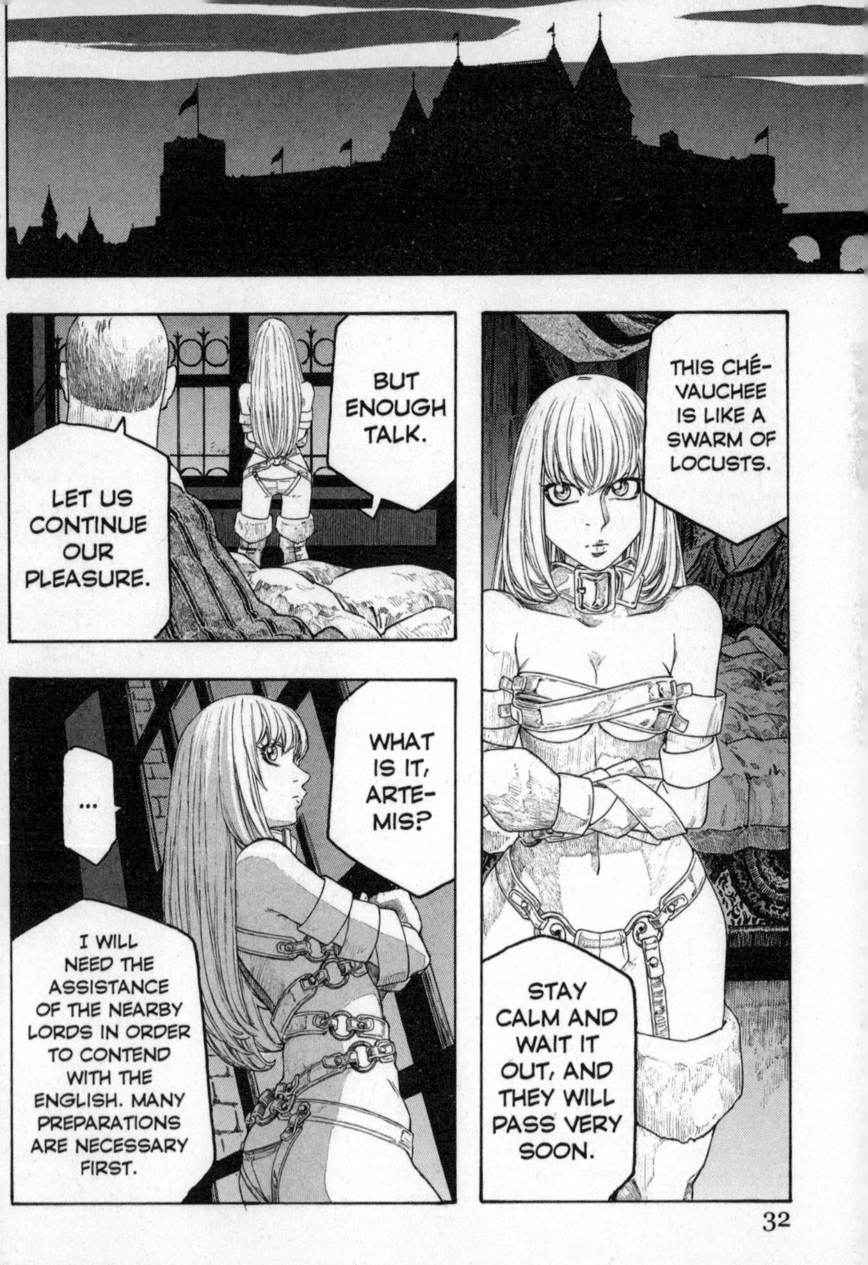
THIS CHÉ-VAUCHEE IS LIKE A SWARM OF LOCUSTS.
STAY CALM AND WAIT IT OUT, AND THEY WILL PASS VERY SOON.
BUT ENOUGH TALK.
LET US CONTINUE OUR PLEASURE.
WHAT IS IT, ARTE-MIS?
...
I WILL NEED THE ASSISTANCE OF THE NEARBY LORDS IN ORDER TO CONTEND WITH THE ENGLISH. MANY PREPARATIONS ARE NECESSARY FIRST.

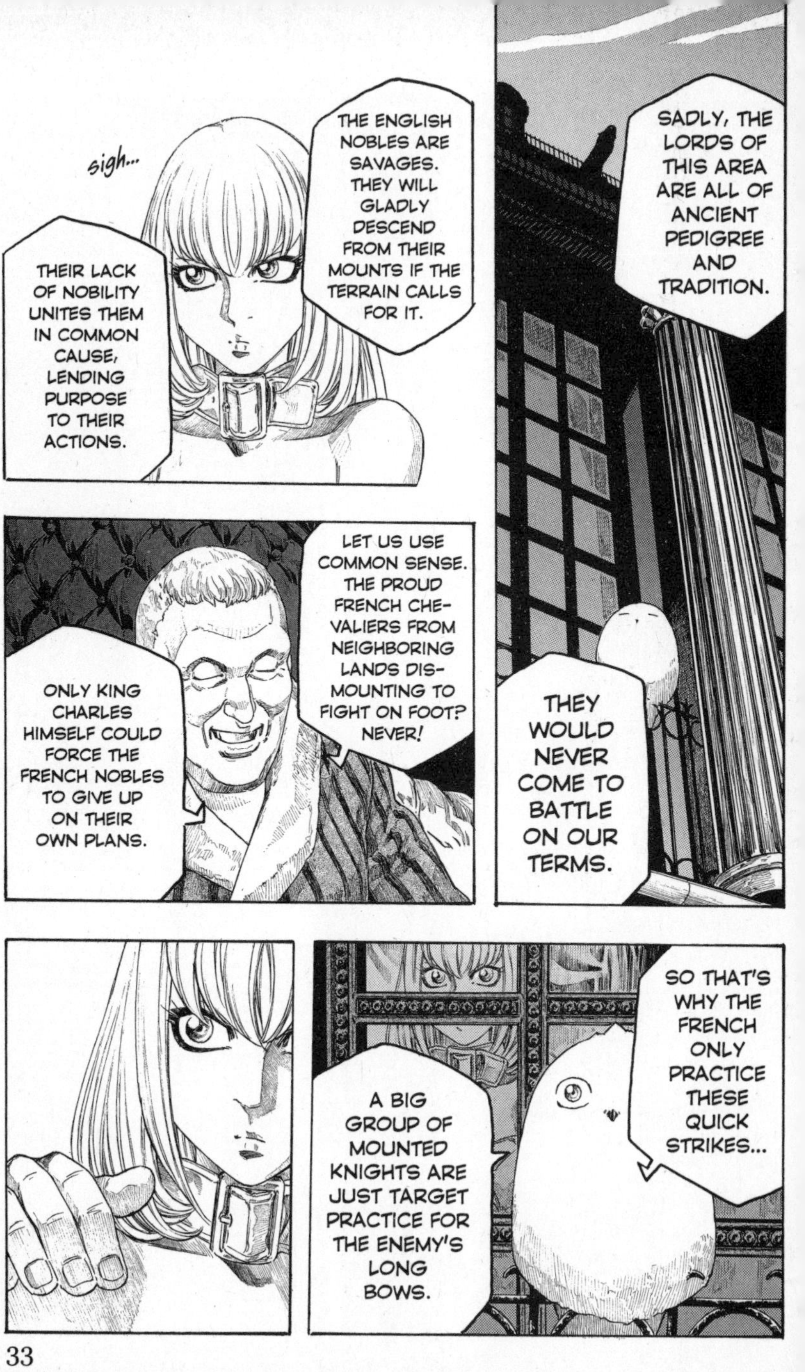
SADLY, THE LORDS OF THIS AREA ARE ALL OF ANCIENT PEDIGREE AND TRADITION.
THEY WOULD NEVER COME TO BATTLE ON OUR TERMS.
THE ENGLISH NOBLES ARE SAVAGES. THEY WILL GLADLY DESCEND FROM THEIR MOUNTS IF THE TERRAIN CALLS FOR IT.
sigh...
THEIR LACK OF NOBILITY UNITES THEM IN COMMON CAUSE, LENDING PURPOSE TO THEIR ACTIONS.
LET US USE COMMON SENSE. THE PROUD FRENCH CHE-VALIERS FROM NEIGHBORING LANDS DIS-MOUNTING TO FIGHT ON FOOT? NEVER!
ONLY KING CHARLES HIMSELF COULD FORCE THE FRENCH NOBLES TO GIVE UP ON THEIR OWN PLANS.
SO THAT'S WHY THE FRENCH ONLY PRACTICE THESE QUICK STRIKES...
A BIG GROUP OF MOUNTED KNIGHTS ARE JUST TARGET PRACTICE FOR THE ENEMY'S LONG BOWS.

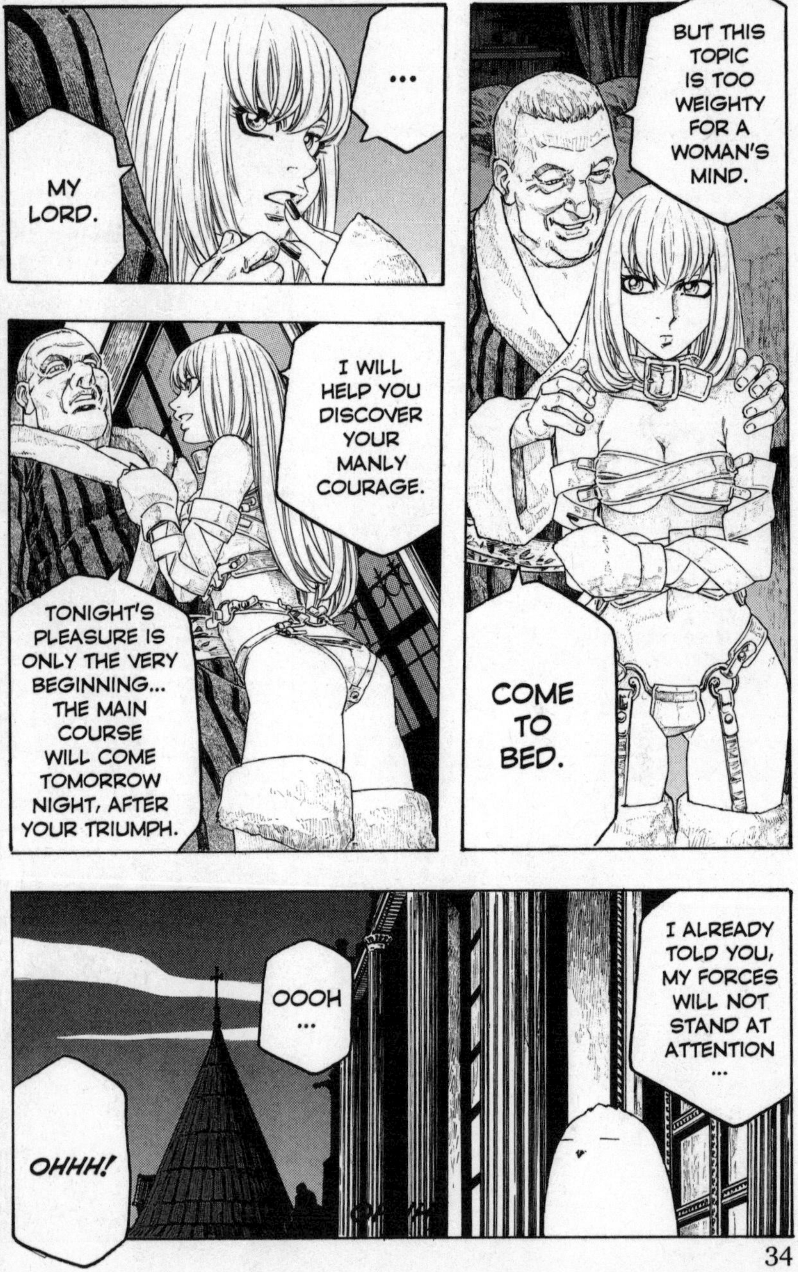
BUT THIS TOPIC IS TOO WEIGHTY FOR A WOMAN'S MIND.
COME TO BED.
...
MY LORD.
I WILL HELP YOU DISCOVER YOUR MANLY COURAGE.
TONIGHT'S PLEASURE IS ONLY THE VERY BEGINNING... THE MAIN COURSE WILL COME TOMORROW NIGHT, AFTER YOUR TRIUMPH.
I ALREADY TOLD YOU, MY FORCES WILL NOT STAND AT ATTENTION ...
OOOH ...
OHHH!

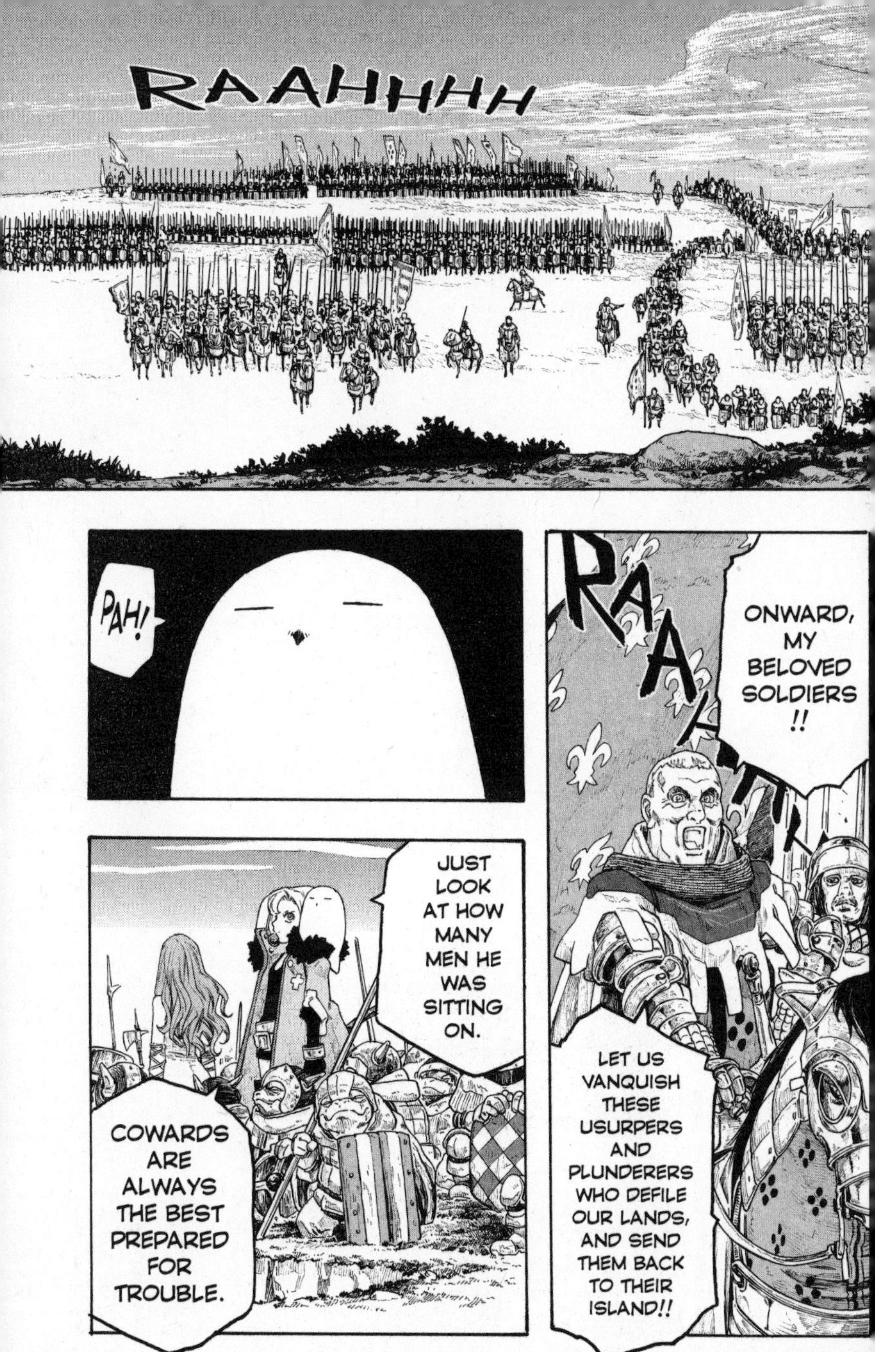
RAAHHHH
ONWARD, MY BELOVED SOLDIERS!!
LET US VANQUISH THESE USURPERS AND PLUNDERERS WHO DEFILE OUR LANDS, AND SEND THEM BACK TO THEIR ISLAND!!
PAH!
JUST LOOK AT HOW MANY MEN HE WAS SITTING ON.
COWARDS ARE ALWAYS THE BEST PREPARED FOR TROUBLE.

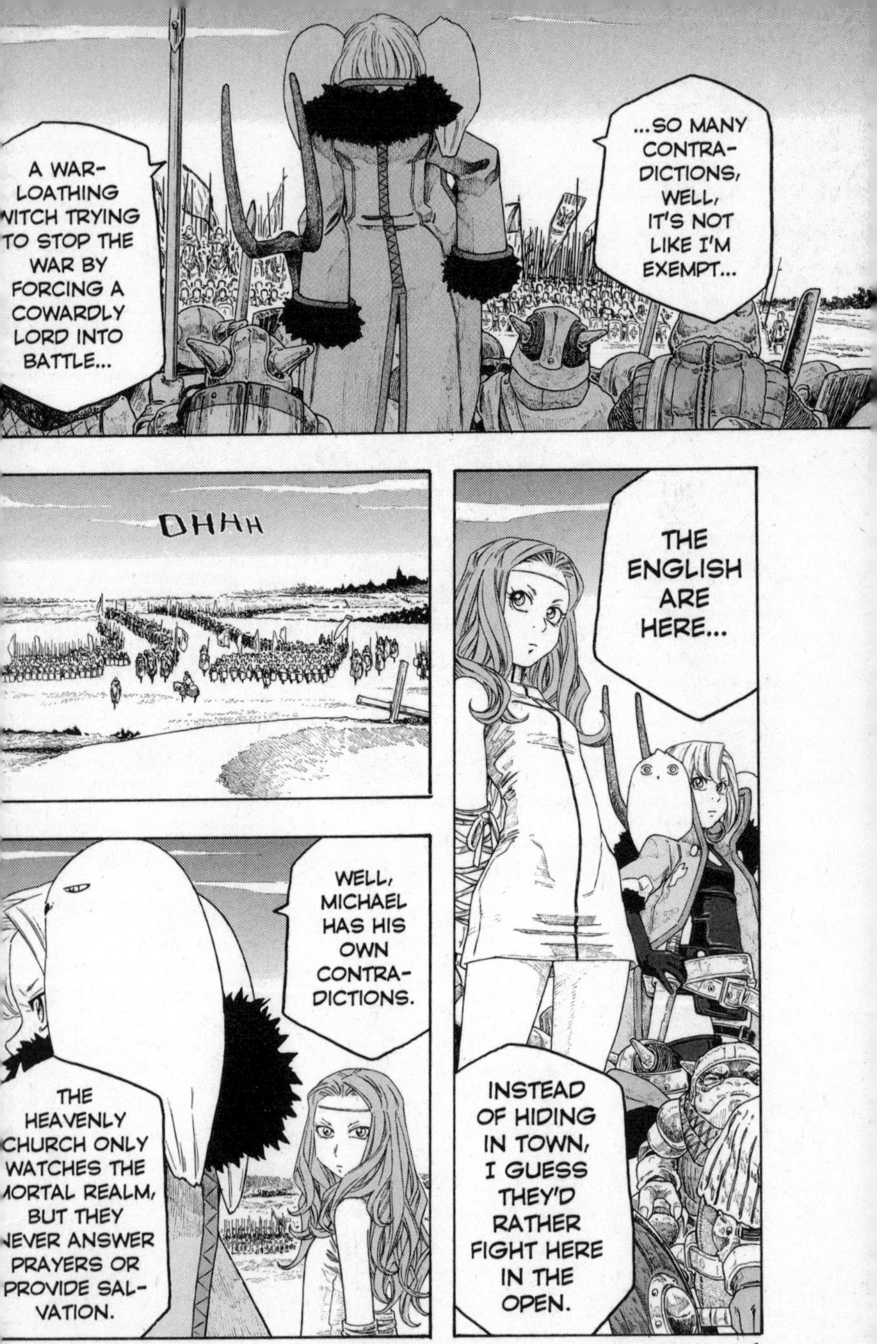
...SO MANY CONTRA-DICTIONS, WELL, IT'S NOT LIKE I'M EXEMPT...
A WAR-LOATHING WITCH TRYING TO STOP THE WAR BY FORCING A COWARDLY LORD INTO BATTLE...
THE ENGLISH ARE HERE...
INSTEAD OF HIDING IN TOWN, I GUESS THEY'D RATHER FIGHT HERE IN THE OPEN.
DHHH
WELL, MICHAEL HAS HIS OWN CONTRA-DICTIONS.
THE HEAVENLY CHURCH ONLY WATCHES THE MORTAL REALM, BUT THEY NEVER ANSWER PRAYERS OR PROVIDE SAL-VATION.

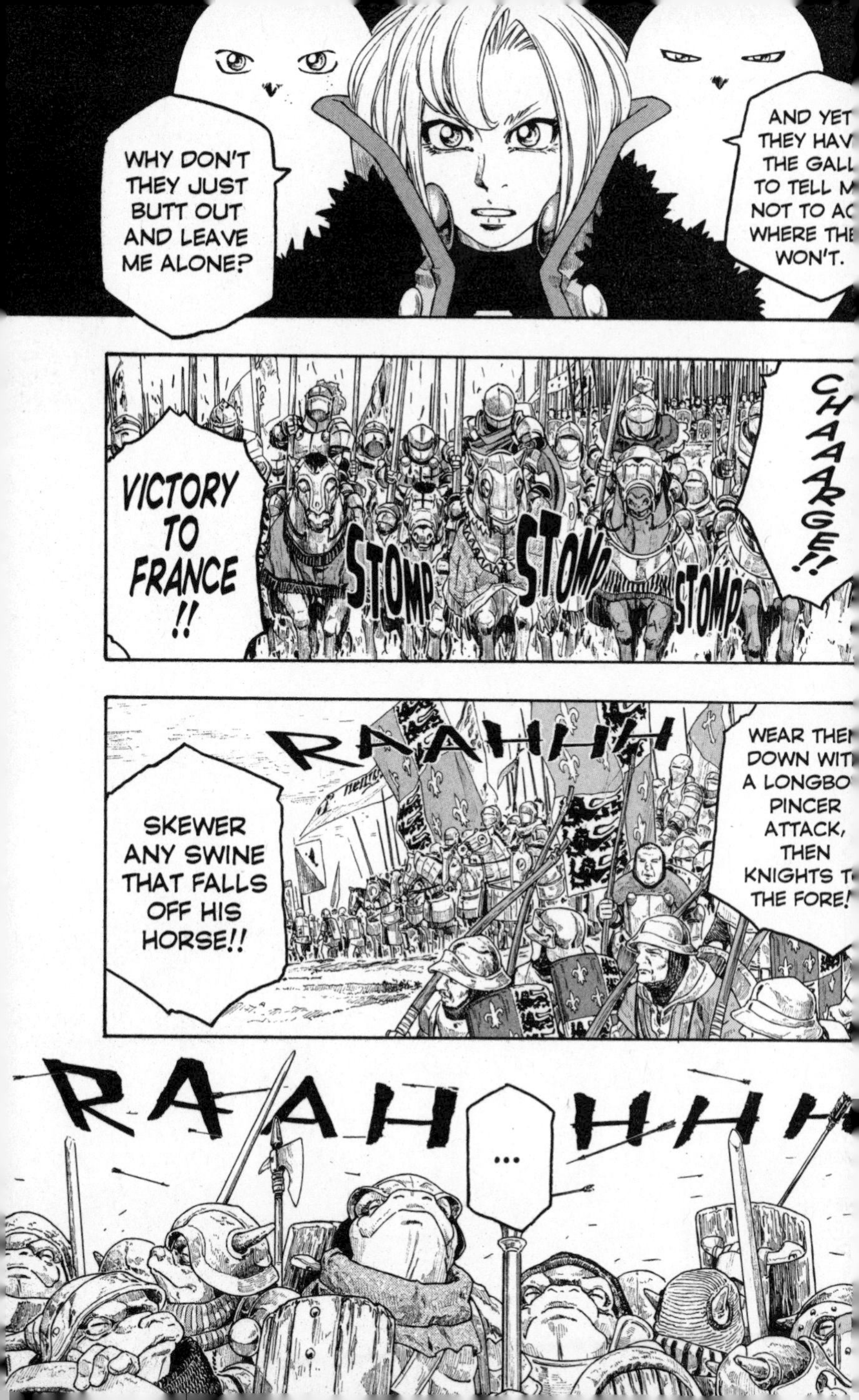
AND YET THEY HAV THE GALL TO TELL M NOT TO AC WHERE THE WON'T.
WHY DON'T THEY JUST BUTT OUT AND LEAVE ME ALONE?
CHAAARGE!!
STOMP
STOMP
STOMP
VICTORY TO FRANCE!!
WEAR THE DOWN WIT A LONGBO PINCER ATTACK, THEN KNIGHTS T THE FORE!
RAHHH
SKEWER ANY SWINE THAT FALLS OFF HIS HORSE!!
RAAHHHH
...

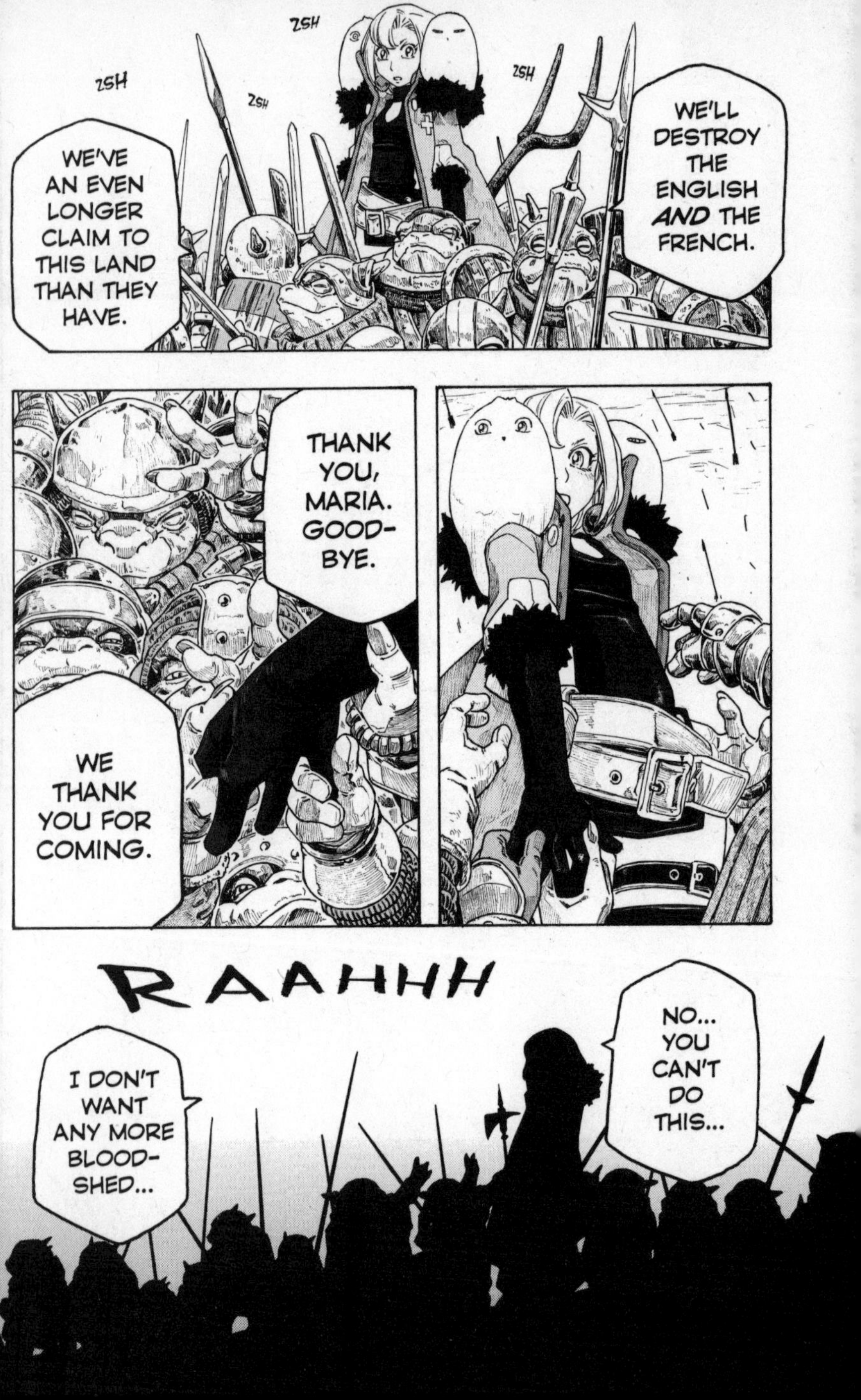
ZSH
ZSH
ZSH
ZSH
WE'LL DESTROY THE ENGLISH *AND* THE FRENCH.
WE'VE AN EVEN LONGER CLAIM TO THIS LAND THAN THEY HAVE.
THANK YOU, MARIA. GOOD-BYE.
WE THANK YOU FOR COMING.
RAAHHH
NO... YOU CAN'T DO THIS...
I DON'T WANT ANY MORE BLOOD-SHED...

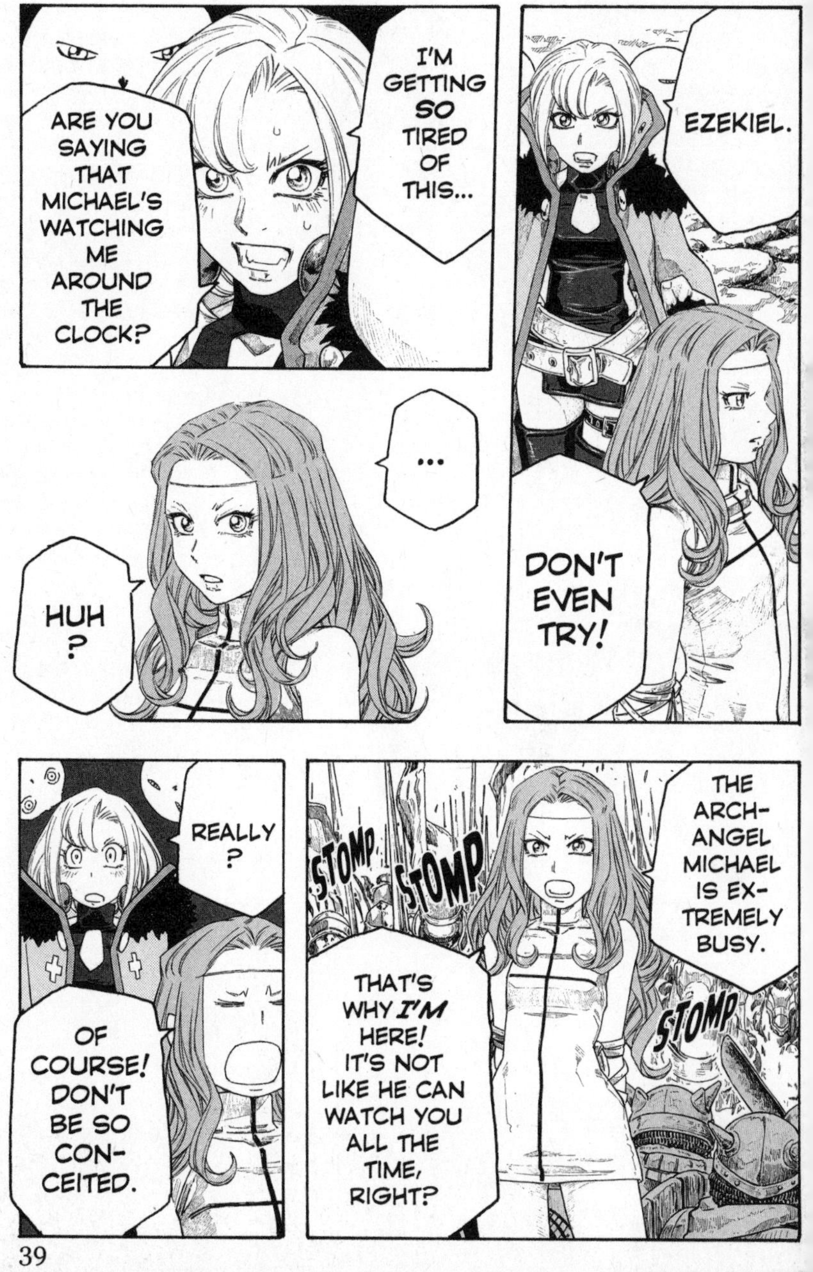
EZEKIEL.
DON'T EVEN TRY!
I'M GETTING SO TIRED OF THIS...
ARE YOU SAYING THAT MICHAEL'S WATCHING ME AROUND THE CLOCK?
...
HUH?
THE ARCH-ANGEL MICHAEL IS EX-TREMELY BUSY.
STOMP
STOMP
STOMP
THAT'S WHY *I'M* HERE! IT'S NOT LIKE HE CAN WATCH YOU ALL THE TIME, RIGHT?
REALLY?
OF COURSE! DON'T BE SO CON-CEITED.

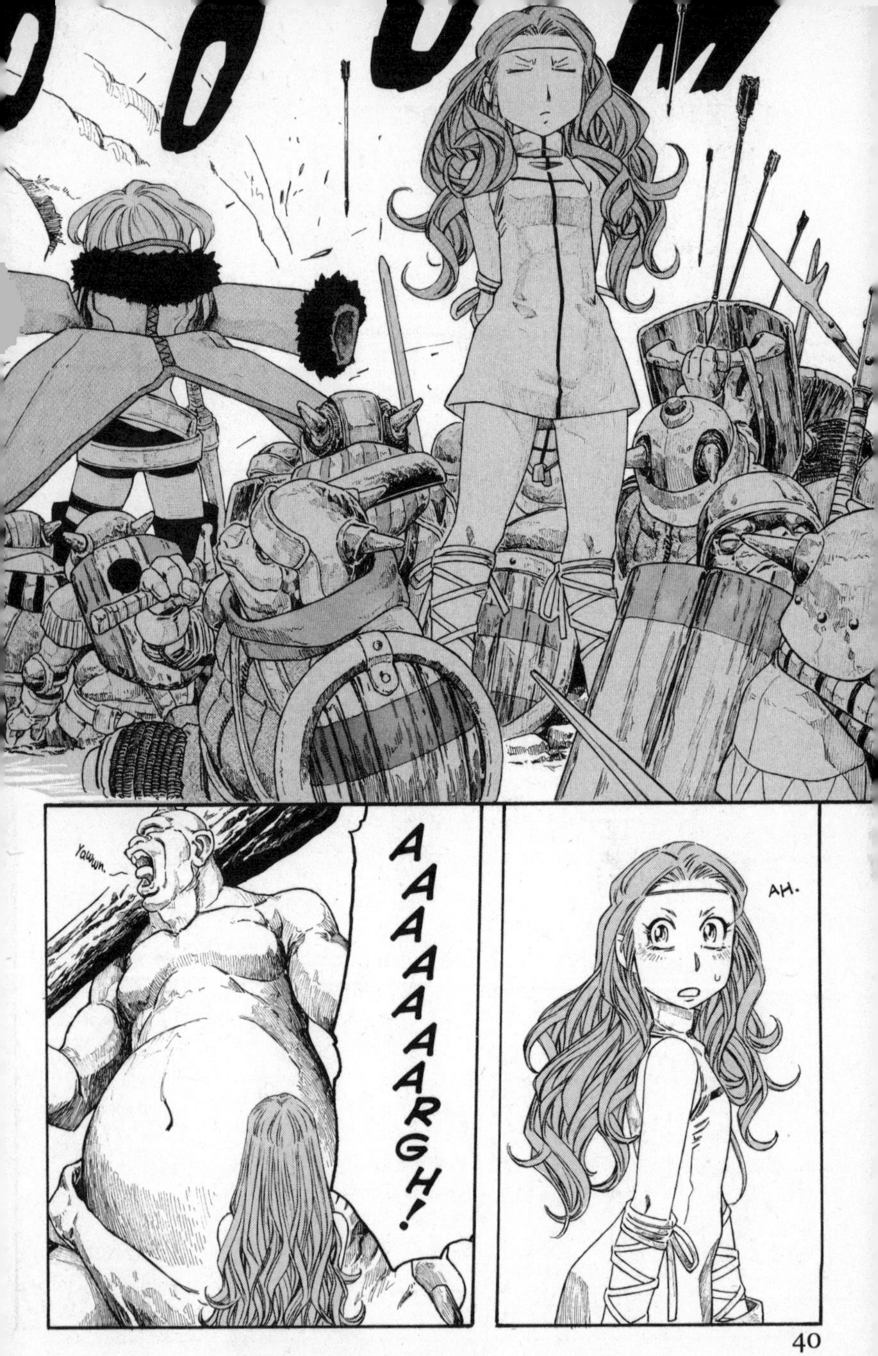
AH.
Yawwn.
AAAAAAARGH!

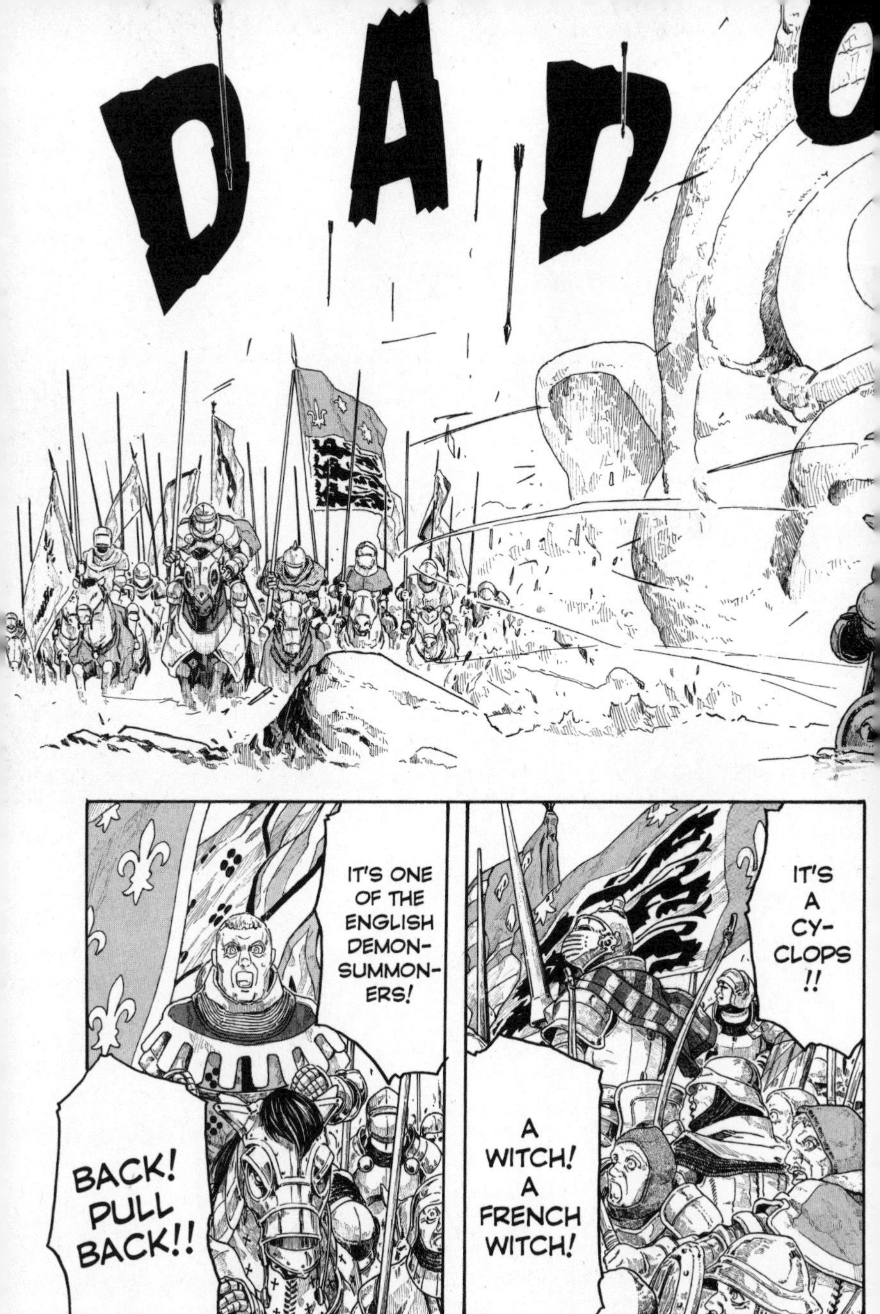
DADO
IT'S A CY-CLOPS!!
A WITCH! A FRENCH WITCH!
IT'S ONE OF THE ENGLISH DEMON-SUMMON-ERS!
BACK! PULL BACK!!

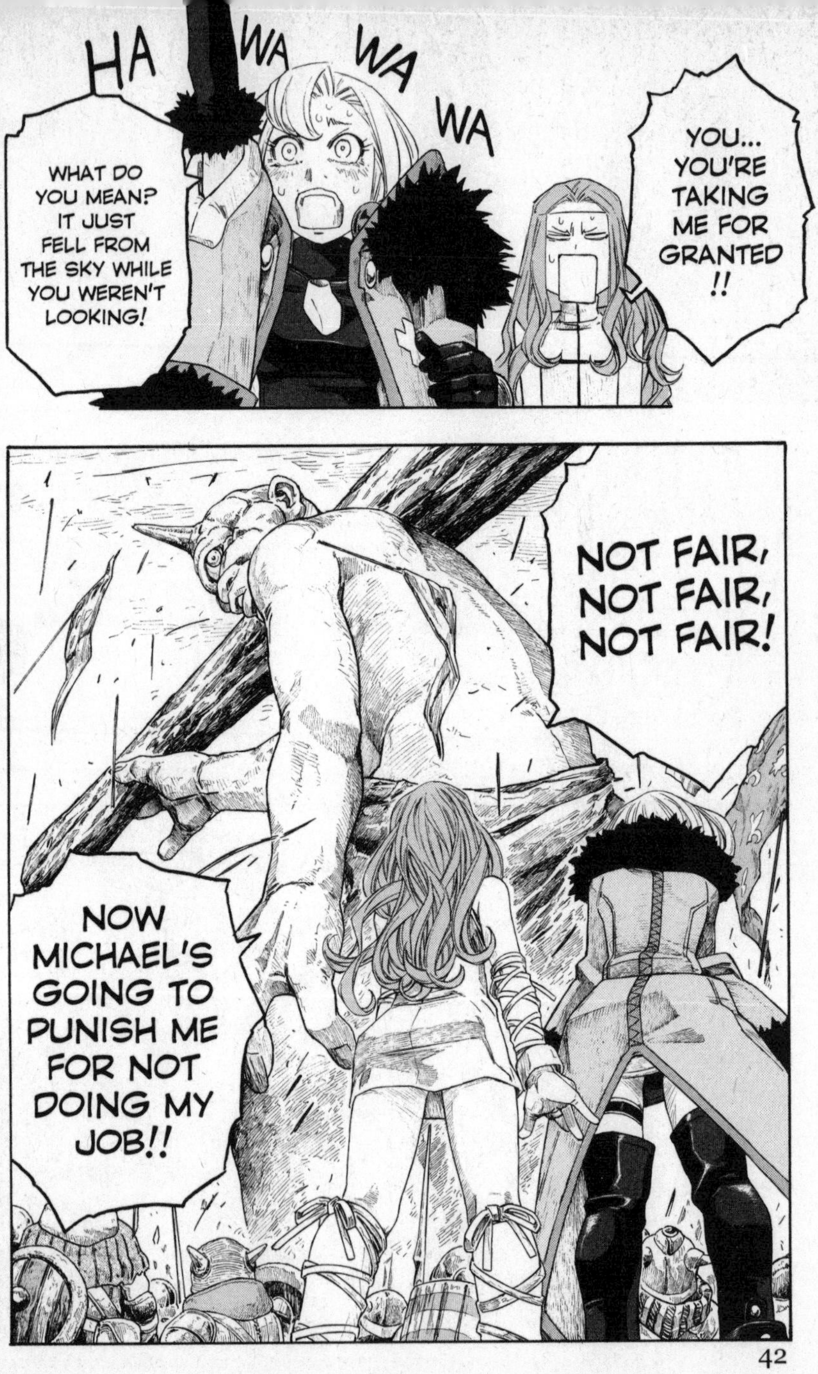
HA WA WA WA
YOU... YOU'RE TAKING ME FOR GRANTED!!
WHAT DO YOU MEAN? IT JUST FELL FROM THE SKY WHILE YOU WEREN'T LOOKING!
NOT FAIR, NOT FAIR, NOT FAIR!
NOW MICHAEL'S GOING TO PUNISH ME FOR NOT DOING MY JOB!!

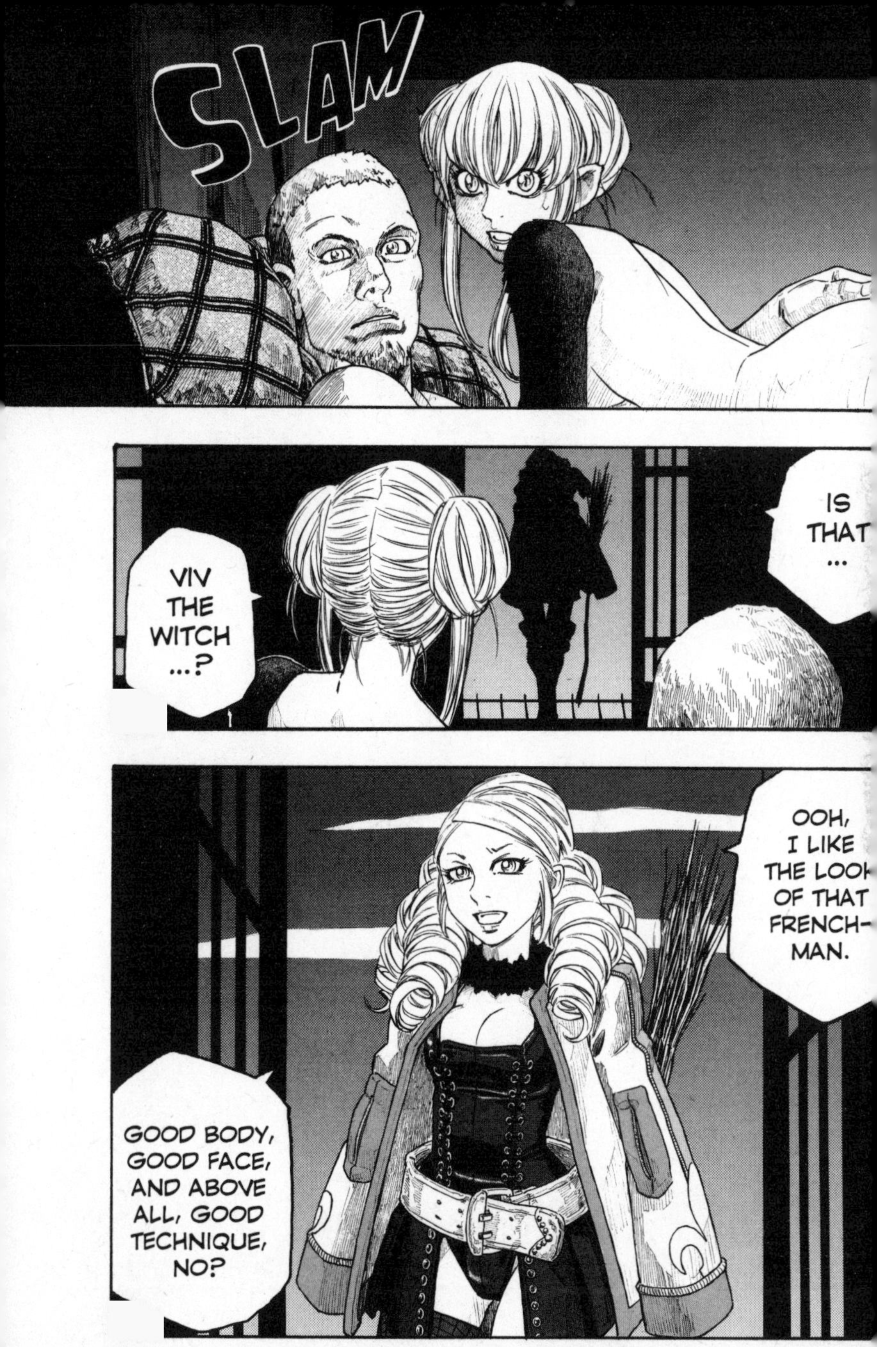
SLAM
IS THAT ...
VIV THE WITCH ...?
OOH, I LIKE THE LOOK OF THAT FRENCH-MAN.
GOOD BODY, GOOD FACE, AND ABOVE ALL, GOOD TECHNIQUE, NO?

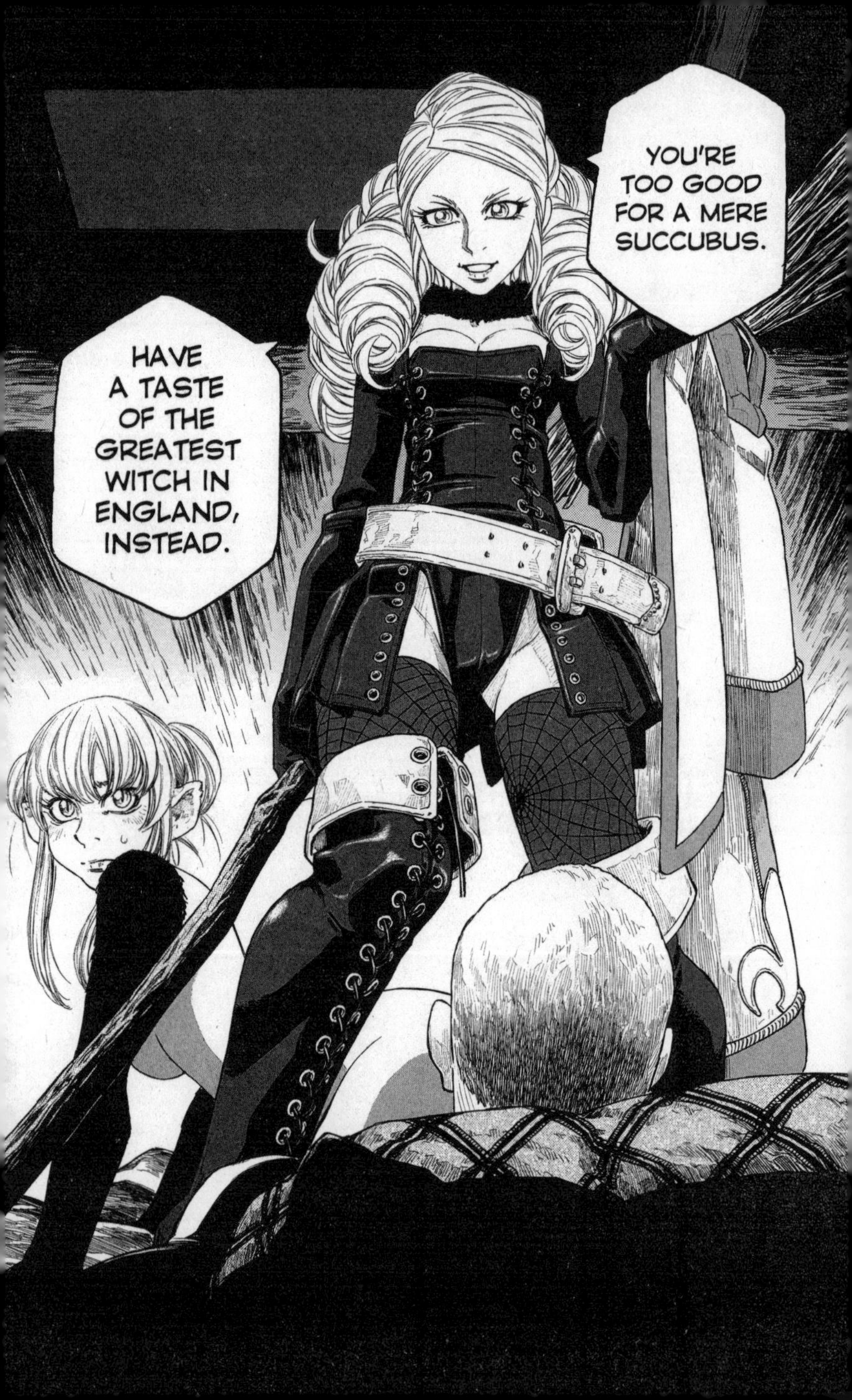
YOU'RE TOO GOOD FOR A MERE SUCCUBUS.
HAVE A TASTE OF THE GREATEST WITCH IN ENGLAND, INSTEAD.

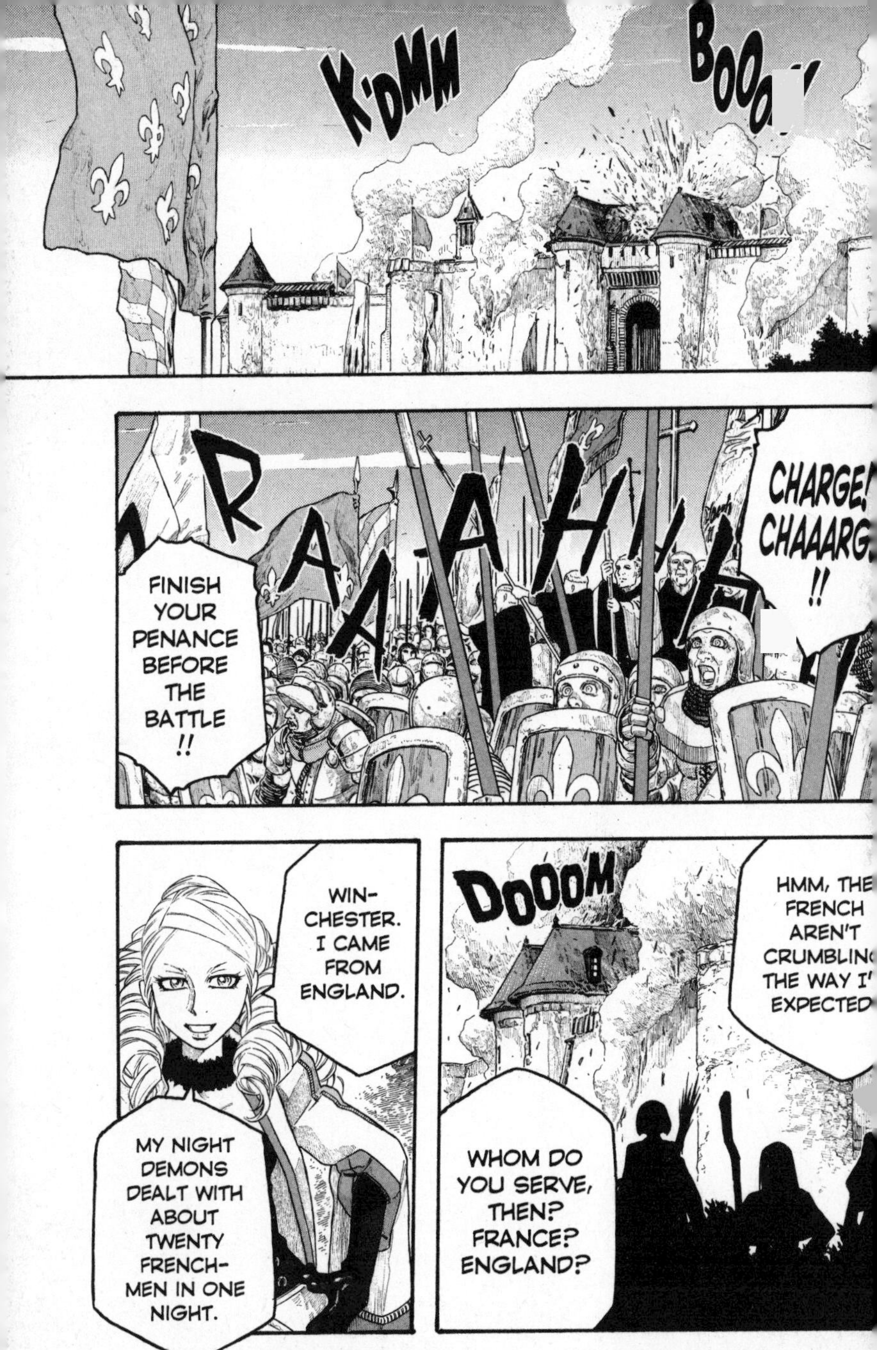
BOOO
K'DMM
CHARGE! CHAAARG !!
RAAAAHH
FINISH YOUR PENANCE BEFORE THE BATTLE !!
HMM, THE FRENCH AREN'T CRUMBLIN THE WAY I' EXPECTED
DOOOM
WHOM DO YOU SERVE, THEN? FRANCE? ENGLAND?
WIN-CHESTER. I CAME FROM ENGLAND.
MY NIGHT DEMONS DEALT WITH ABOUT TWENTY FRENCH-MEN IN ONE NIGHT.

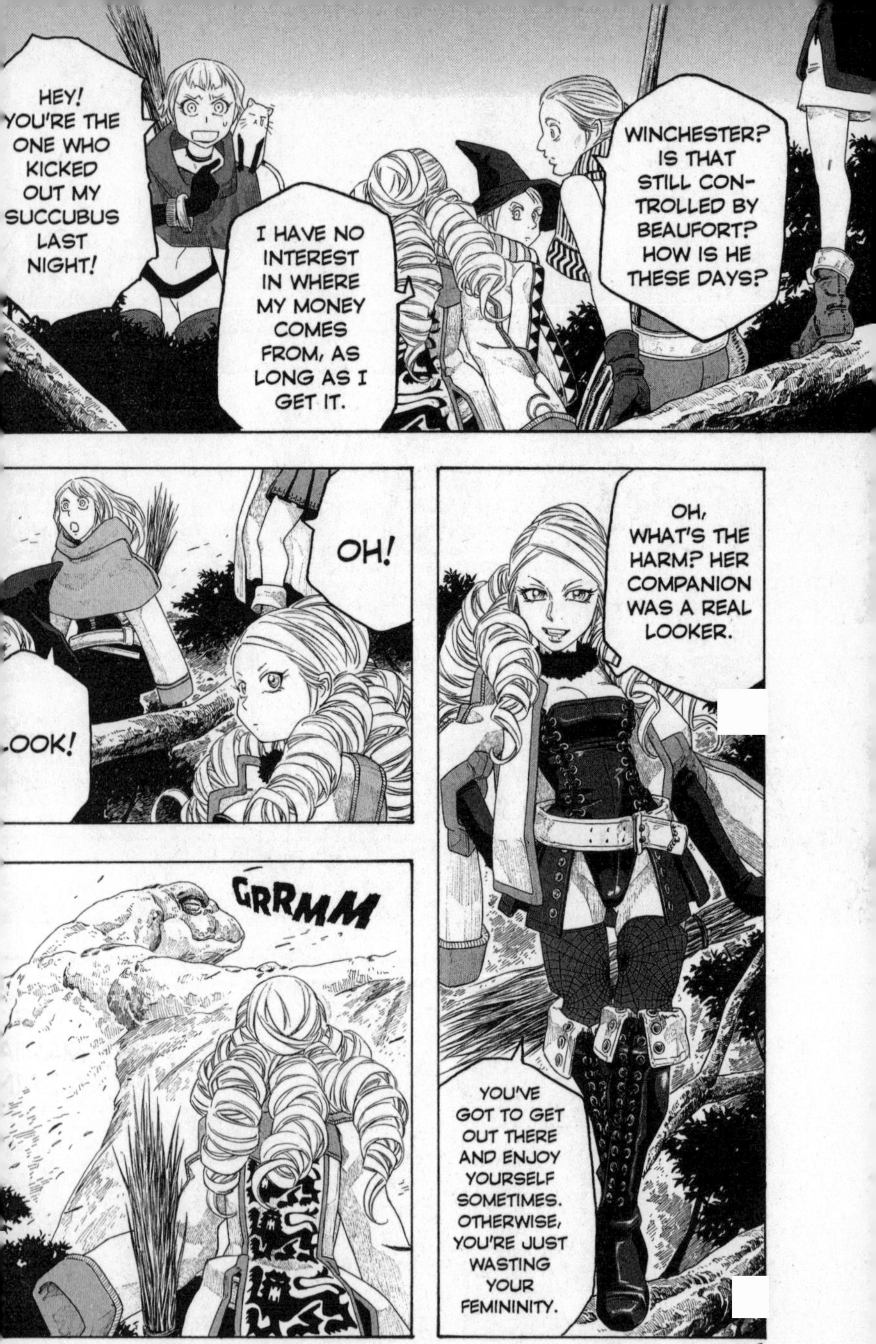
WINCHESTER? IS THAT STILL CON-TROLLED BY BEAUFORT? HOW IS HE THESE DAYS?
I HAVE NO INTEREST IN WHERE MY MONEY COMES FROM, AS LONG AS I GET IT.
HEY! YOU'RE THE ONE WHO KICKED OUT MY SUCCUBUS LAST NIGHT!
OH, WHAT'S THE HARM? HER COMPANION WAS A REAL LOOKER.
YOU'VE GOT TO GET OUT THERE AND ENJOY YOURSELF SOMETIMES. OTHERWISE, YOU'RE JUST WASTING YOUR FEMININITY.
OH!
OOK!
GRRMM

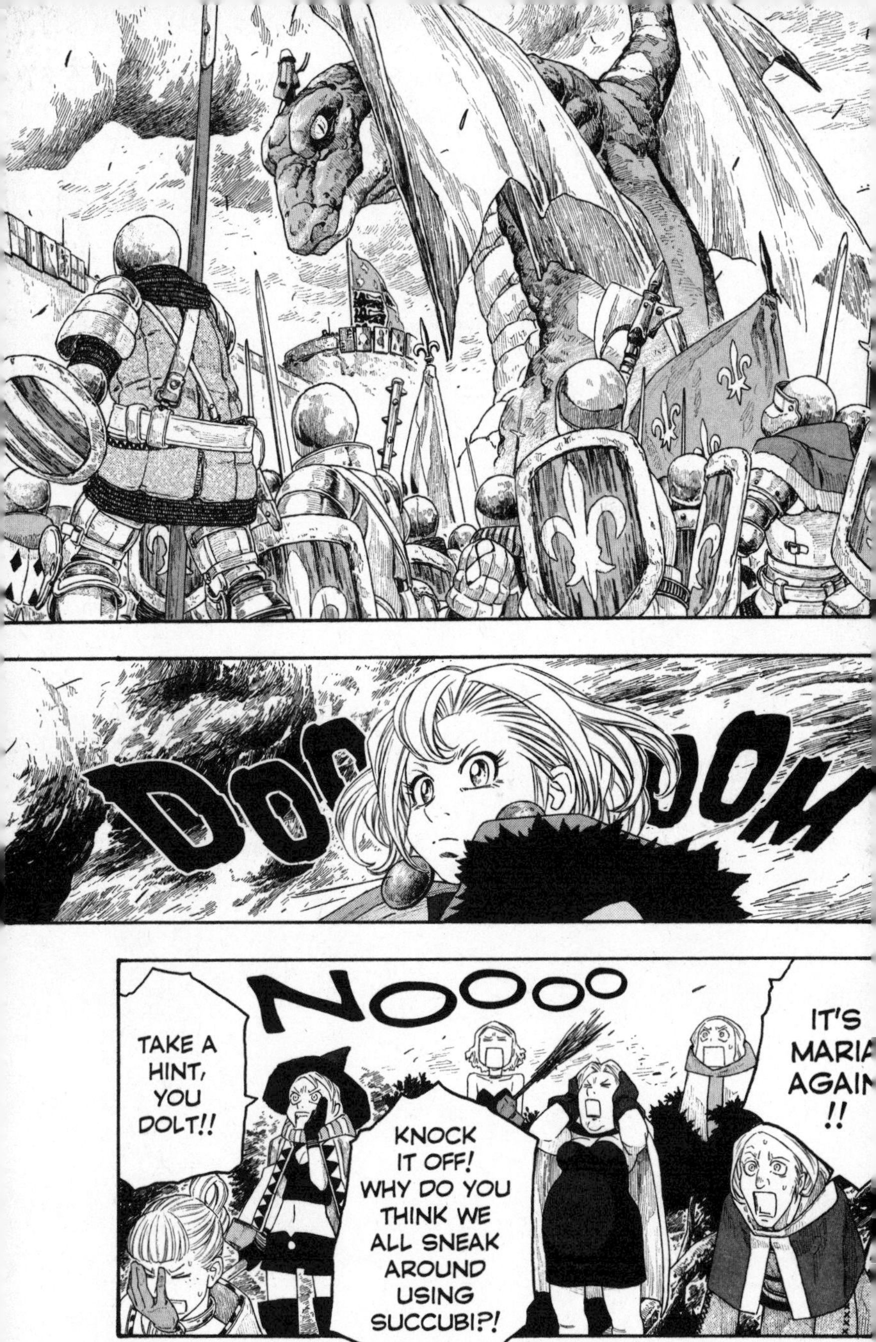
DOO
OOM
IT'S MARIA AGAIN!!
NOOOO
TAKE A HINT, YOU DOLT!!
KNOCK IT OFF! WHY DO YOU THINK WE ALL SNEAK AROUND USING SUCCUBI?!

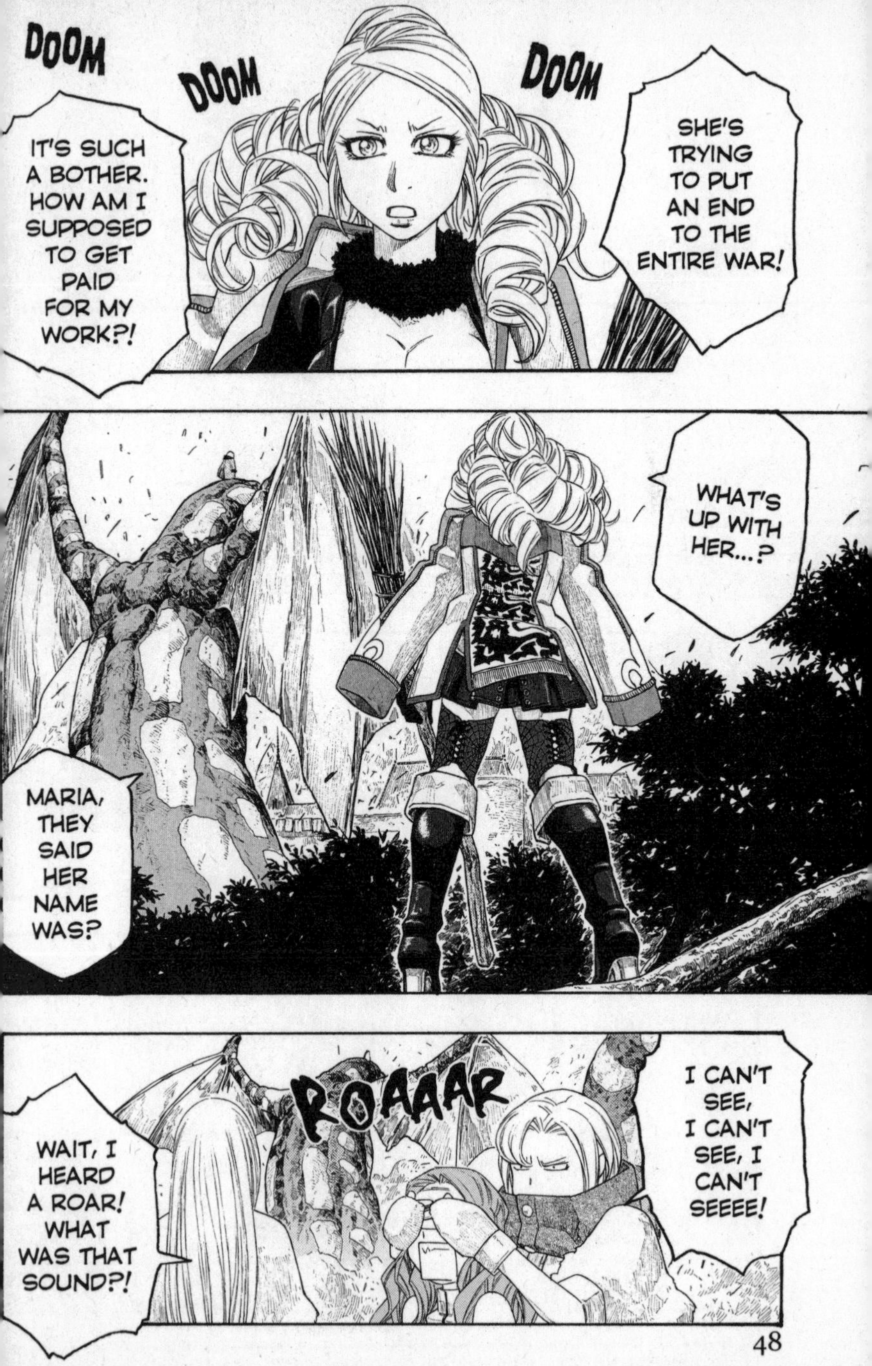
DOOM
DOOM
DOOM
SHE'S TRYING TO PUT AN END TO THE ENTIRE WAR!
IT'S SUCH A BOTHER. HOW AM I SUPPOSED TO GET PAID FOR MY WORK?!
WHAT'S UP WITH HER...?
MARIA, THEY SAID HER NAME WAS?
ROAAAR
I CAN'T SEE, I CAN'T SEE, I CAN'T SEEEE!
WAIT, I HEARD A ROAR! WHAT WAS THAT SOUND?!

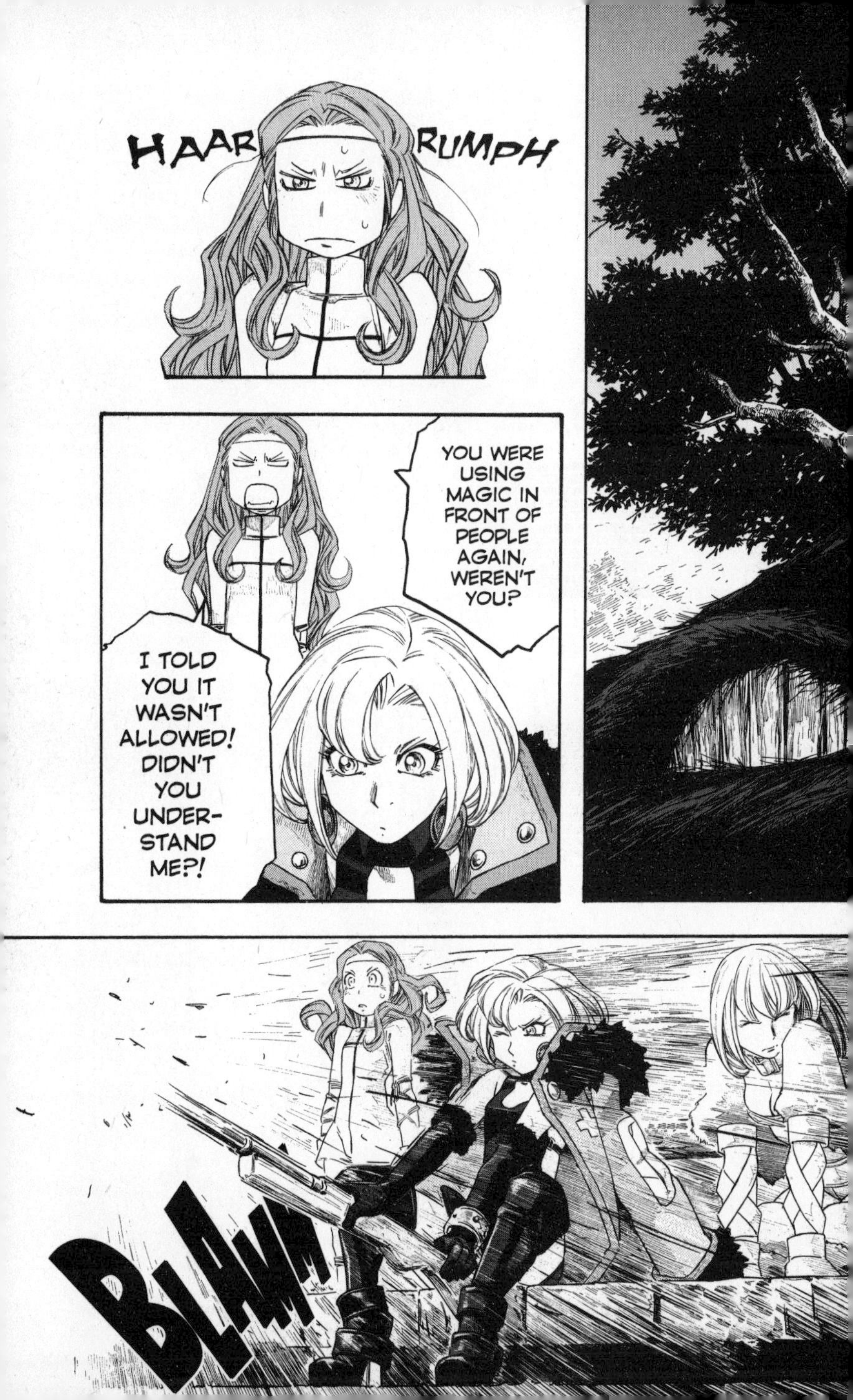
HAAR RUMPH
YOU WERE USING MAGIC IN FRONT OF PEOPLE AGAIN, WEREN'T YOU?
I TOLD YOU IT WASN'T ALLOWED! DIDN'T YOU UNDER-STAND ME?!
BLAMM

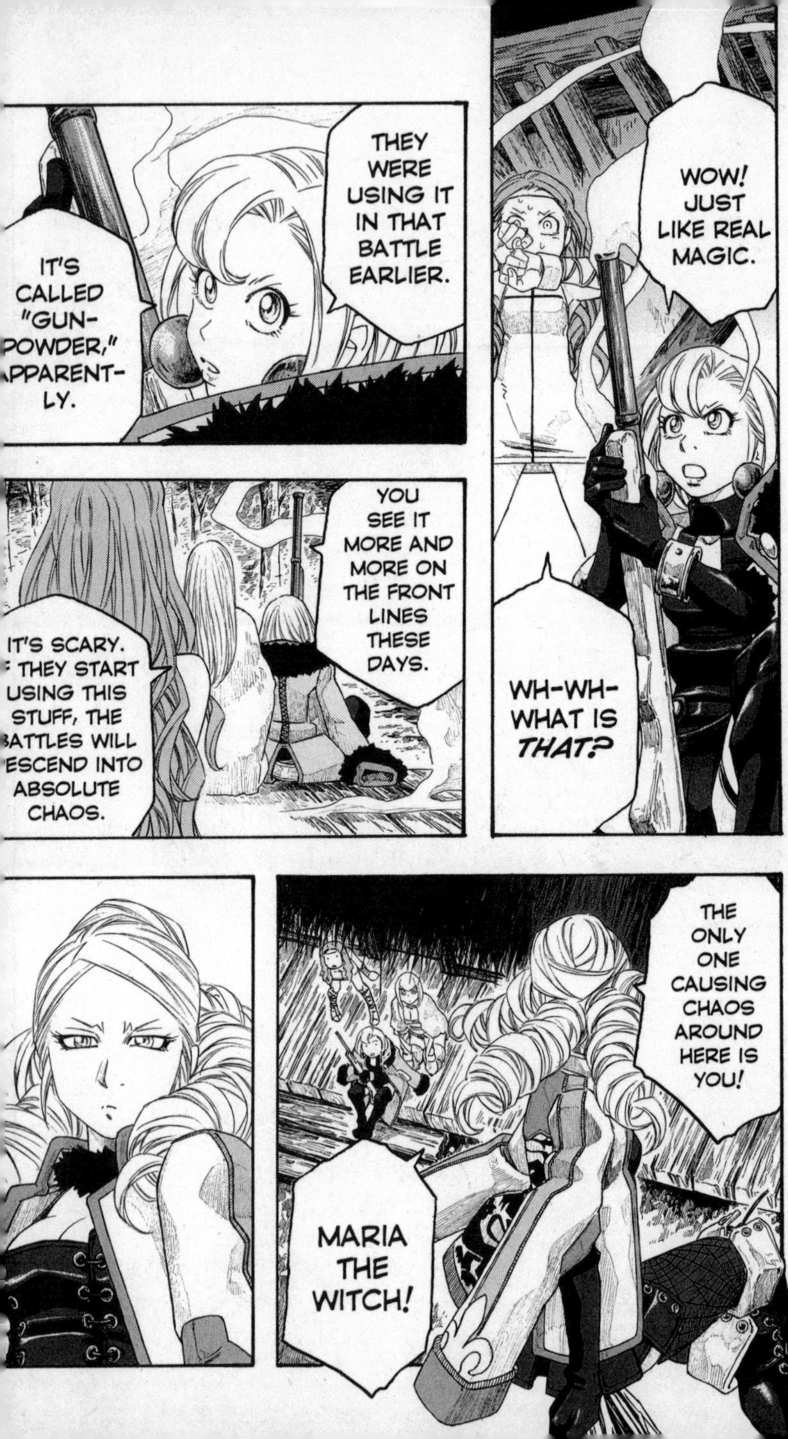

WOW! JUST LIKE REAL MAGIC.
WH-WH-WHAT IS *THAT?*
THEY WERE USING IT IN THAT BATTLE EARLIER.
IT'S CALLED "GUN-POWDER," PPARENT-LY.
YOU SEE IT MORE AND MORE ON THE FRONT LINES THESE DAYS.
IT'S SCARY. F THEY START USING THIS STUFF, THE ATTLES WILL ESCEND INTO ABSOLUTE CHAOS.
THE ONLY ONE CAUSING CHAOS AROUND HERE IS YOU!
MARIA THE WITCH!

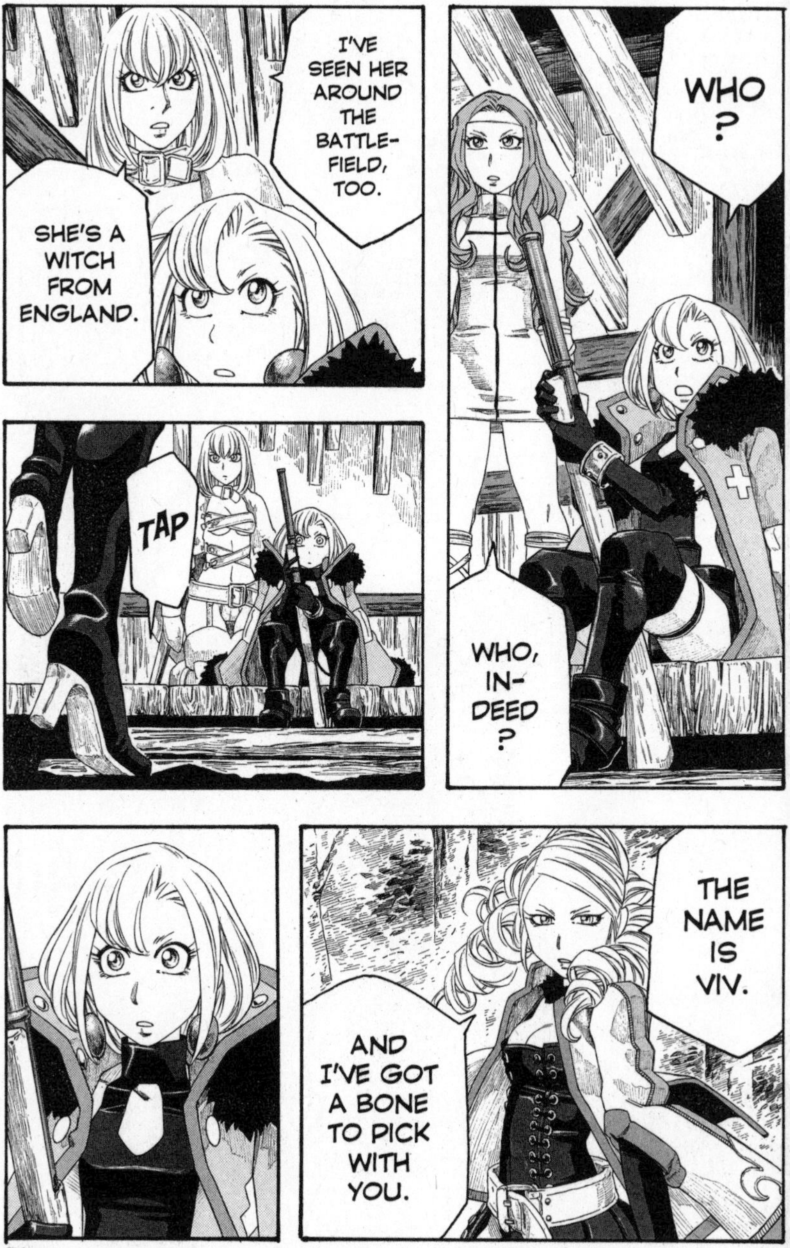
WHO ?
WHO, IN-DEED ?
I'VE SEEN HER AROUND THE BATTLE-FIELD, TOO.
SHE'S A WITCH FROM ENGLAND.
TAP
THE NAME IS VIV.
AND I'VE GOT A BONE TO PICK WITH YOU.

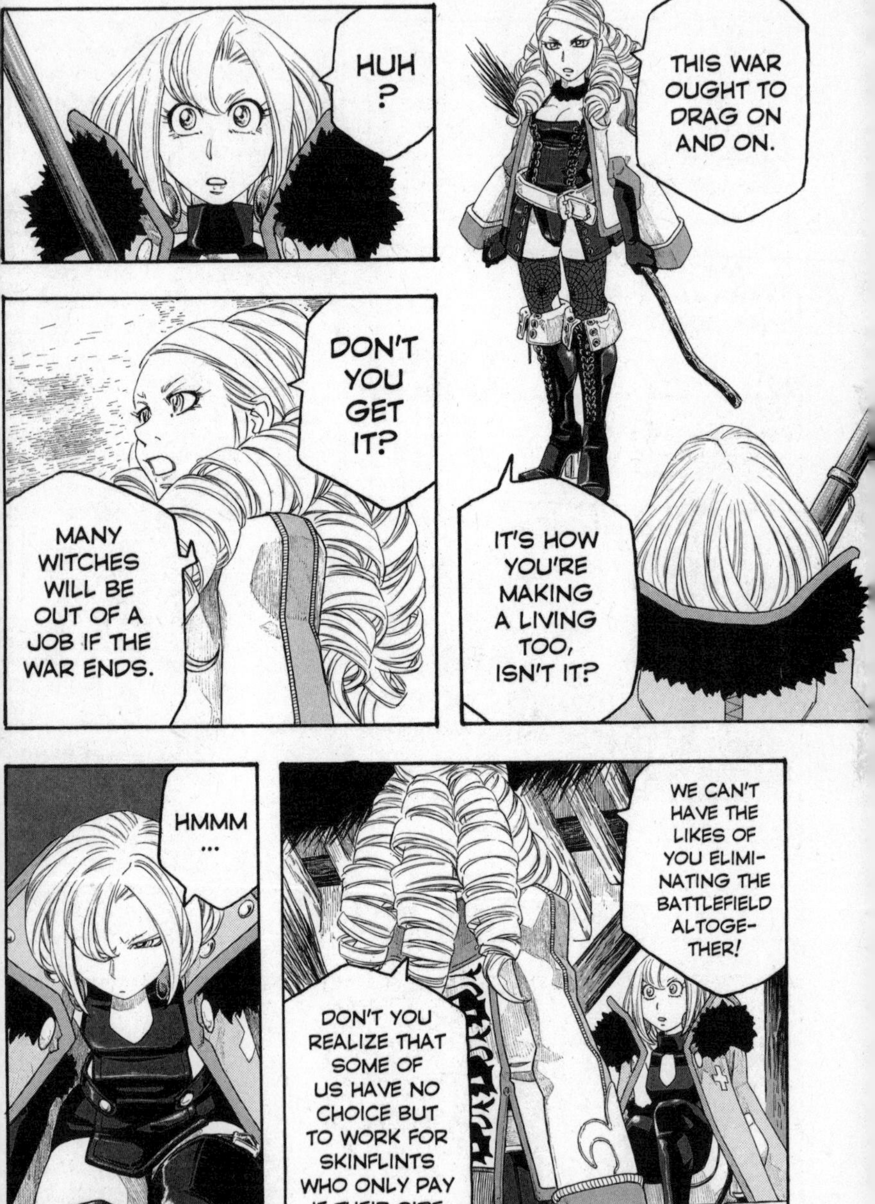
THIS WAR OUGHT TO DRAG ON AND ON.
HUH?
IT'S HOW YOU'RE MAKING A LIVING TOO, ISN'T IT?
DON'T YOU GET IT?
MANY WITCHES WILL BE OUT OF A JOB IF THE WAR ENDS.
WE CAN'T HAVE THE LIKES OF YOU ELIMINATING THE BATTLEFIELD ALTOGETHER!
DON'T YOU REALIZE THAT SOME OF US HAVE NO CHOICE BUT TO WORK FOR SKINFLINTS WHO ONLY PAY IF THEIR SIDE WINS?
HMMM...

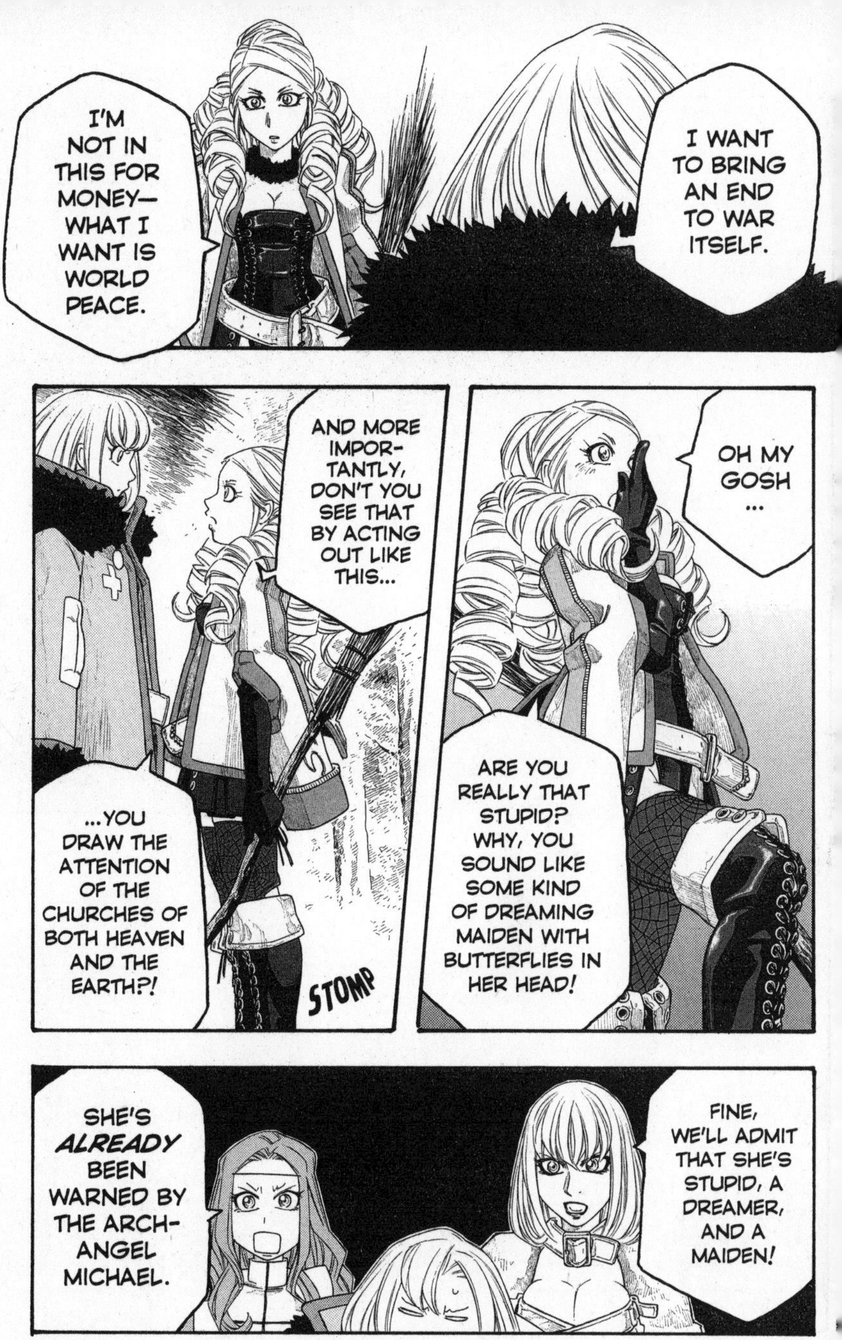
I WANT TO BRING AN END TO WAR ITSELF.
I'M NOT IN THIS FOR MONEY— WHAT I WANT IS WORLD PEACE.
OH MY GOSH ...
ARE YOU REALLY THAT STUPID? WHY, YOU SOUND LIKE SOME KIND OF DREAMING MAIDEN WITH BUTTERFLIES IN HER HEAD!
AND MORE IMPOR-TANTLY, DON'T YOU SEE THAT BY ACTING OUT LIKE THIS...
...YOU DRAW THE ATTENTION OF THE CHURCHES OF BOTH HEAVEN AND THE EARTH?!
STOMP
FINE, WE'LL ADMIT THAT SHE'S STUPID, A DREAMER, AND A MAIDEN!
SHE'S *ALREADY* BEEN WARNED BY THE ARCH-ANGEL MICHAEL.

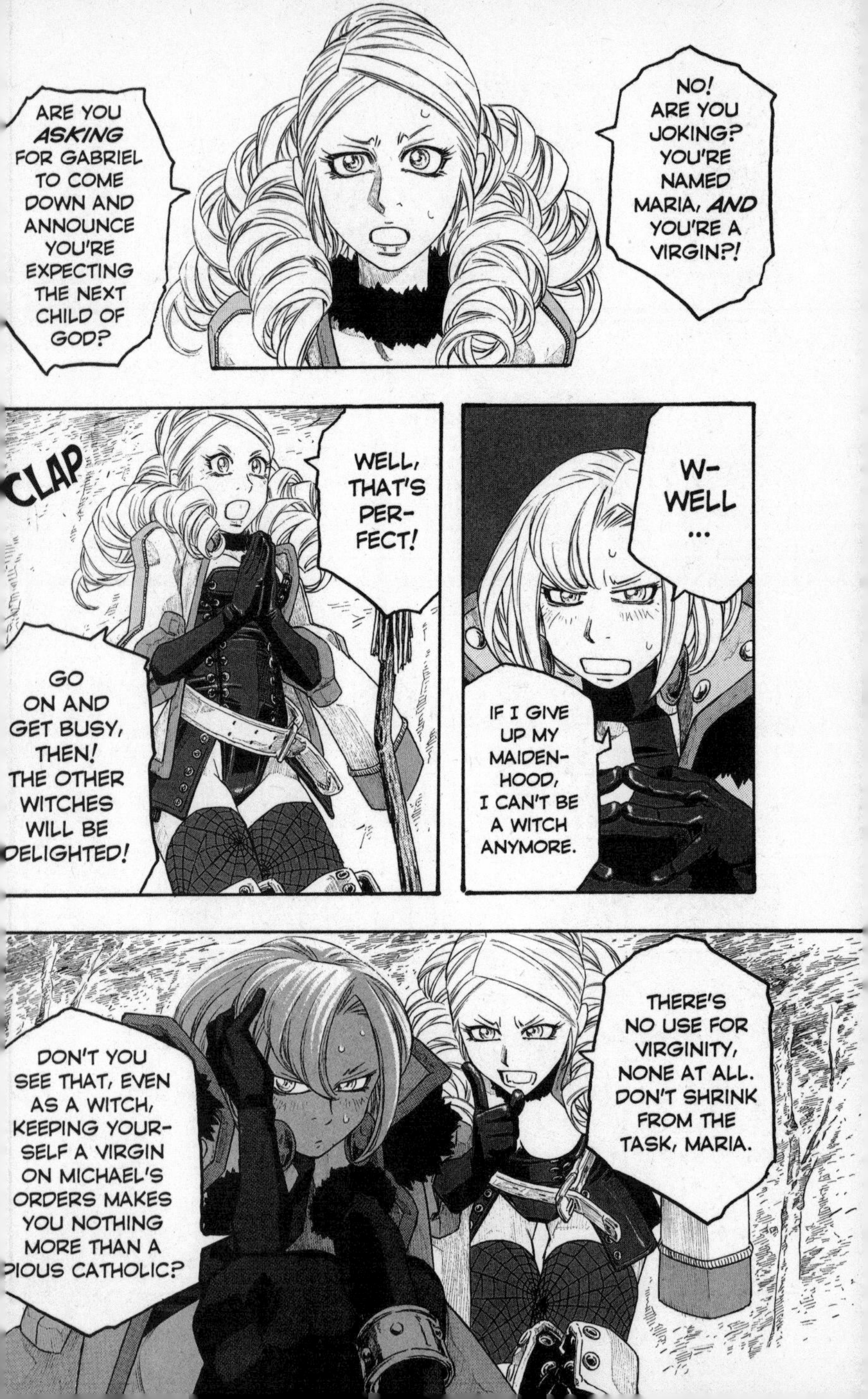
NO! ARE YOU JOKING? YOU'RE NAMED MARIA, *AND* YOU'RE A VIRGIN?!
ARE YOU *ASKING* FOR GABRIEL TO COME DOWN AND ANNOUNCE YOU'RE EXPECTING THE NEXT CHILD OF GOD?
W-WELL ...
IF I GIVE UP MY MAIDEN-HOOD, I CAN'T BE A WITCH ANYMORE.
WELL, THAT'S PER-FECT!
CLAP
GO ON AND GET BUSY, THEN! THE OTHER WITCHES WILL BE DELIGHTED!
THERE'S NO USE FOR VIRGINITY, NONE AT ALL. DON'T SHRINK FROM THE TASK, MARIA.
DON'T YOU SEE THAT, EVEN AS A WITCH, KEEPING YOUR-SELF A VIRGIN ON MICHAEL'S ORDERS MAKES YOU NOTHING MORE THAN A PIOUS CATHOLIC?

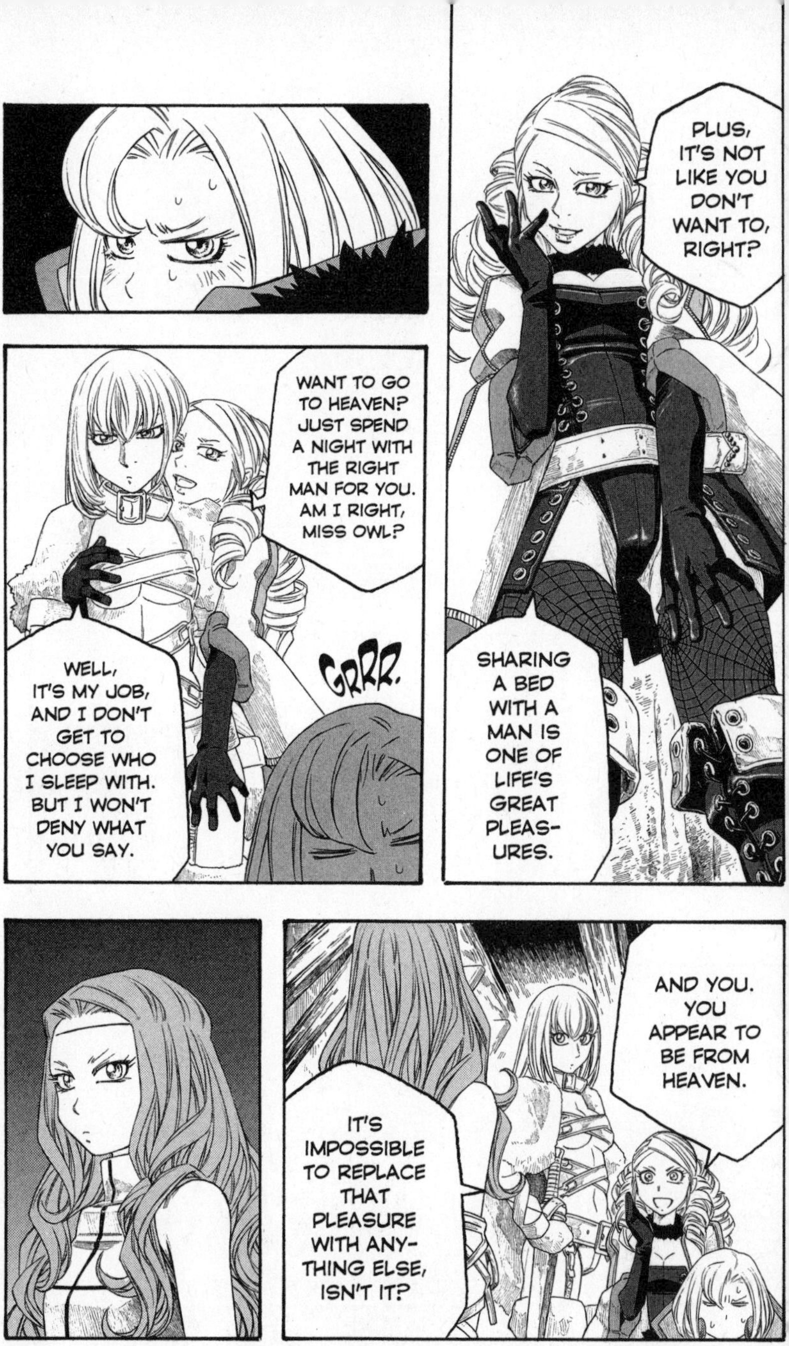
PLUS, IT'S NOT LIKE YOU DON'T WANT TO, RIGHT?
SHARING A BED WITH A MAN IS ONE OF LIFE'S GREAT PLEAS- URES.
WANT TO GO TO HEAVEN? JUST SPEND A NIGHT WITH THE RIGHT MAN FOR YOU. AM I RIGHT, MISS OWL?
GRRR.
WELL, IT'S MY JOB, AND I DON'T GET TO CHOOSE WHO I SLEEP WITH. BUT I WON'T DENY WHAT YOU SAY.
AND YOU. YOU APPEAR TO BE FROM HEAVEN.
IT'S IMPOSSIBLE TO REPLACE THAT PLEASURE WITH ANY- THING ELSE, ISN'T IT?

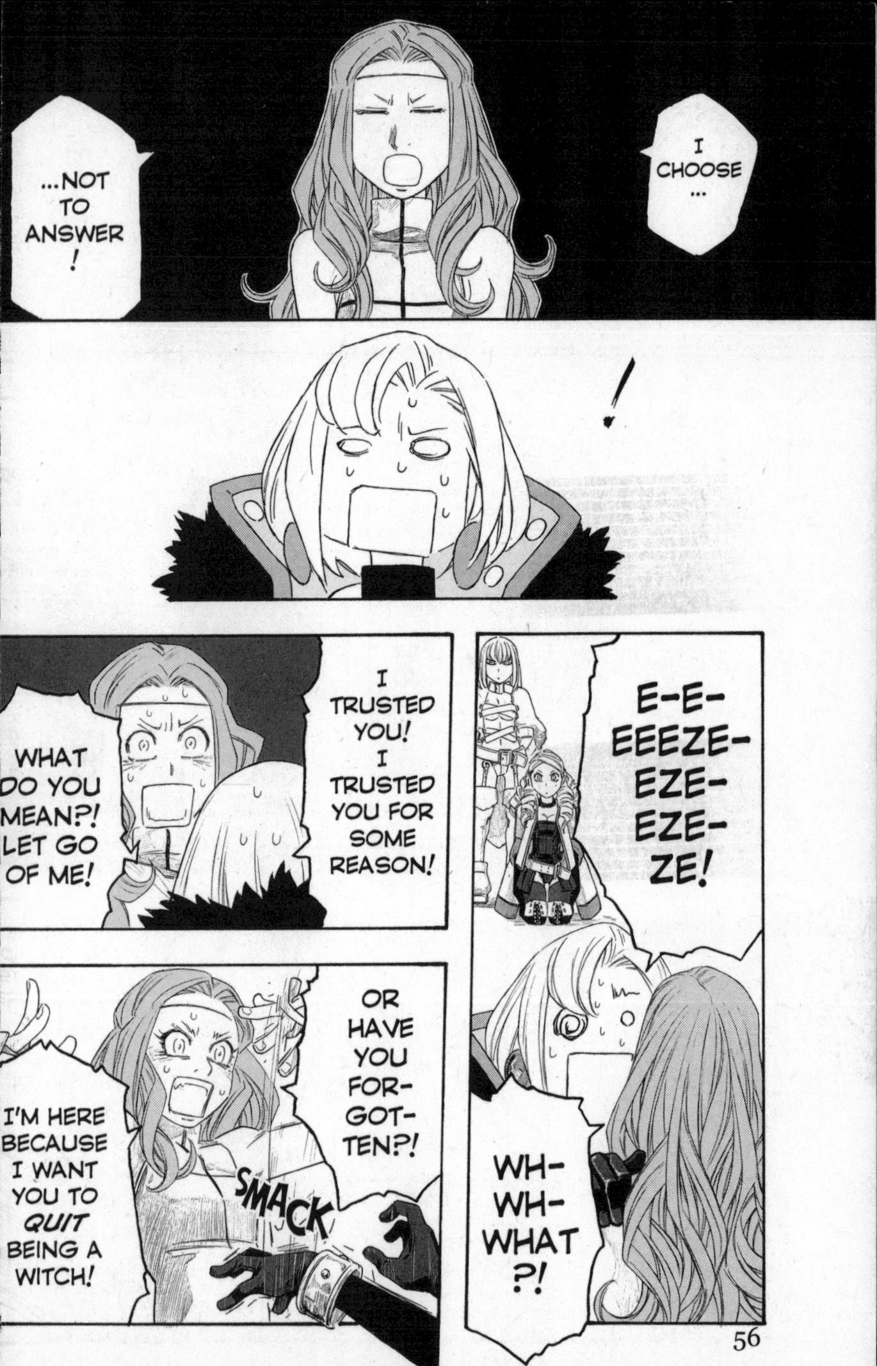
I CHOOSE ...
...NOT TO ANSWER!
!
E-E-EEEZE-EZE-EZE-ZE!
WH-WH-WHAT?!
I TRUSTED YOU! I TRUSTED YOU FOR SOME REASON!
WHAT DO YOU MEAN?! LET GO OF ME!
OR HAVE YOU FOR-GOT-TEN?!
I'M HERE BECAUSE I WANT YOU TO *QUIT* BEING A WITCH!
SMACK

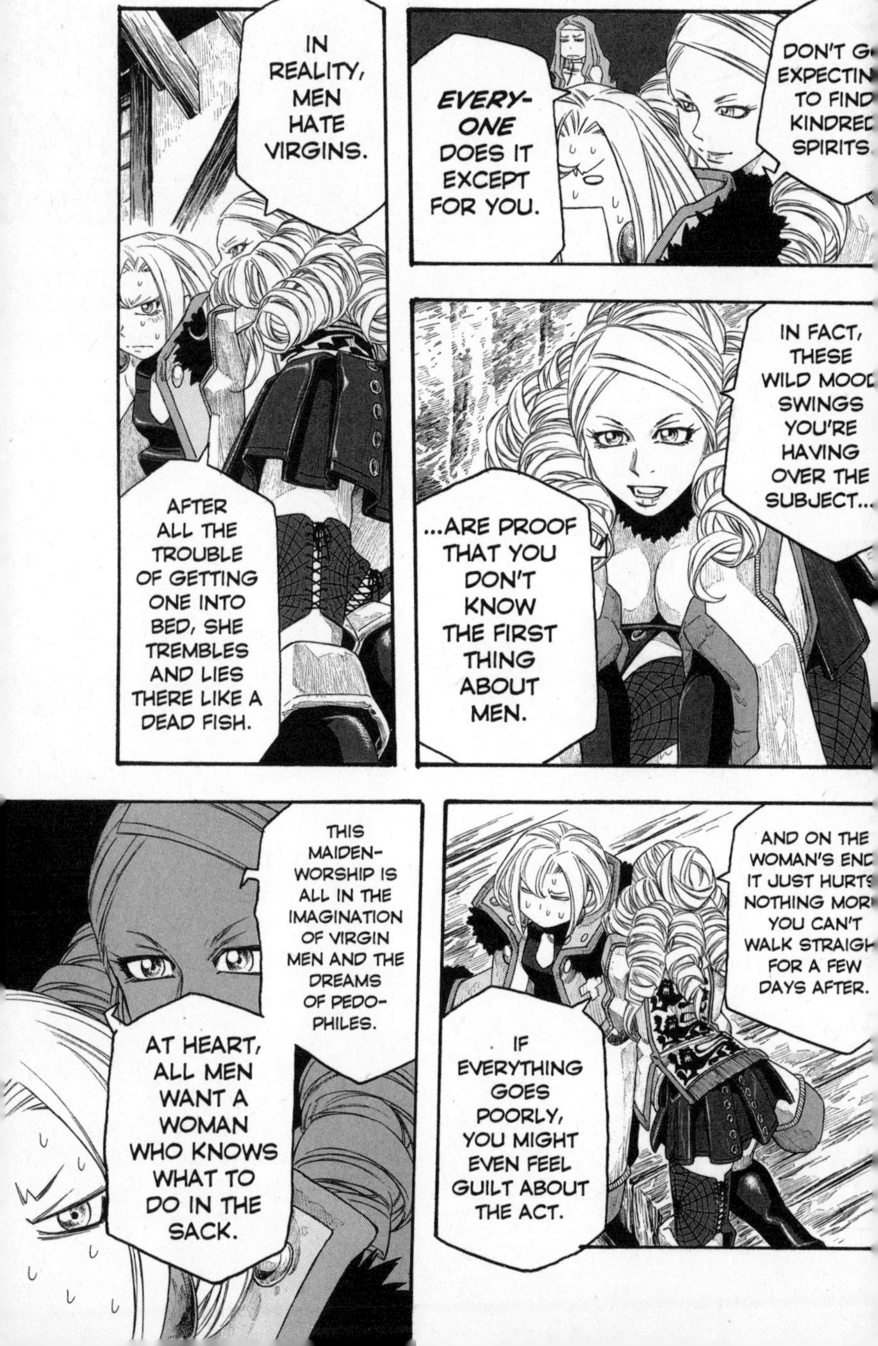
DON'T G EXPECTIN TO FIND KINDRED SPIRITS.
EVERY-ONE DOES IT EXCEPT FOR YOU.
IN FACT, THESE WILD MOOD SWINGS YOU'RE HAVING OVER THE SUBJECT...
...ARE PROOF THAT YOU DON'T KNOW THE FIRST THING ABOUT MEN.
IN REALITY, MEN HATE VIRGINS.
AFTER ALL THE TROUBLE OF GETTING ONE INTO BED, SHE TREMBLES AND LIES THERE LIKE A DEAD FISH.
AND ON THE WOMAN'S END IT JUST HURTS NOTHING MOR YOU CAN'T WALK STRAIGH FOR A FEW DAYS AFTER.
IF EVERYTHING GOES POORLY, YOU MIGHT EVEN FEEL GUILT ABOUT THE ACT.
THIS MAIDEN-WORSHIP IS ALL IN THE IMAGINATION OF VIRGIN MEN AND THE DREAMS OF PEDO-PHILES.
AT HEART, ALL MEN WANT A WOMAN WHO KNOWS WHAT TO DO IN THE SACK.

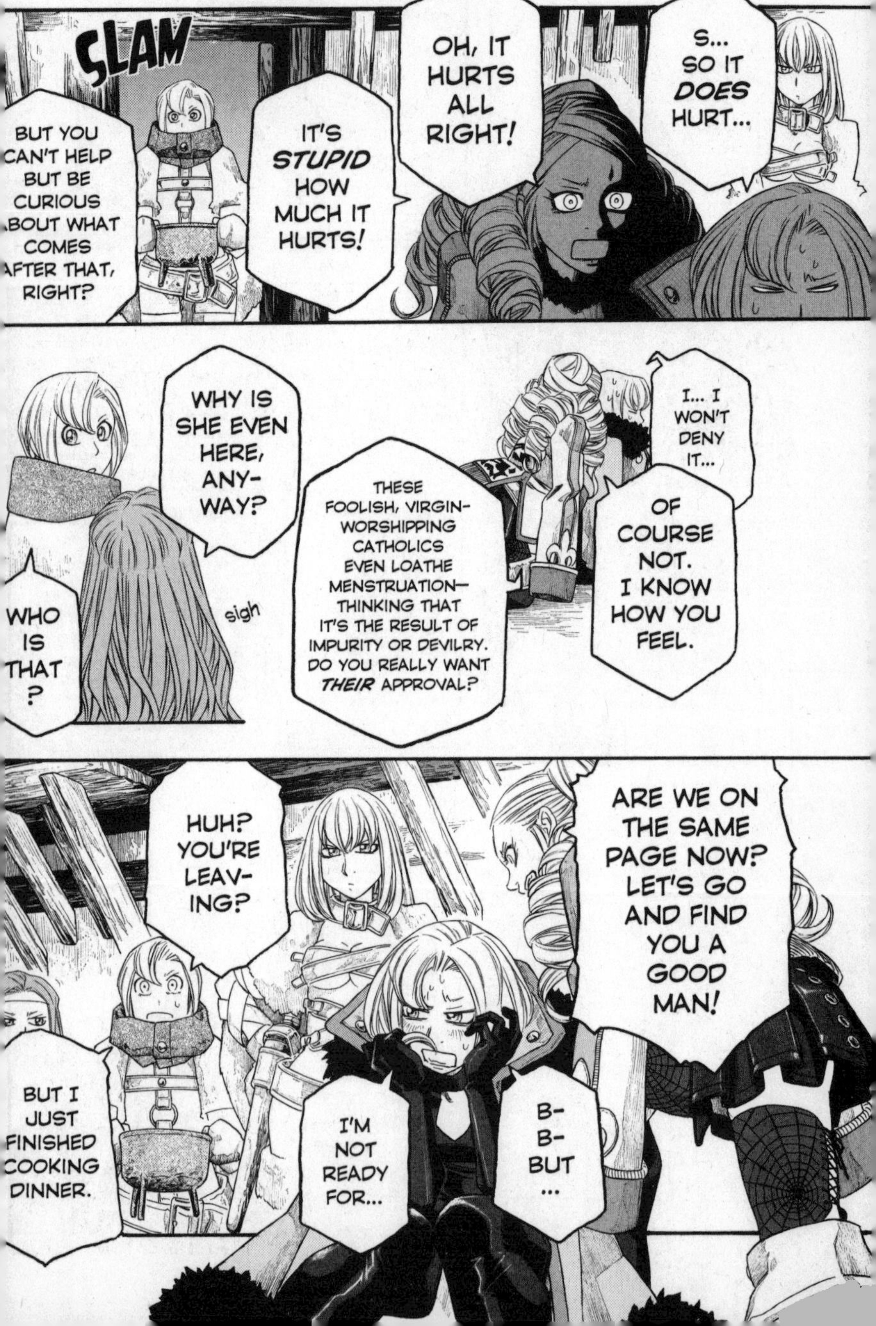
S... SO IT *DOES* HURT...
OH, IT HURTS ALL RIGHT!
IT'S *STUPID* HOW MUCH IT HURTS!
SLAM
BUT YOU CAN'T HELP BUT BE CURIOUS ABOUT WHAT COMES AFTER THAT, RIGHT?
I... I WON'T DENY IT...
OF COURSE NOT. I KNOW HOW YOU FEEL.
THESE FOOLISH, VIRGIN-WORSHIPPING CATHOLICS EVEN LOATHE MENSTRUATION—THINKING THAT IT'S THE RESULT OF IMPURITY OR DEVILRY. DO YOU REALLY WANT *THEIR* APPROVAL?
WHY IS SHE EVEN HERE, ANY-WAY?
sigh
WHO IS THAT?
ARE WE ON THE SAME PAGE NOW? LET'S GO AND FIND YOU A GOOD MAN!
B-B-BUT...
I'M NOT READY FOR...
HUH? YOU'RE LEAV-ING?
BUT I JUST FINISHED COOKING DINNER.

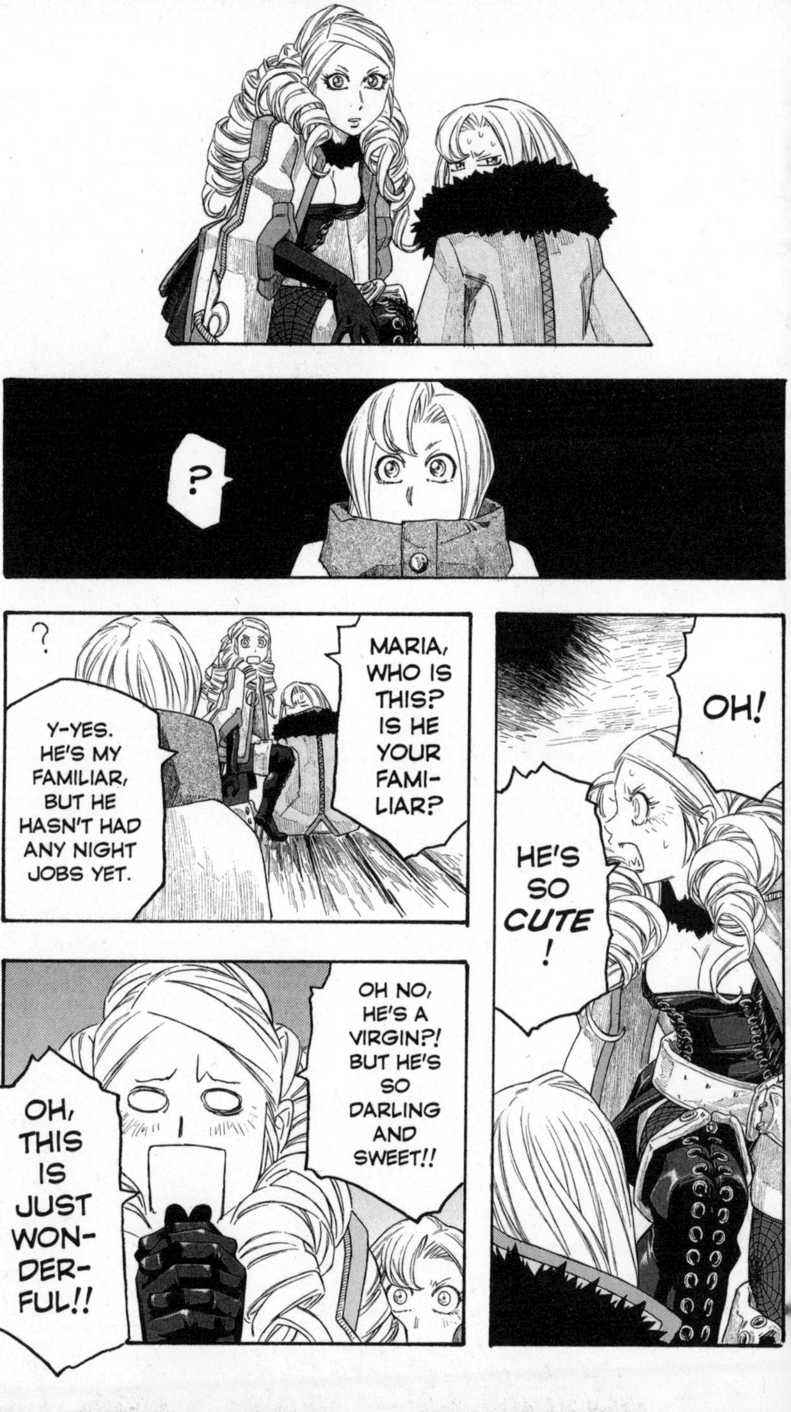
?
OH!
HE'S SO CUTE!
MARIA, WHO IS THIS? IS HE YOUR FAMILIAR?
?
Y-YES. HE'S MY FAMILIAR, BUT HE HASN'T HAD ANY NIGHT JOBS YET.
OH NO, HE'S A VIRGIN?! BUT HE'S SO DARLING AND SWEET!!
OH, THIS IS JUST WONDERFUL!!

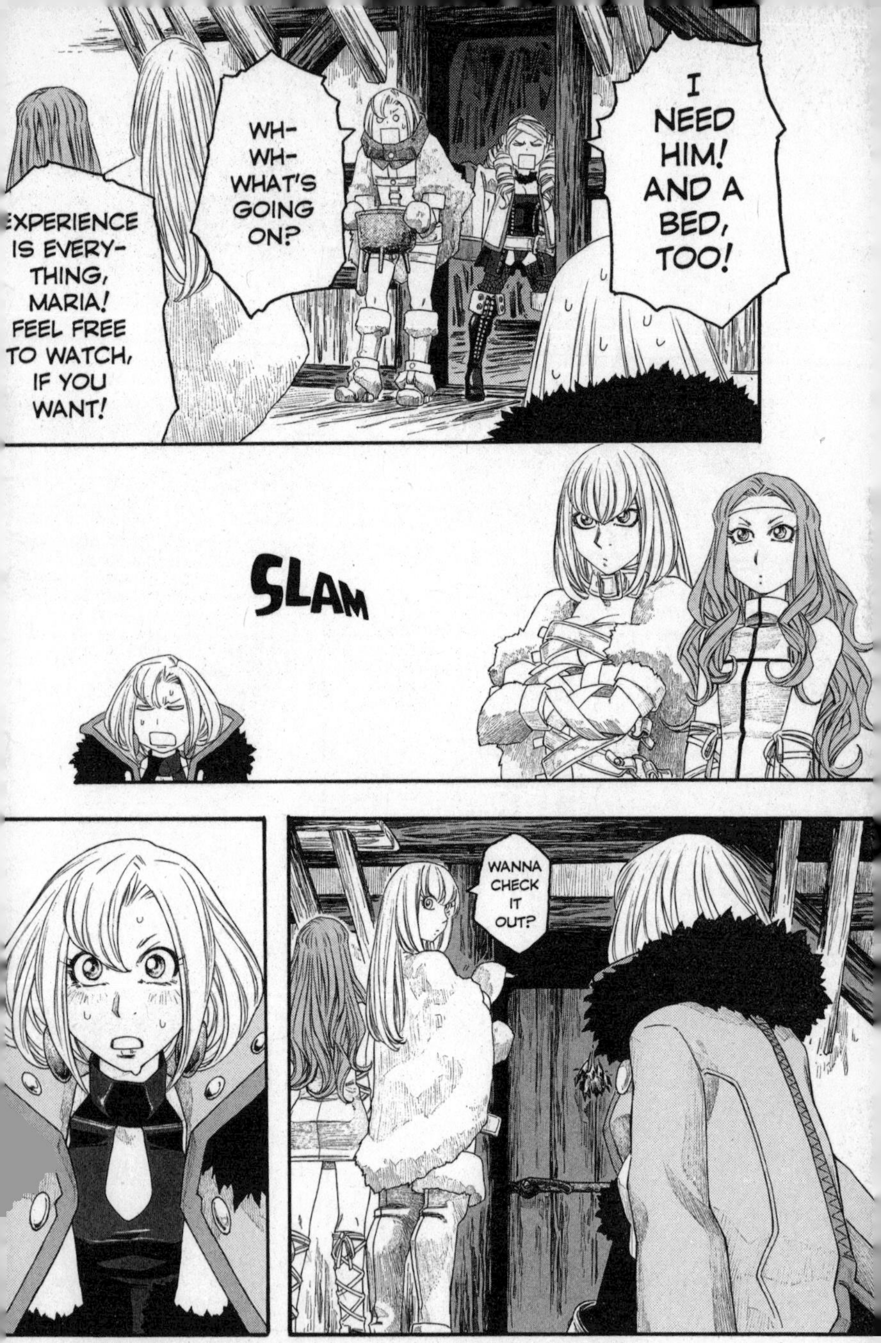
I NEED HIM! AND A BED, TOO!
WH-WH-WHAT'S GOING ON?
EXPERIENCE IS EVERYTHING, MARIA! FEEL FREE TO WATCH, IF YOU WANT!
SLAM
WANNA CHECK IT OUT?

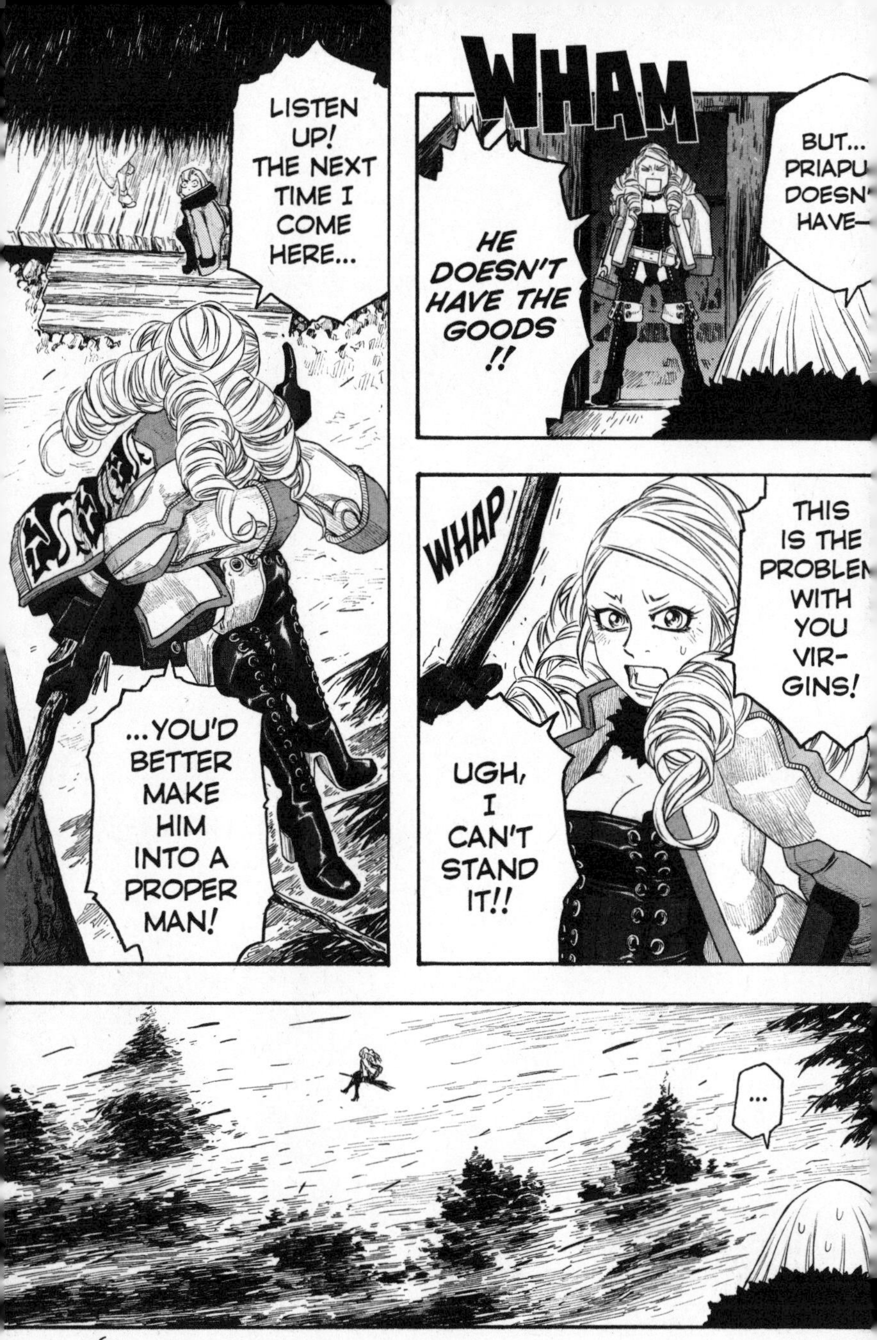
BUT... PRIAPU DOESN' HAVE—
WHAM
HE DOESN'T HAVE THE GOODS!!
WHAP
THIS IS THE PROBLEM WITH YOU VIR-GINS!
UGH, I CAN'T STAND IT!!
LISTEN UP! THE NEXT TIME I COME HERE...
...YOU'D BETTER MAKE HIM INTO A PROPER MAN!
...

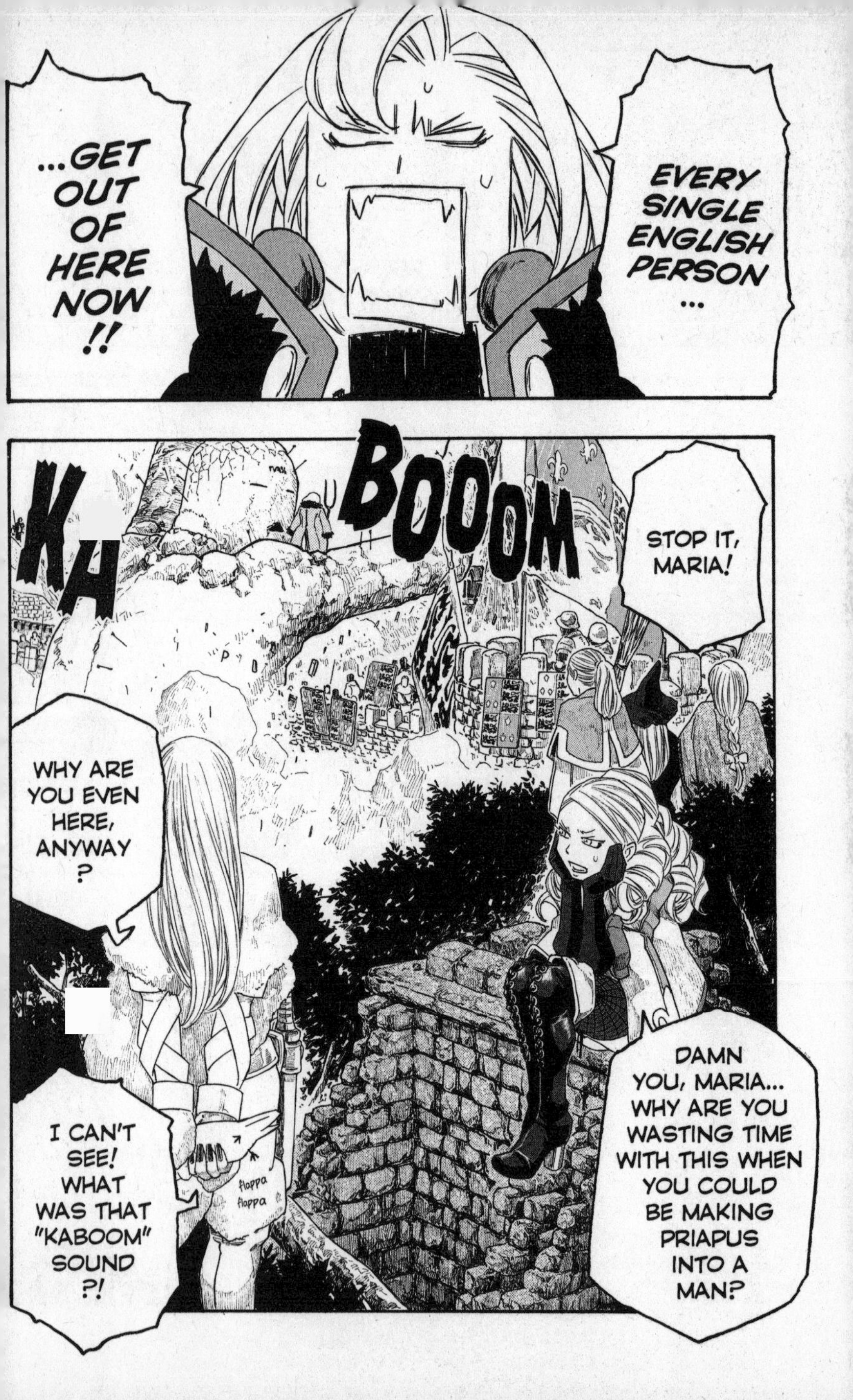
EVERY SINGLE ENGLISH PERSON...
...GET OUT OF HERE NOW!!
STOP IT, MARIA!
KA BOOOM
WHY ARE YOU EVEN HERE, ANYWAY?
DAMN YOU, MARIA... WHY ARE YOU WASTING TIME WITH THIS WHEN YOU COULD BE MAKING PRIAPUS INTO A MAN?
I CAN'T SEE! WHAT WAS THAT "KABOOM" SOUND?!
flappa flappa

Chapter 11 A Witch's Regret and a Bouquet from an Angel's Servant

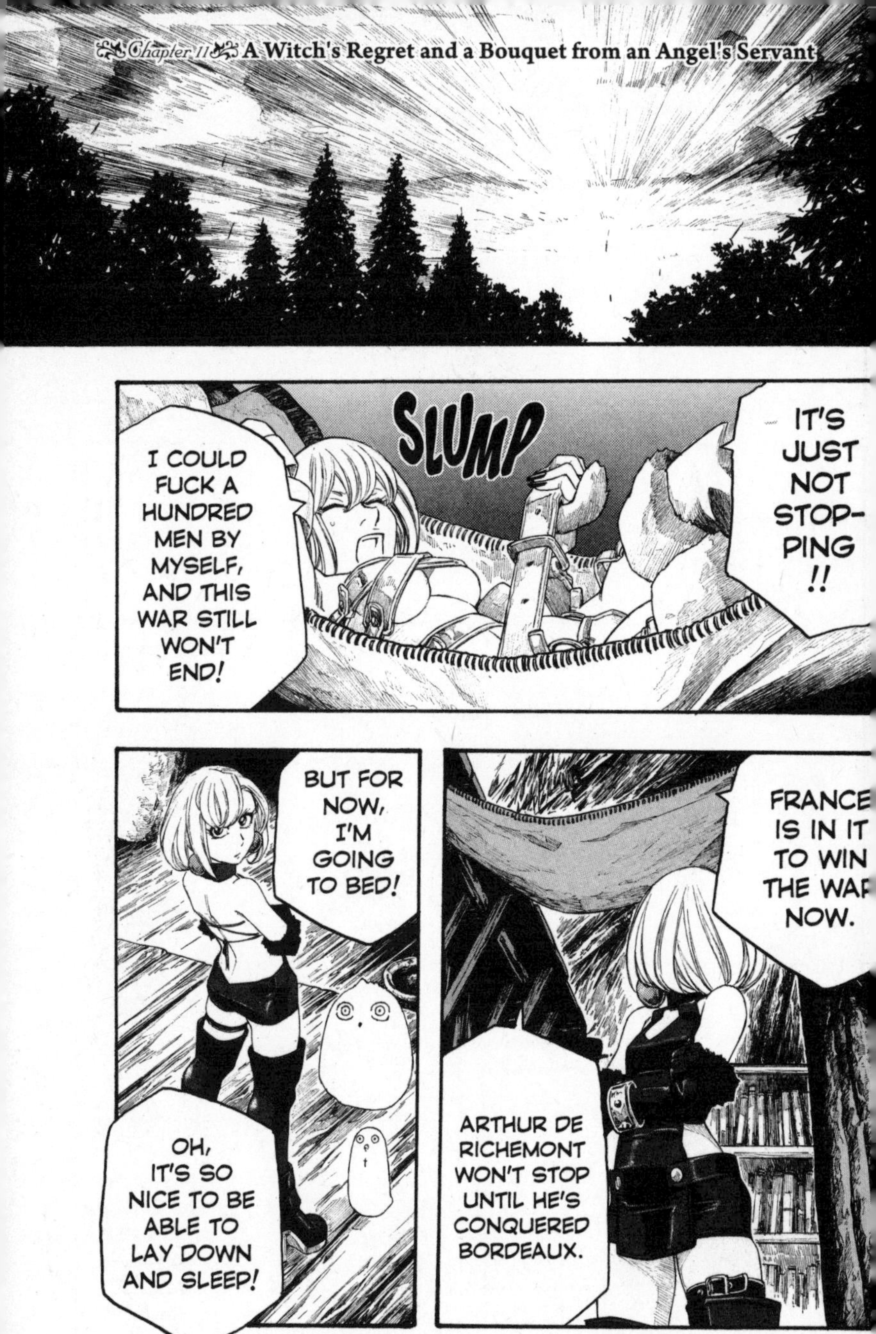
IT'S JUST NOT STOPPING!!
SLUMP
I COULD FUCK A HUNDRED MEN BY MYSELF, AND THIS WAR STILL WON'T END!
FRANCE IS IN IT TO WIN THE WAR NOW.
ARTHUR DE RICHEMONT WON'T STOP UNTIL HE'S CONQUERED BORDEAUX.
BUT FOR NOW, I'M GOING TO BED!
OH, IT'S SO NICE TO BE ABLE TO LAY DOWN AND SLEEP!

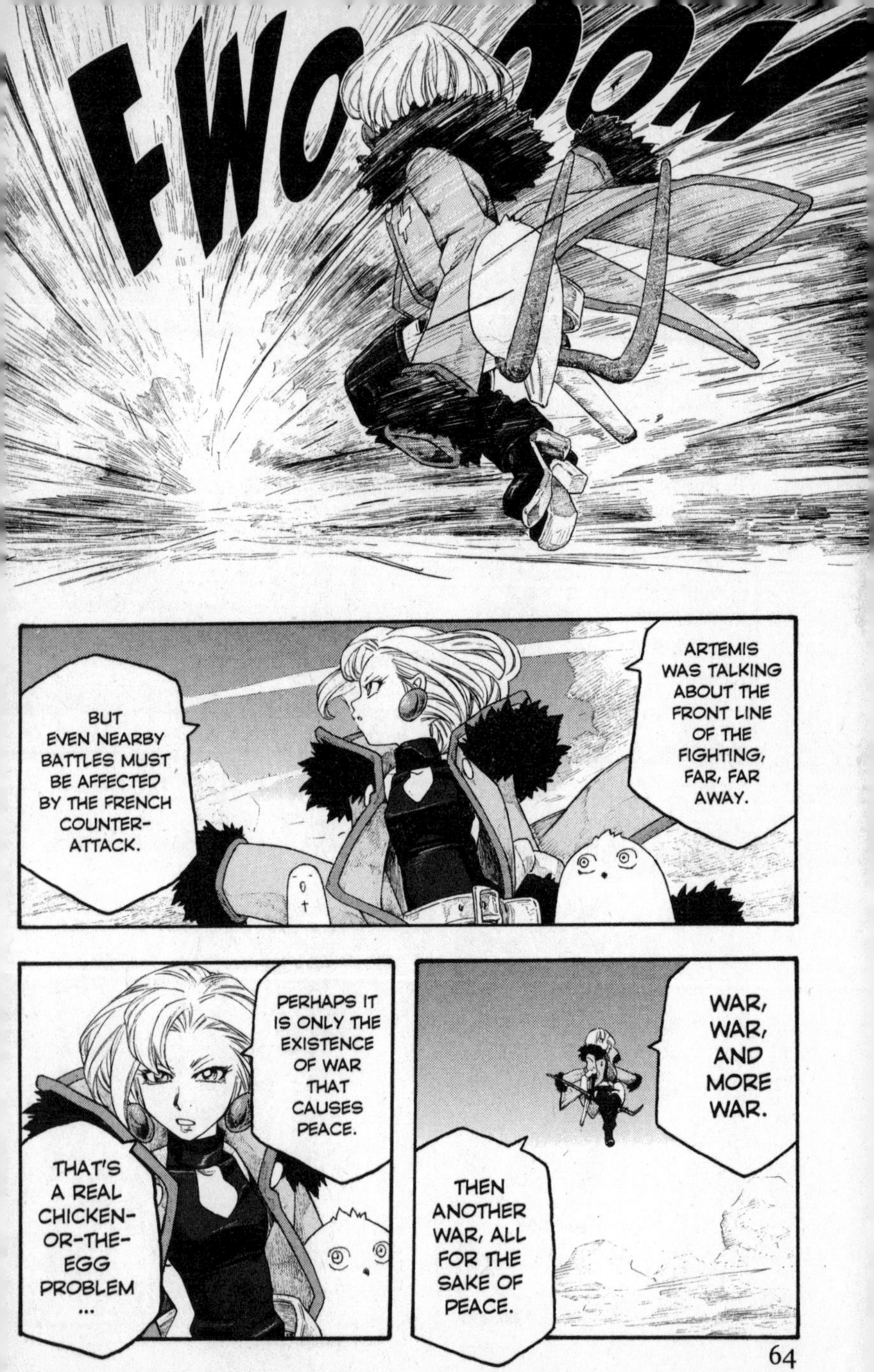
FWOOOM
ARTEMIS WAS TALKING ABOUT THE FRONT LINE OF THE FIGHTING, FAR, FAR AWAY.
BUT EVEN NEARBY BATTLES MUST BE AFFECTED BY THE FRENCH COUNTER-ATTACK.
WAR, WAR, AND MORE WAR.
THEN ANOTHER WAR, ALL FOR THE SAKE OF PEACE.
PERHAPS IT IS ONLY THE EXISTENCE OF WAR THAT CAUSES PEACE.
THAT'S A REAL CHICKEN-OR-THE-EGG PROBLEM ...

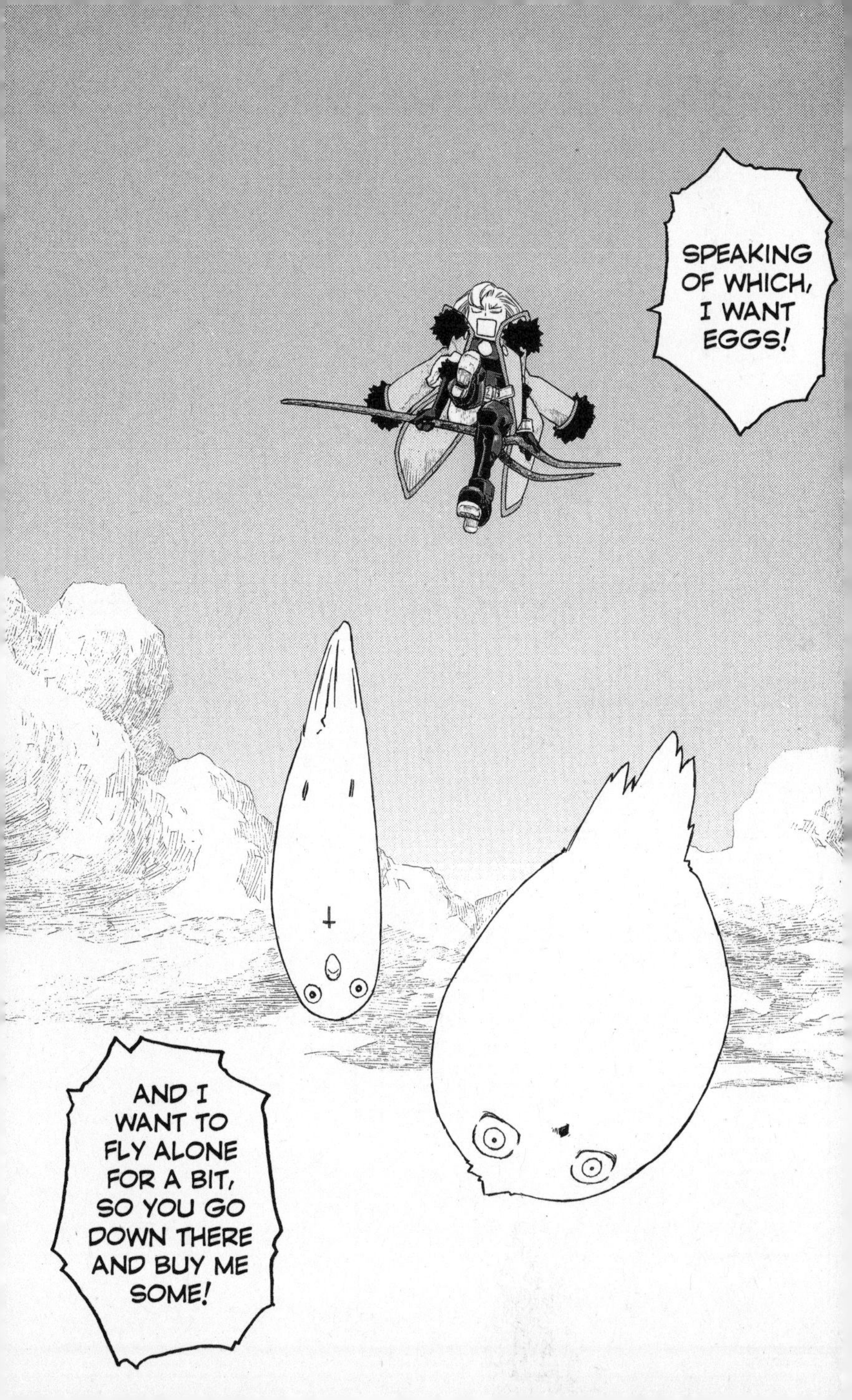
SPEAKING OF WHICH, I WANT EGGS!
AND I WANT TO FLY ALONE FOR A BIT, SO YOU GO DOWN THERE AND BUY ME SOME!

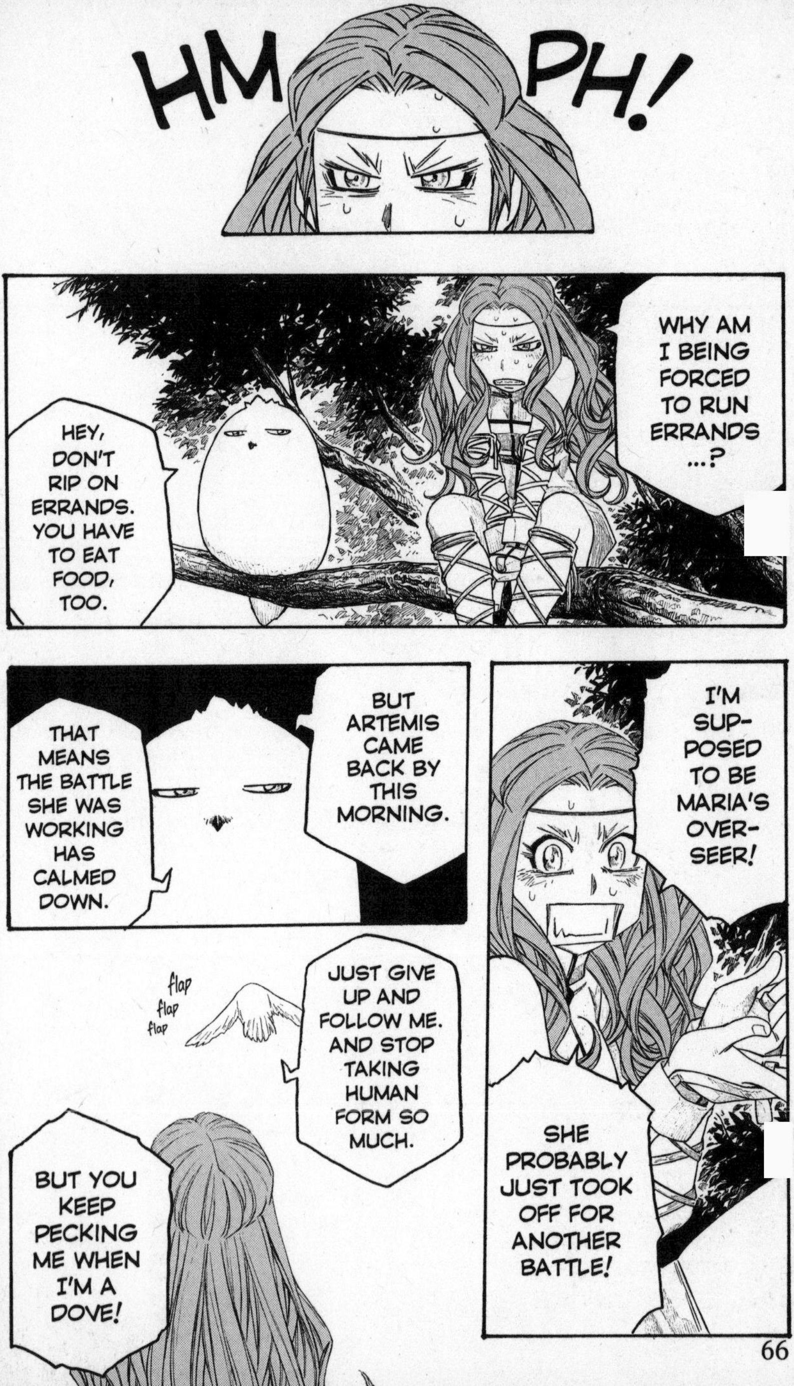
HMPH!
WHY AM I BEING FORCED TO RUN ERRANDS ...?
HEY, DON'T RIP ON ERRANDS. YOU HAVE TO EAT FOOD, TOO.
I'M SUP-POSED TO BE MARIA'S OVER-SEER!
SHE PROBABLY JUST TOOK OFF FOR ANOTHER BATTLE!
BUT ARTEMIS CAME BACK BY THIS MORNING.
THAT MEANS THE BATTLE SHE WAS WORKING HAS CALMED DOWN.
JUST GIVE UP AND FOLLOW ME. AND STOP TAKING HUMAN FORM SO MUCH.
flap flap flap
BUT YOU KEEP PECKING ME WHEN I'M A DOVE!

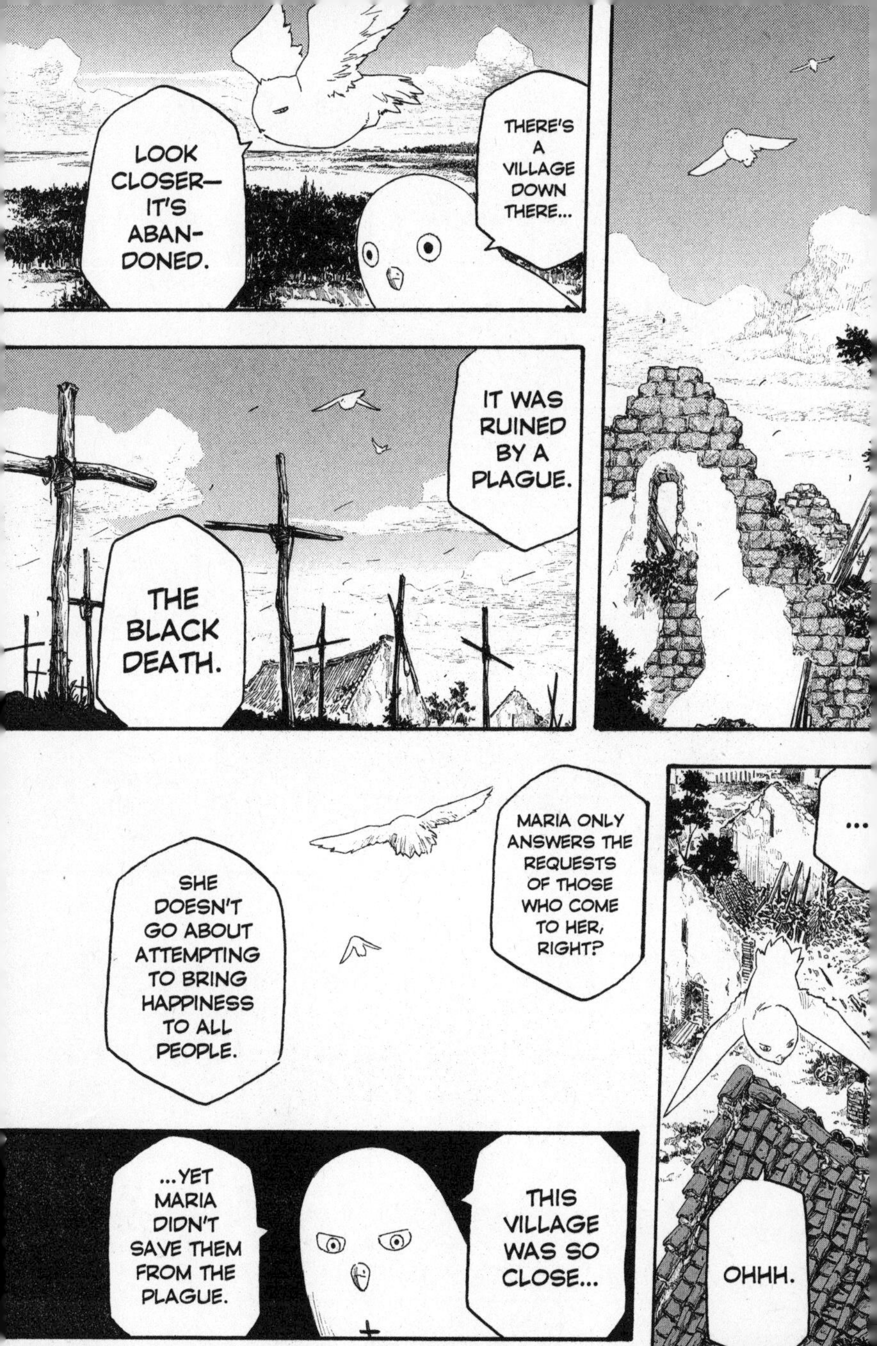
THERE'S A VILLAGE DOWN THERE...
LOOK CLOSER—IT'S ABAN-DONED.
IT WAS RUINED BY A PLAGUE.
THE BLACK DEATH.
...
OHHH.
MARIA ONLY ANSWERS THE REQUESTS OF THOSE WHO COME TO HER, RIGHT?
SHE DOESN'T GO ABOUT ATTEMPTING TO BRING HAPPINESS TO ALL PEOPLE.
THIS VILLAGE WAS SO CLOSE...
...YET MARIA DIDN'T SAVE THEM FROM THE PLAGUE.

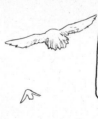

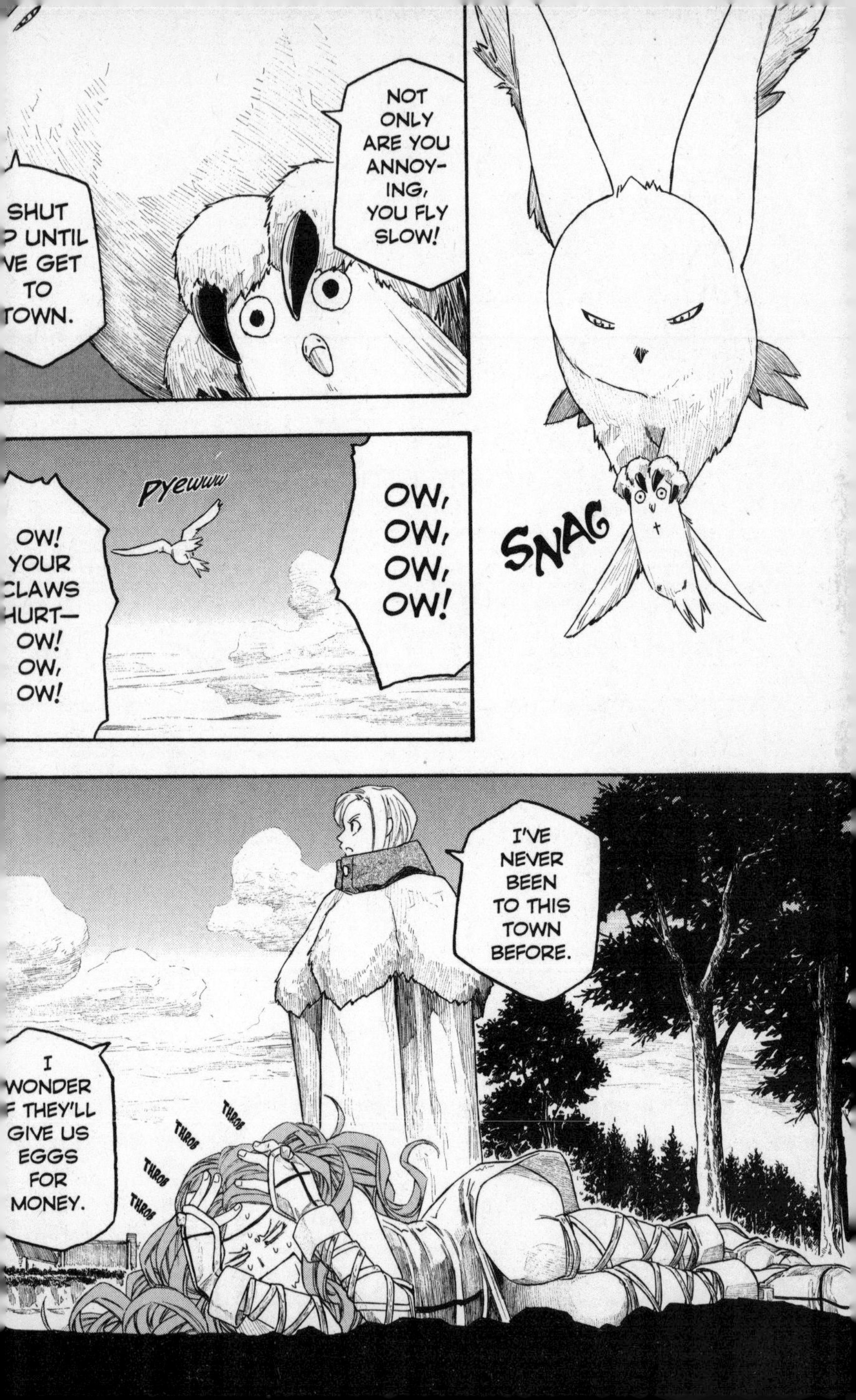

SNAG
NOT ONLY ARE YOU ANNOY-ING, YOU FLY SLOW!
SHUT P UNTIL VE GET TO TOWN.
OW, OW, OW, OW!
PYEWWW
OW! YOUR CLAWS HURT— OW! OW, OW!
I'VE NEVER BEEN TO THIS TOWN BEFORE.
I WONDER F THEY'LL GIVE US EGGS FOR MONEY.
THROB
THROB
THROB
THROB

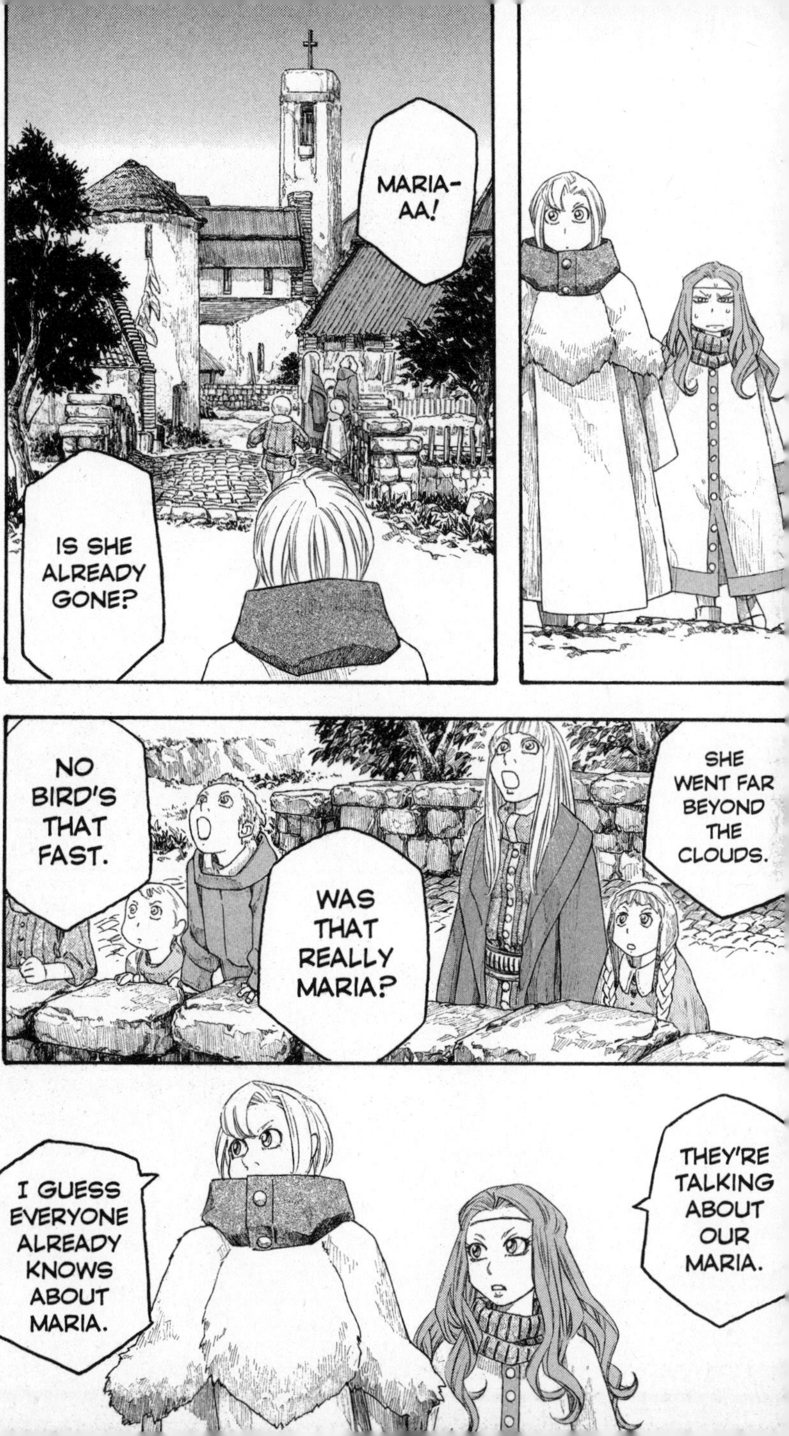
MARIA-AA!
IS SHE ALREADY GONE?
SHE WENT FAR BEYOND THE CLOUDS.
WAS THAT REALLY MARIA?
NO BIRD'S THAT FAST.
THEY'RE TALKING ABOUT OUR MARIA.
I GUESS EVERYONE ALREADY KNOWS ABOUT MARIA.

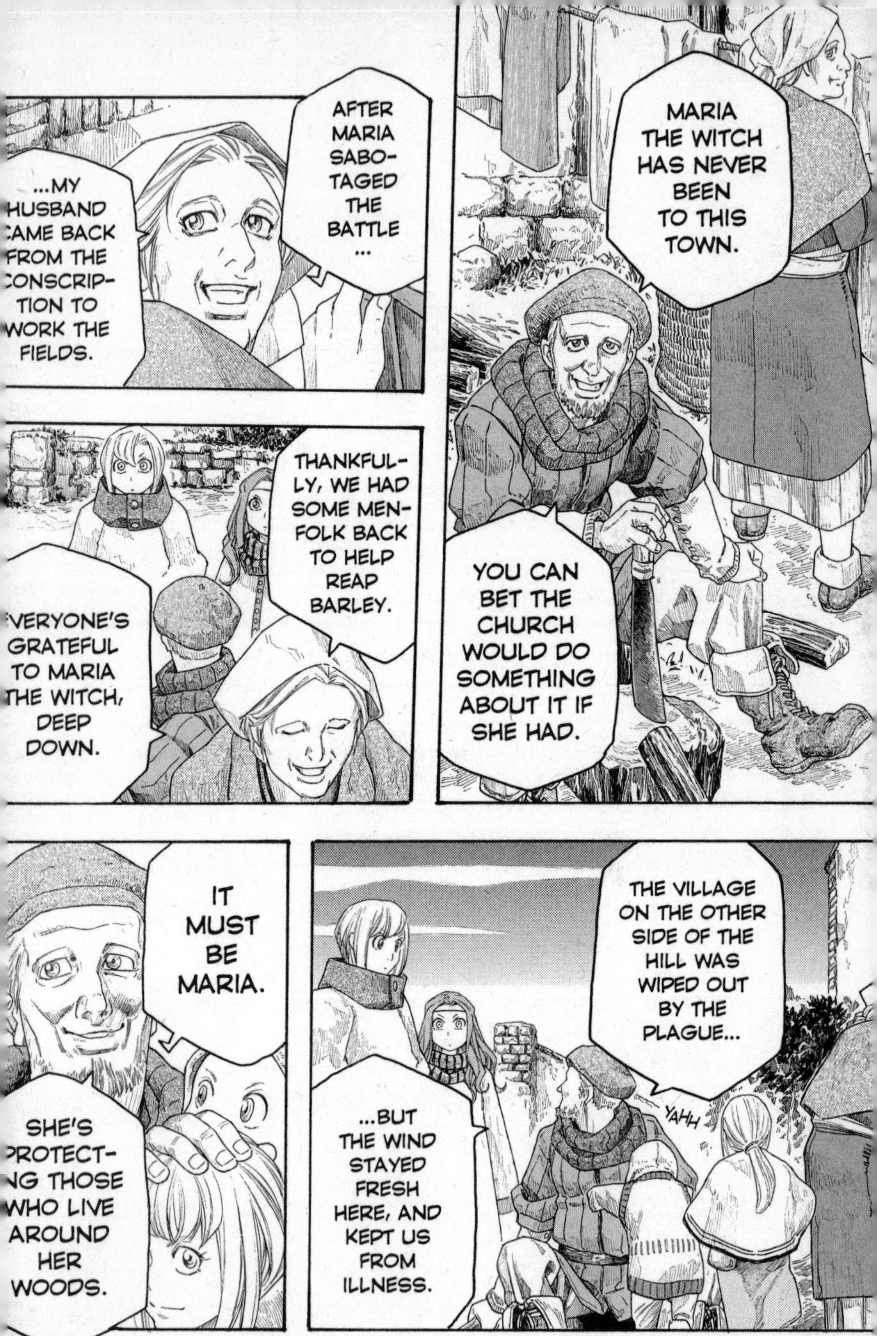
MARIA THE WITCH HAS NEVER BEEN TO THIS TOWN.
YOU CAN BET THE CHURCH WOULD DO SOMETHING ABOUT IT IF SHE HAD.
AFTER MARIA SABOTAGED THE BATTLE ...
...MY HUSBAND CAME BACK FROM THE CONSCRIPTION TO WORK THE FIELDS.
THANKFULLY, WE HAD SOME MENFOLK BACK TO HELP REAP BARLEY.
EVERYONE'S GRATEFUL TO MARIA THE WITCH, DEEP DOWN.
THE VILLAGE ON THE OTHER SIDE OF THE HILL WAS WIPED OUT BY THE PLAGUE...
YAHH
...BUT THE WIND STAYED FRESH HERE, AND KEPT US FROM ILLNESS.
IT MUST BE MARIA.
SHE'S PROTECTING THOSE WHO LIVE AROUND HER WOODS.

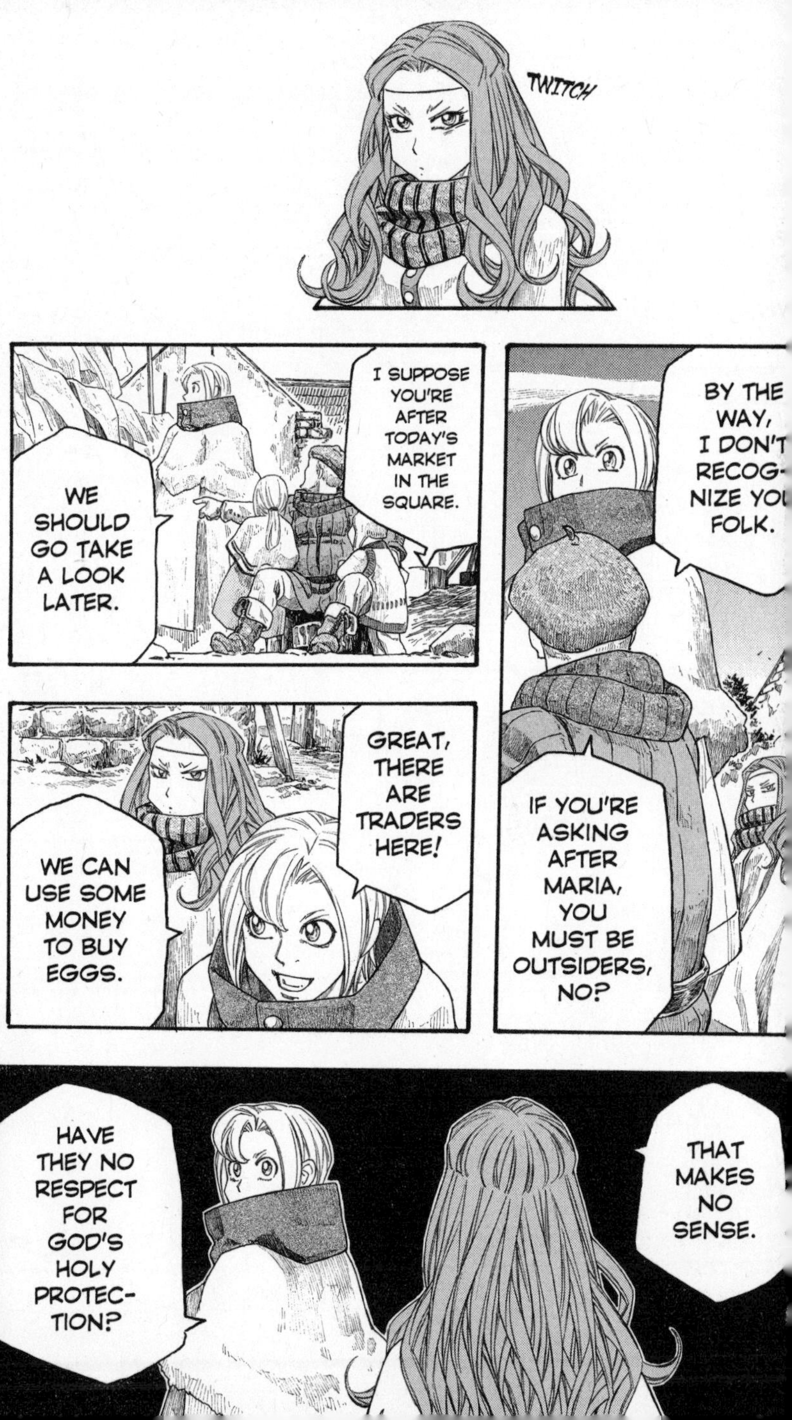
TWITCH
BY THE WAY, I DON'T RECOGNIZE YOU FOLK.
IF YOU'RE ASKING AFTER MARIA, YOU MUST BE OUTSIDERS, NO?
I SUPPOSE YOU'RE AFTER TODAY'S MARKET IN THE SQUARE.
WE SHOULD GO TAKE A LOOK LATER.
GREAT, THERE ARE TRADERS HERE!
WE CAN USE SOME MONEY TO BUY EGGS.
THAT MAKES NO SENSE.
HAVE THEY NO RESPECT FOR GOD'S HOLY PROTECTION?

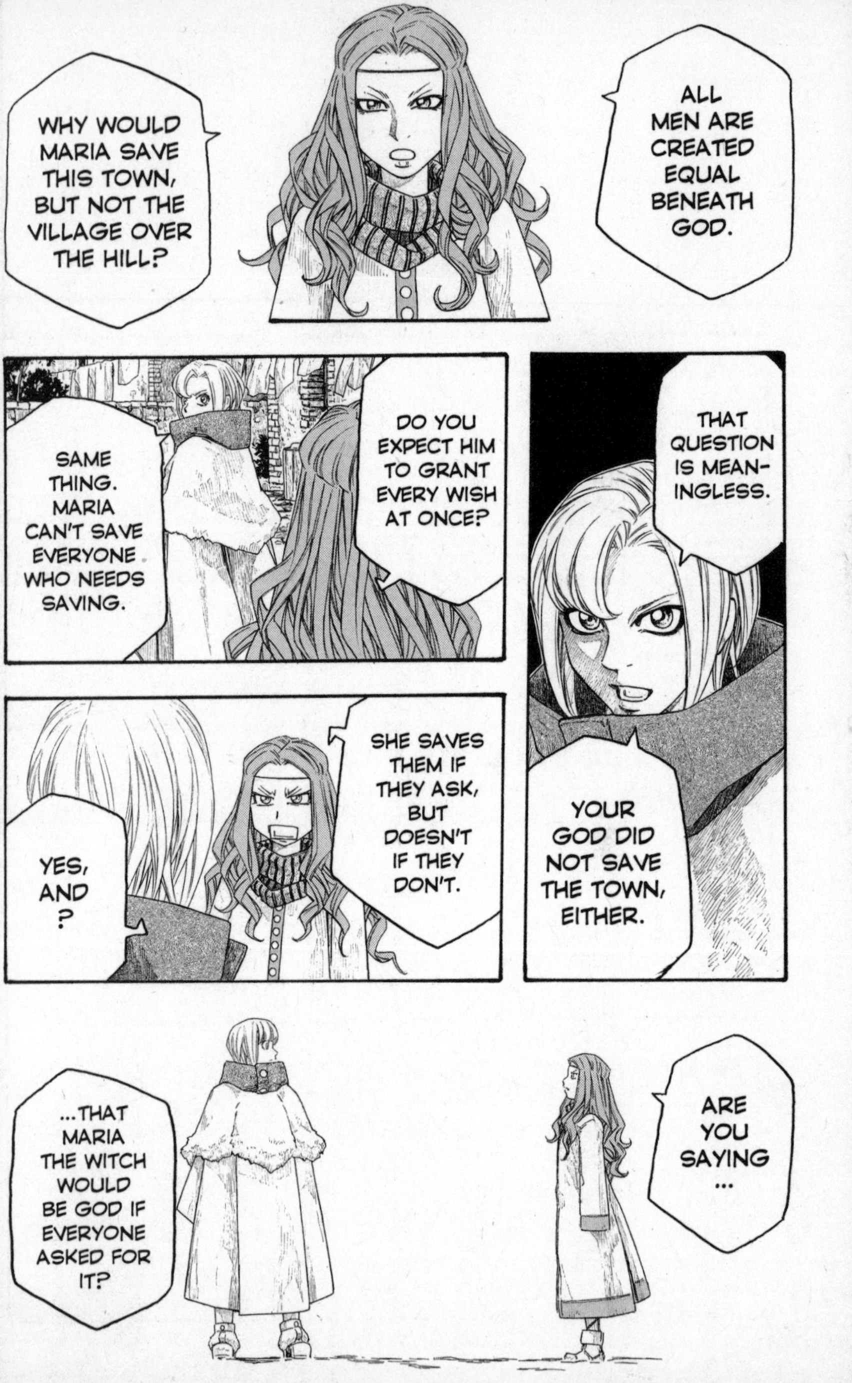
ALL MEN ARE CREATED EQUAL BENEATH GOD.
WHY WOULD MARIA SAVE THIS TOWN, BUT NOT THE VILLAGE OVER THE HILL?
THAT QUESTION IS MEAN-INGLESS.
YOUR GOD DID NOT SAVE THE TOWN, EITHER.
DO YOU EXPECT HIM TO GRANT EVERY WISH AT ONCE?
SAME THING. MARIA CAN'T SAVE EVERYONE WHO NEEDS SAVING.
SHE SAVES THEM IF THEY ASK, BUT DOESN'T IF THEY DON'T.
YES, AND ?
ARE YOU SAYING ...
...THAT MARIA THE WITCH WOULD BE GOD IF EVERYONE ASKED FOR IT?

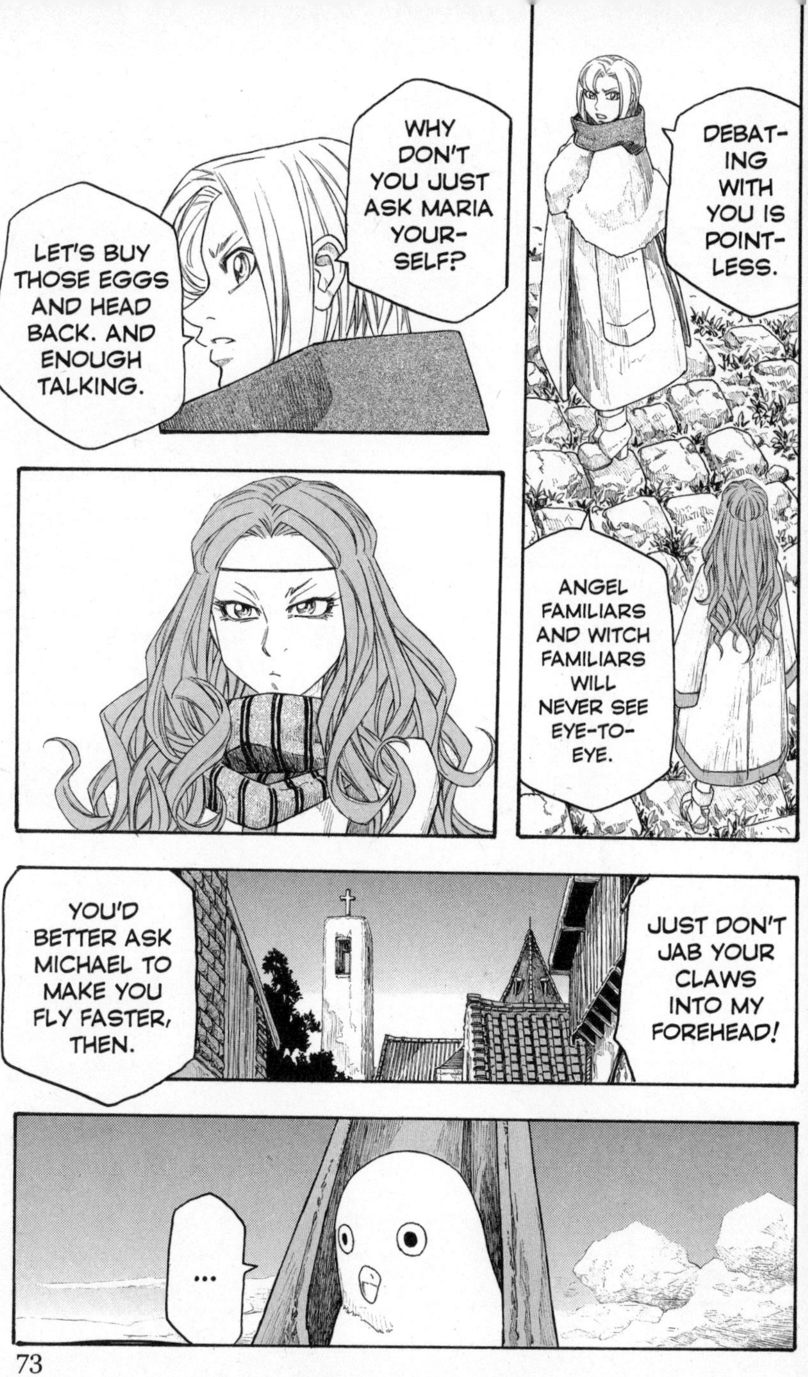
DEBAT-ING WITH YOU IS POINT-LESS.
ANGEL FAMILIARS AND WITCH FAMILIARS WILL NEVER SEE EYE-TO-EYE.
WHY DON'T YOU JUST ASK MARIA YOUR-SELF?
LET'S BUY THOSE EGGS AND HEAD BACK. AND ENOUGH TALKING.
JUST DON'T JAB YOUR CLAWS INTO MY FOREHEAD!
YOU'D BETTER ASK MICHAEL TO MAKE YOU FLY FASTER, THEN.
...

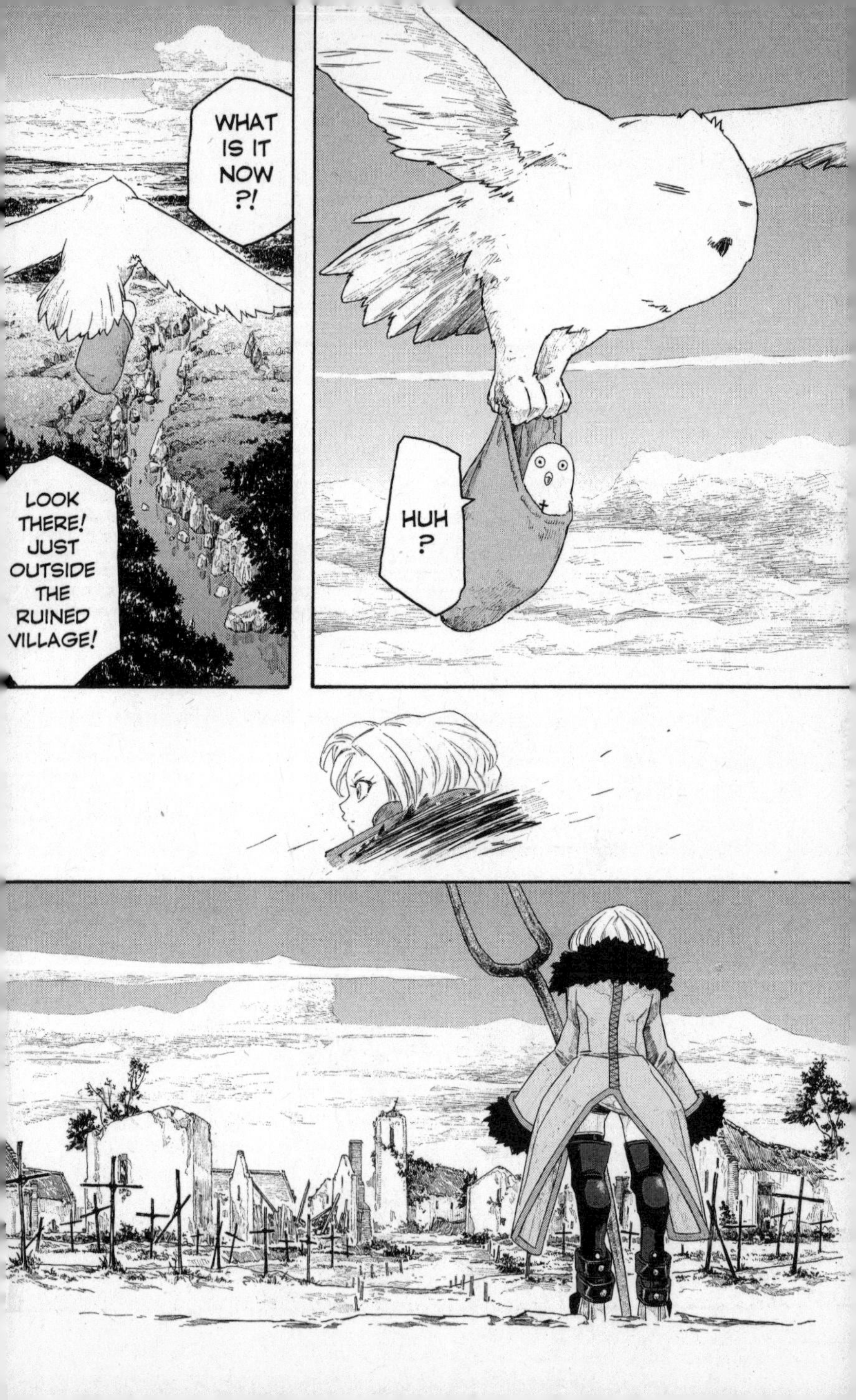
HUH ?
WHAT IS IT NOW ?!
LOOK THERE! JUST OUTSIDE THE RUINED VILLAGE!

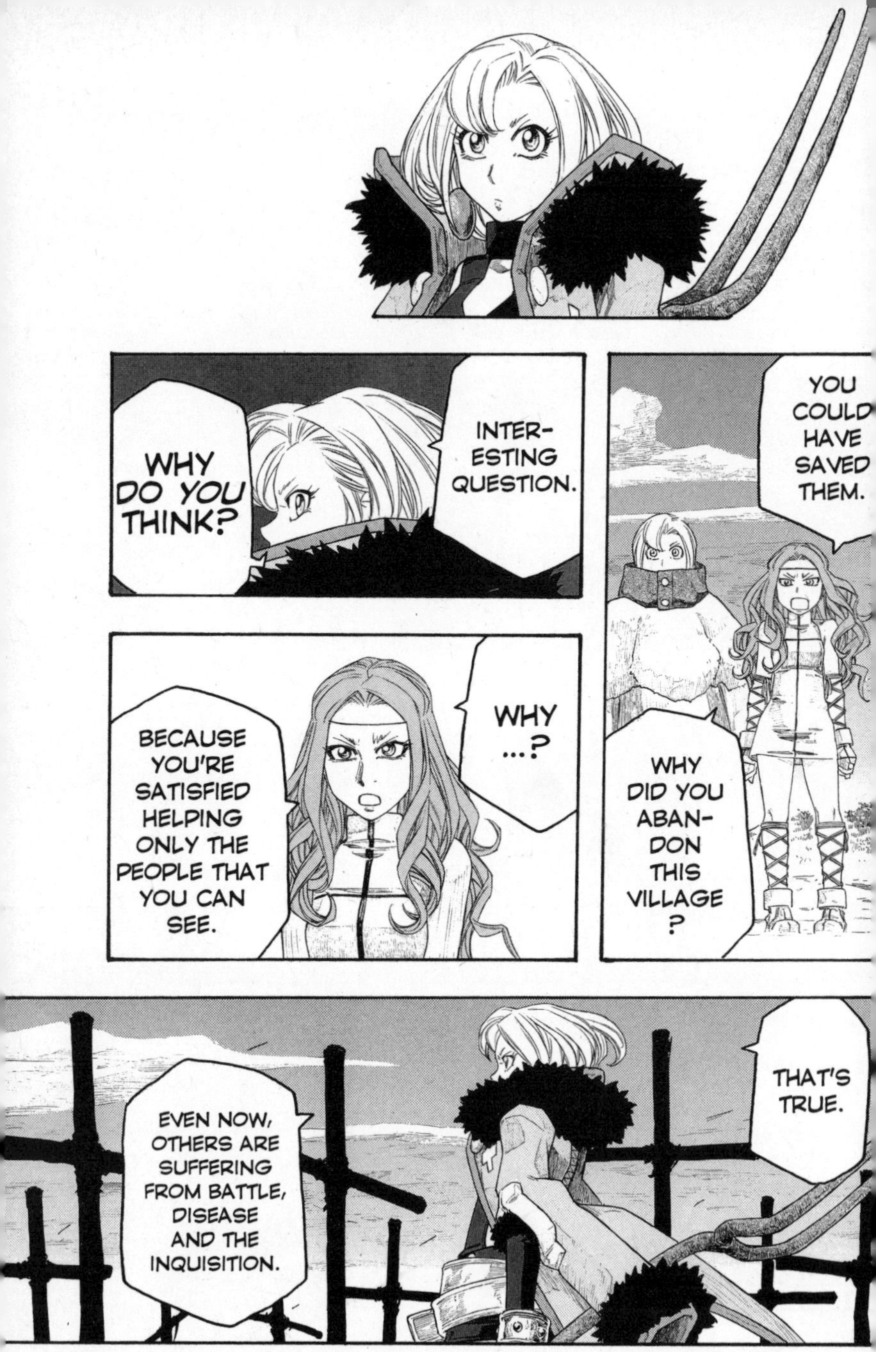

YOU COULD HAVE SAVED THEM.
WHY DID YOU ABANDON THIS VILLAGE?
INTERESTING QUESTION.
WHY DO YOU THINK?
WHY...?
BECAUSE YOU'RE SATISFIED HELPING ONLY THE PEOPLE THAT YOU CAN SEE.
THAT'S TRUE.
EVEN NOW, OTHERS ARE SUFFERING FROM BATTLE, DISEASE AND THE INQUISITION.

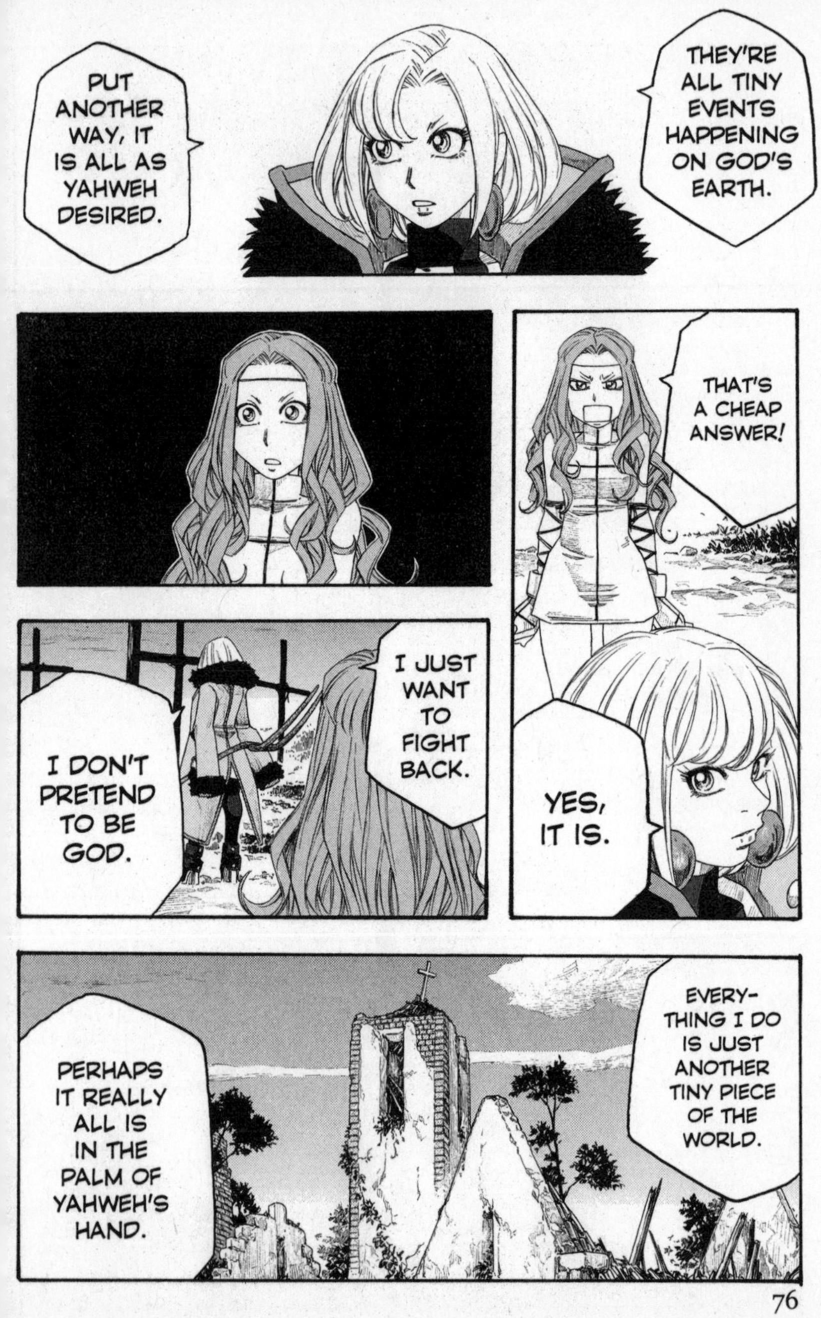
THEY'RE ALL TINY EVENTS HAPPENING ON GOD'S EARTH.
PUT ANOTHER WAY, IT IS ALL AS YAHWEH DESIRED.
THAT'S A CHEAP ANSWER!
YES, IT IS.
I JUST WANT TO FIGHT BACK.
I DON'T PRETEND TO BE GOD.
EVERY-THING I DO IS JUST ANOTHER TINY PIECE OF THE WORLD.
PERHAPS IT REALLY ALL IS IN THE PALM OF YAHWEH'S HAND.

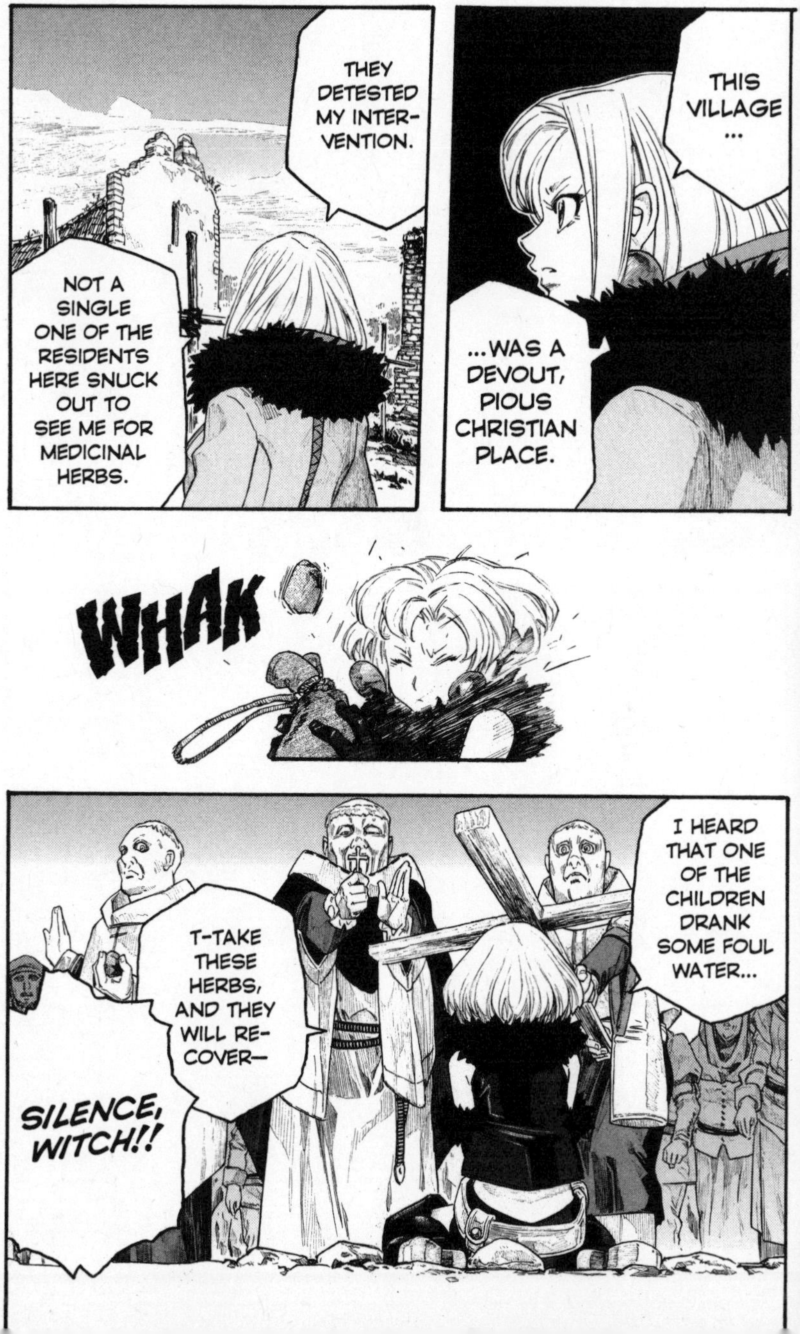
THIS VILLAGE ...
...WAS A DEVOUT, PIOUS CHRISTIAN PLACE.
THEY DETESTED MY INTER-VENTION.
NOT A SINGLE ONE OF THE RESIDENTS HERE SNUCK OUT TO SEE ME FOR MEDICINAL HERBS.
WHAK
I HEARD THAT ONE OF THE CHILDREN DRANK SOME FOUL WATER...
T-TAKE THESE HERBS, AND THEY WILL RE-COVER—
SILENCE, WITCH!!

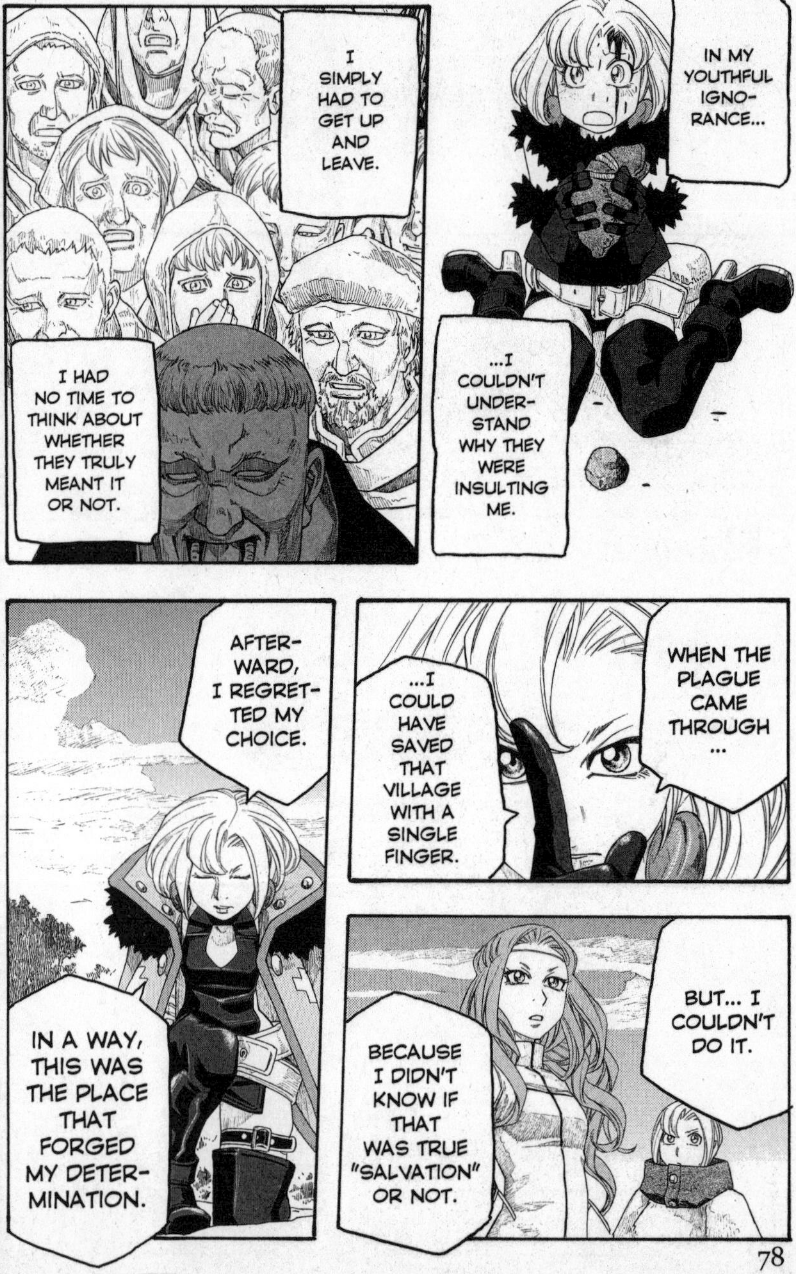
IN MY YOUTHFUL IGNO-RANCE...
...I COULDN'T UNDER-STAND WHY THEY WERE INSULTING ME.
I SIMPLY HAD TO GET UP AND LEAVE.
I HAD NO TIME TO THINK ABOUT WHETHER THEY TRULY MEANT IT OR NOT.
WHEN THE PLAGUE CAME THROUGH ...
...I COULD HAVE SAVED THAT VILLAGE WITH A SINGLE FINGER.
BUT... I COULDN'T DO IT.
BECAUSE I DIDN'T KNOW IF THAT WAS TRUE "SALVATION" OR NOT.
AFTER-WARD, I REGRET-TED MY CHOICE.
IN A WAY, THIS WAS THE PLACE THAT FORGED MY DETER-MINATION.

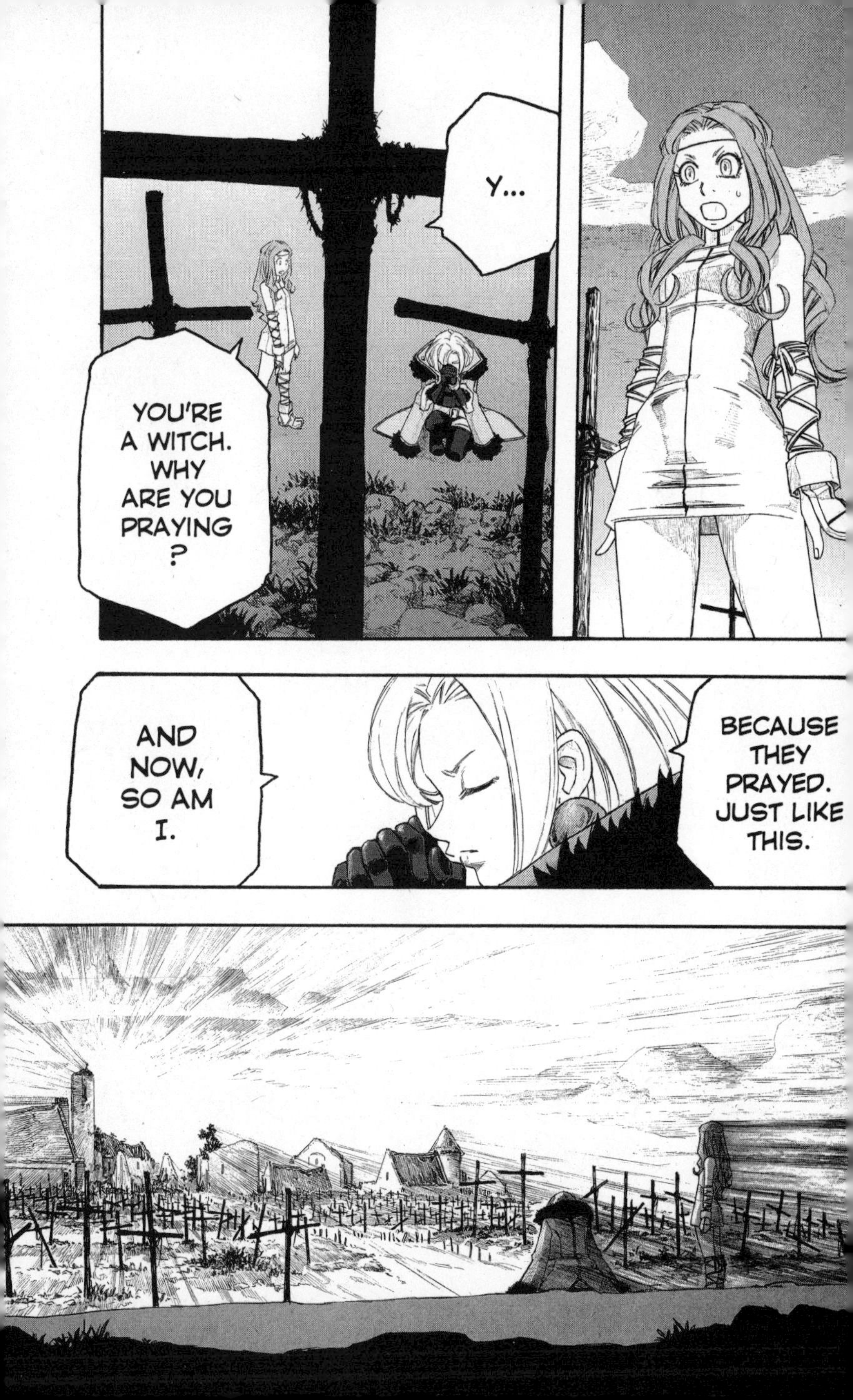
Y...
YOU'RE A WITCH. WHY ARE YOU PRAYING ?
BECAUSE THEY PRAYED. JUST LIKE THIS.
AND NOW, SO AM I.

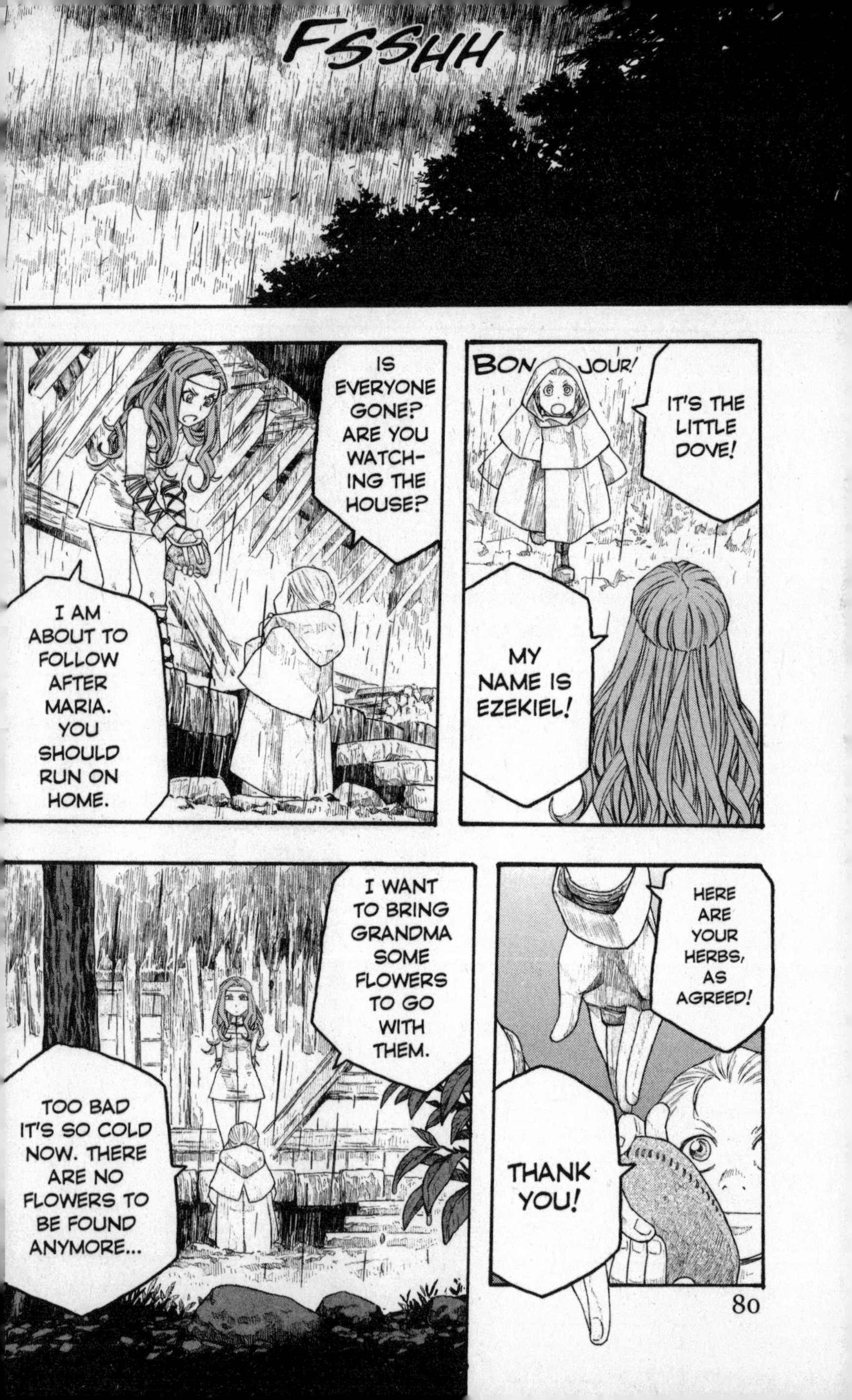
FSSHH
BONJOUR!
IT'S THE LITTLE DOVE!
MY NAME IS EZEKIEL!
IS EVERYONE GONE? ARE YOU WATCHING THE HOUSE?
I AM ABOUT TO FOLLOW AFTER MARIA. YOU SHOULD RUN ON HOME.
HERE ARE YOUR HERBS, AS AGREED!
THANK YOU!
I WANT TO BRING GRANDMA SOME FLOWERS TO GO WITH THEM.
TOO BAD IT'S SO COLD NOW. THERE ARE NO FLOWERS TO BE FOUND ANYMORE...

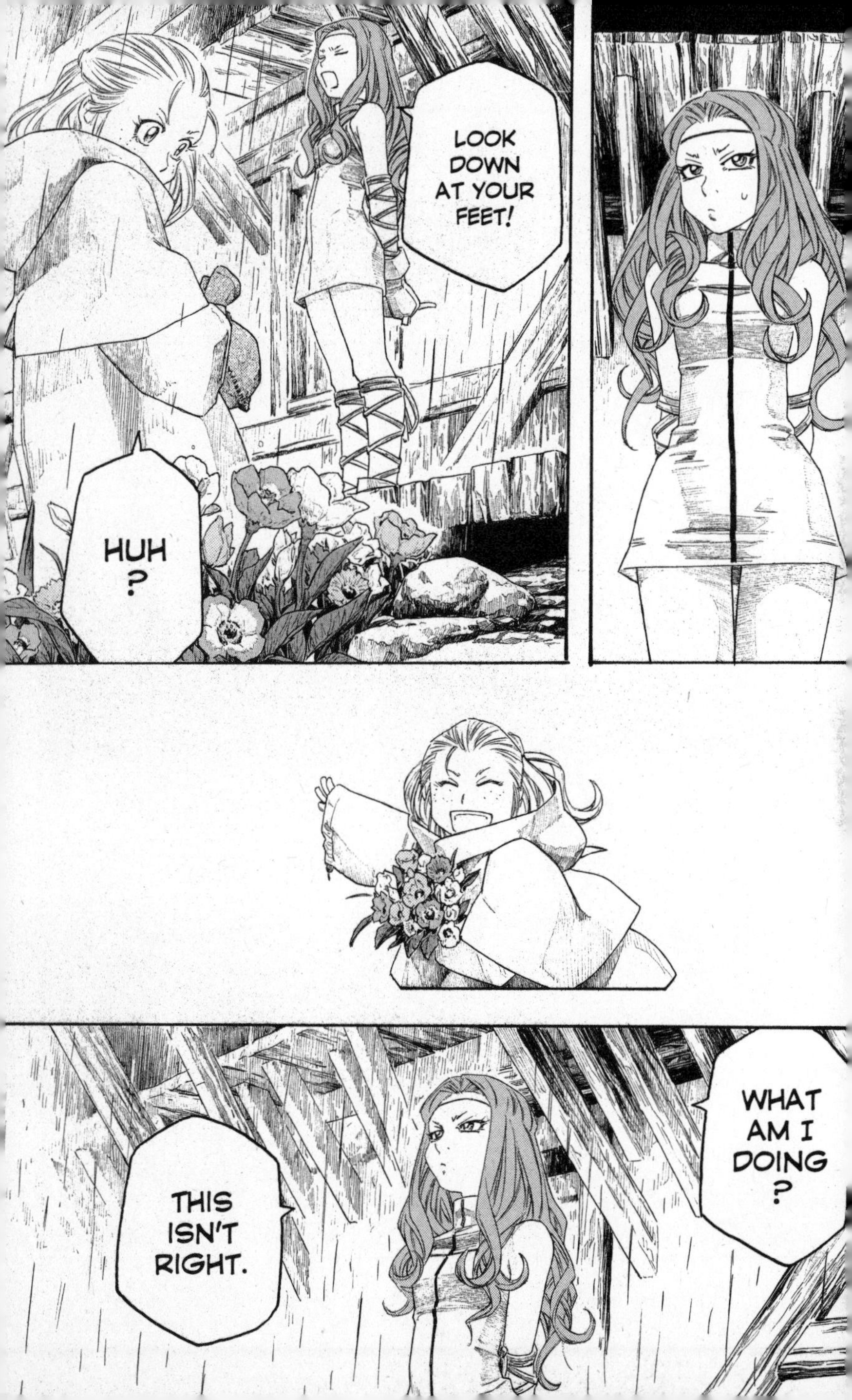
LOOK DOWN AT YOUR FEET!
HUH?
WHAT AM I DOING?
THIS ISN'T RIGHT.

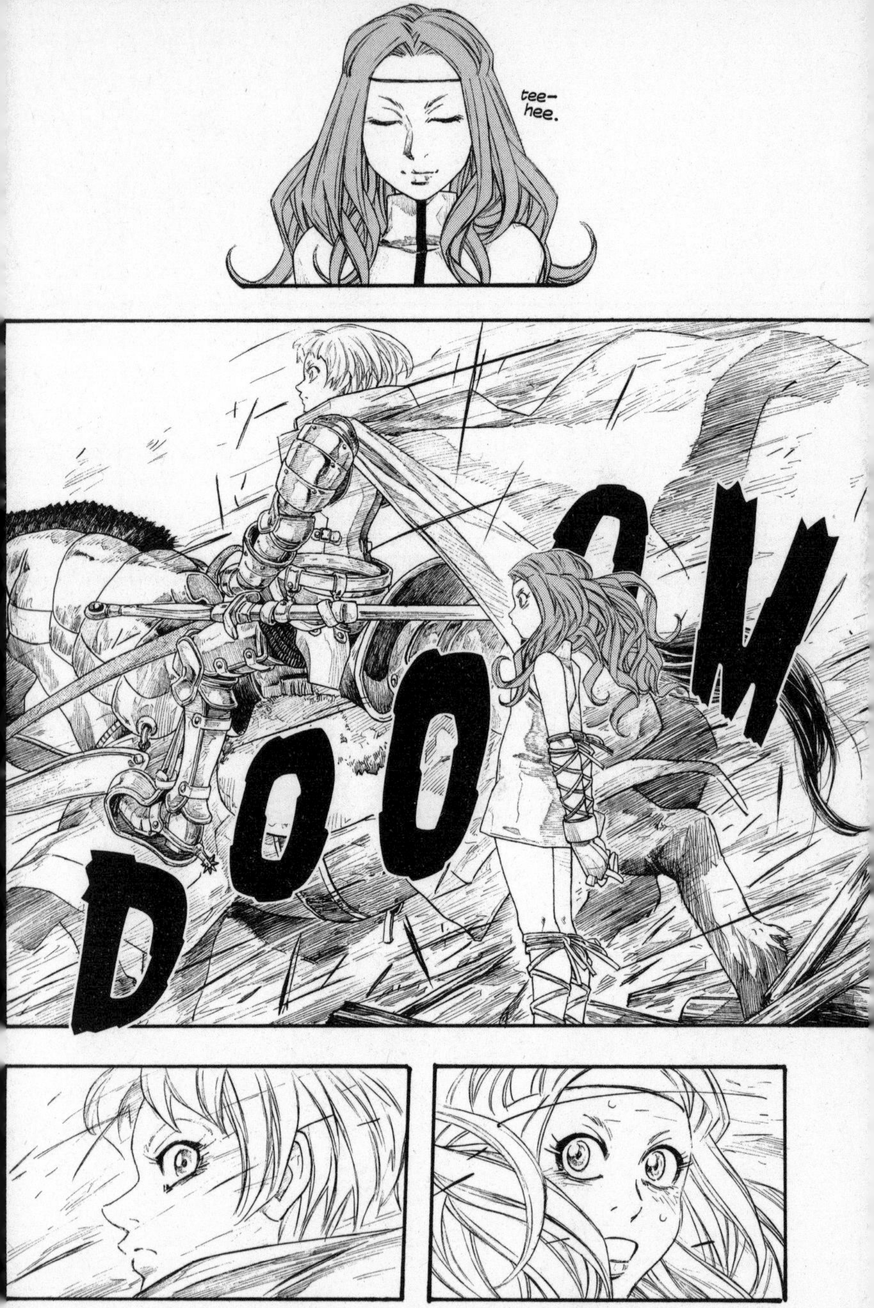
tee-hee.
DOOOW

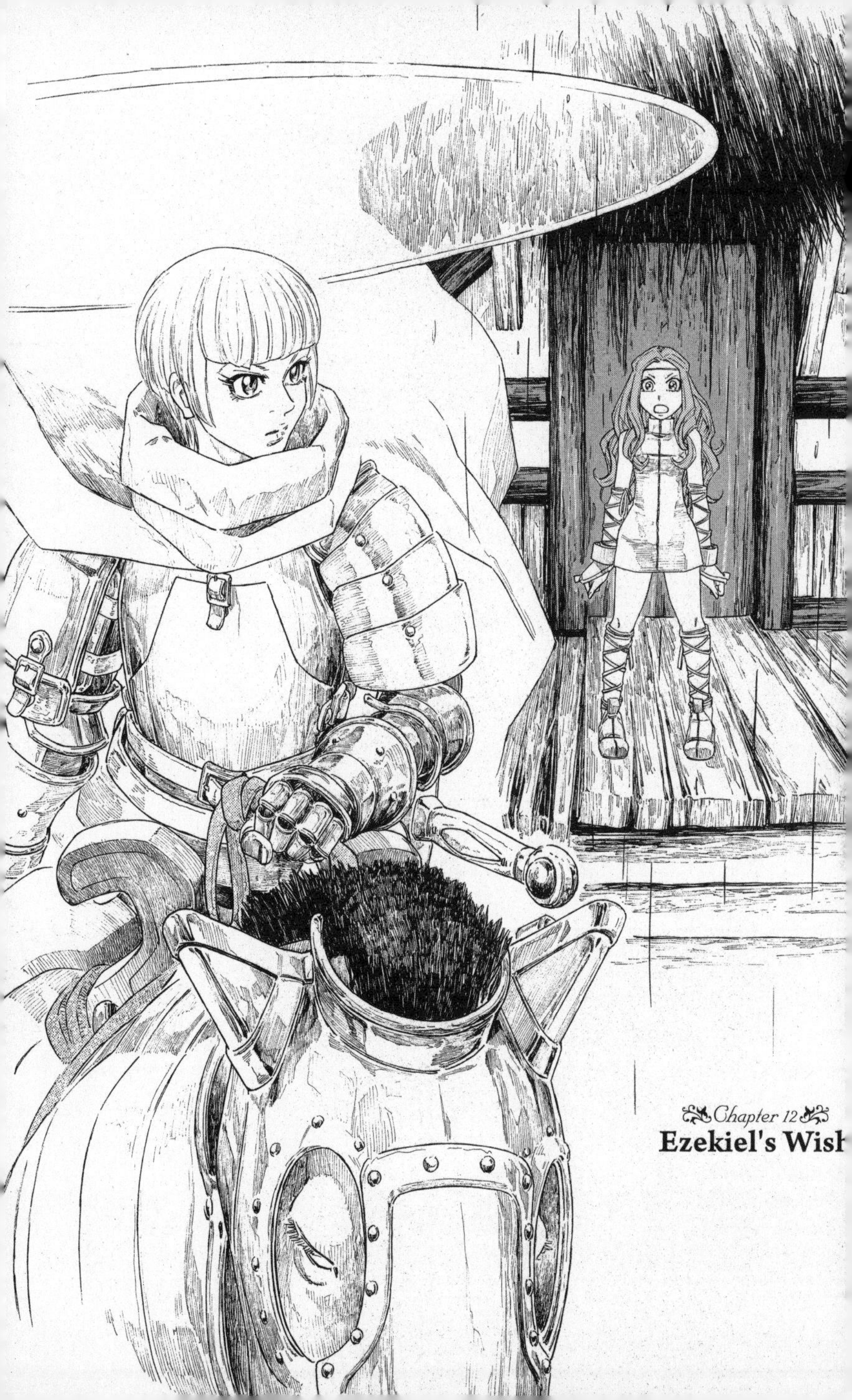

Chapter 12

Ezekiel's Wish

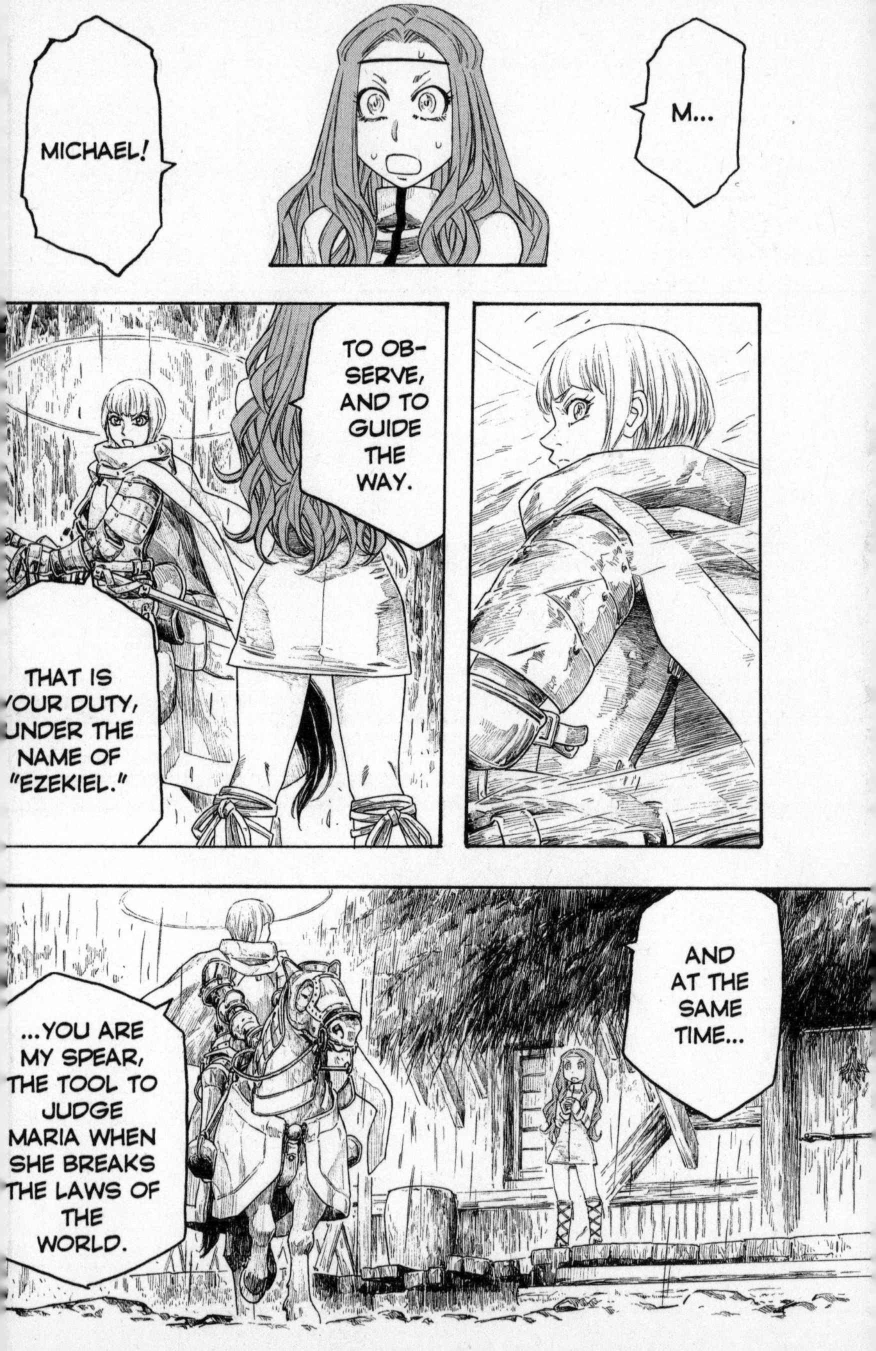
M...
MICHAEL!
TO OB-SERVE, AND TO GUIDE THE WAY.
THAT IS YOUR DUTY, UNDER THE NAME OF "EZEKIEL."
AND AT THE SAME TIME...
...YOU ARE MY SPEAR, THE TOOL TO JUDGE MARIA WHEN SHE BREAKS THE LAWS OF THE WORLD.

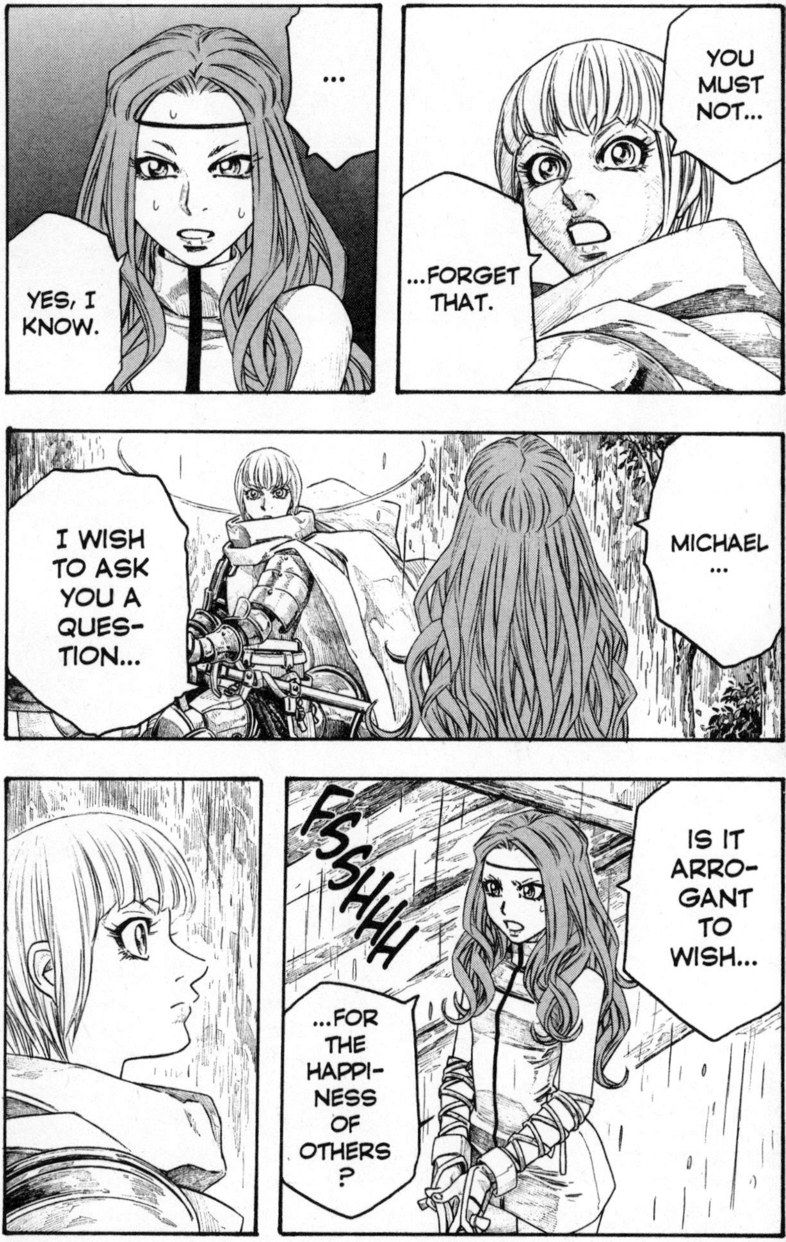
YOU MUST NOT...
...FORGET THAT.
...
YES, I KNOW.
MICHAEL ...
I WISH TO ASK YOU A QUES- TION...
IS IT ARRO- GANT TO WISH...
FSSHHH
...FOR THE HAPPI- NESS OF OTHERS ?

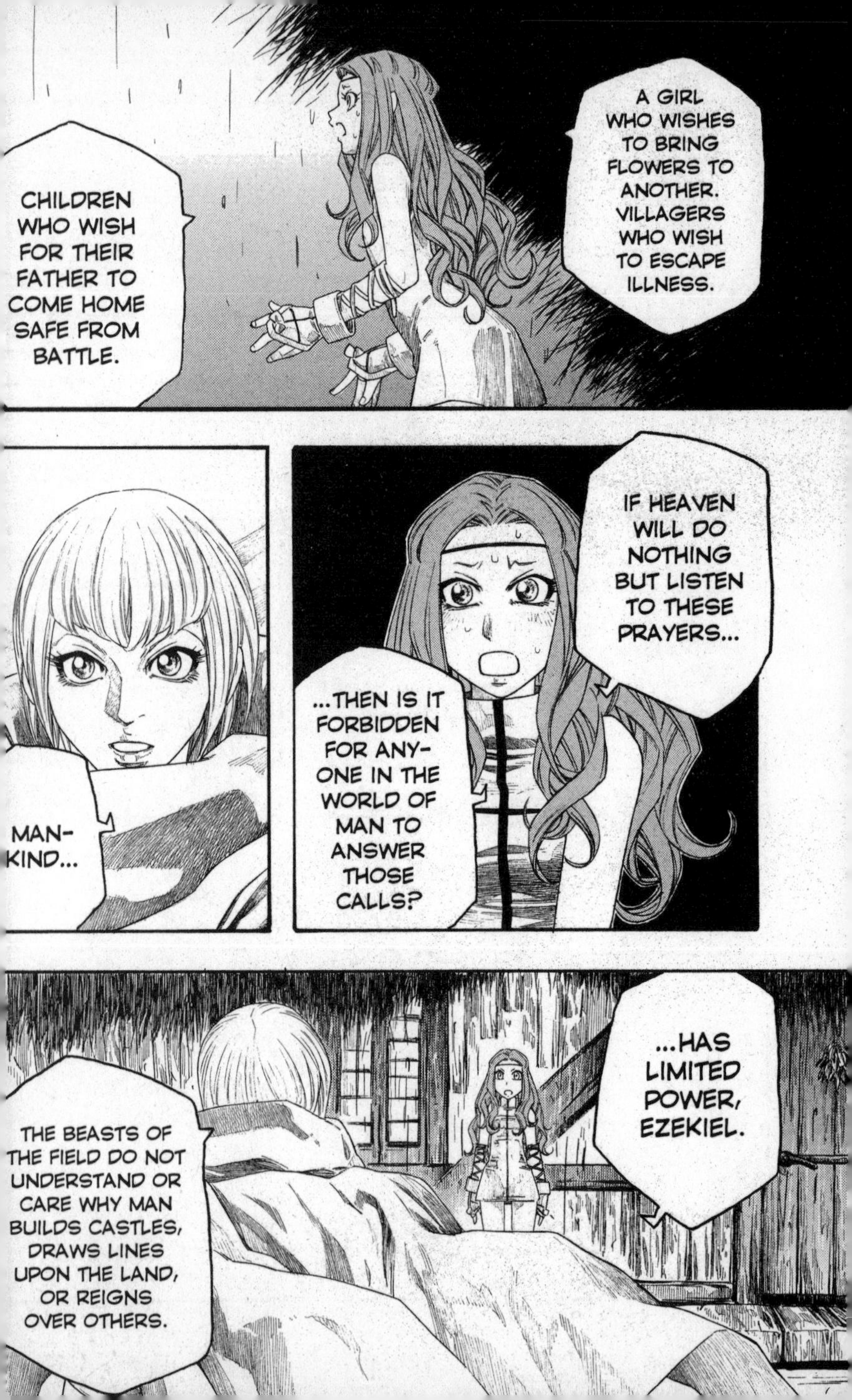
A GIRL WHO WISHES TO BRING FLOWERS TO ANOTHER. VILLAGERS WHO WISH TO ESCAPE ILLNESS.
CHILDREN WHO WISH FOR THEIR FATHER TO COME HOME SAFE FROM BATTLE.
IF HEAVEN WILL DO NOTHING BUT LISTEN TO THESE PRAYERS...
...THEN IS IT FORBIDDEN FOR ANY-ONE IN THE WORLD OF MAN TO ANSWER THOSE CALLS?
MAN-KIND...
...HAS LIMITED POWER, EZEKIEL.
THE BEASTS OF THE FIELD DO NOT UNDERSTAND OR CARE WHY MAN BUILDS CASTLES, DRAWS LINES UPON THE LAND, OR REIGNS OVER OTHERS.

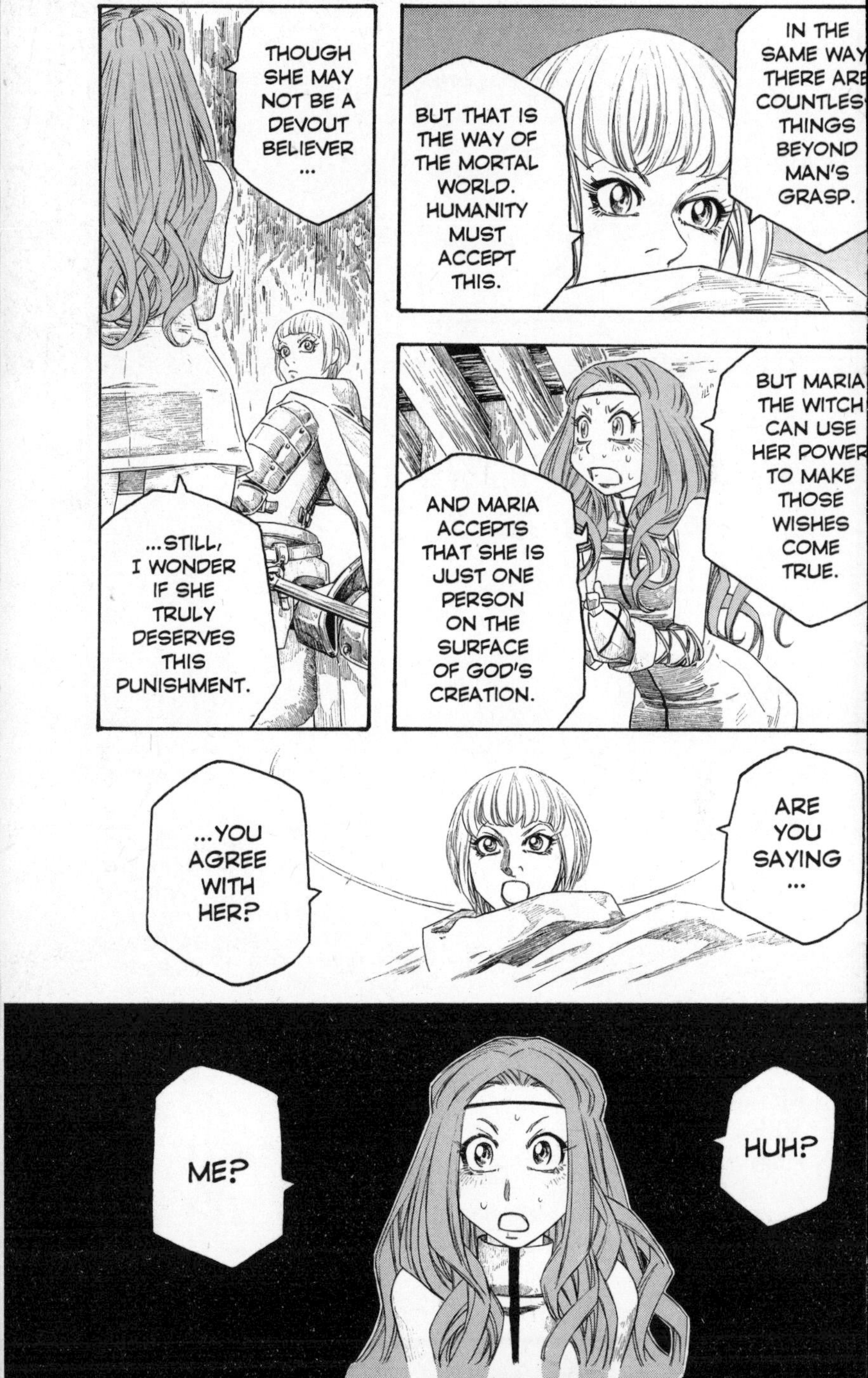
IN THE SAME WAY THERE ARE COUNTLESS THINGS BEYOND MAN'S GRASP.
BUT THAT IS THE WAY OF THE MORTAL WORLD. HUMANITY MUST ACCEPT THIS.
BUT MARIA THE WITCH CAN USE HER POWER TO MAKE THOSE WISHES COME TRUE.
AND MARIA ACCEPTS THAT SHE IS JUST ONE PERSON ON THE SURFACE OF GOD'S CREATION.
THOUGH SHE MAY NOT BE A DEVOUT BELIEVER ...
...STILL, I WONDER IF SHE TRULY DESERVES THIS PUNISHMENT.
ARE YOU SAYING ...
...YOU AGREE WITH HER?
HUH?
ME?

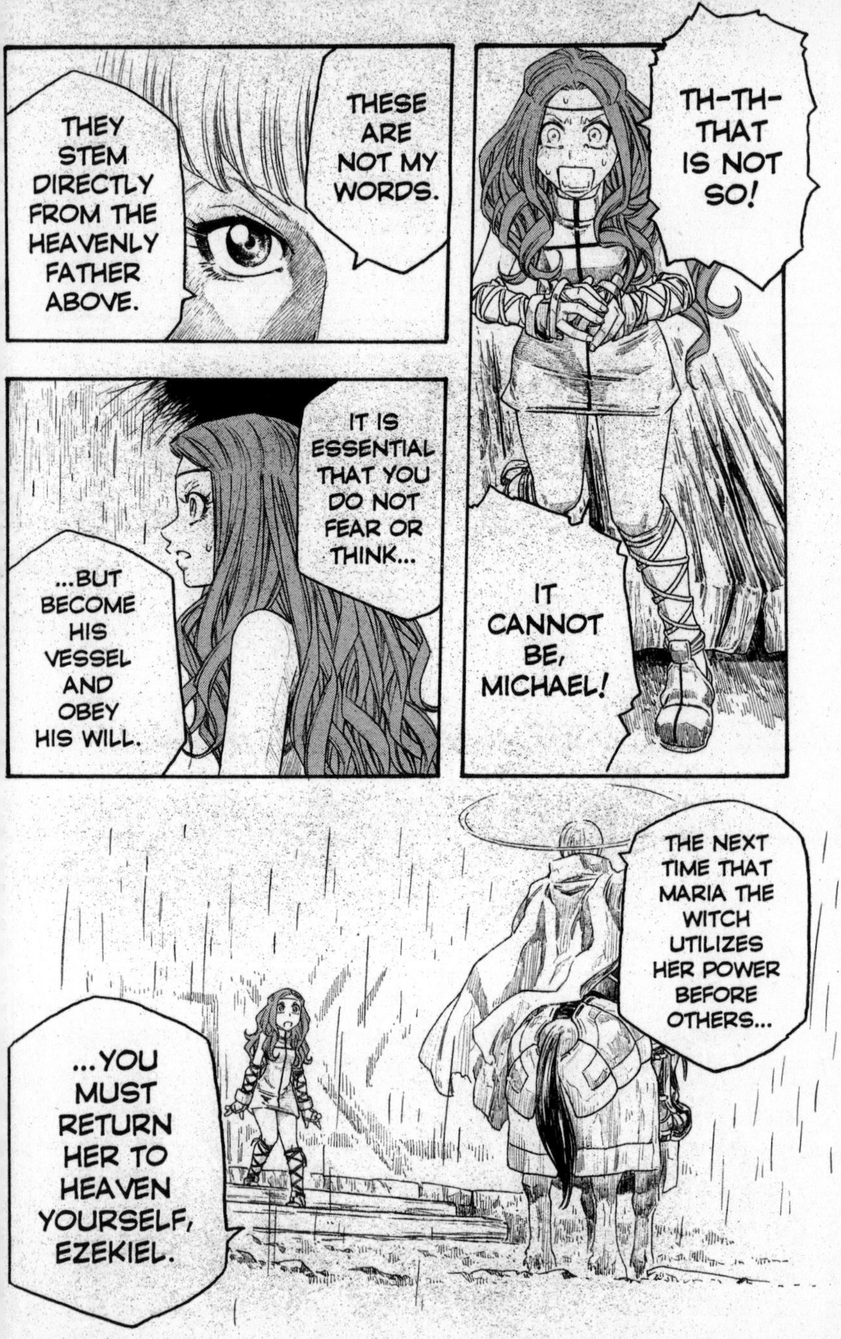
TH-TH-THAT IS NOT SO!
IT CANNOT BE, MICHAEL!
THESE ARE NOT MY WORDS.
THEY STEM DIRECTLY FROM THE HEAVENLY FATHER ABOVE.
IT IS ESSENTIAL THAT YOU DO NOT FEAR OR THINK...
...BUT BECOME HIS VESSEL AND OBEY HIS WILL.
THE NEXT TIME THAT MARIA THE WITCH UTILIZES HER POWER BEFORE OTHERS...
...YOU MUST RETURN HER TO HEAVEN YOURSELF, EZEKIEL.

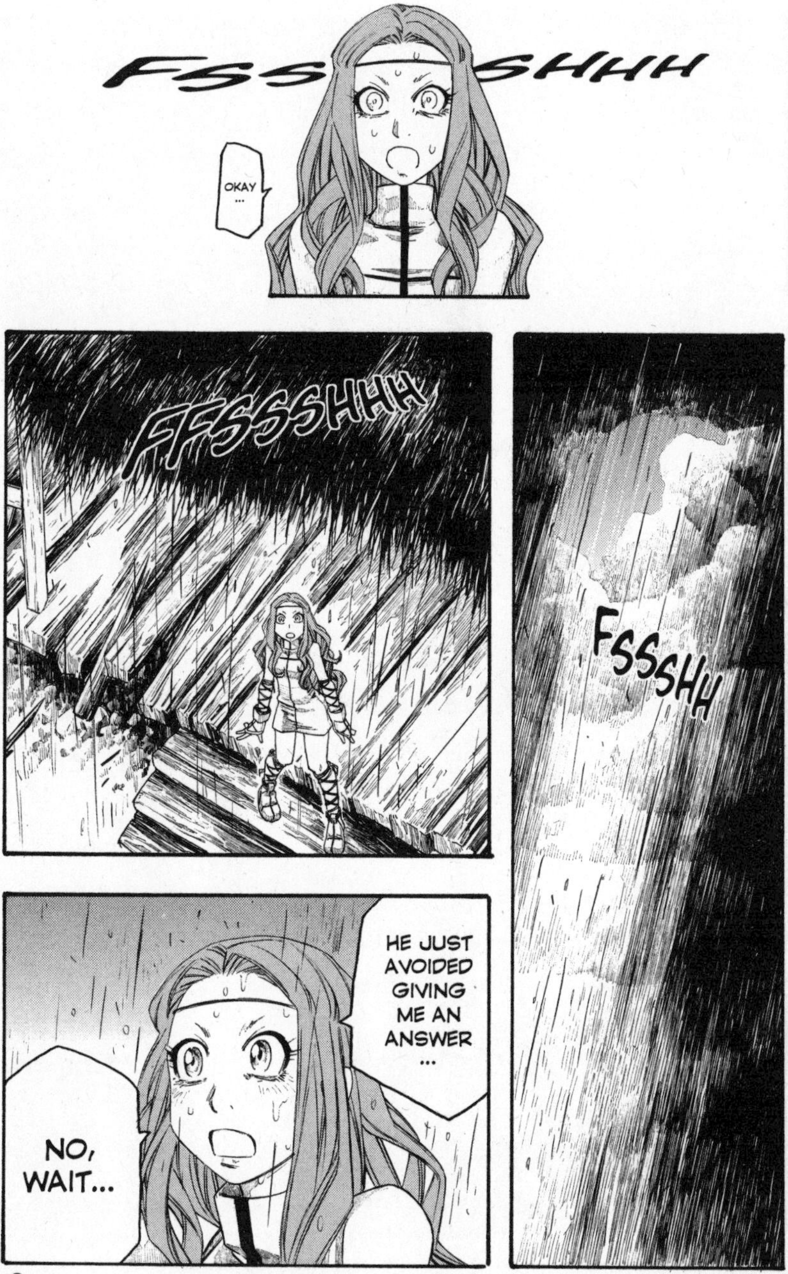
FSSSHHH
OKAY ...
FSSSHH
FFSSSSHHH
HE JUST AVOIDED GIVING ME AN ANSWER ...
NO, WAIT...

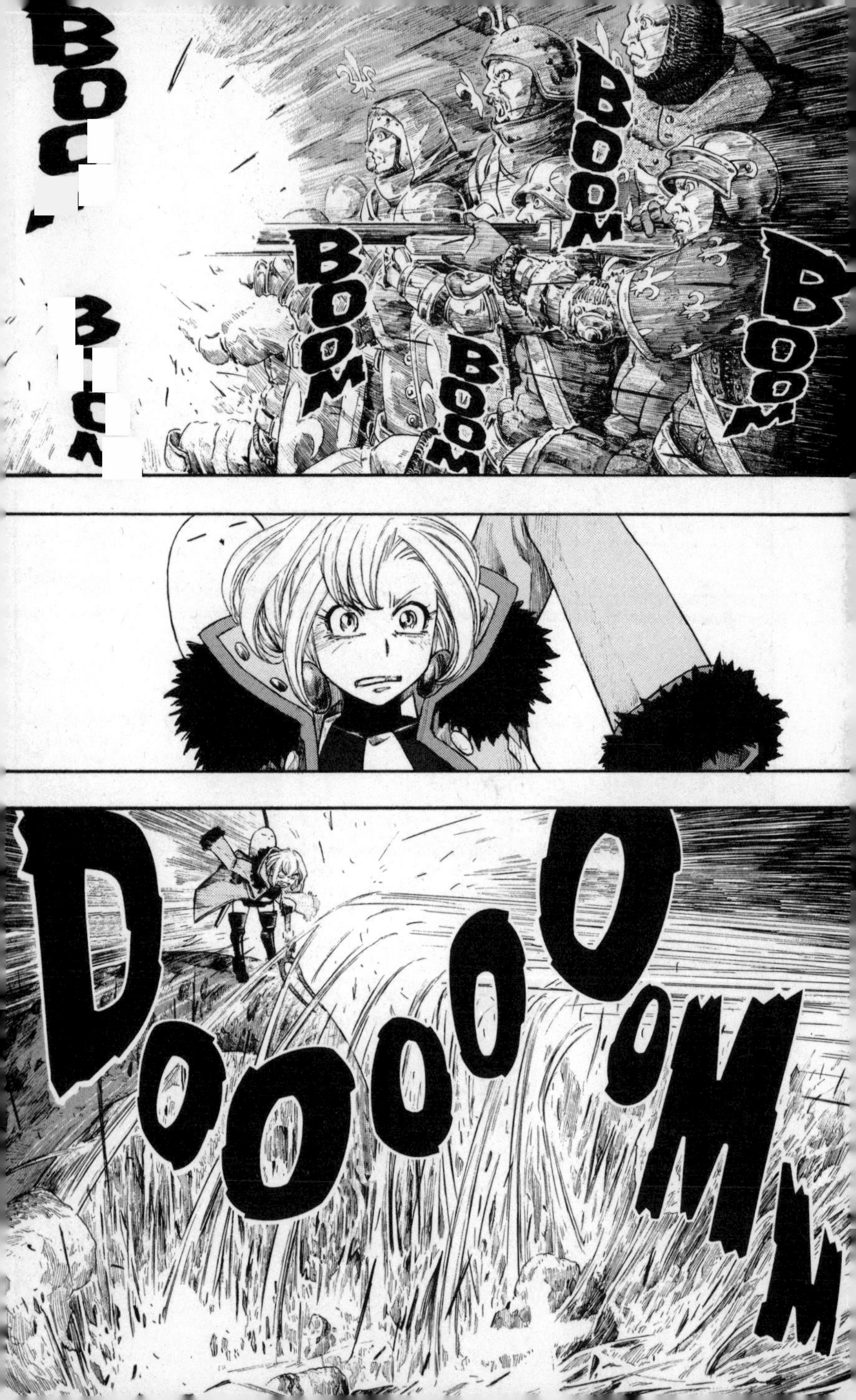

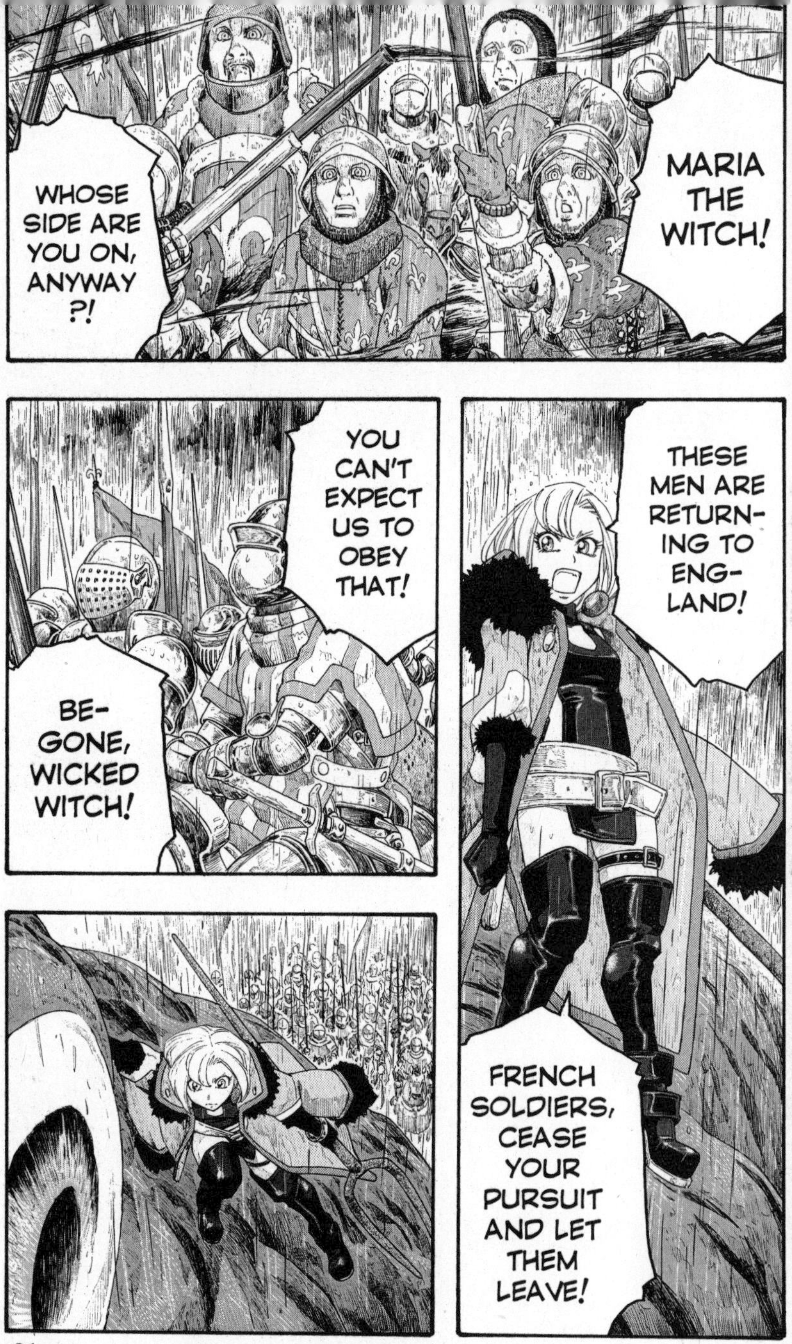
MARIA THE WITCH!
WHOSE SIDE ARE YOU ON, ANYWAY?!
THESE MEN ARE RETURNING TO ENGLAND!
FRENCH SOLDIERS, CEASE YOUR PURSUIT AND LET THEM LEAVE!
YOU CAN'T EXPECT US TO OBEY THAT!
BEGONE, WICKED WITCH!

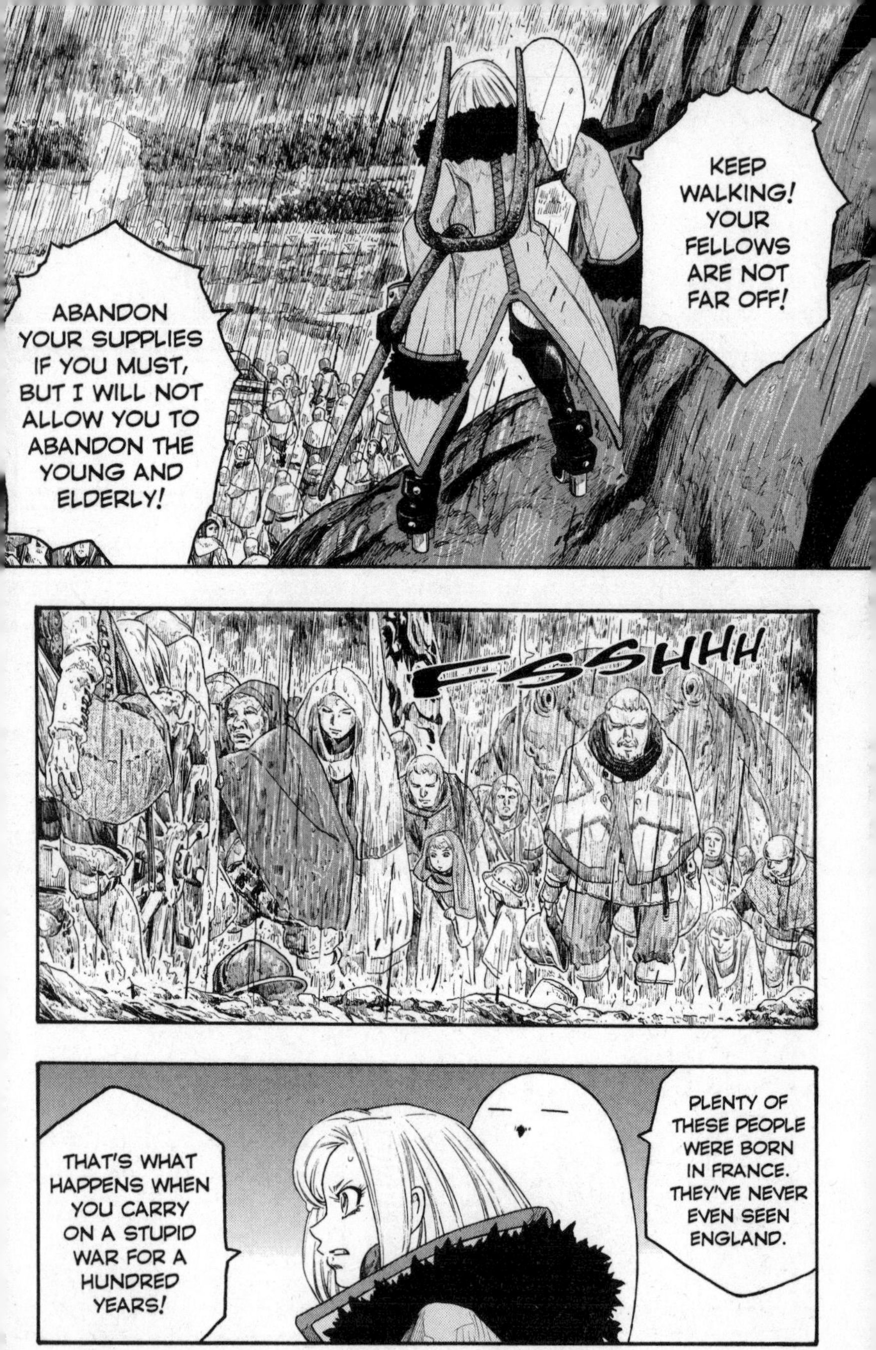
KEEP WALKING! YOUR FELLOWS ARE NOT FAR OFF!
ABANDON YOUR SUPPLIES IF YOU MUST, BUT I WILL NOT ALLOW YOU TO ABANDON THE YOUNG AND ELDERLY!
FSSHHH
PLENTY OF THESE PEOPLE WERE BORN IN FRANCE. THEY'VE NEVER EVEN SEEN ENGLAND.
THAT'S WHAT HAPPENS WHEN YOU CARRY ON A STUPID WAR FOR A HUNDRED YEARS!

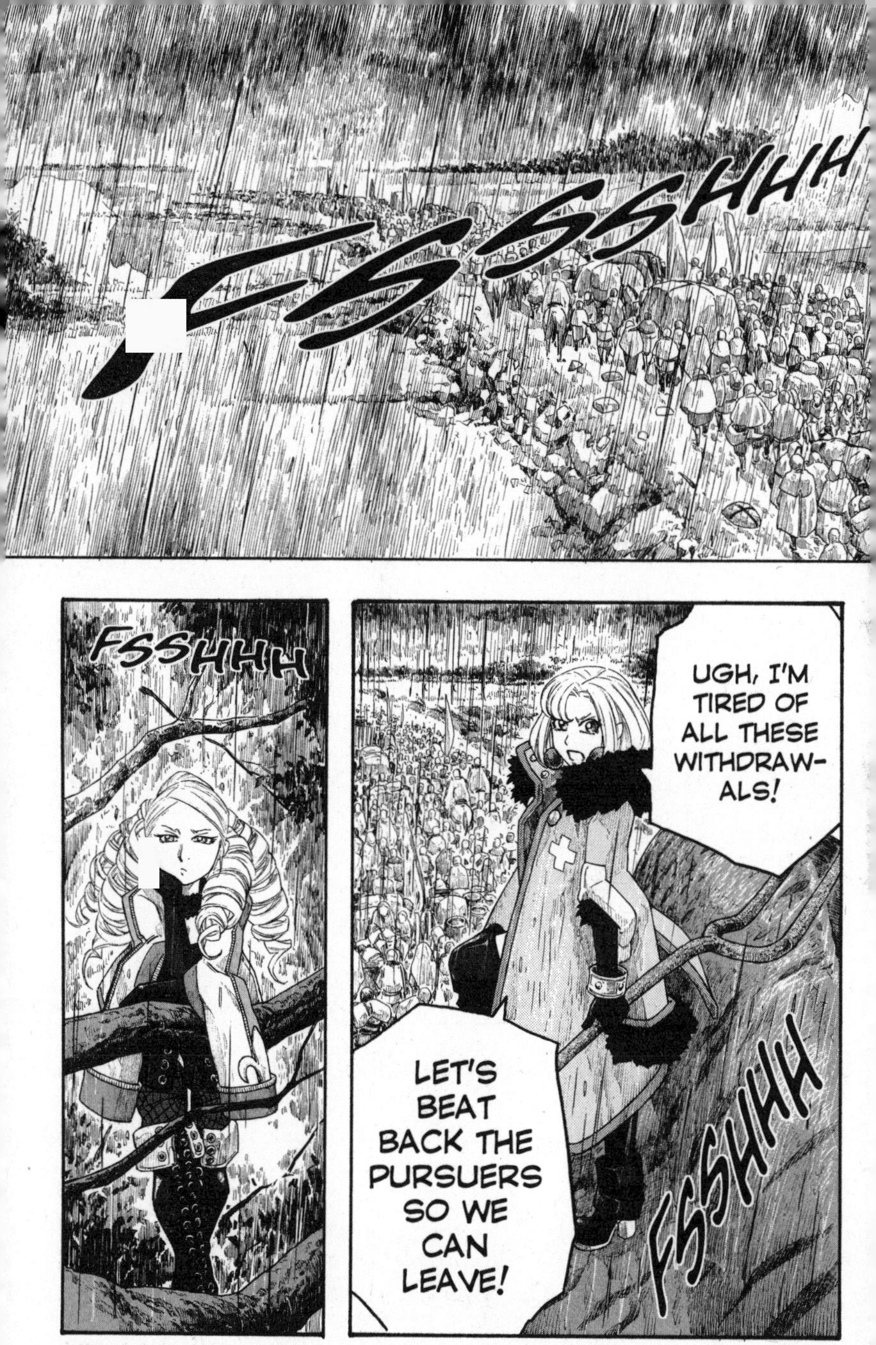
FSSSHHH
UGH, I'M TIRED OF ALL THESE WITHDRAW-ALS!
LET'S BEAT BACK THE PURSUERS SO WE CAN LEAVE!
FSSHHH
FSSHHH

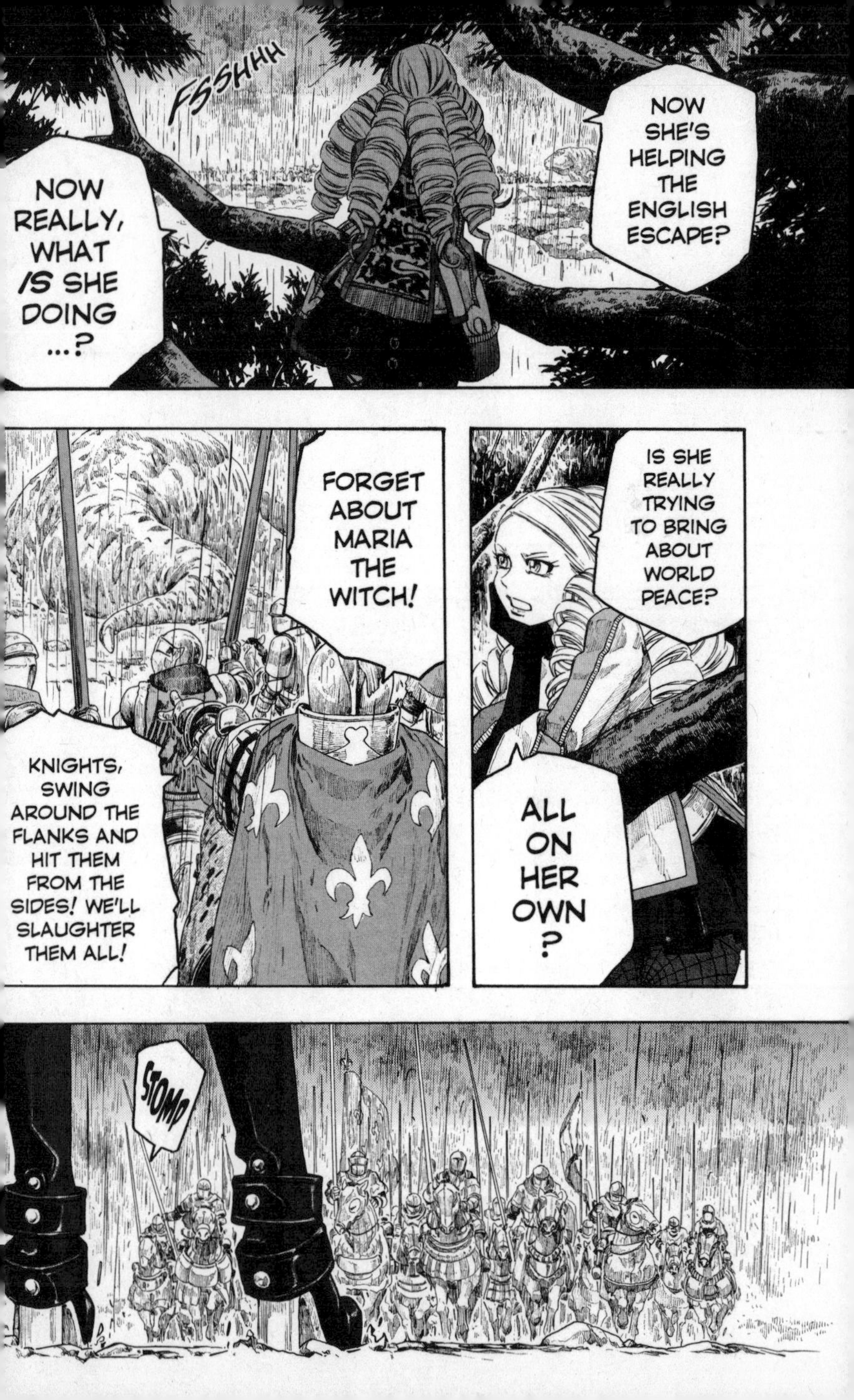
NOW SHE'S HELPING THE ENGLISH ESCAPE?
FSSHHH
NOW REALLY, WHAT *IS* SHE DOING ...?
IS SHE REALLY TRYING TO BRING ABOUT WORLD PEACE?
ALL ON HER OWN?
FORGET ABOUT MARIA THE WITCH!
KNIGHTS, SWING AROUND THE FLANKS AND HIT THEM FROM THE SIDES! WE'LL SLAUGHTER THEM ALL!
STOMP

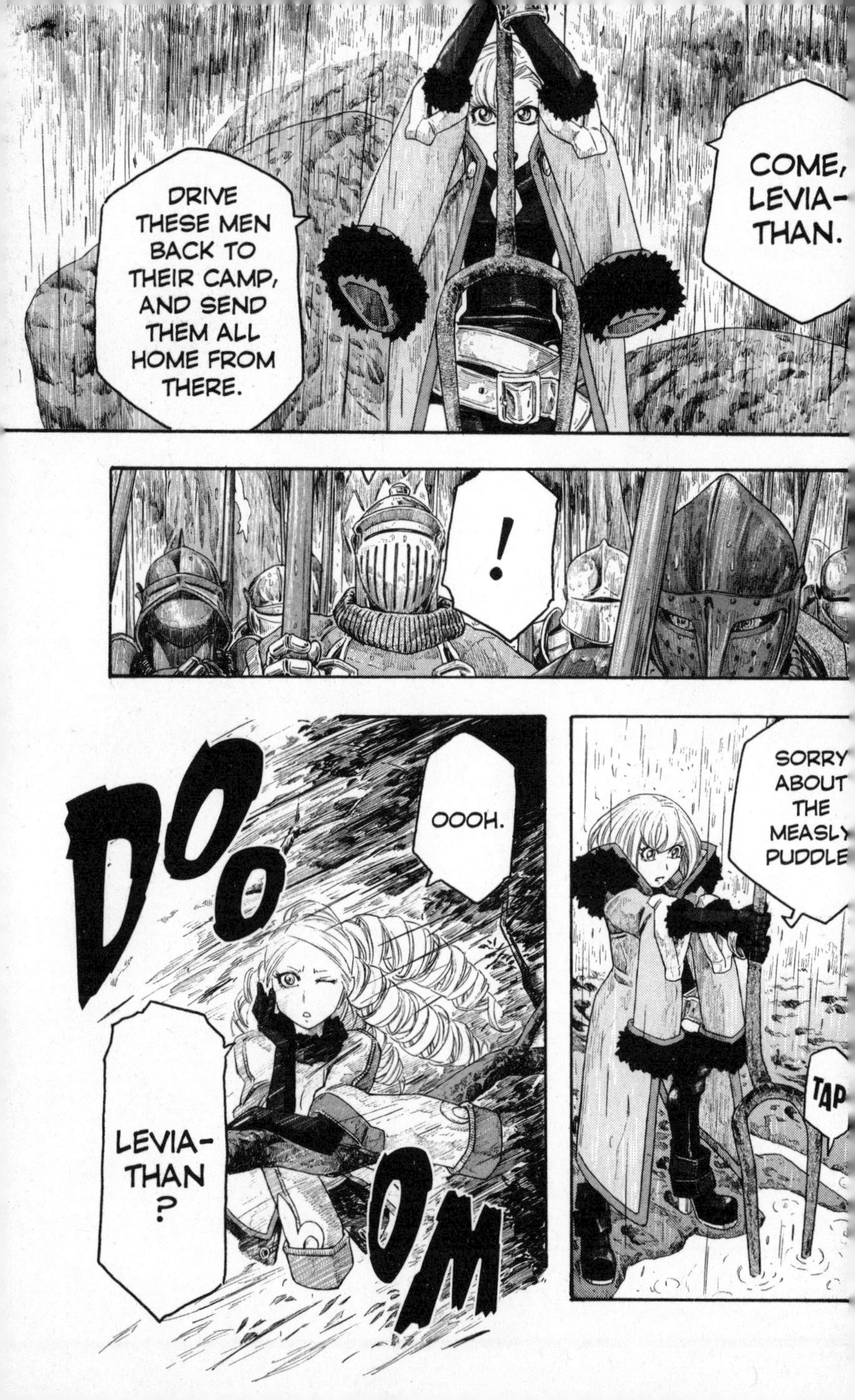
COME, LEVIA-THAN.
DRIVE THESE MEN BACK TO THEIR CAMP, AND SEND THEM ALL HOME FROM THERE.
!
SORRY ABOUT THE MEASLY PUDDLE
TAP
OOOH.
DOOOM
LEVIA-THAN?

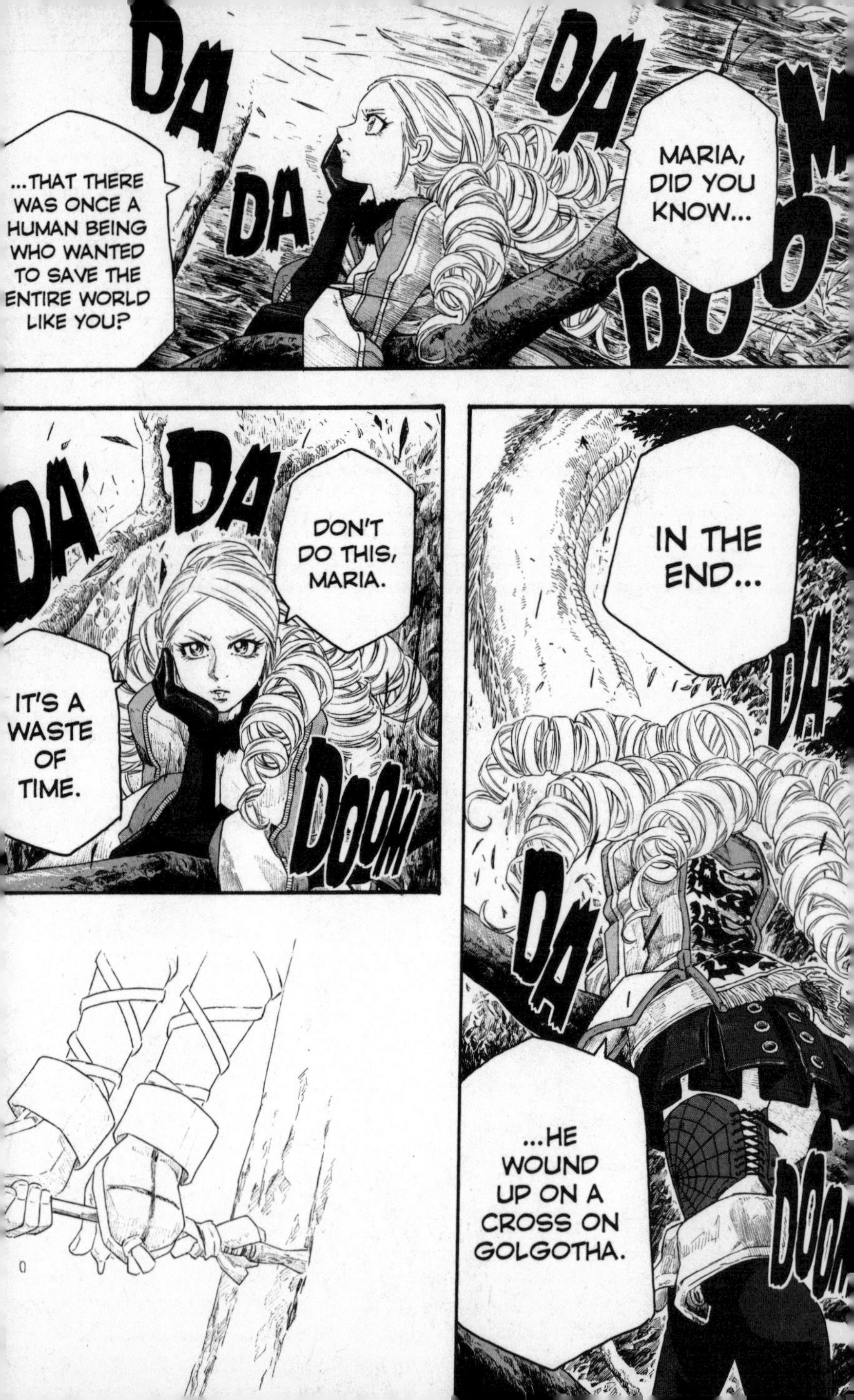
DA
MARIA, DID YOU KNOW...
DA
DA
...THAT THERE WAS ONCE A HUMAN BEING WHO WANTED TO SAVE THE ENTIRE WORLD LIKE YOU?
IN THE END...
DA
DA
...HE WOUND UP ON A CROSS ON GOLGOTHA.
DOOM
DA
DA
DON'T DO THIS, MARIA.
IT'S A WASTE OF TIME.
DOOM

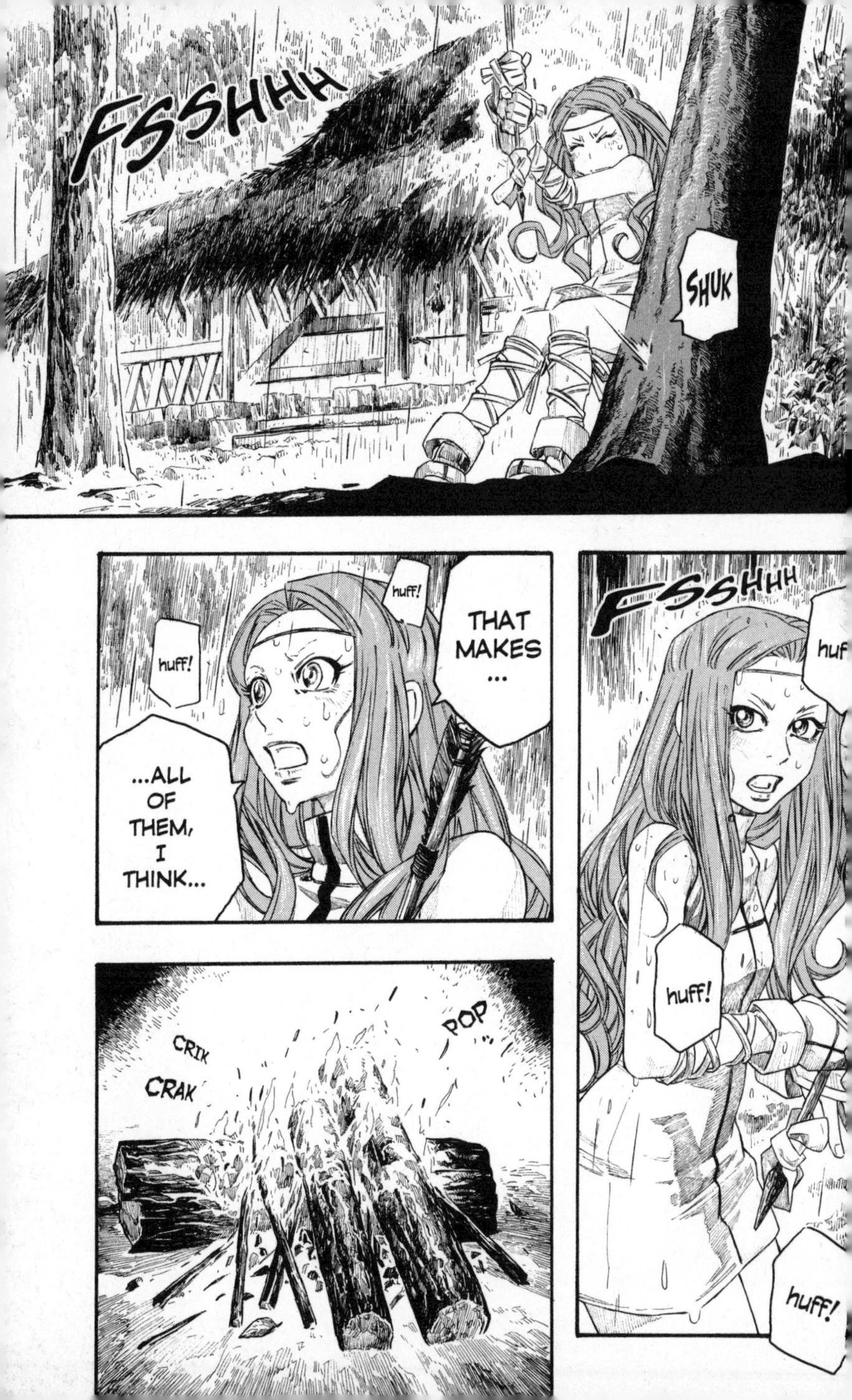
FSSHHH
SHUK
FSSHHH
huf
huff!
huff!
THAT MAKES...
huff!
huff!
...ALL OF THEM, I THINK...
POP
CRIK
CRAK

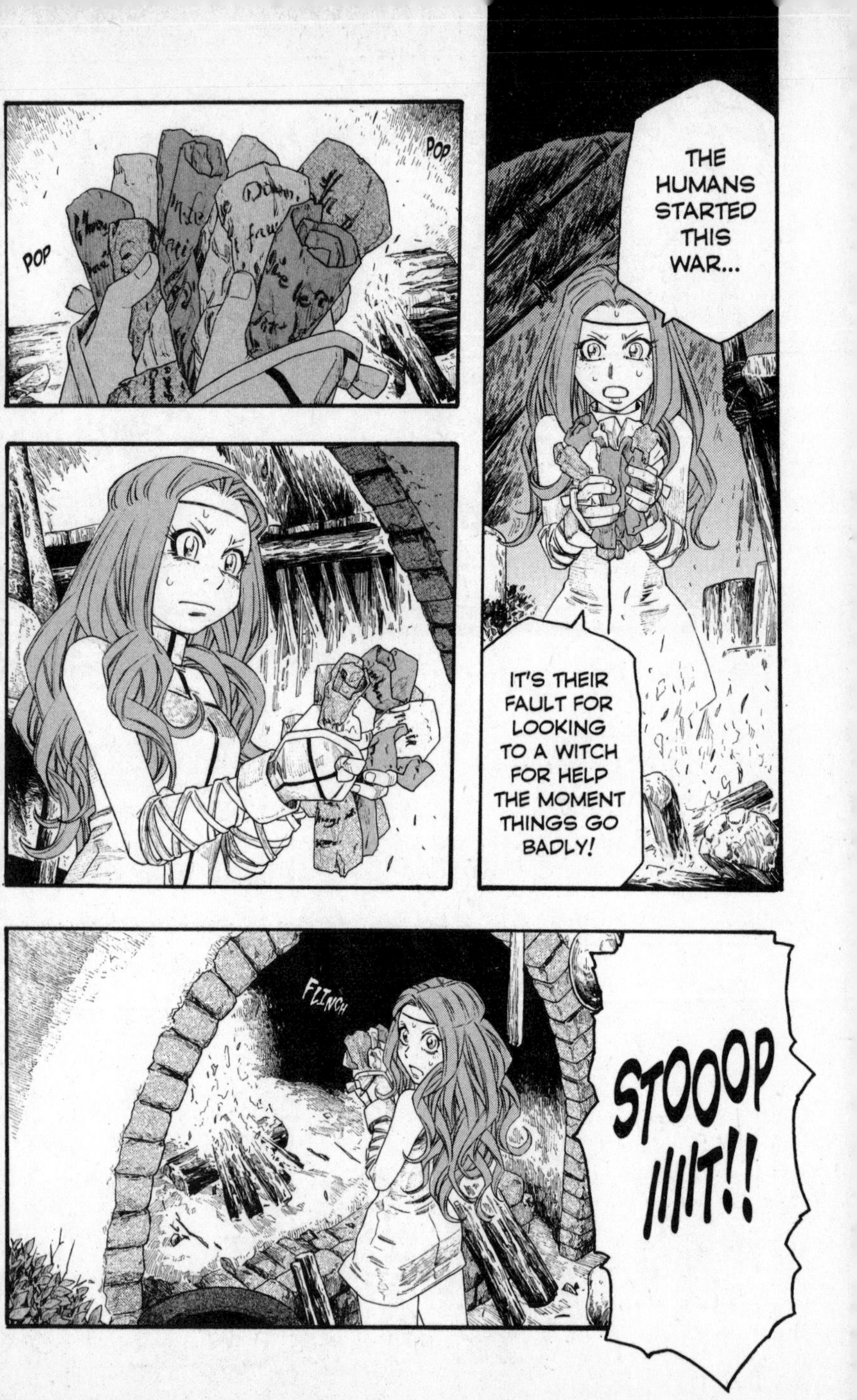
THE HUMANS STARTED THIS WAR...
IT'S THEIR FAULT FOR LOOKING TO A WITCH FOR HELP THE MOMENT THINGS GO BADLY!
POP
POP
FLINCH
STOOOP IIIIT!!

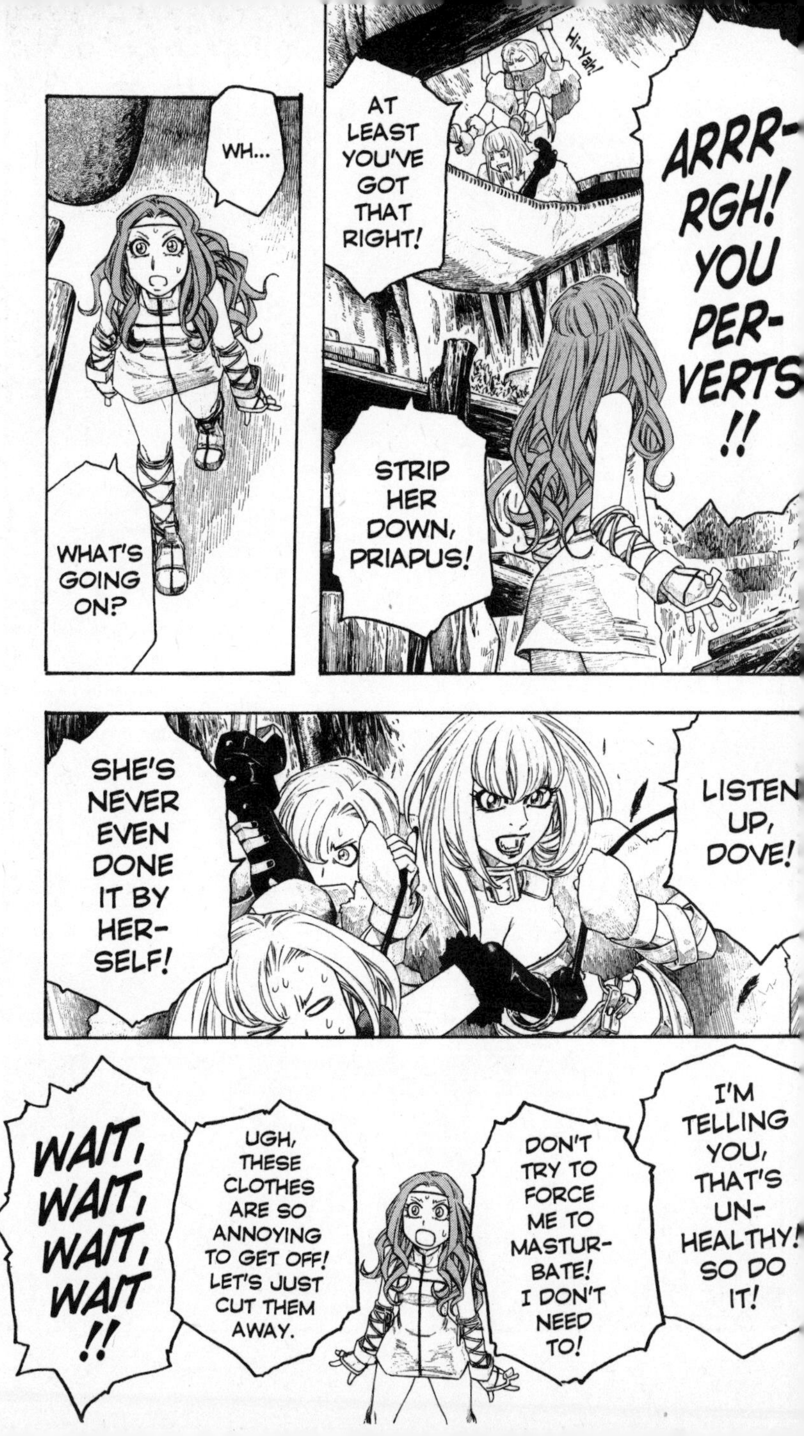
ARRRRGH! YOU PERVERTS!!
Hi-yah!
AT LEAST YOU'VE GOT THAT RIGHT!
STRIP HER DOWN, PRIAPUS!
WH...
WHAT'S GOING ON?
LISTEN UP, DOVE!
SHE'S NEVER EVEN DONE IT BY HERSELF!
I'M TELLING YOU, THAT'S UNHEALTHY! SO DO IT!
DON'T TRY TO FORCE ME TO MASTURBATE! I DON'T NEED TO!
UGH, THESE CLOTHES ARE SO ANNOYING TO GET OFF! LET'S JUST CUT THEM AWAY.
WAIT, WAIT, WAIT, WAIT!!

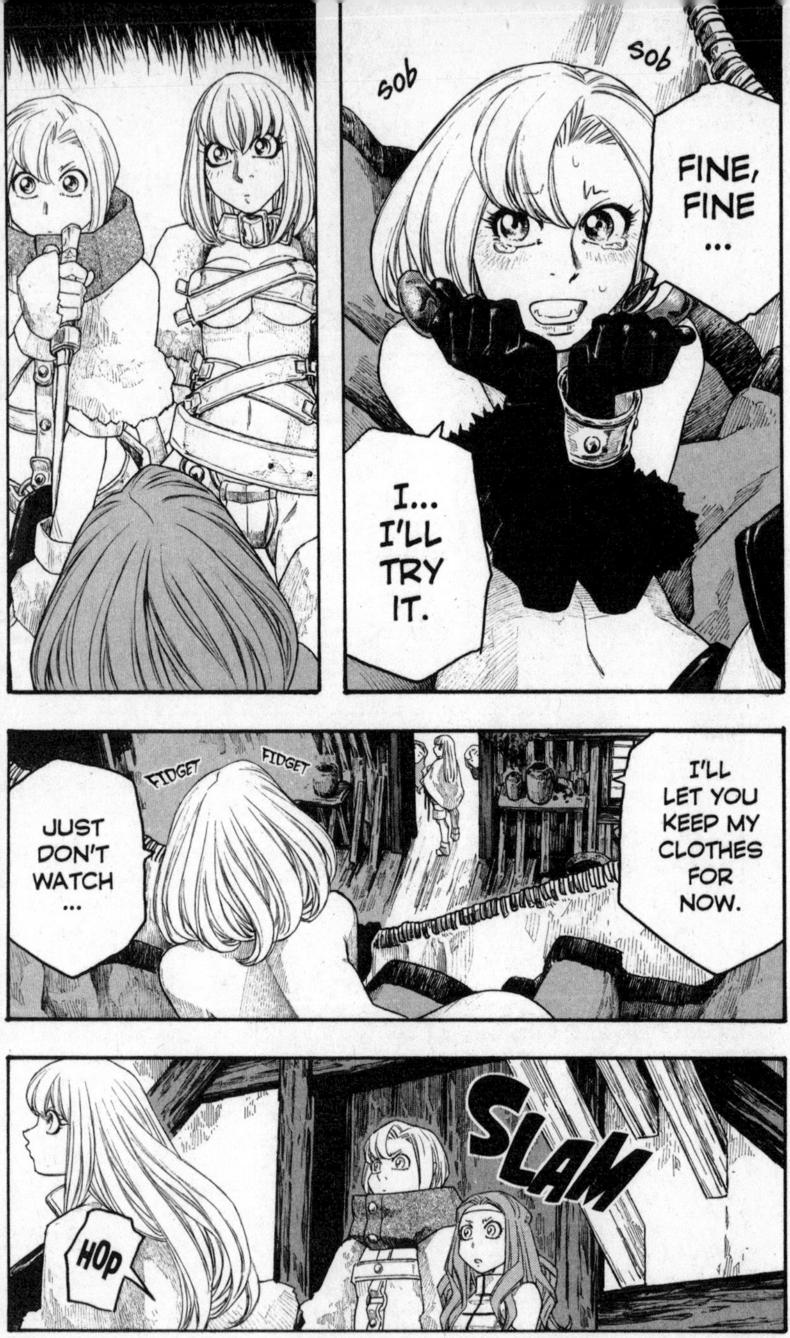
sob
sob
FINE, FINE ...
I... I'LL TRY IT.
I'LL LET YOU KEEP MY CLOTHES FOR NOW.
FIDGET
FIDGET
JUST DON'T WATCH ...
SLAM
HOp

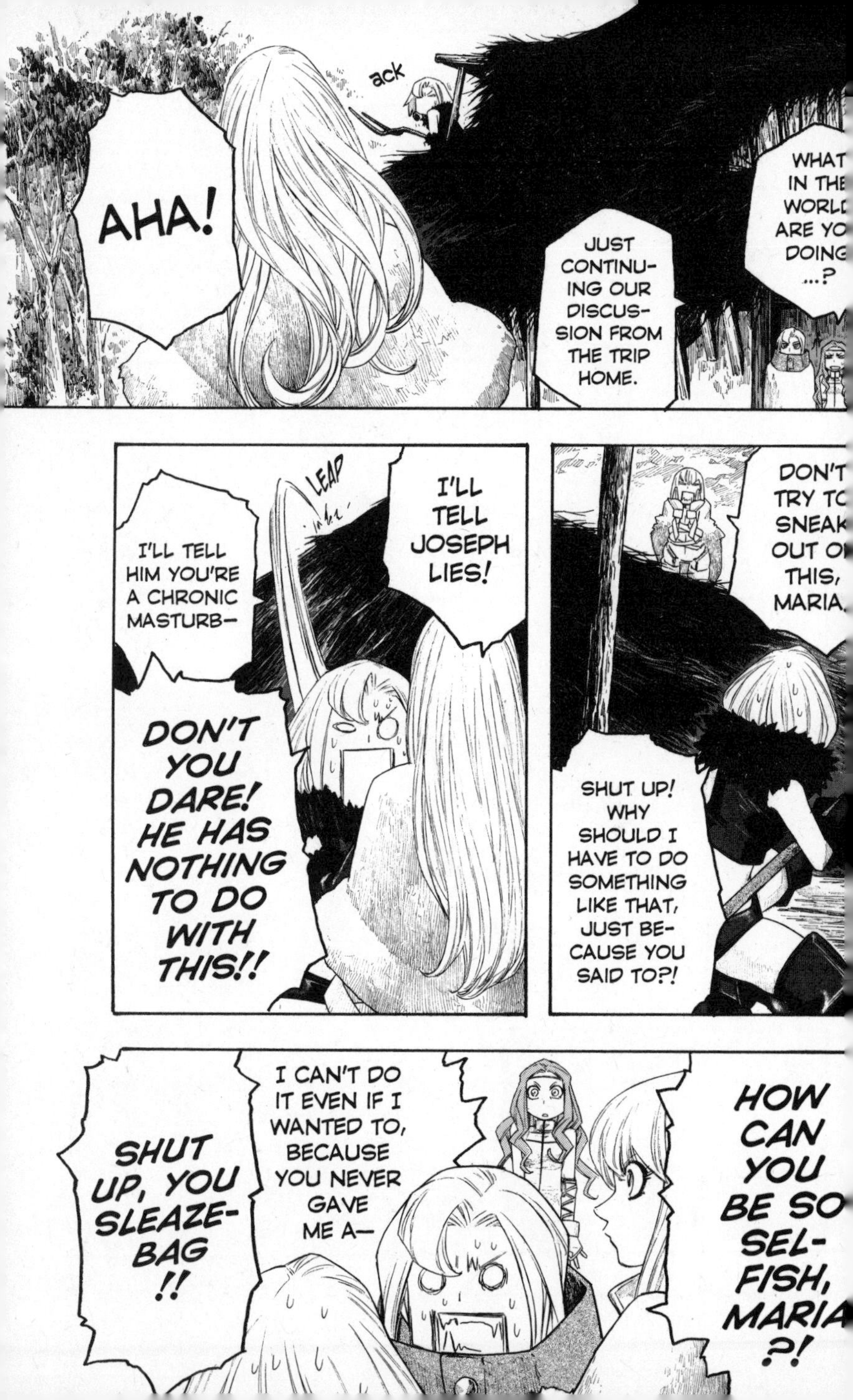
WHAT IN THE WORLD ARE YO DOING ...?
JUST CONTINUING OUR DISCUSSION FROM THE TRIP HOME.
ack
AHA!
DON'T TRY TO SNEAK OUT O THIS, MARIA.
SHUT UP! WHY SHOULD I HAVE TO DO SOMETHING LIKE THAT, JUST BECAUSE YOU SAID TO?!
I'LL TELL JOSEPH LIES!
LEAP
I'LL TELL HIM YOU'RE A CHRONIC MASTURB—
DON'T YOU DARE! HE HAS NOTHING TO DO WITH THIS!!
HOW CAN YOU BE SO SELFISH, MARIA ?!
I CAN'T DO IT EVEN IF I WANTED TO, BECAUSE YOU NEVER GAVE ME A—
SHUT UP, YOU SLEAZEBAG !!

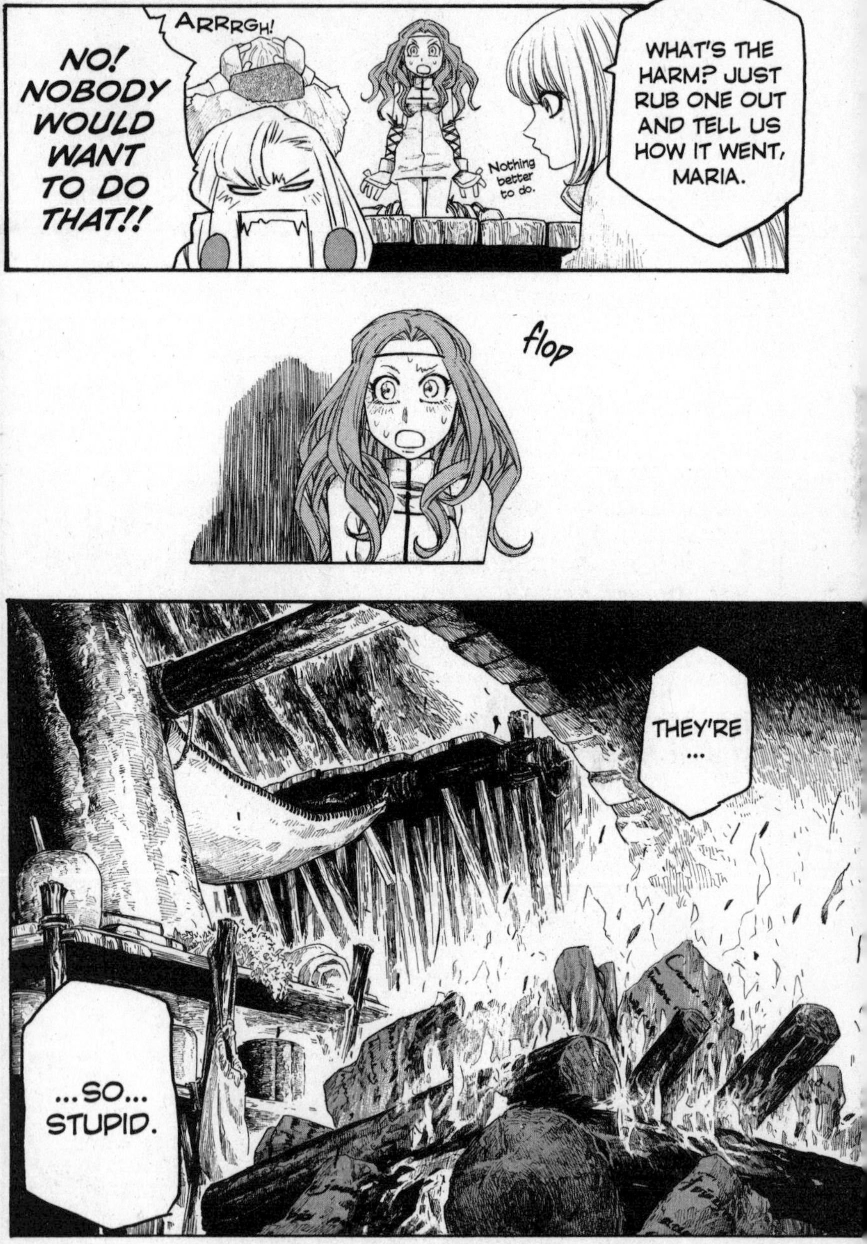
WHAT'S THE HARM? JUST RUB ONE OUT AND TELL US HOW IT WENT, MARIA.
Nothing better to do.
ARRRGH!
NO! NOBODY WOULD WANT TO DO THAT!!
flop
THEY'RE ...
...SO... STUPID.

huff!

huff!

GLUG!

GLUG!

huff!

GOT TO...

huff!

huff!

...WATER MY HORSE...

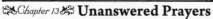

Chapter 13 **Unanswered Prayers**

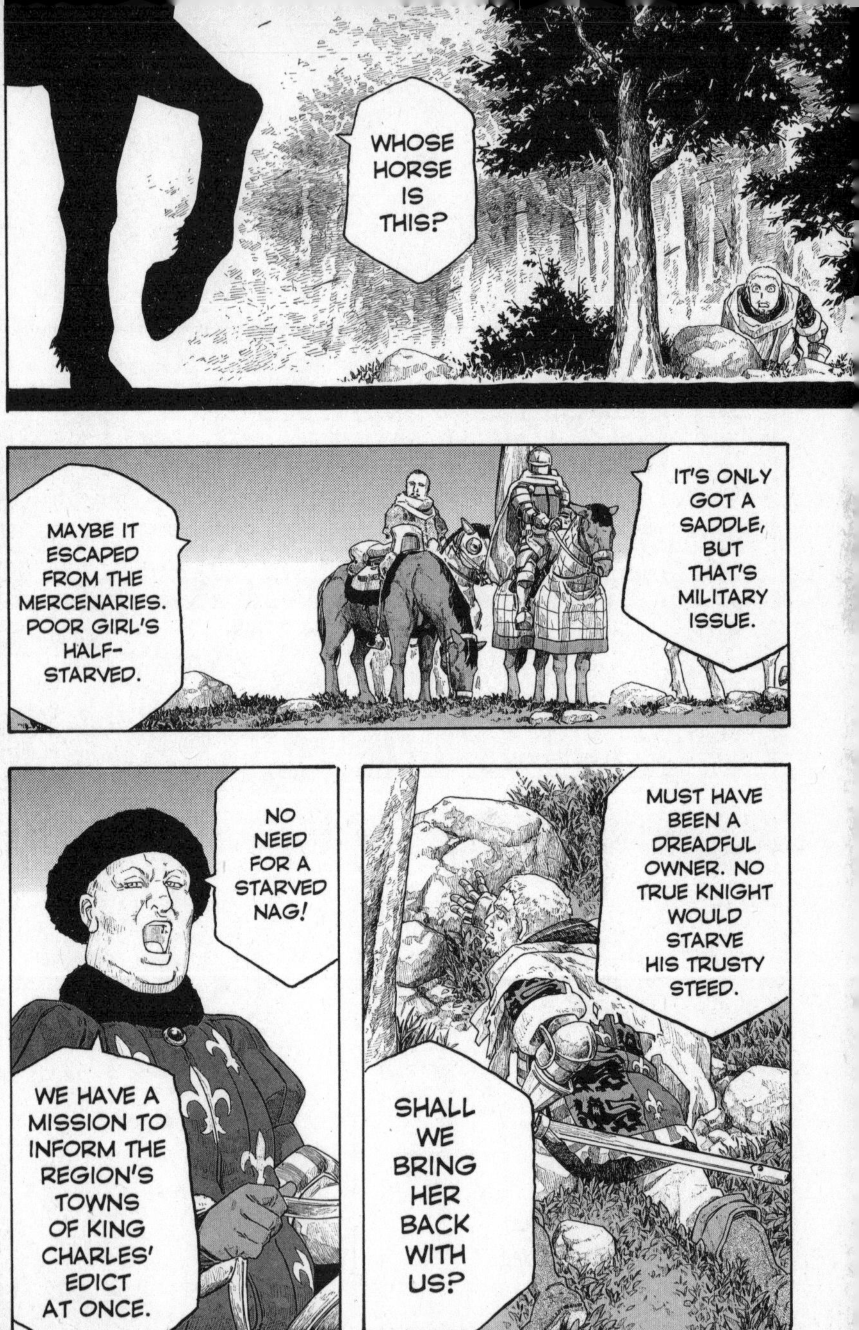
WHOSE HORSE IS THIS?
IT'S ONLY GOT A SADDLE, BUT THAT'S MILITARY ISSUE.
MAYBE IT ESCAPED FROM THE MERCENARIES. POOR GIRL'S HALF-STARVED.
MUST HAVE BEEN A DREADFUL OWNER. NO TRUE KNIGHT WOULD STARVE HIS TRUSTY STEED.
SHALL WE BRING HER BACK WITH US?
NO NEED FOR A STARVED NAG!
WE HAVE A MISSION TO INFORM THE REGION'S TOWNS OF KING CHARLES' EDICT AT ONCE.

THE WITCH MARIA'S WOODS ARE ALONG THIS STRETCH.

EERIE PLACE! LET US BE OFF.

SHIVER SHIVER

WHEWWW!

SLOSH

SLOSH

RUMORS SAY THAT MARIA'S WOODS ARE SHROUDED IN MIST ALL DAY, EVEN WHEN THE SUN SHINES. THAT'S HOW YOU CAN RECOGNIZE THEM.

SORRY GIRL... I'VE GOT NOTHING BUT WATER FOR YOU

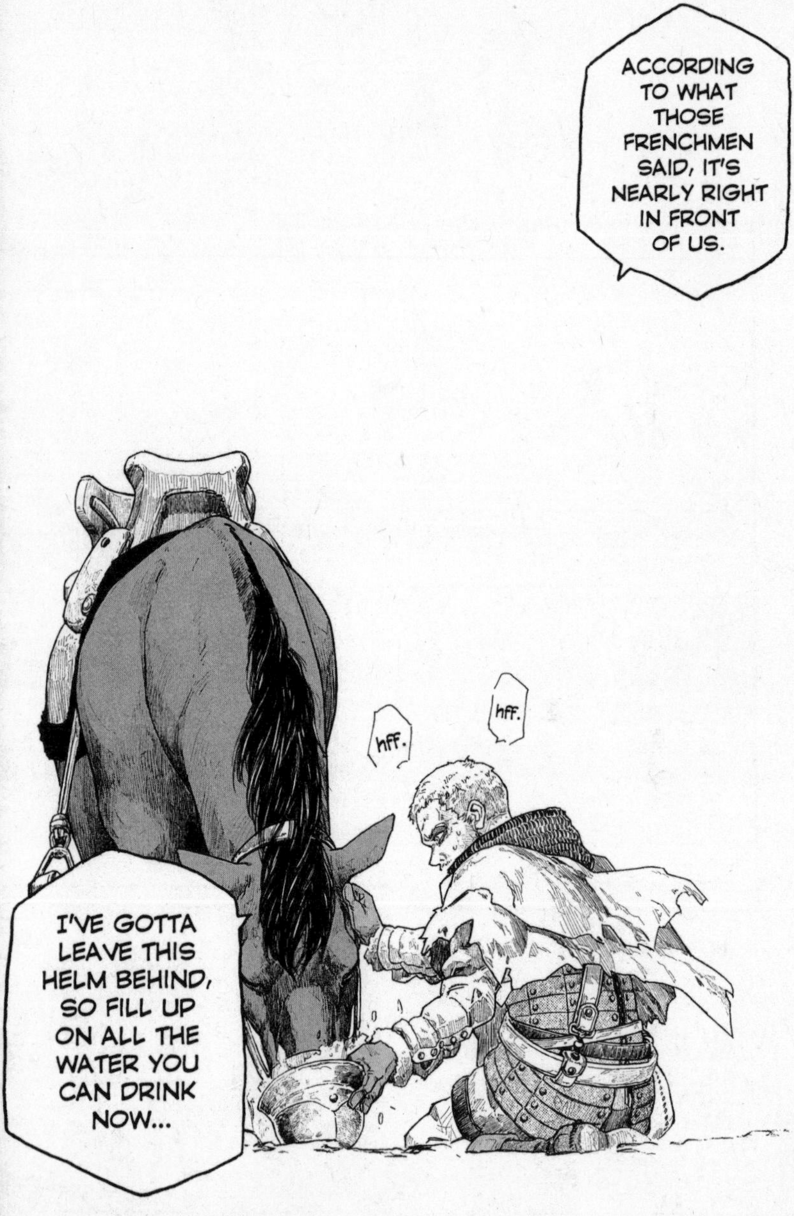
ACCORDING TO WHAT THOSE FRENCHMEN SAID, IT'S NEARLY RIGHT IN FRONT OF US.
hff.
hff.
I'VE GOTTA LEAVE THIS HELM BEHIND, SO FILL UP ON ALL THE WATER YOU CAN DRINK NOW...

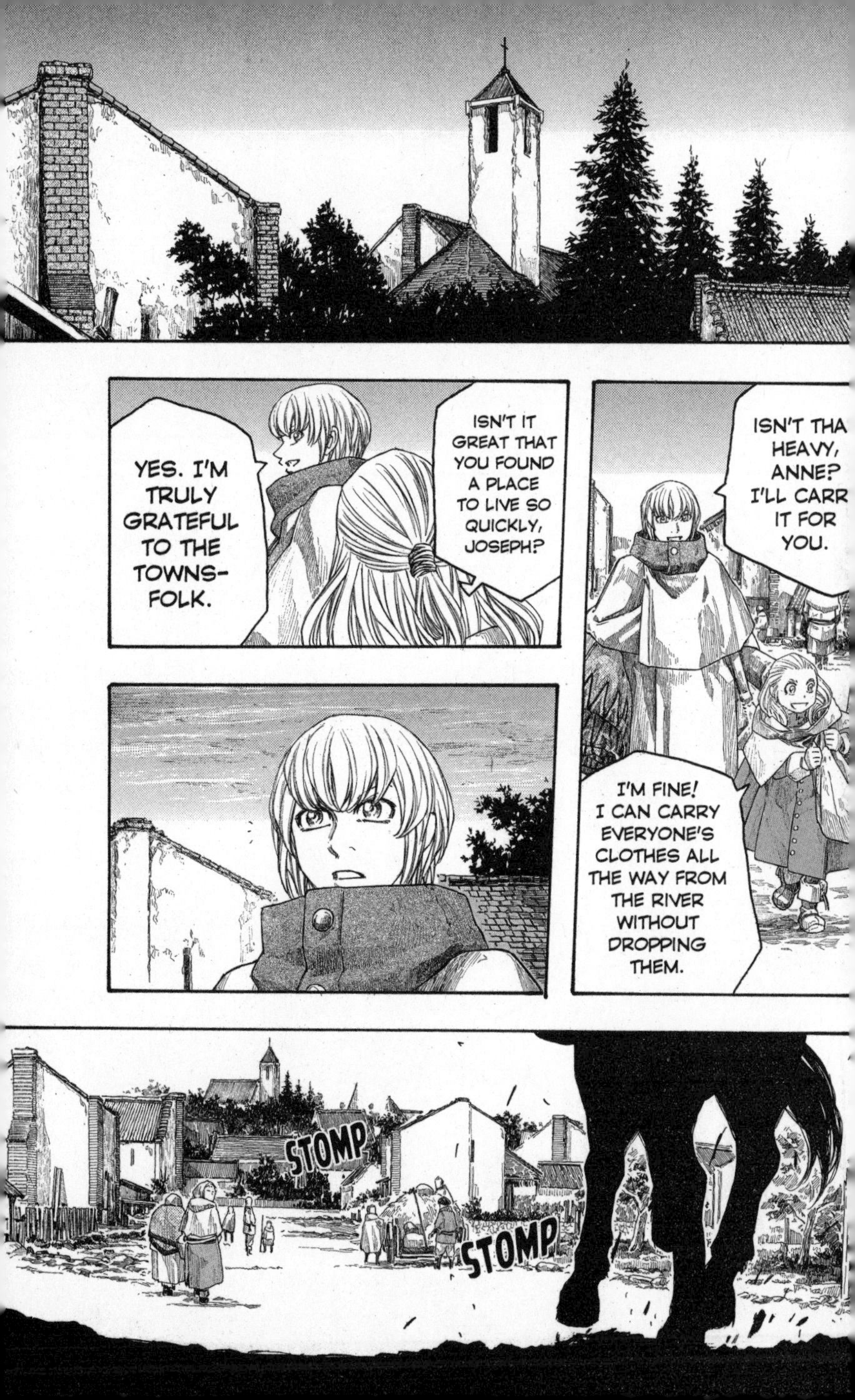
ISN'T THA HEAVY, ANNE? I'LL CARR IT FOR YOU.
I'M FINE! I CAN CARRY EVERYONE'S CLOTHES ALL THE WAY FROM THE RIVER WITHOUT DROPPING THEM.
ISN'T IT GREAT THAT YOU FOUND A PLACE TO LIVE SO QUICKLY, JOSEPH?
YES. I'M TRULY GRATEFUL TO THE TOWNS-FOLK.
STOMP
STOMP

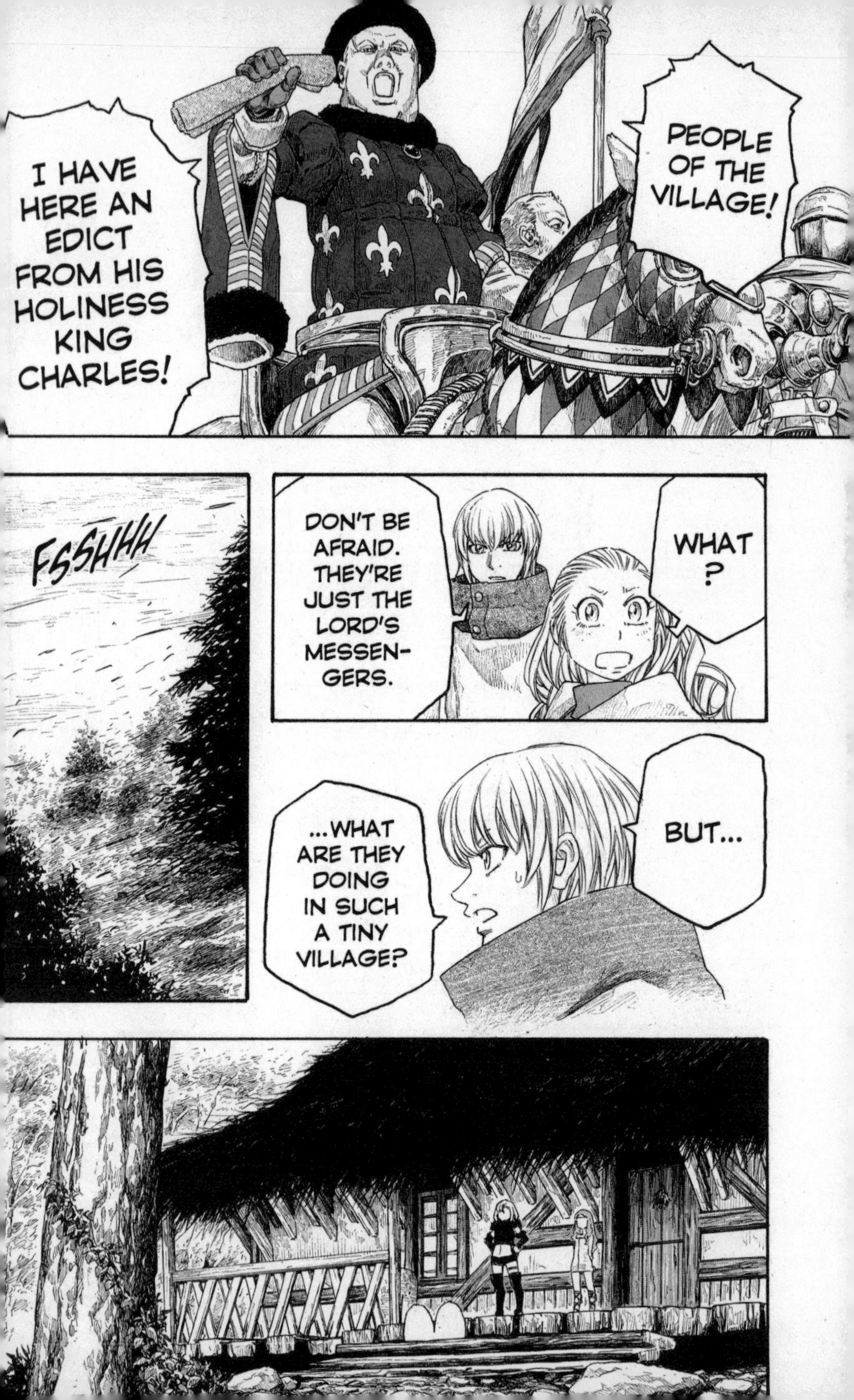
PEOPLE OF THE VILLAGE!
I HAVE HERE AN EDICT FROM HIS HOLINESS KING CHARLES!
WHAT?
DON'T BE AFRAID. THEY'RE JUST THE LORD'S MESSEN-GERS.
BUT...
...WHAT ARE THEY DOING IN SUCH A TINY VILLAGE?
FSSHHH

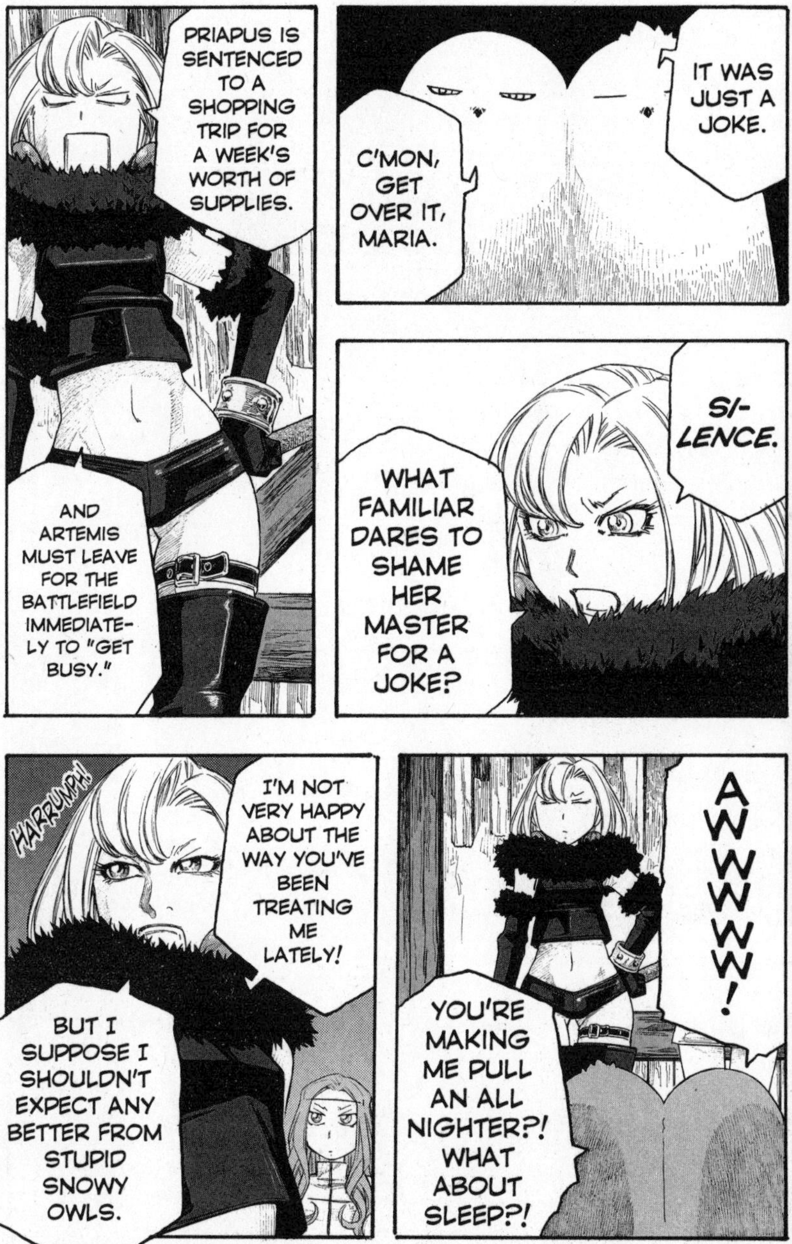
IT WAS JUST A JOKE.
C'MON, GET OVER IT, MARIA.
SI-LENCE.
WHAT FAMILIAR DARES TO SHAME HER MASTER FOR A JOKE?
PRIAPUS IS SENTENCED TO A SHOPPING TRIP FOR A WEEK'S WORTH OF SUPPLIES.
AND ARTEMIS MUST LEAVE FOR THE BATTLEFIELD IMMEDIATE-LY TO "GET BUSY."
AWWWWWW!
YOU'RE MAKING ME PULL AN ALL NIGHTER?! WHAT ABOUT SLEEP?!
I'M NOT VERY HAPPY ABOUT THE WAY YOU'VE BEEN TREATING ME LATELY!
HARRUMPH!
BUT I SUPPOSE I SHOULDN'T EXPECT ANY BETTER FROM STUPID SNOWY OWLS.

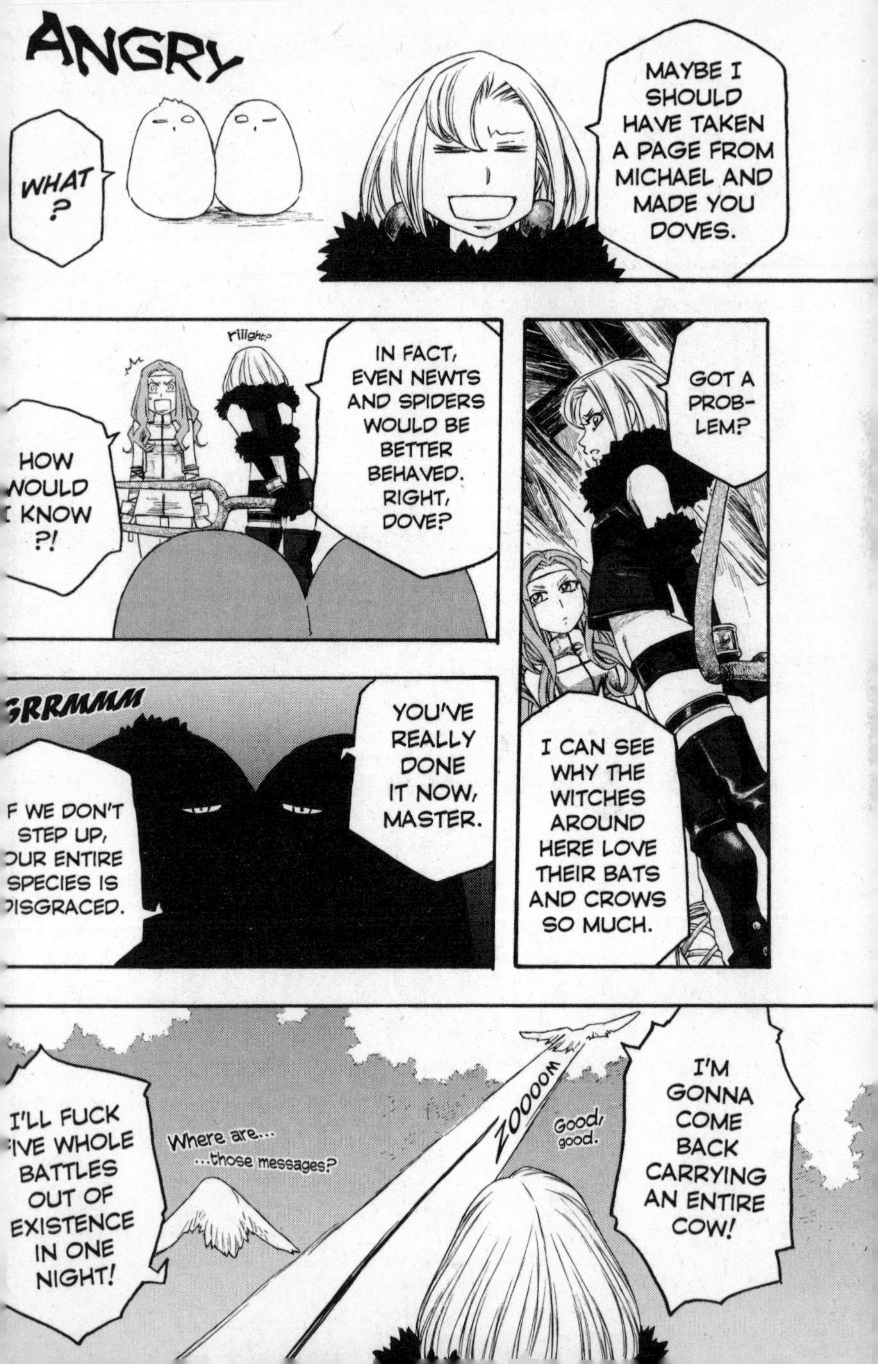
MAYBE I SHOULD HAVE TAKEN A PAGE FROM MICHAEL AND MADE YOU DOVES.
ANGRY
WHAT?
GOT A PROB-LEM?
I CAN SEE WHY THE WITCHES AROUND HERE LOVE THEIR BATS AND CROWS SO MUCH.
IN FACT, EVEN NEWTS AND SPIDERS WOULD BE BETTER BEHAVED. RIGHT, DOVE?
riiight?
HOW WOULD I KNOW?!
YOU'VE REALLY DONE IT NOW, MASTER.
GRRMMM
IF WE DON'T STEP UP, OUR ENTIRE SPECIES IS DISGRACED.
I'M GONNA COME BACK CARRYING AN ENTIRE COW!
Good, good.
ZOOOOM
Where are...
...those messages?
I'LL FUCK FIVE WHOLE BATTLES OUT OF EXISTENCE IN ONE NIGHT!

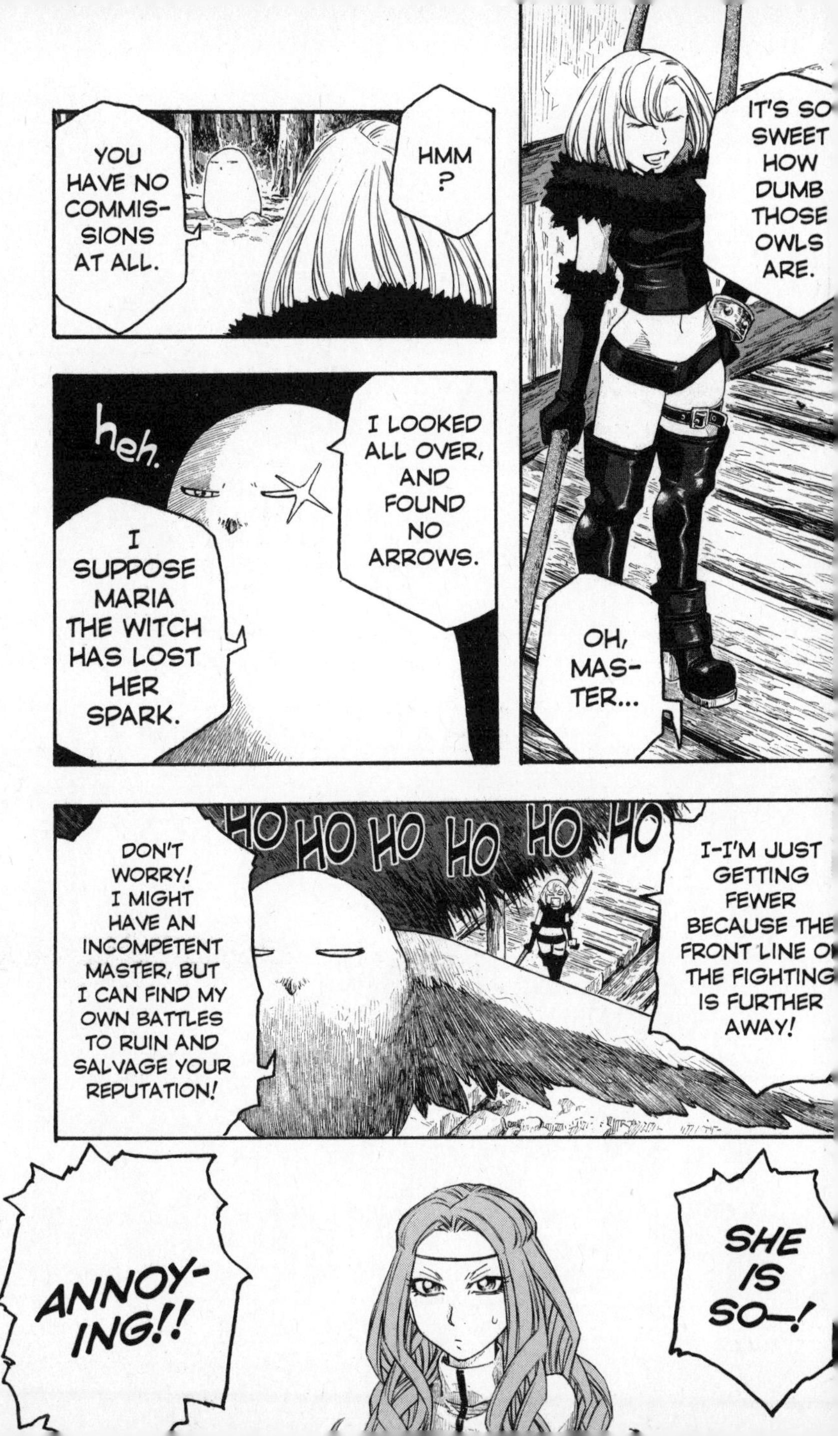
IT'S SO SWEET HOW DUMB THOSE OWLS ARE.
OH, MASTER...
HMM?
YOU HAVE NO COMMISSIONS AT ALL.
I LOOKED ALL OVER, AND FOUND NO ARROWS.
heh.
I SUPPOSE MARIA THE WITCH HAS LOST HER SPARK.
I-I'M JUST GETTING FEWER BECAUSE THE FRONT LINE OF THE FIGHTING IS FURTHER AWAY!
HO HO HO HO HO HO HO
DON'T WORRY! I MIGHT HAVE AN INCOMPETENT MASTER, BUT I CAN FIND MY OWN BATTLES TO RUIN AND SALVAGE YOUR REPUTATION!
SHE IS SO—!
ANNOYING!!

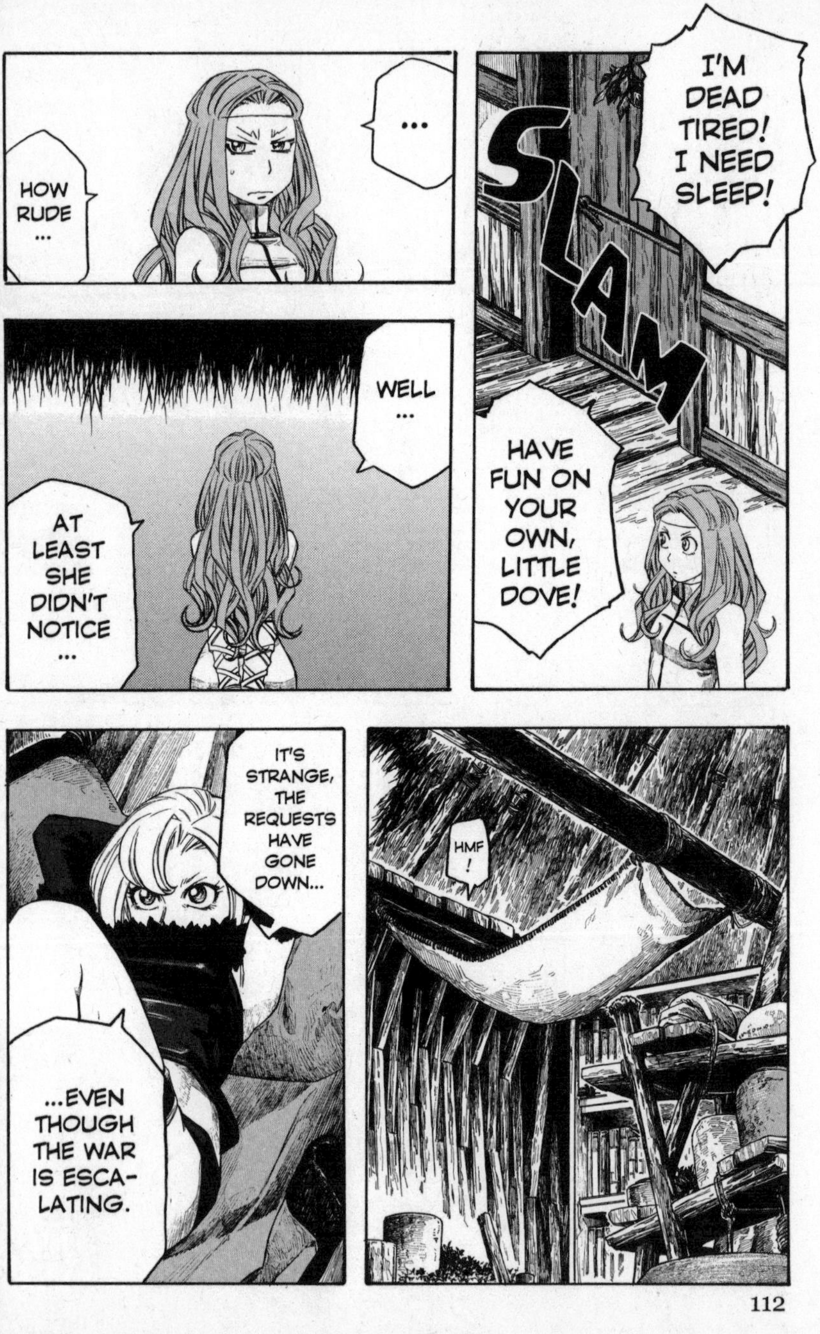
I'M DEAD TIRED! I NEED SLEEP!
SLAM
HAVE FUN ON YOUR OWN, LITTLE DOVE!
...
HOW RUDE ...
WELL ...
AT LEAST SHE DIDN'T NOTICE ...
HMF!
IT'S STRANGE, THE REQUESTS HAVE GONE DOWN...
...EVEN THOUGH THE WAR IS ESCA-LATING.

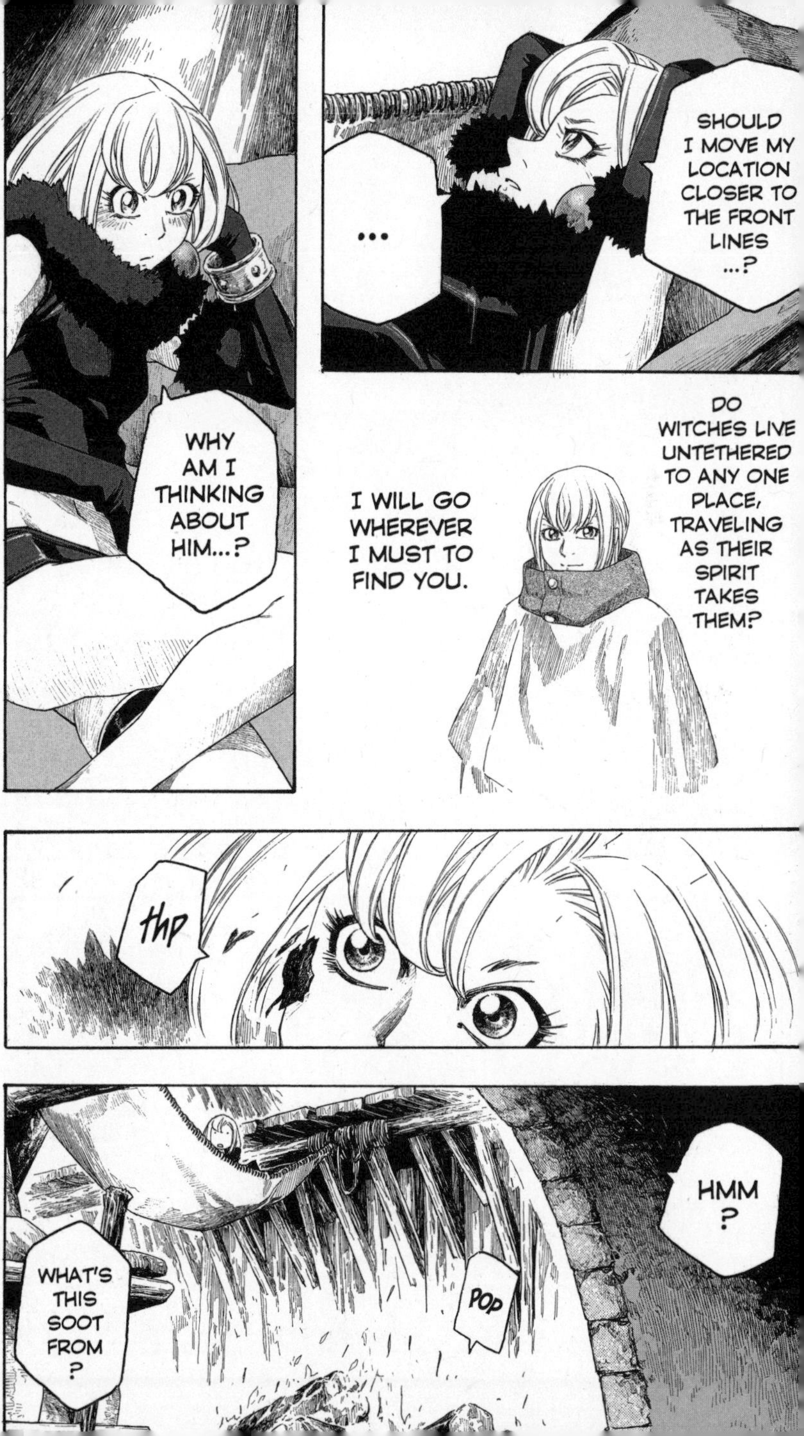
SHOULD I MOVE MY LOCATION CLOSER TO THE FRONT LINES ...?
...
DO WITCHES LIVE UNTETHERED TO ANY ONE PLACE, TRAVELING AS THEIR SPIRIT TAKES THEM?
I WILL GO WHEREVER I MUST TO FIND YOU.
WHY AM I THINKING ABOUT HIM...?
thp
HMM ?
POP
WHAT'S THIS SOOT FROM ?

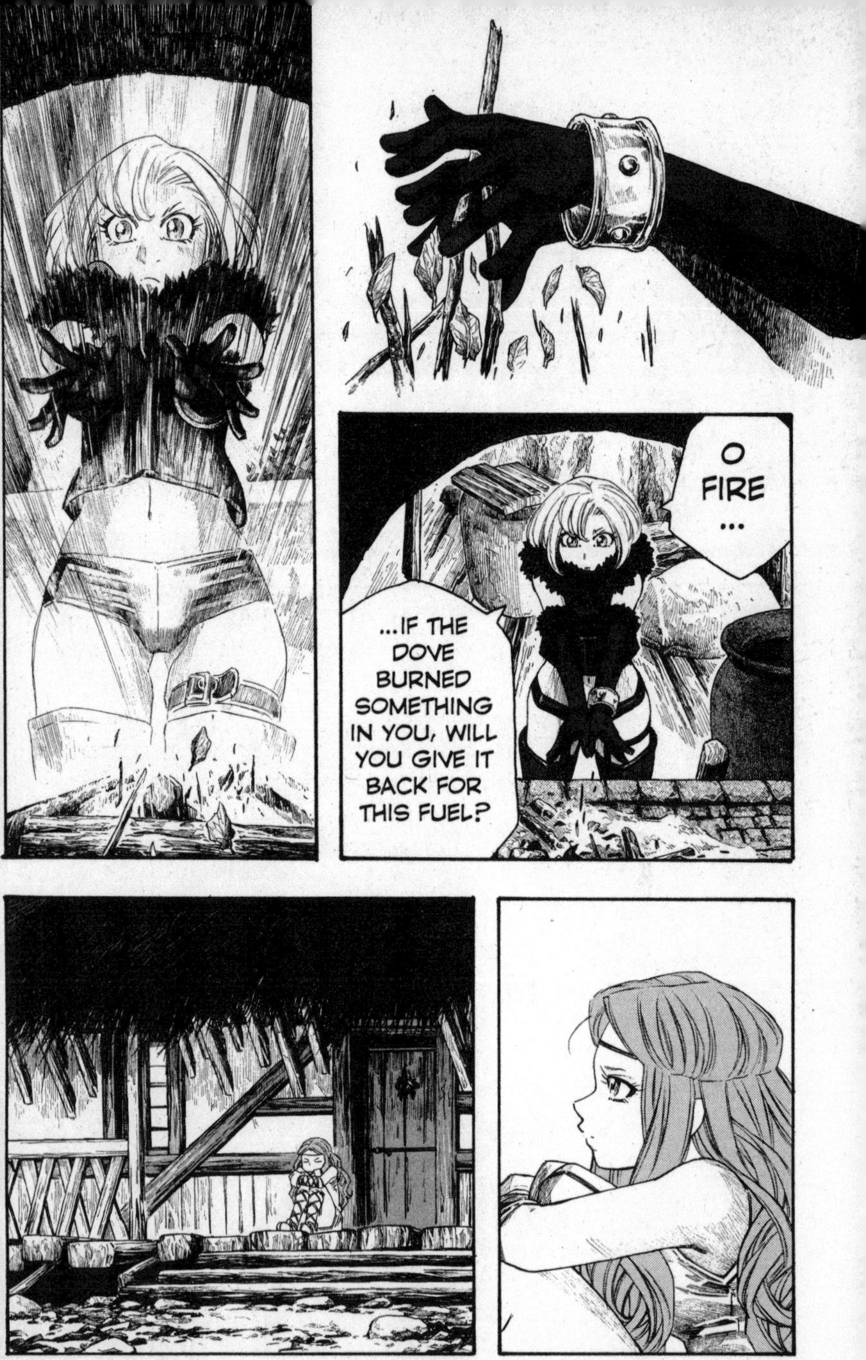
O FIRE ...
...IF THE DOVE BURNED SOMETHING IN YOU, WILL YOU GIVE IT BACK FOR THIS FUEL?

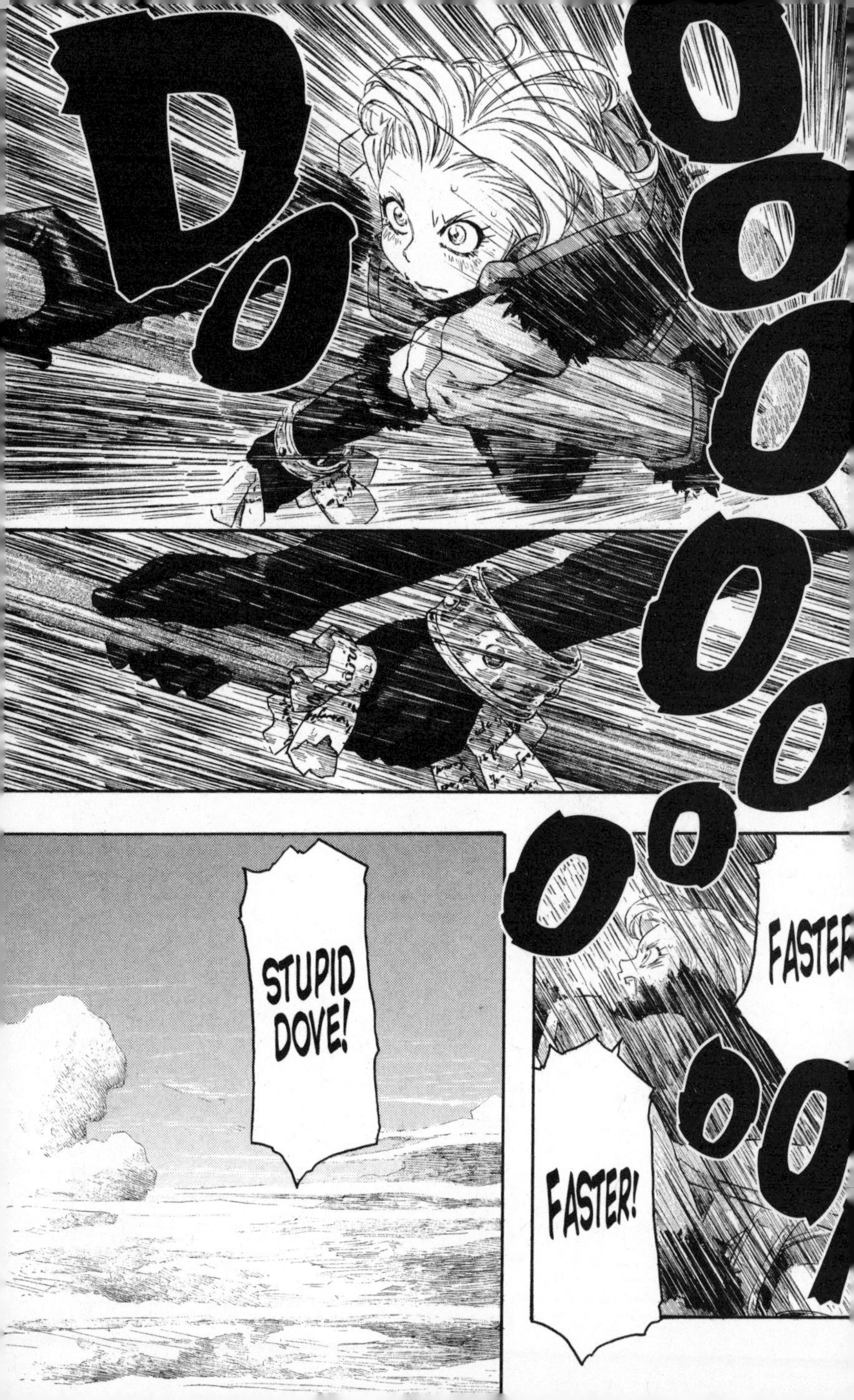
DOOOOOOOOOOOOO
FASTER
FASTER!
STUPID DOVE!

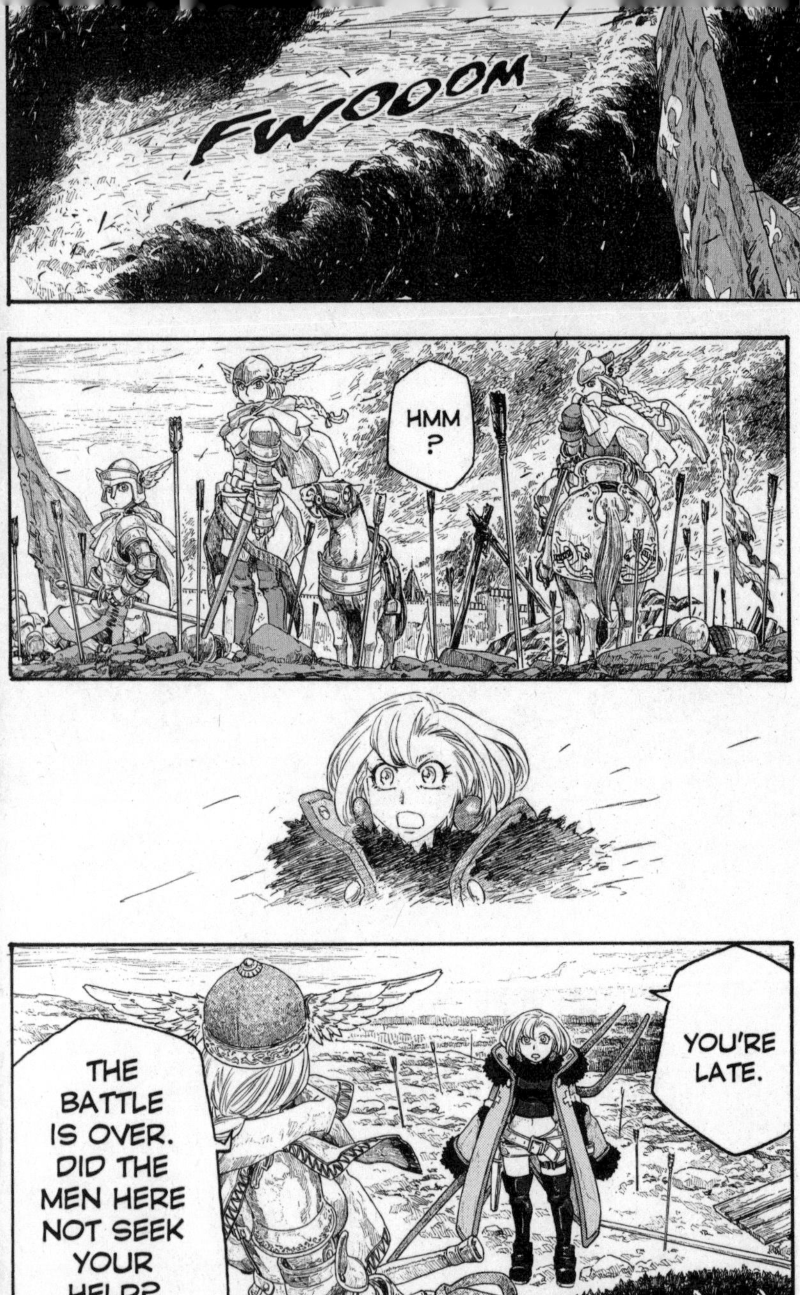
FWOOOM
HMM?
YOU'RE LATE.
THE BATTLE IS OVER. DID THE MEN HERE NOT SEEK YOUR HELP?

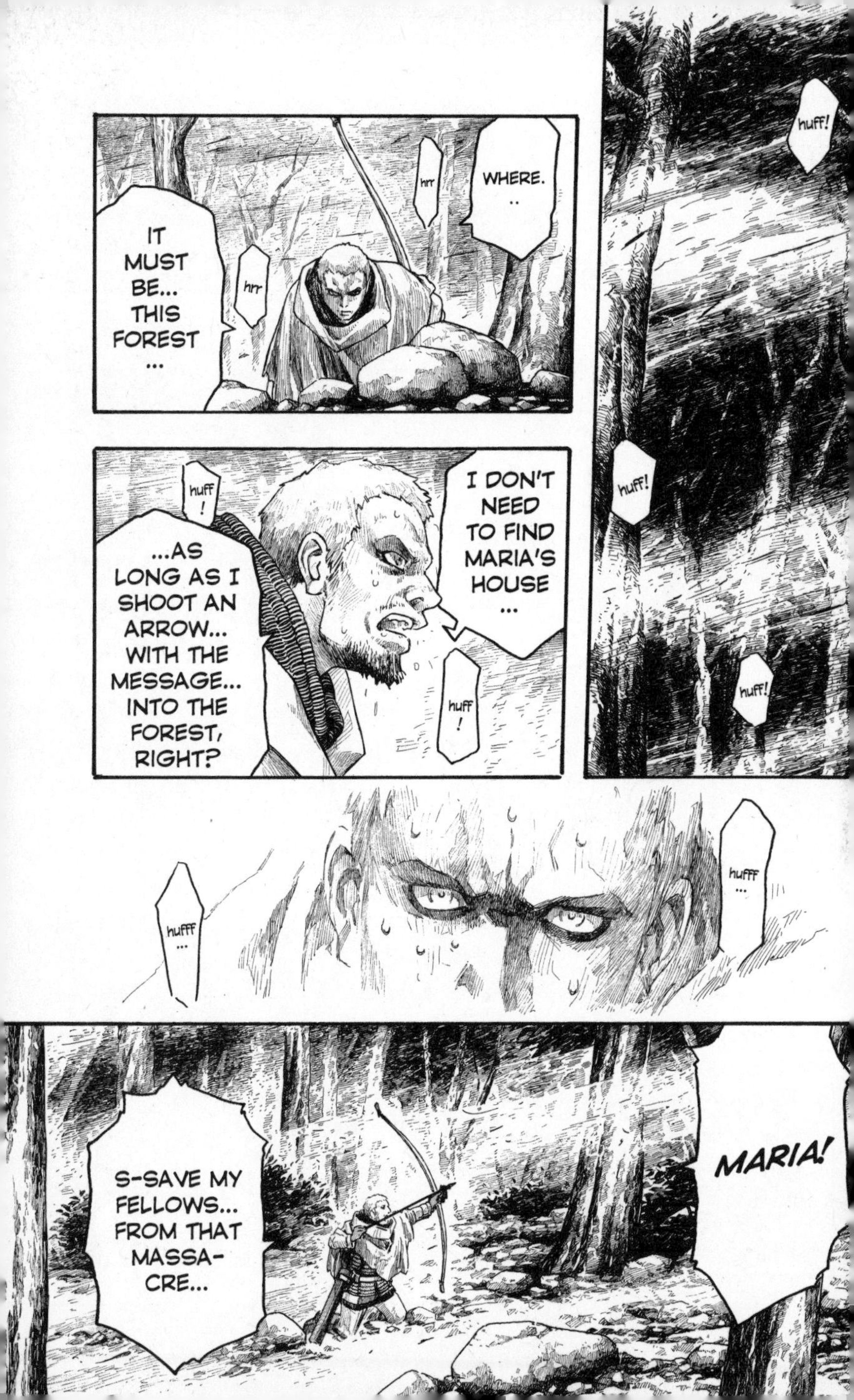
huff!
huff!
huff!
WHERE. ..
hrr
hrr
IT MUST BE... THIS FOREST ...
I DON'T NEED TO FIND MARIA'S HOUSE ...
huff !
...AS LONG AS I SHOOT AN ARROW... WITH THE MESSAGE... INTO THE FOREST, RIGHT?
huff !
hufff ...
hufff ...
MARIA!
S-SAVE MY FELLOWS... FROM THAT MASSA- CRE...

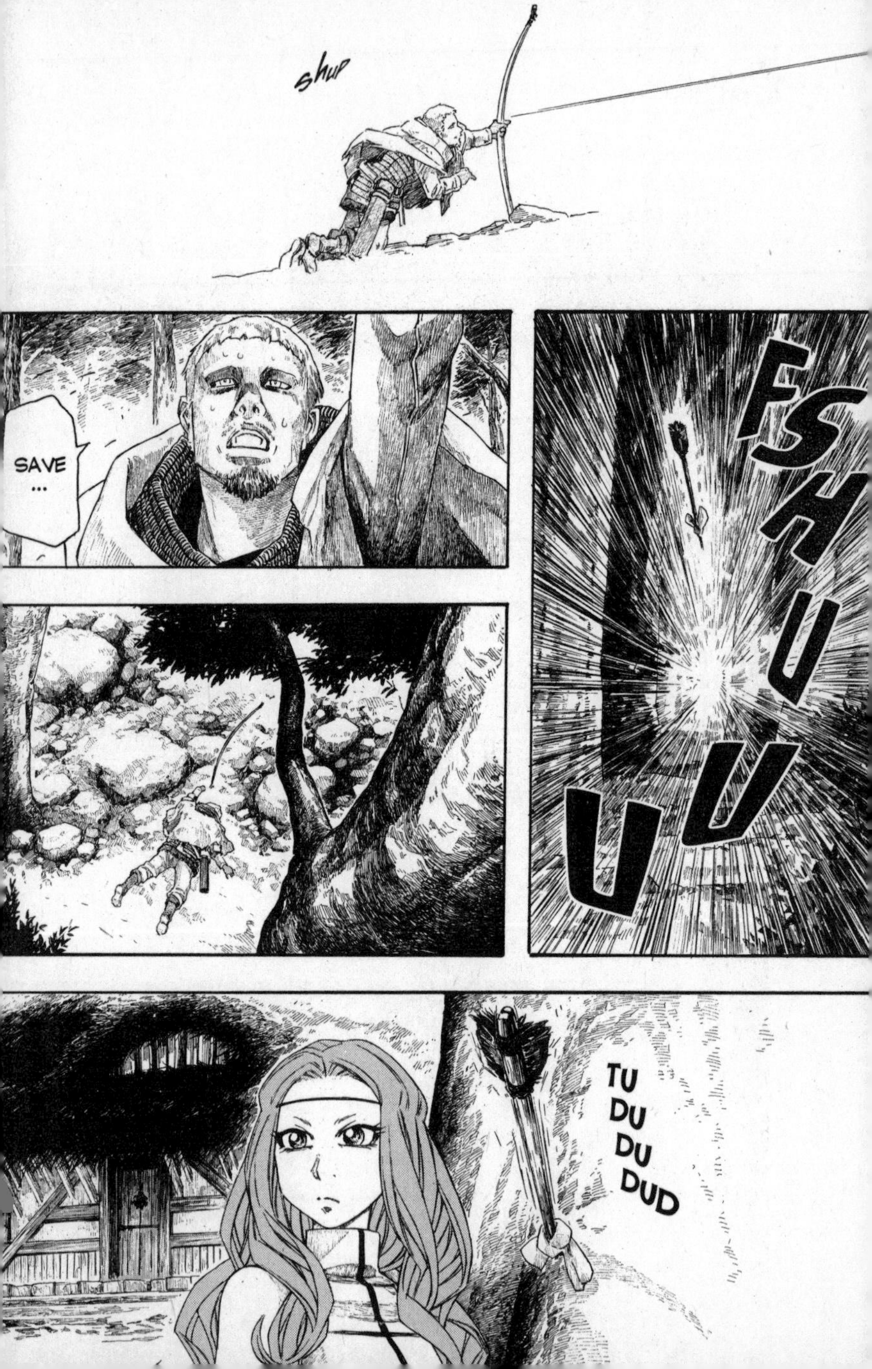
shup
FSHUUU
SAVE ...
TU DU DU DUD

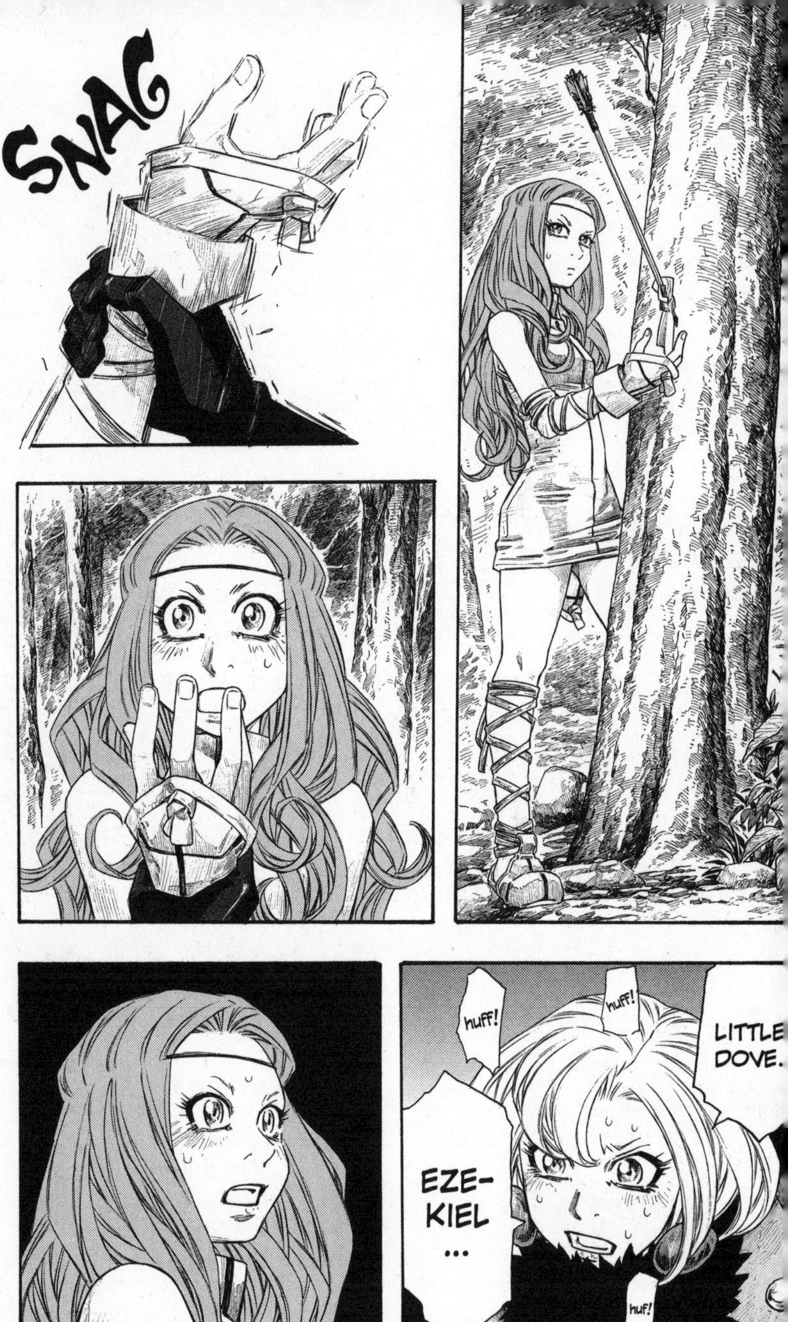
SNAG
huff!
huff!
LITTLE DOVE.
EZE-KIEL...
huf!

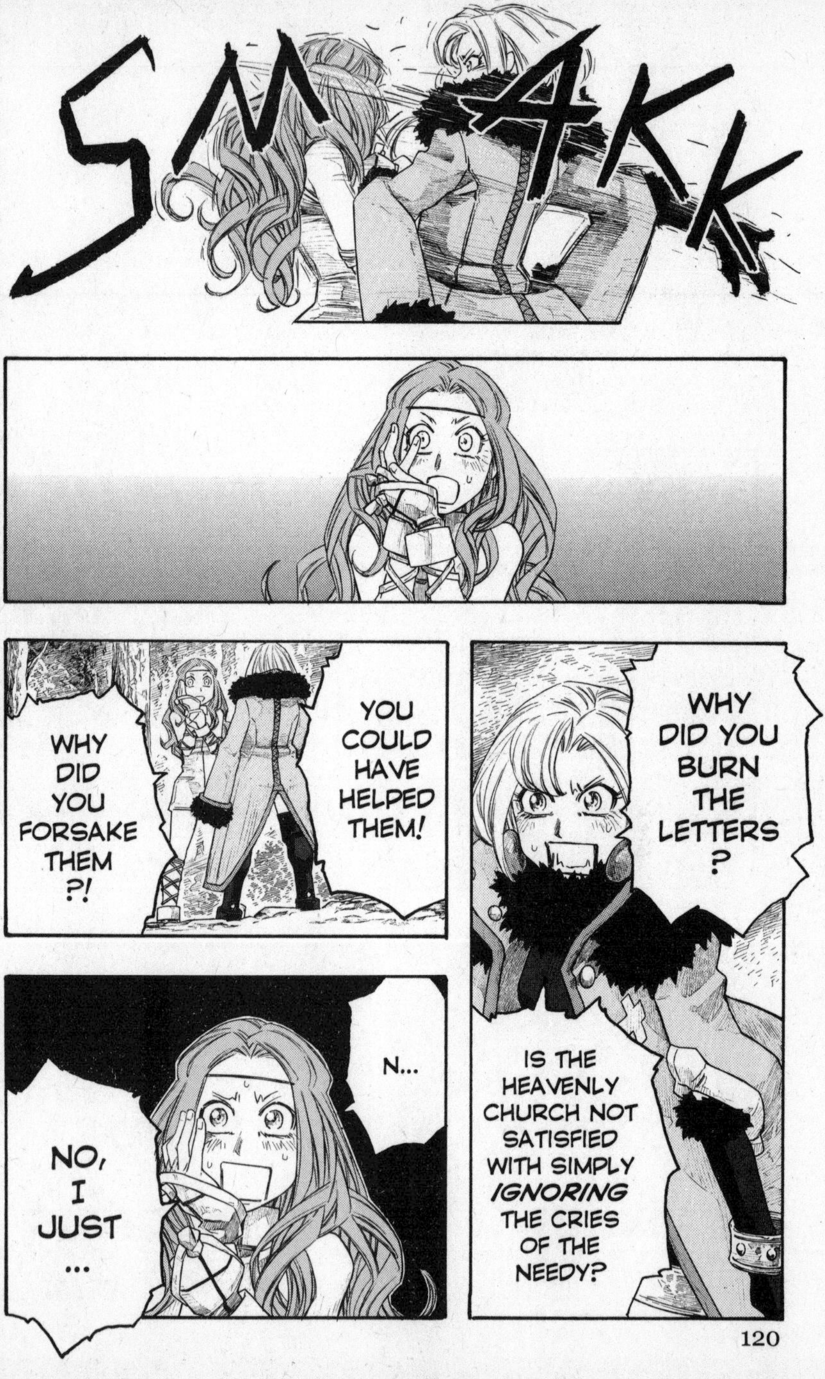
SMAKK
WHY DID YOU BURN THE LETTERS?
IS THE HEAVENLY CHURCH NOT SATISFIED WITH SIMPLY *IGNORING* THE CRIES OF THE NEEDY?
YOU COULD HAVE HELPED THEM!
WHY DID YOU FORSAKE THEM?!
N...
NO, I JUST...

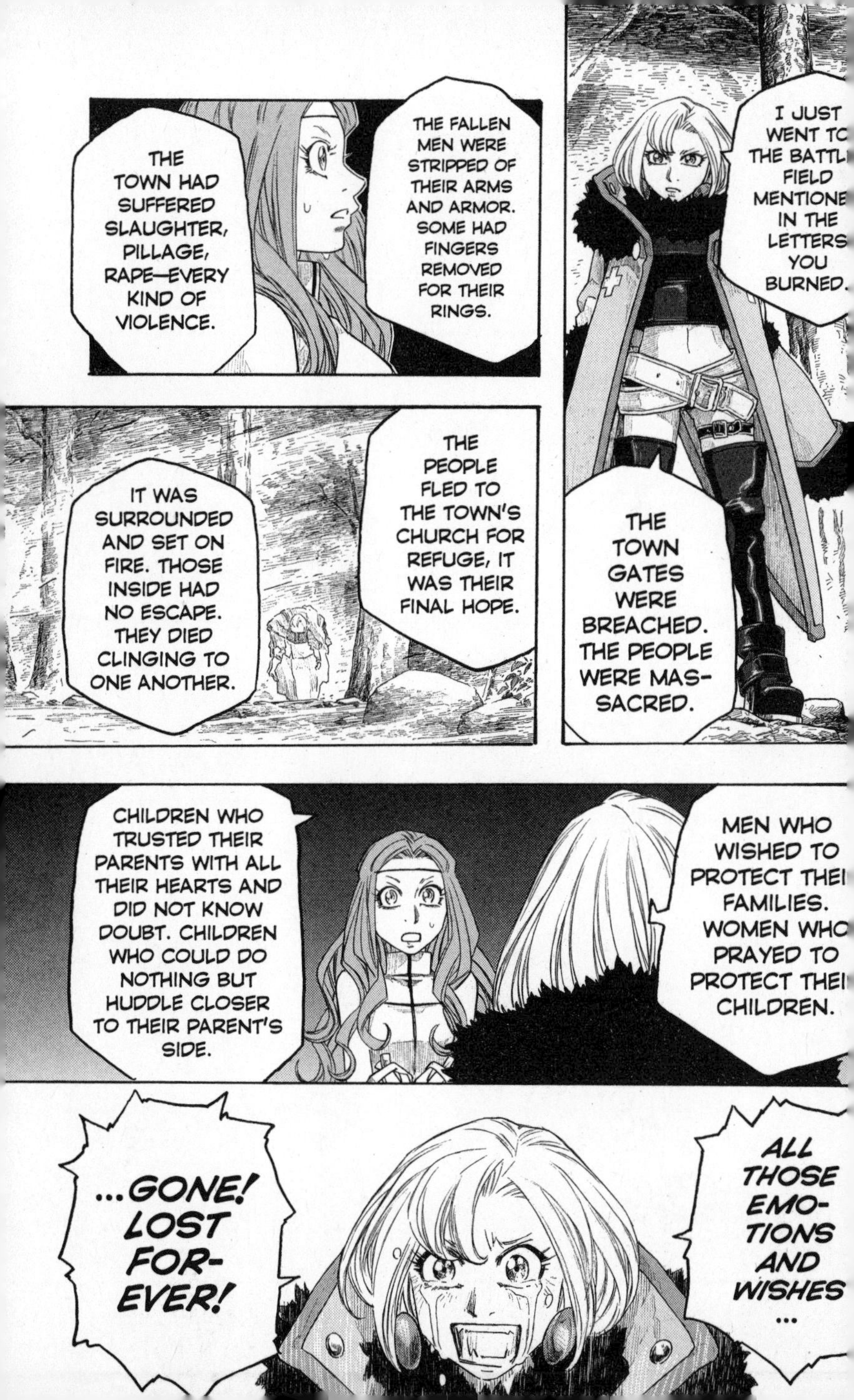
I JUST WENT TO THE BATTL FIELD MENTIONE IN THE LETTERS YOU BURNED.
THE TOWN GATES WERE BREACHED. THE PEOPLE WERE MAS-SACRED.
THE FALLEN MEN WERE STRIPPED OF THEIR ARMS AND ARMOR. SOME HAD FINGERS REMOVED FOR THEIR RINGS.
THE TOWN HAD SUFFERED SLAUGHTER, PILLAGE, RAPE—EVERY KIND OF VIOLENCE.
THE PEOPLE FLED TO THE TOWN'S CHURCH FOR REFUGE, IT WAS THEIR FINAL HOPE.
IT WAS SURROUNDED AND SET ON FIRE. THOSE INSIDE HAD NO ESCAPE. THEY DIED CLINGING TO ONE ANOTHER.
MEN WHO WISHED TO PROTECT THEI FAMILIES. WOMEN WHO PRAYED TO PROTECT THEI CHILDREN.
CHILDREN WHO TRUSTED THEIR PARENTS WITH ALL THEIR HEARTS AND DID NOT KNOW DOUBT. CHILDREN WHO COULD DO NOTHING BUT HUDDLE CLOSER TO THEIR PARENT'S SIDE.
ALL THOSE EMO-TIONS AND WISHES ...
...GONE! LOST FOR-EVER!

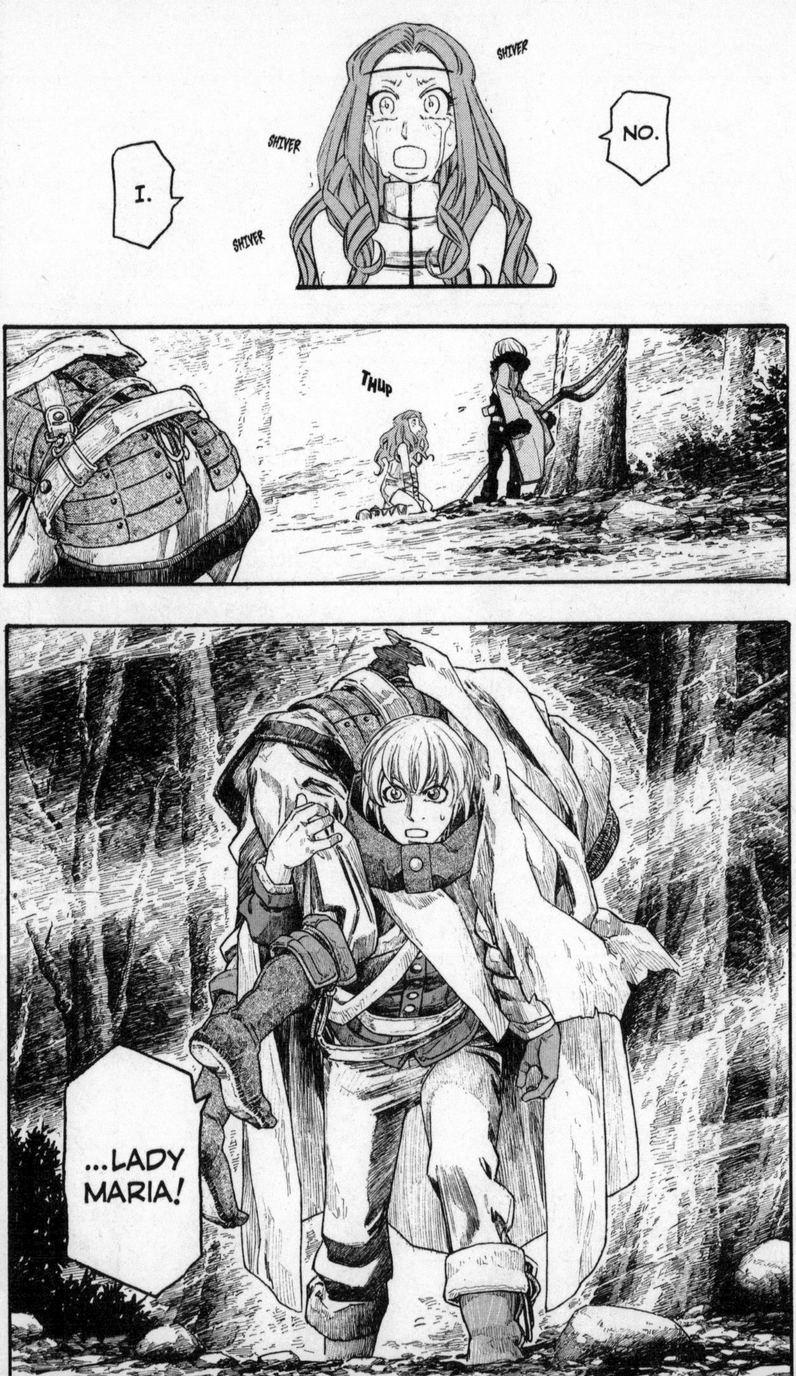
SHIVER
NO.
SHIVER
I.
SHIVER
THUP
...LADY MARIA!

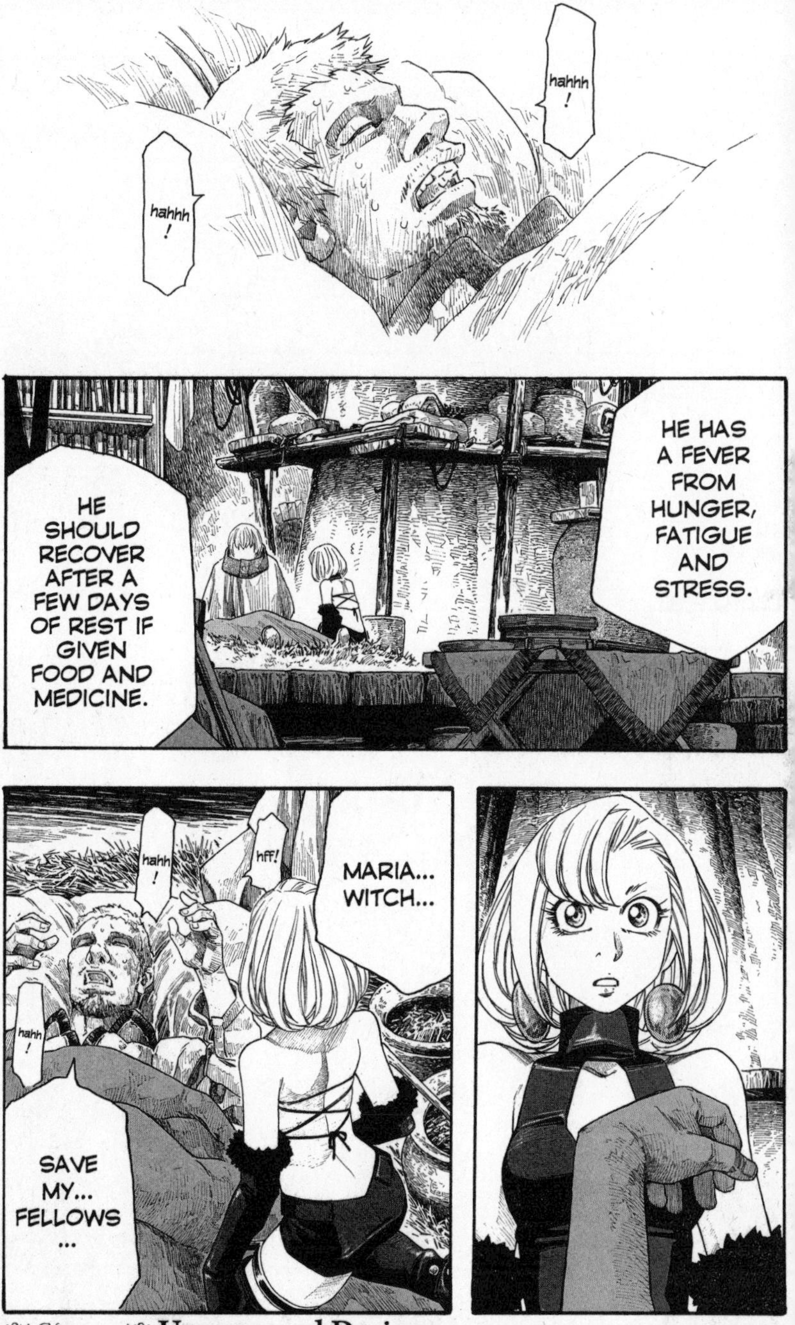
hahhh!
hahhh!
HE HAS A FEVER FROM HUNGER, FATIGUE AND STRESS.
HE SHOULD RECOVER AFTER A FEW DAYS OF REST IF GIVEN FOOD AND MEDICINE.
hff!
MARIA... WITCH...
hahh!
hahh!
SAVE MY... FELLOWS ...

Chapter 14 Unanswered Desires

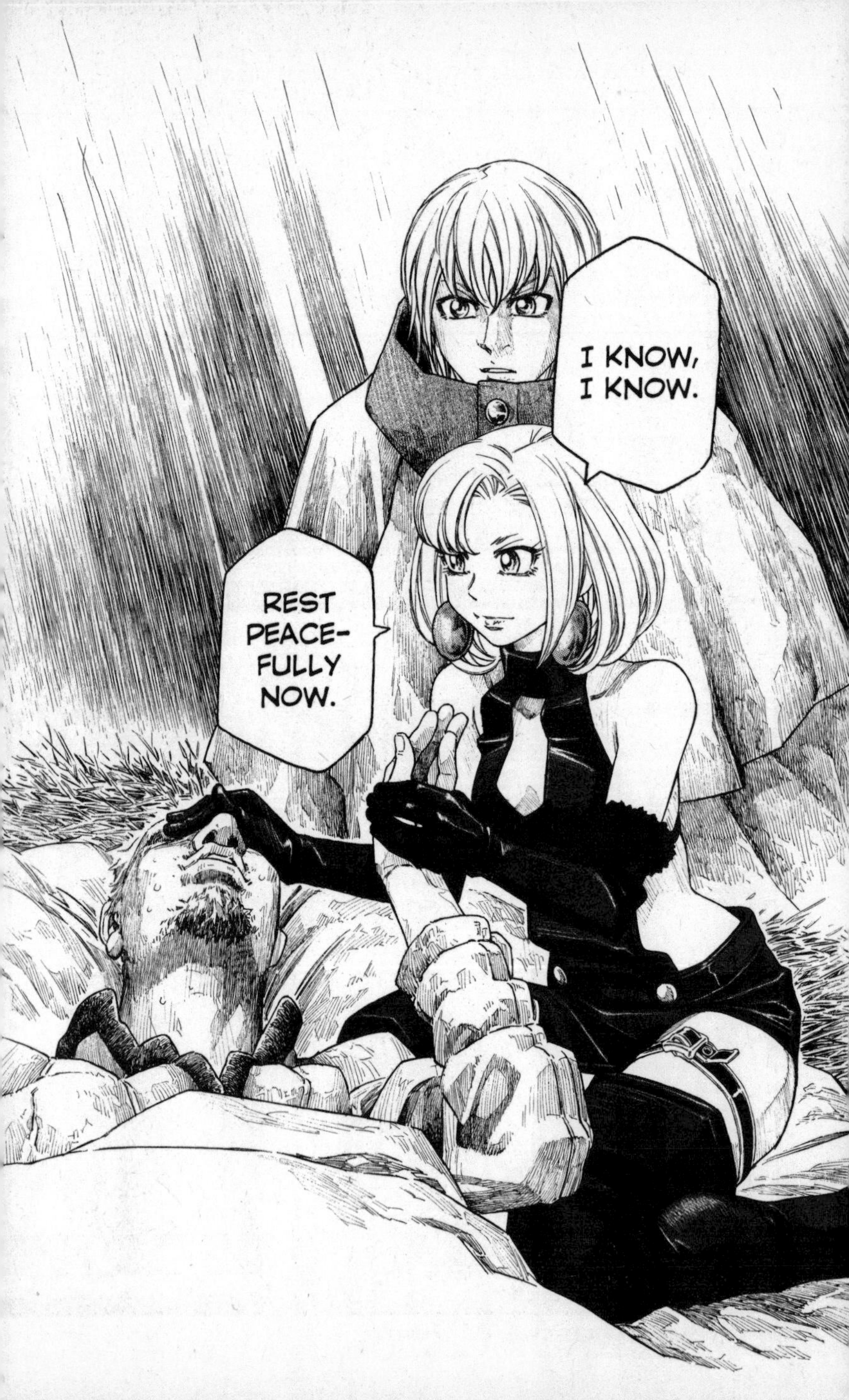
I KNOW, I KNOW.
REST PEACE-FULLY NOW.

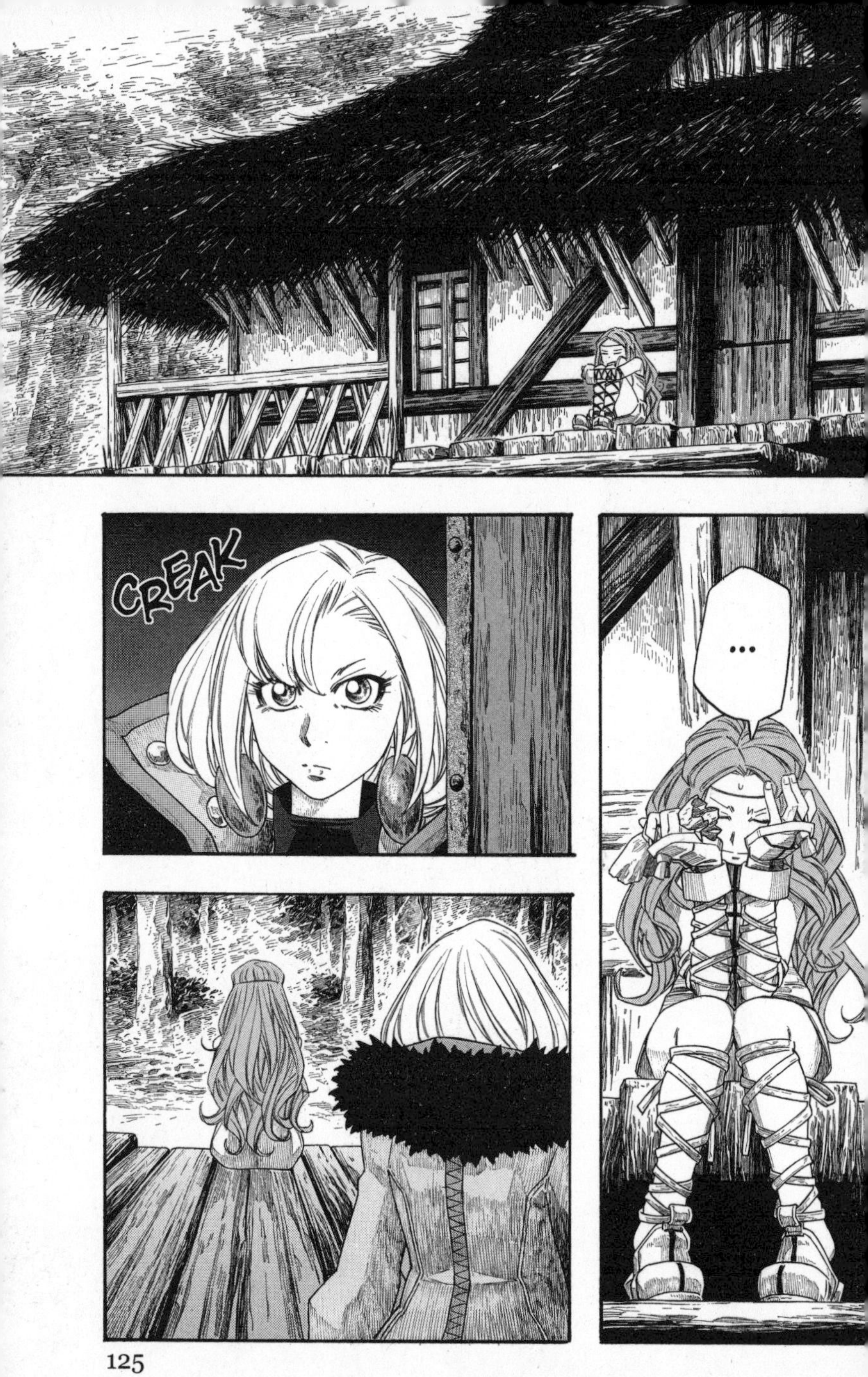
...
CREAK

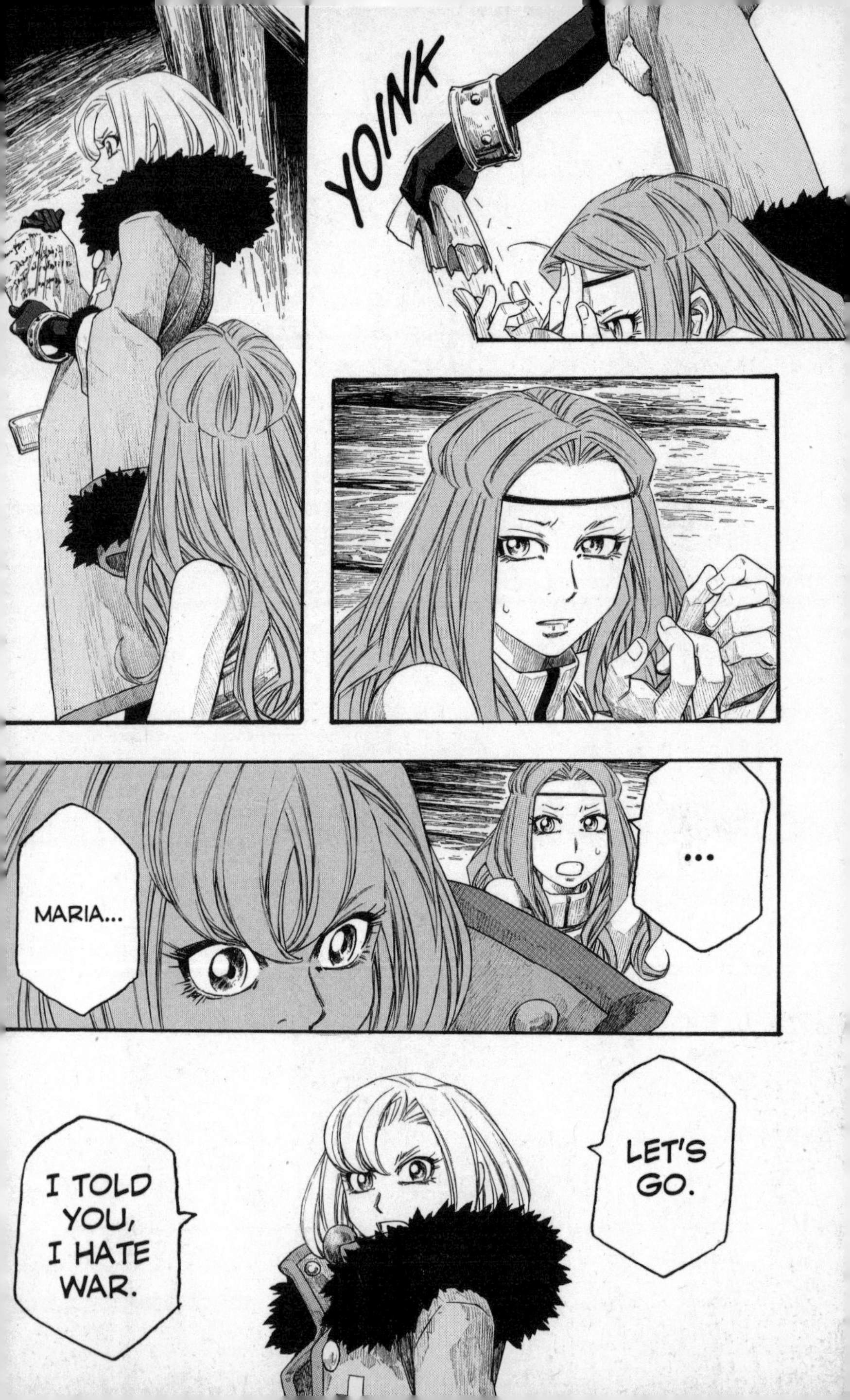

YOINK
...
MARIA...
LET'S GO.
I TOLD YOU, I HATE WAR.

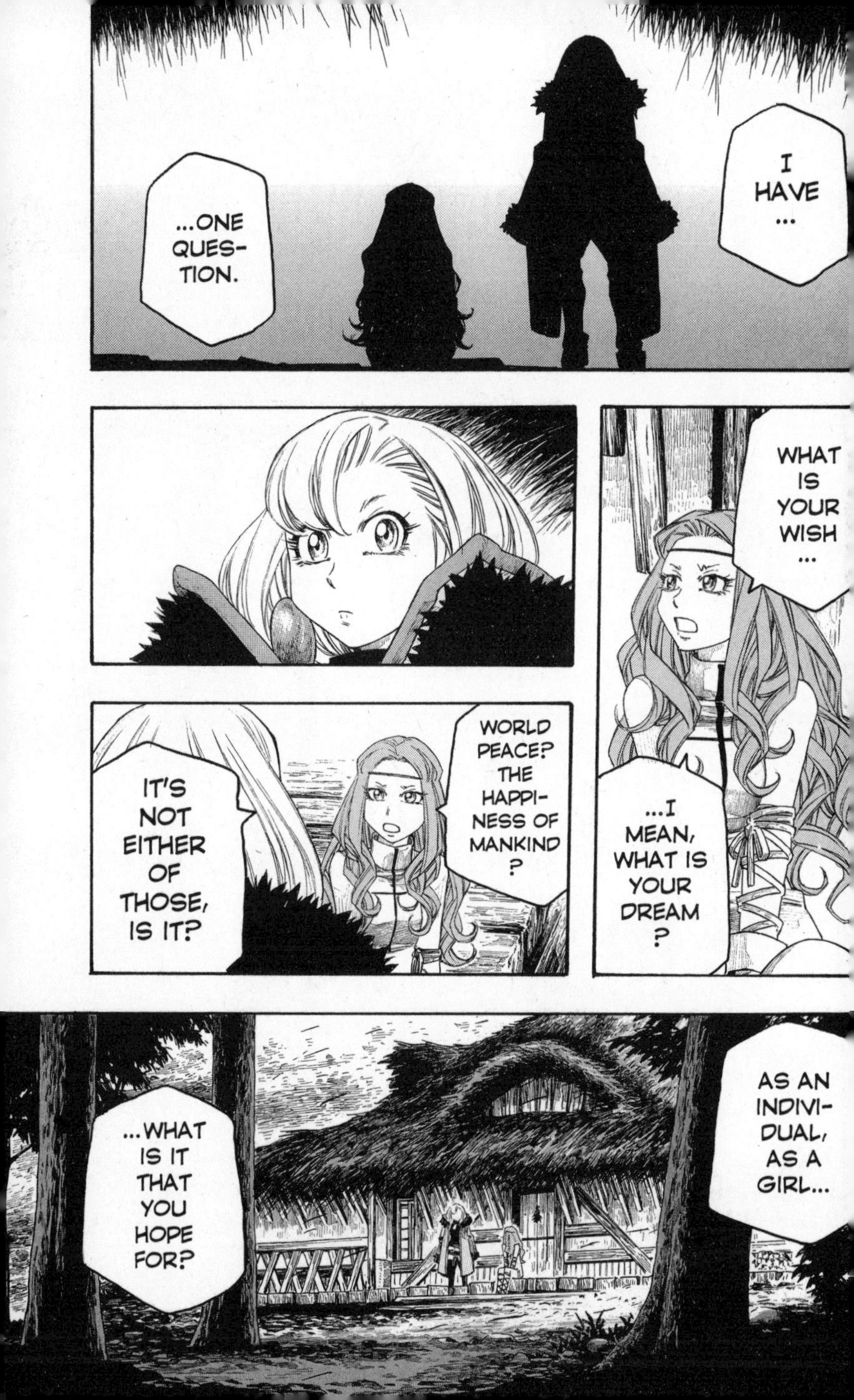
I HAVE...
...ONE QUESTION.
WHAT IS YOUR WISH...
...I MEAN, WHAT IS YOUR DREAM?
WORLD PEACE? THE HAPPINESS OF MANKIND?
IT'S NOT EITHER OF THOSE, IS IT?
AS AN INDIVIDUAL, AS A GIRL...
...WHAT IS IT THAT YOU HOPE FOR?

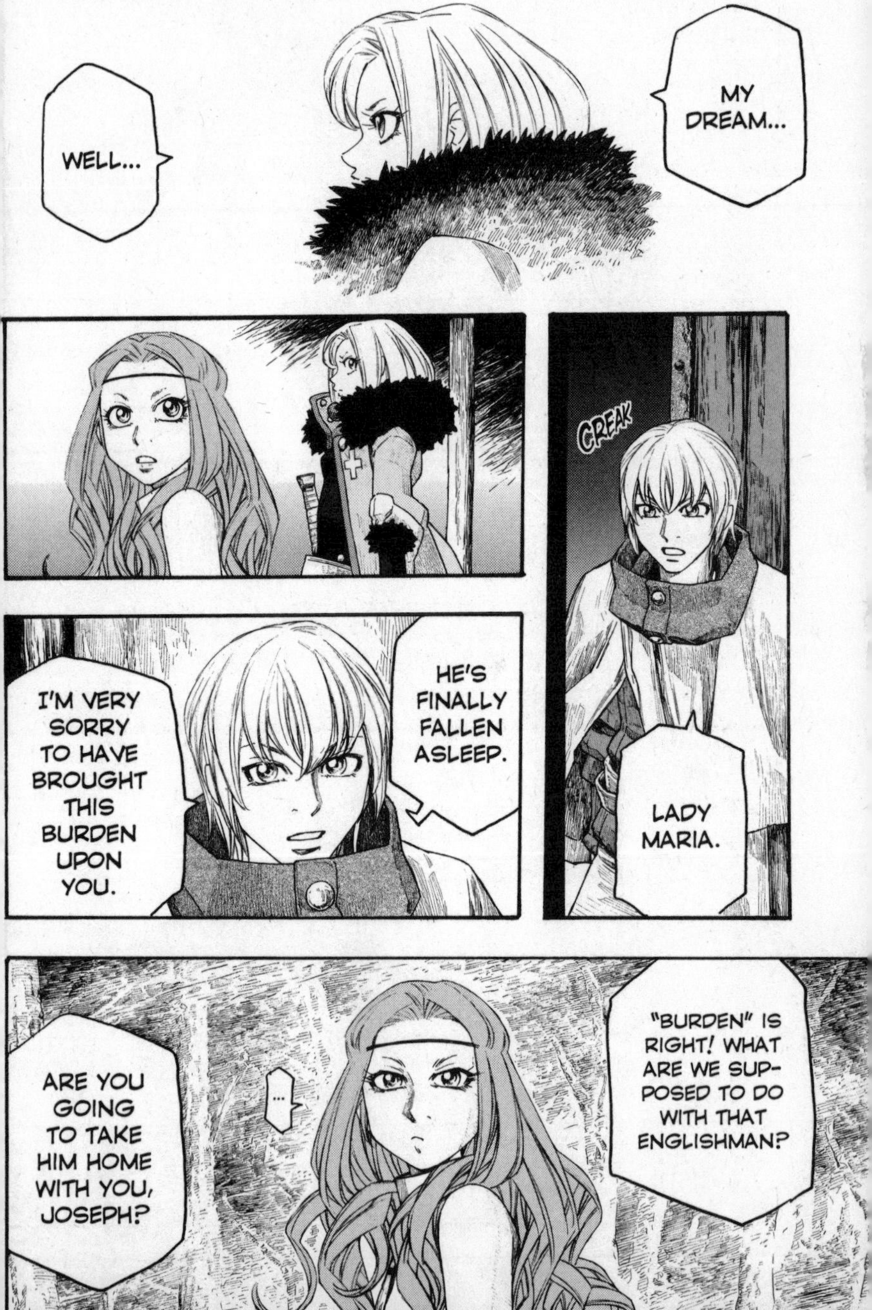
MY DREAM...
WELL...
CREAK
LADY MARIA.
HE'S FINALLY FALLEN ASLEEP.
I'M VERY SORRY TO HAVE BROUGHT THIS BURDEN UPON YOU.
"BURDEN" IS RIGHT! WHAT ARE WE SUP-POSED TO DO WITH THAT ENGLISHMAN?
...
ARE YOU GOING TO TAKE HIM HOME WITH YOU, JOSEPH?

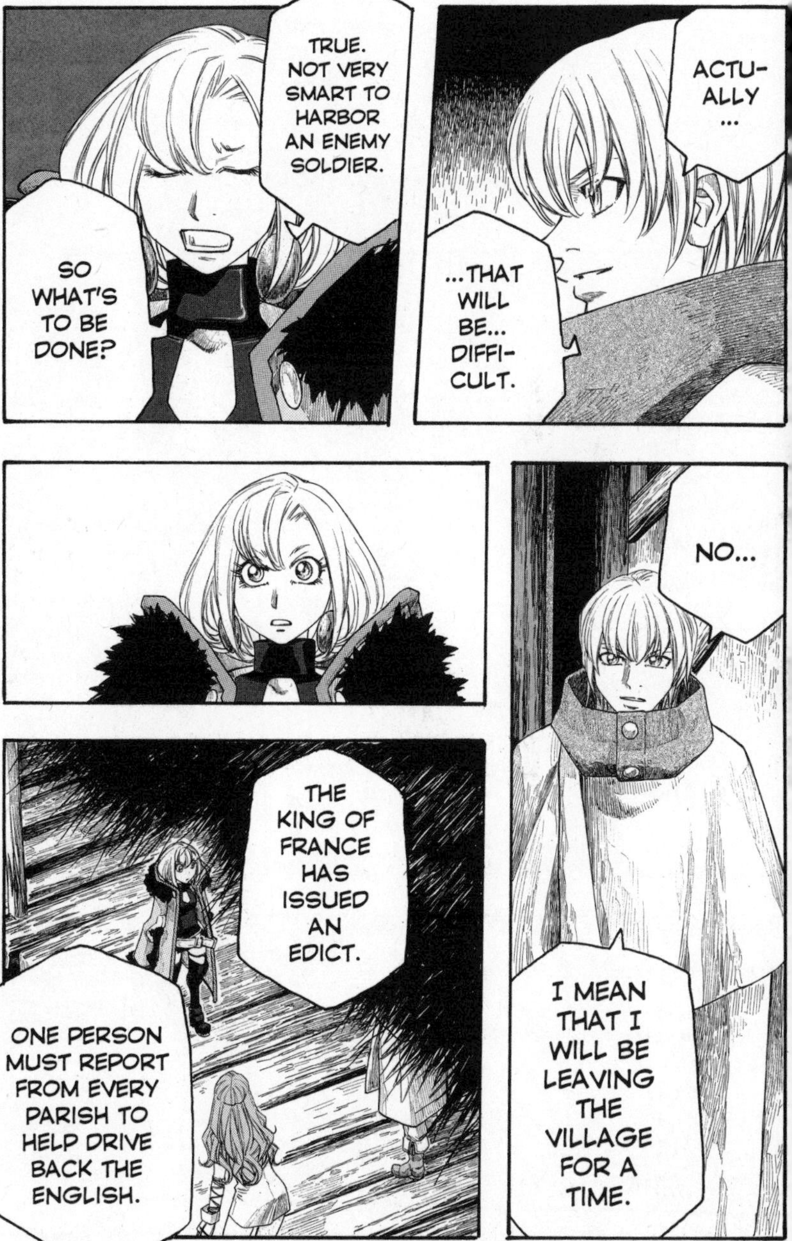
ACTU-ALLY...
...THAT WILL BE... DIFFI-CULT.
TRUE. NOT VERY SMART TO HARBOR AN ENEMY SOLDIER.
SO WHAT'S TO BE DONE?
NO...
I MEAN THAT I WILL BE LEAVING THE VILLAGE FOR A TIME.
THE KING OF FRANCE HAS ISSUED AN EDICT.
ONE PERSON MUST REPORT FROM EVERY PARISH TO HELP DRIVE BACK THE ENGLISH.

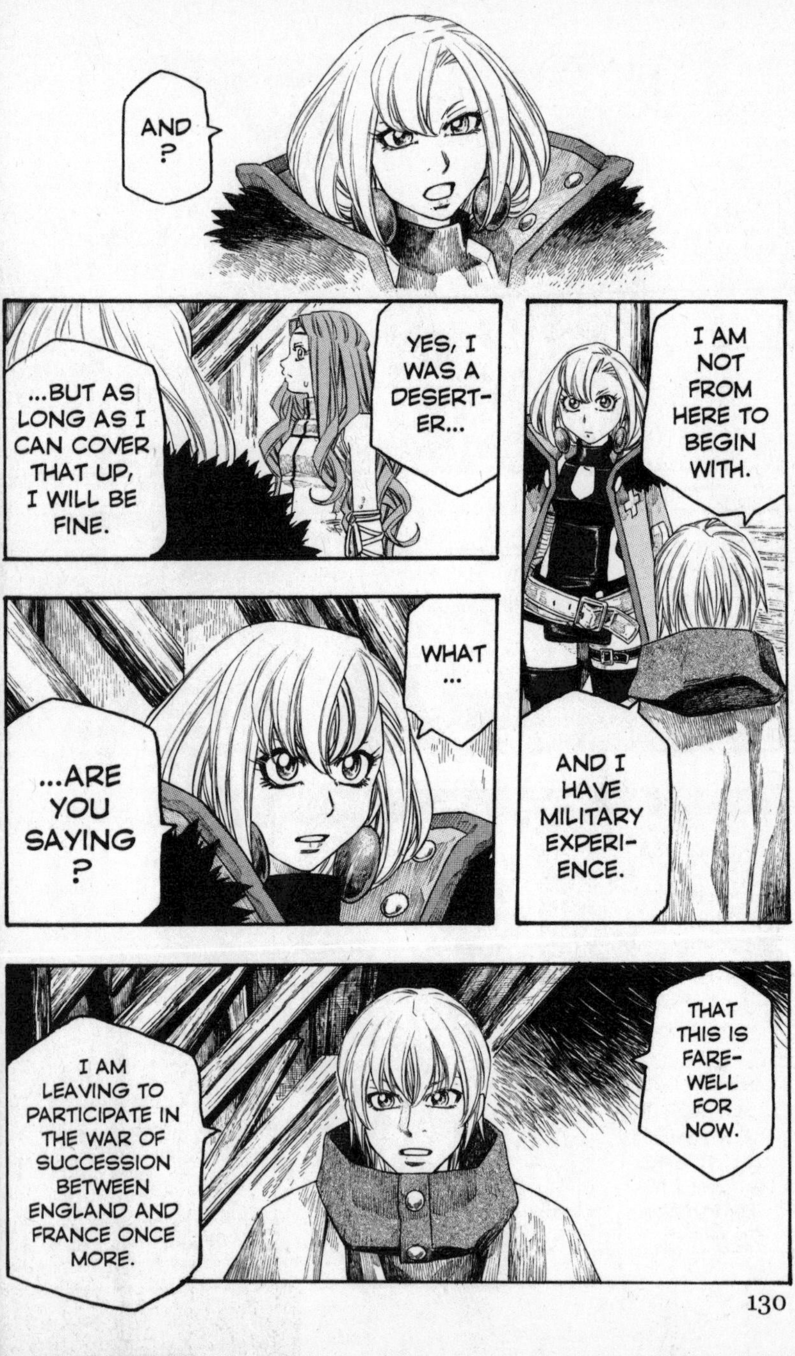
AND ?
I AM NOT FROM HERE TO BEGIN WITH.
AND I HAVE MILITARY EXPERIENCE.
YES, I WAS A DESERTER...
...BUT AS LONG AS I CAN COVER THAT UP, I WILL BE FINE.
WHAT ...
...ARE YOU SAYING ?
THAT THIS IS FAREWELL FOR NOW.
I AM LEAVING TO PARTICIPATE IN THE WAR OF SUCCESSION BETWEEN ENGLAND AND FRANCE ONCE MORE.

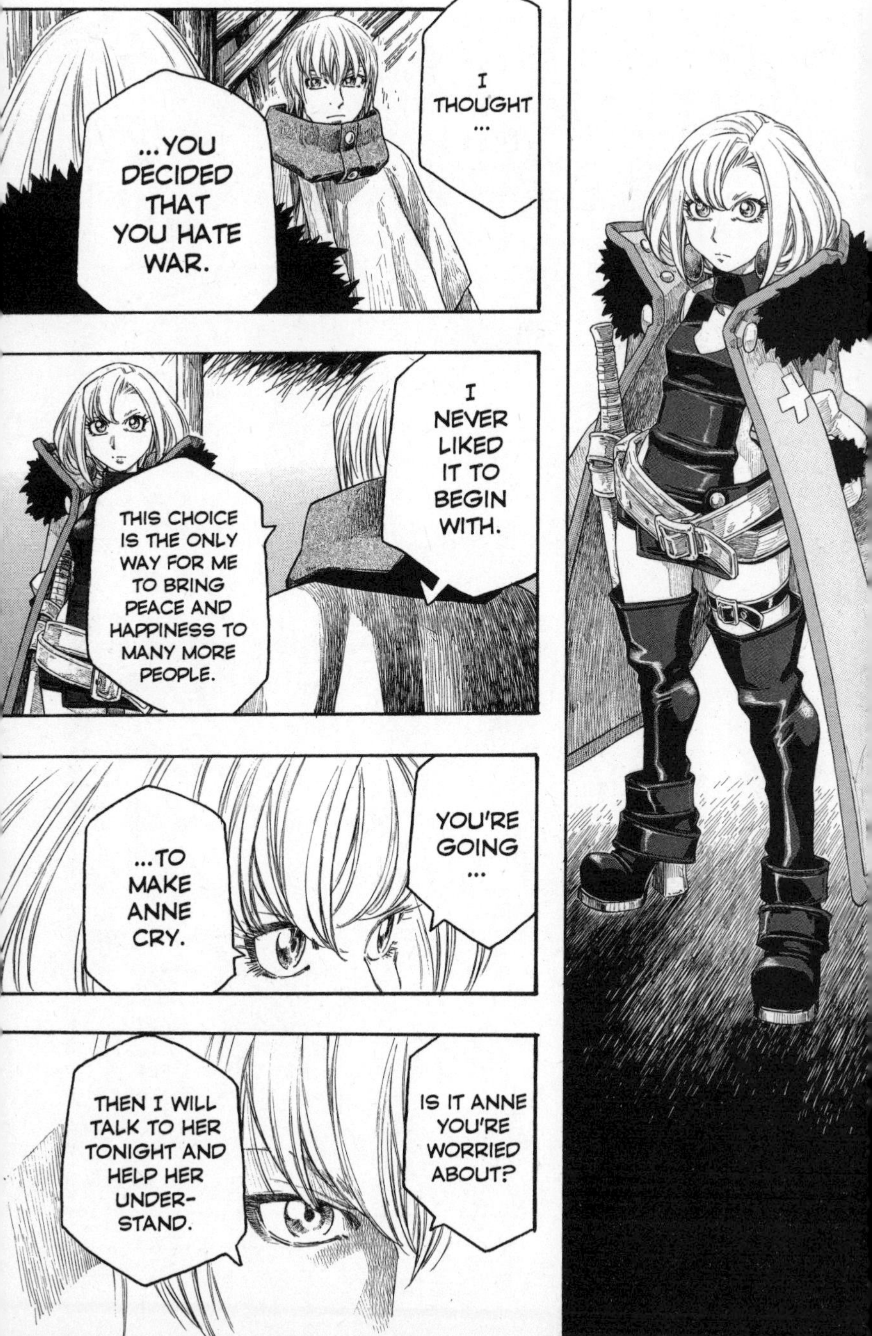
I THOUGHT ...
...YOU DECIDED THAT YOU HATE WAR.
I NEVER LIKED IT TO BEGIN WITH.
THIS CHOICE IS THE ONLY WAY FOR ME TO BRING PEACE AND HAPPINESS TO MANY MORE PEOPLE.
YOU'RE GOING ...
...TO MAKE ANNE CRY.
IS IT ANNE YOU'RE WORRIED ABOUT?
THEN I WILL TALK TO HER TONIGHT AND HELP HER UNDER-STAND.

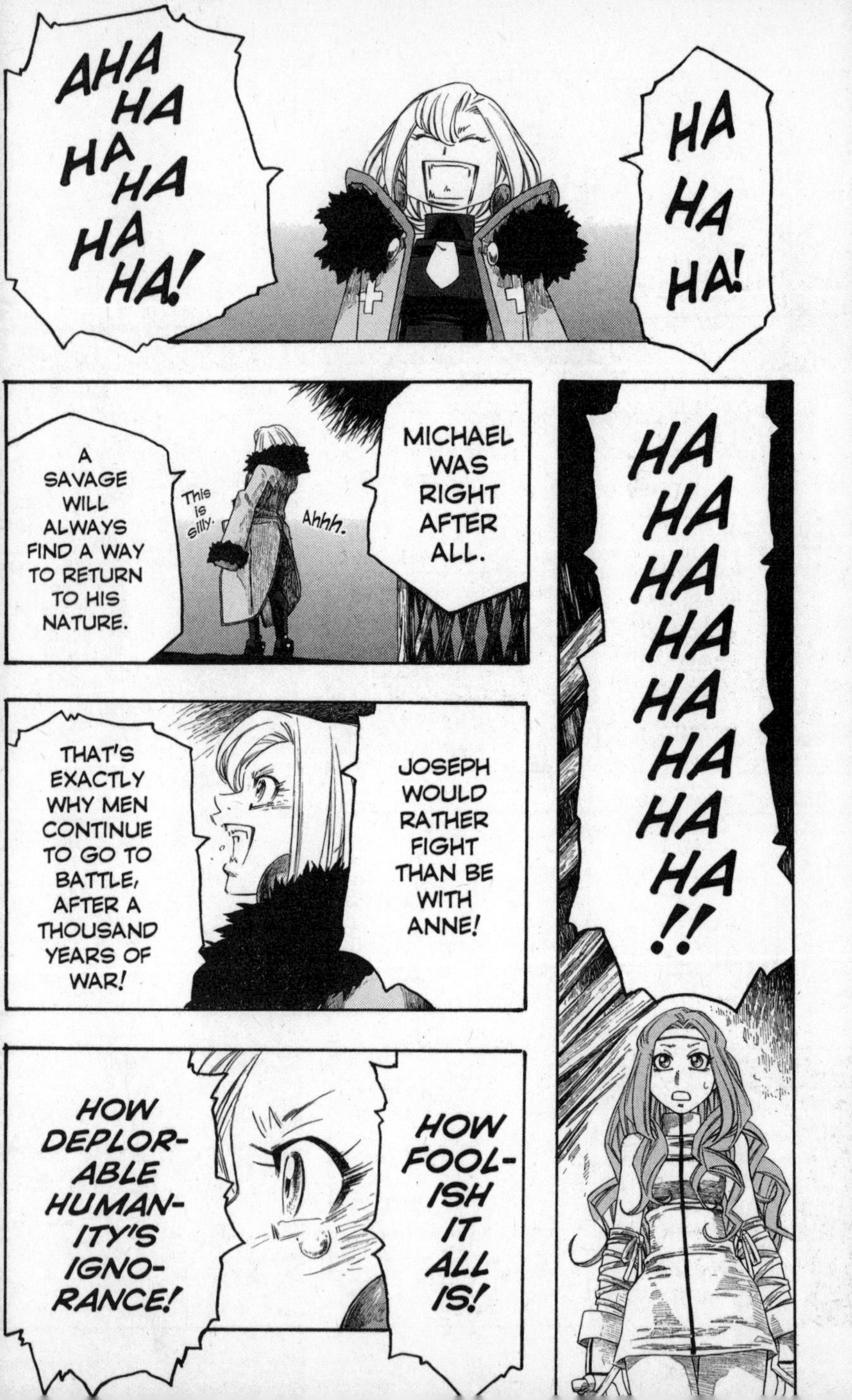
HA HA HA HA!
AHA HA HA HA HA HA!
HA HA HA HA HA HA HA HA!!
MICHAEL WAS RIGHT AFTER ALL.
Ahhh.
This is silly.
A SAVAGE WILL ALWAYS FIND A WAY TO RETURN TO HIS NATURE.
JOSEPH WOULD RATHER FIGHT THAN BE WITH ANNE!
THAT'S EXACTLY WHY MEN CONTINUE TO GO TO BATTLE, AFTER A THOUSAND YEARS OF WAR!
HOW FOOLISH IT ALL IS!
HOW DEPLORABLE HUMANITY'S IGNORANCE!

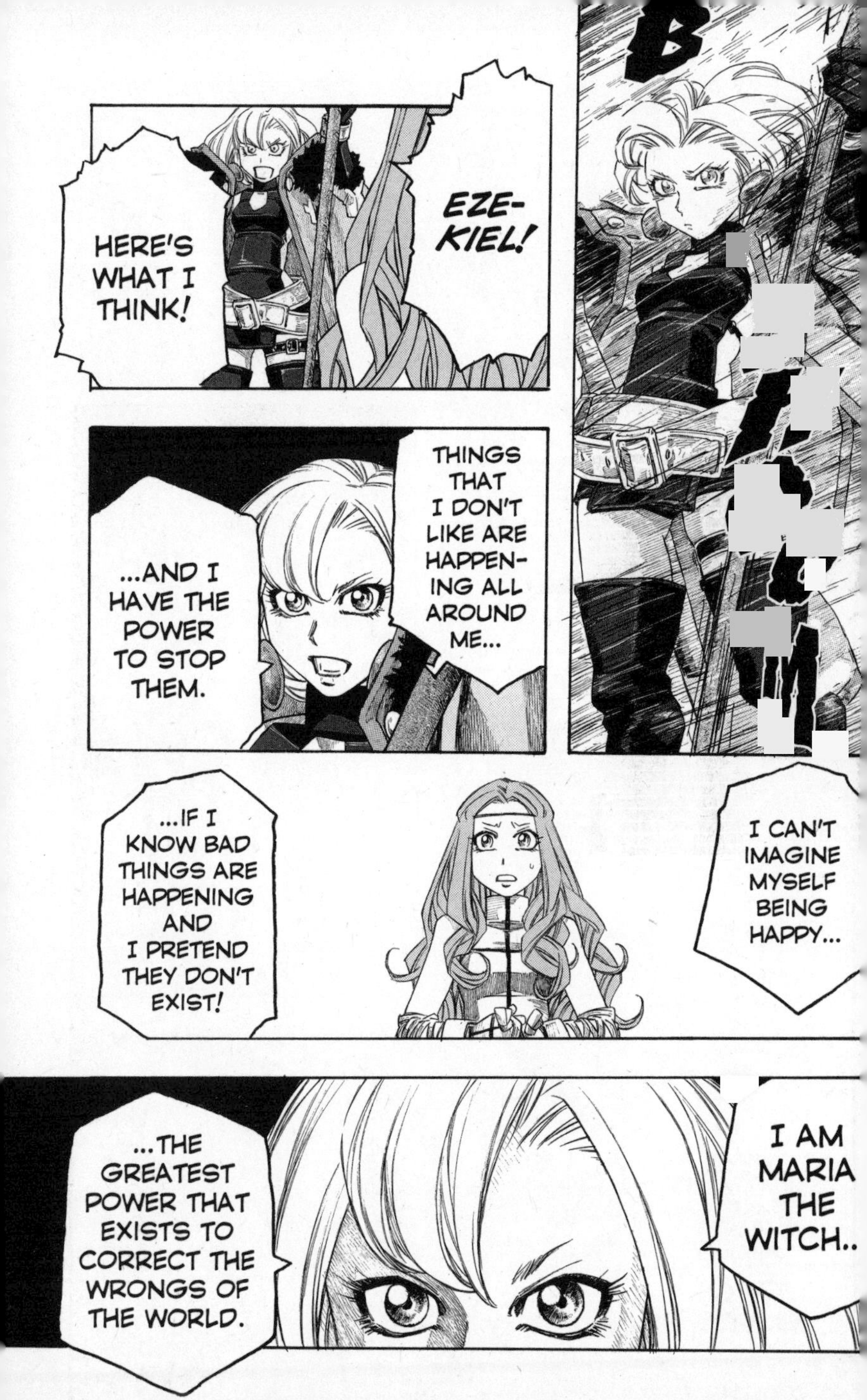
B
EZE-KIEL!
HERE'S WHAT I THINK!
THINGS THAT I DON'T LIKE ARE HAPPEN-ING ALL AROUND ME...
...AND I HAVE THE POWER TO STOP THEM.
I CAN'T IMAGINE MYSELF BEING HAPPY...
...IF I KNOW BAD THINGS ARE HAPPENING AND I PRETEND THEY DON'T EXIST!
I AM MARIA THE WITCH..
...THE GREATEST POWER THAT EXISTS TO CORRECT THE WRONGS OF THE WORLD.

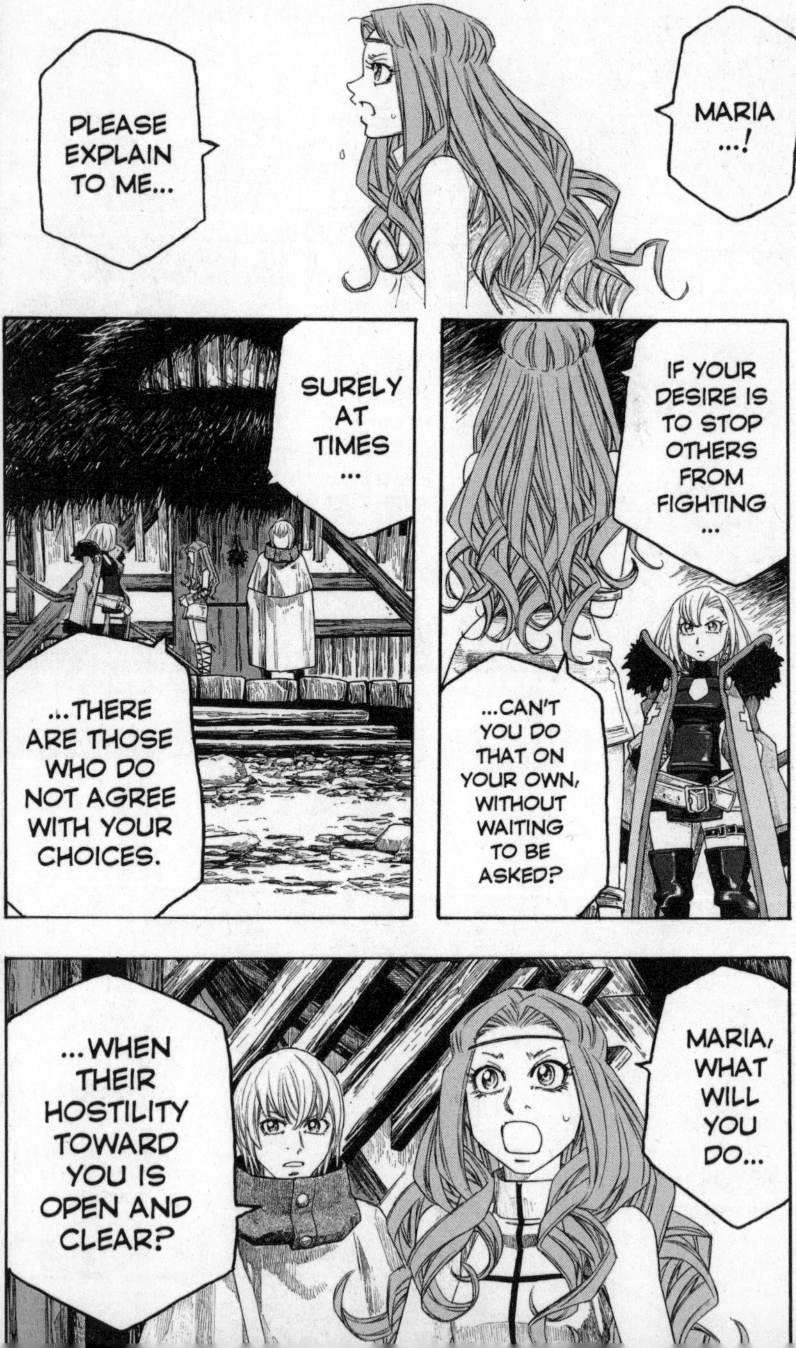
MARIA ...!
PLEASE EXPLAIN TO ME...
IF YOUR DESIRE IS TO STOP OTHERS FROM FIGHTING ...
...CAN'T YOU DO THAT ON YOUR OWN, WITHOUT WAITING TO BE ASKED?
SURELY AT TIMES ...
...THERE ARE THOSE WHO DO NOT AGREE WITH YOUR CHOICES.
MARIA, WHAT WILL YOU DO...
...WHEN THEIR HOSTILITY TOWARD YOU IS OPEN AND CLEAR?

SORRY.

I'LL DECIDE WHEN IT COMES TO THAT.

I WILL GO TO BATTLE IN YOUR PLACE.

JO-SEPH.

...HELP HIM RETURN HOME.

WHEN THE ENGLISH-MAN IS WELL...

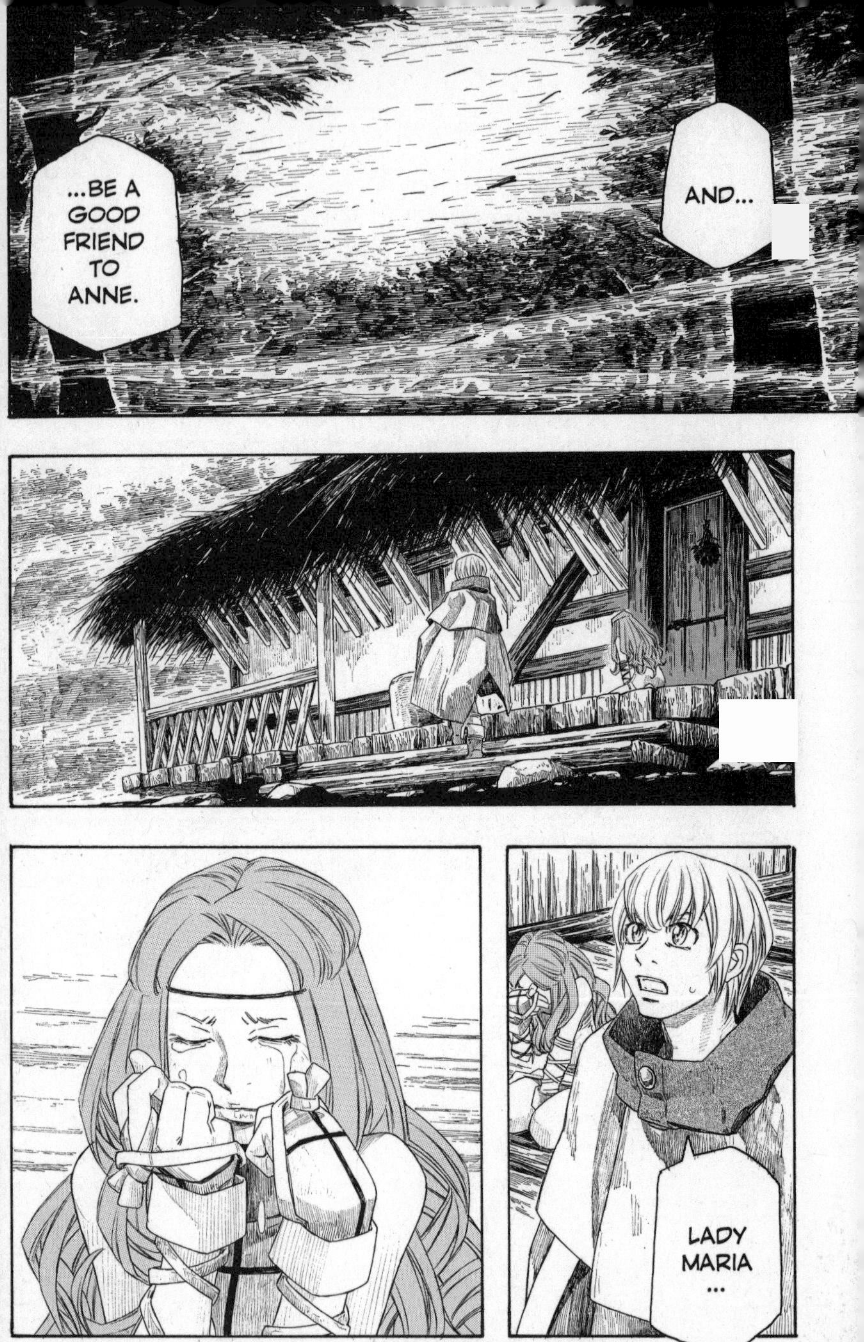
AND...
...BE A GOOD FRIEND TO ANNE.
LADY MARIA ...

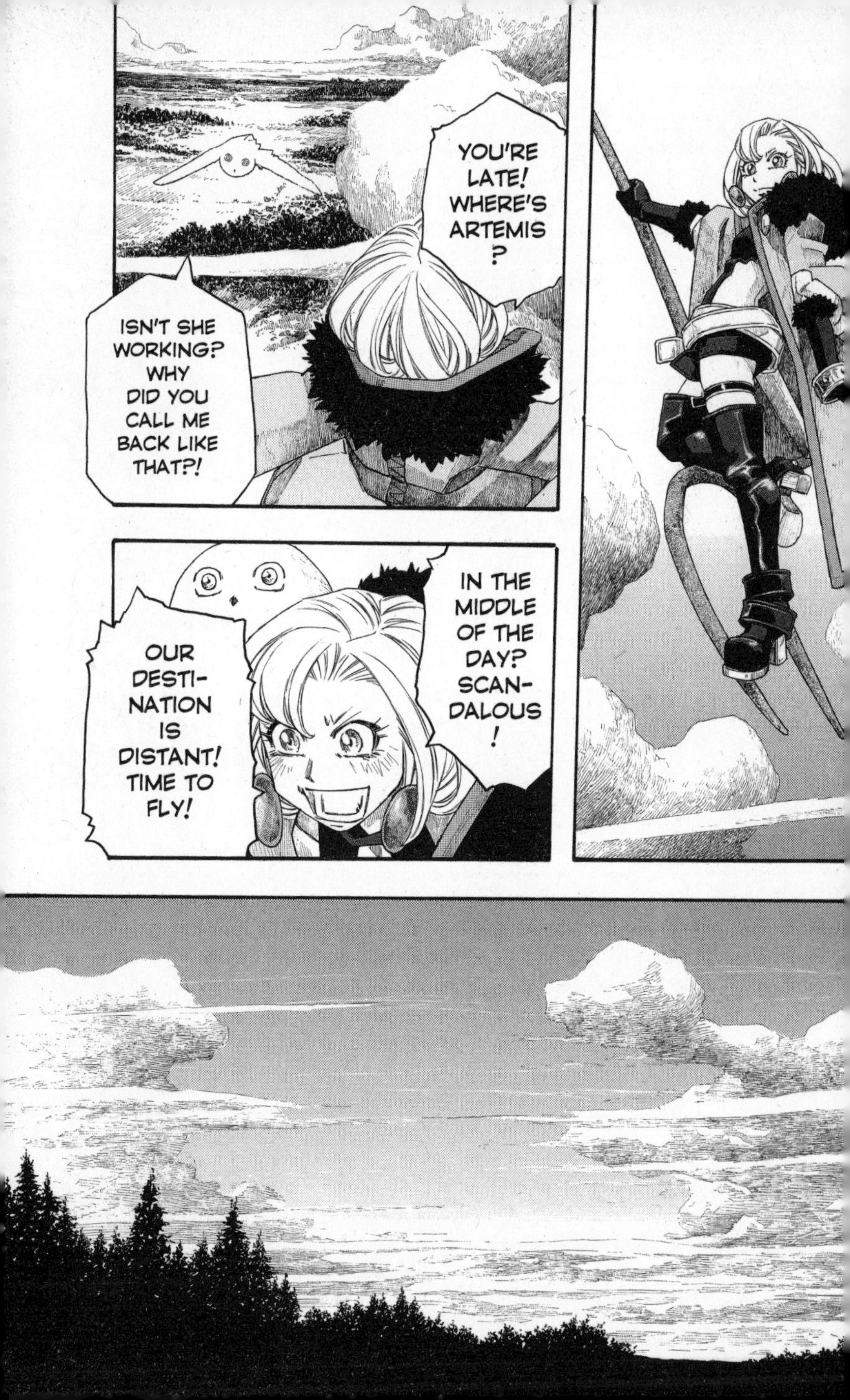
YOU'RE LATE! WHERE'S ARTEMIS?
ISN'T SHE WORKING? WHY DID YOU CALL ME BACK LIKE THAT?!
IN THE MIDDLE OF THE DAY? SCANDALOUS!
OUR DESTINATION IS DISTANT! TIME TO FLY!

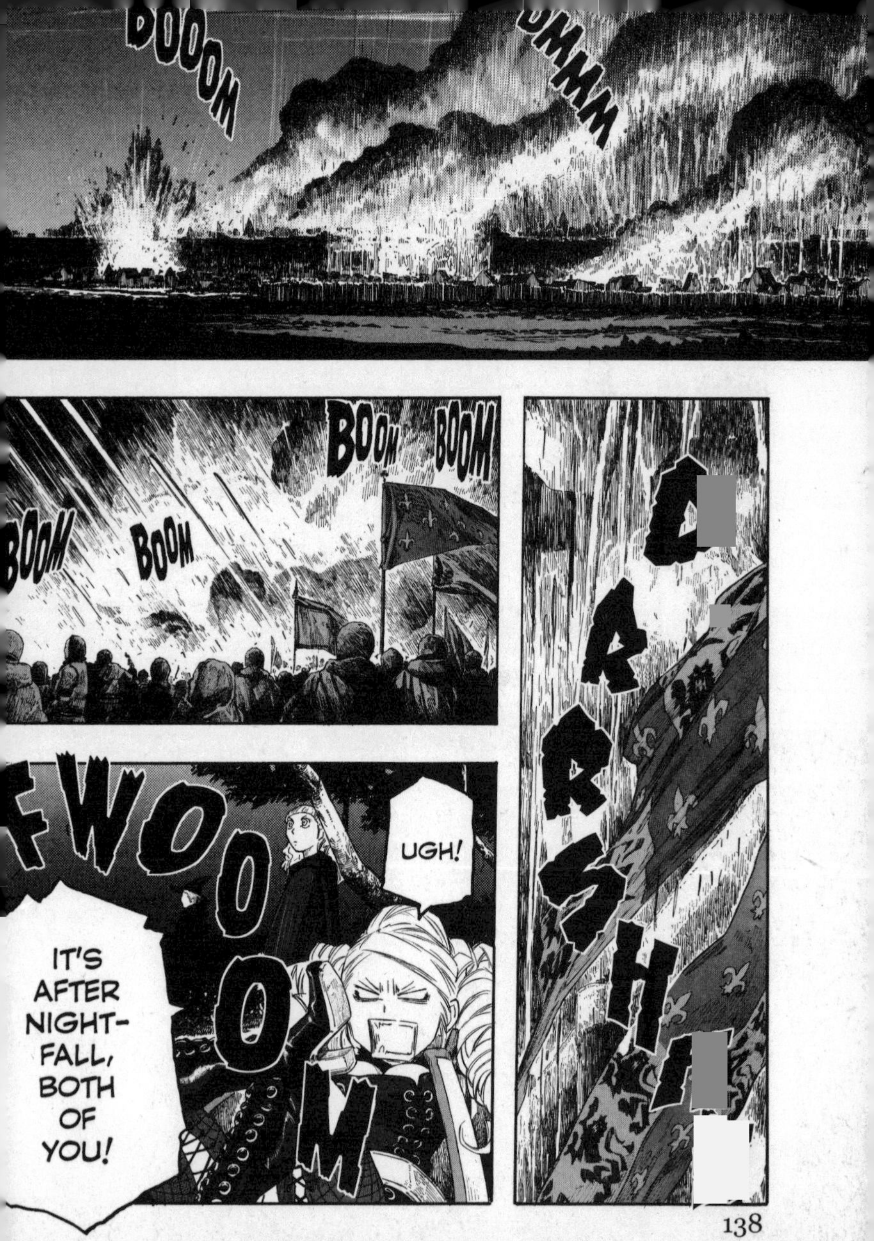
BOOOM
MMMM
CRASH
BOOM
BOOM
BOOM
BOOM
FWOOOOM
UGH!
IT'S AFTER NIGHT-FALL, BOTH OF YOU!

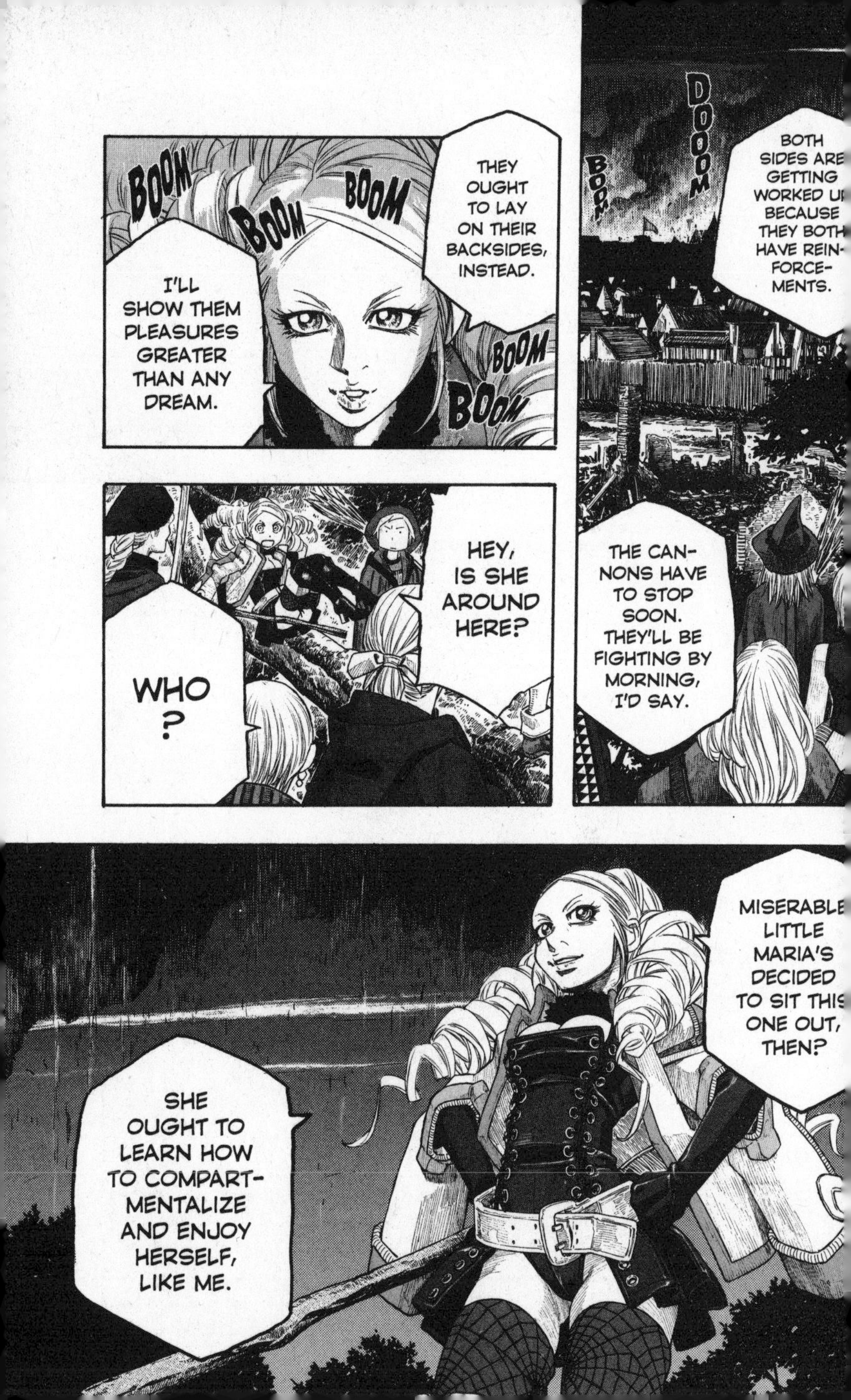
DOOOOM
BOOM
BOTH SIDES ARE GETTING WORKED UP BECAUSE THEY BOTH HAVE REIN-FORCE-MENTS.
THE CAN-NONS HAVE TO STOP SOON. THEY'LL BE FIGHTING BY MORNING, I'D SAY.
BOOM BOOM BOOM
THEY OUGHT TO LAY ON THEIR BACKSIDES, INSTEAD.
I'LL SHOW THEM PLEASURES GREATER THAN ANY DREAM.
BOOM BOOM
HEY, IS SHE AROUND HERE?
WHO ?
MISERABLE LITTLE MARIA'S DECIDED TO SIT THIS ONE OUT, THEN?
SHE OUGHT TO LEARN HOW TO COMPART-MENTALIZE AND ENJOY HERSELF, LIKE ME.

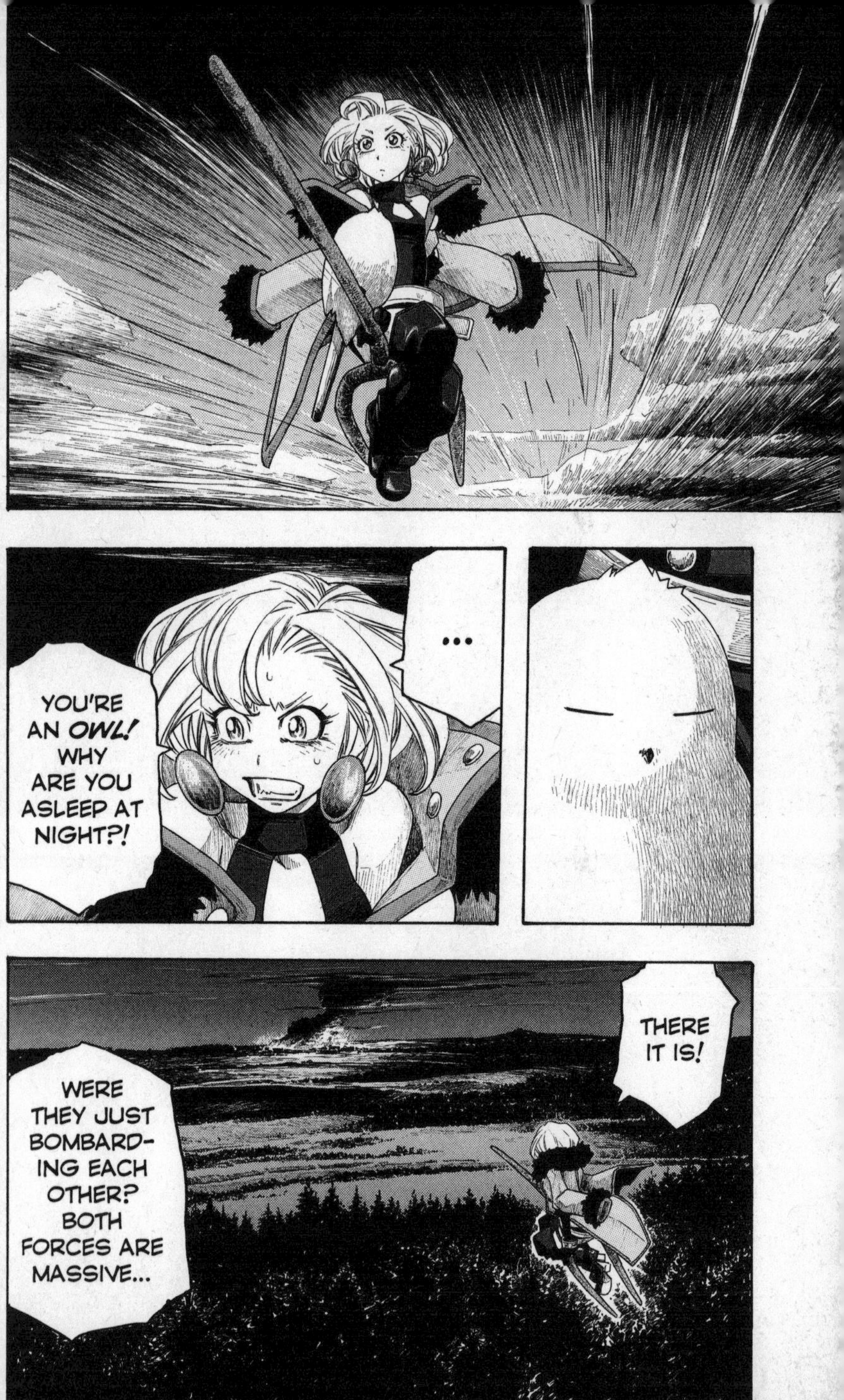
...
YOU'RE AN *OWL!* WHY ARE YOU ASLEEP AT NIGHT?!
THERE IT IS!
WERE THEY JUST BOMBARD-ING EACH OTHER? BOTH FORCES ARE MASSIVE...

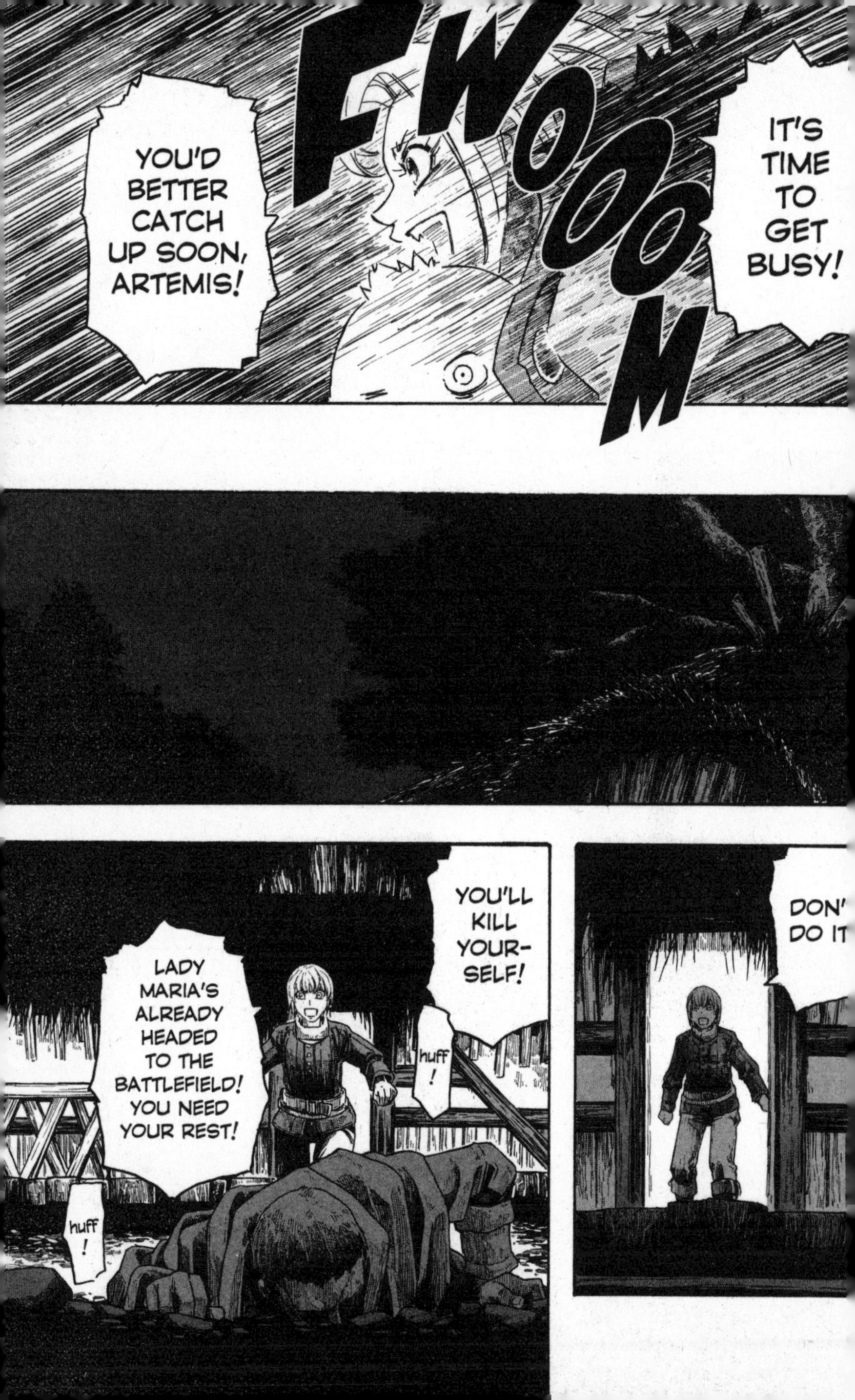
IT'S TIME TO GET BUSY!
FWOOOOM
YOU'D BETTER CATCH UP SOON, ARTEMIS!
DON' DO IT
YOU'LL KILL YOUR-SELF!
huff!
LADY MARIA'S ALREADY HEADED TO THE BATTLEFIELD! YOU NEED YOUR REST!
huff!

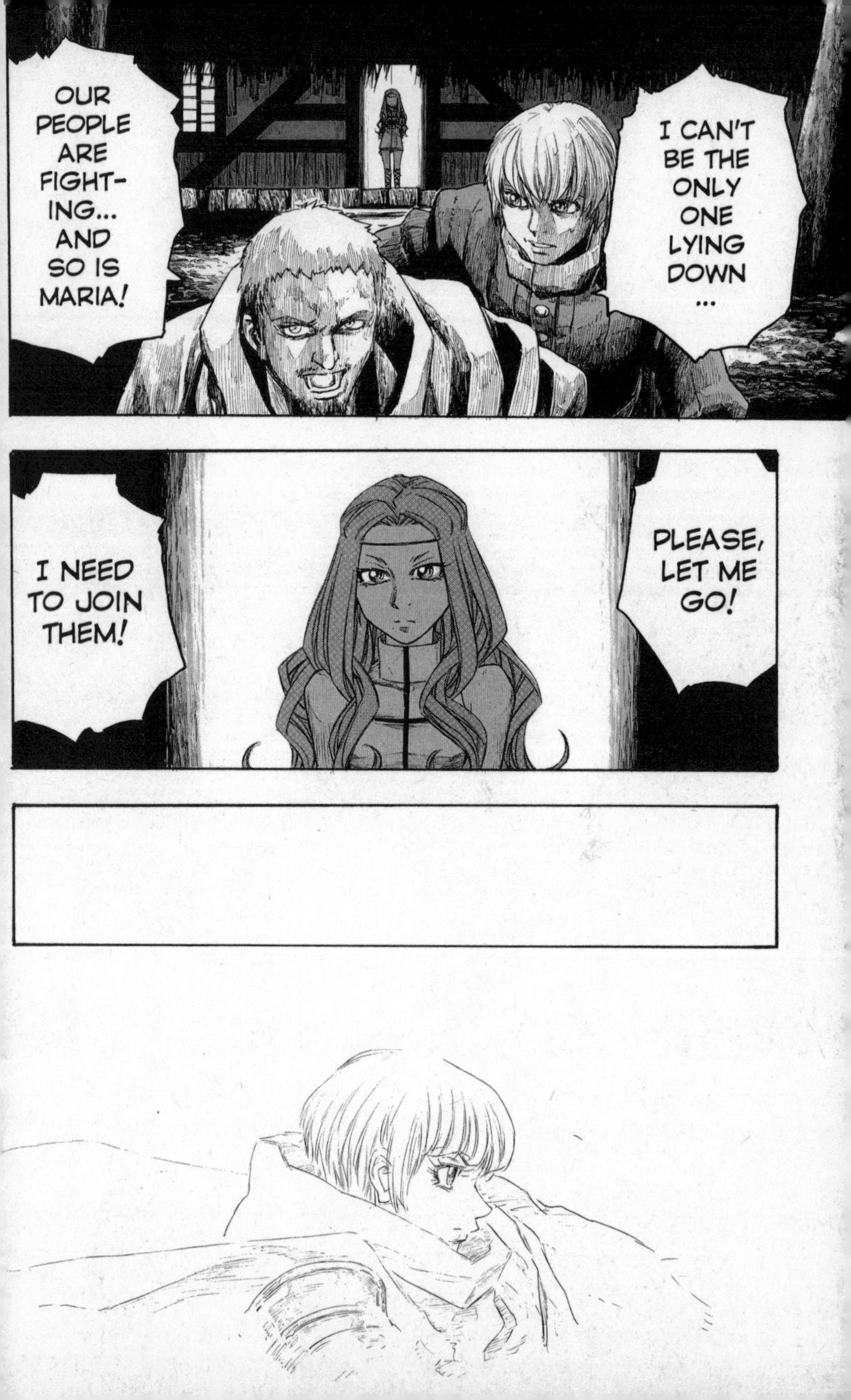
I CAN'T BE THE ONLY ONE LYING DOWN ...
OUR PEOPLE ARE FIGHTING... AND SO IS MARIA!
PLEASE, LET ME GO!
I NEED TO JOIN THEM!

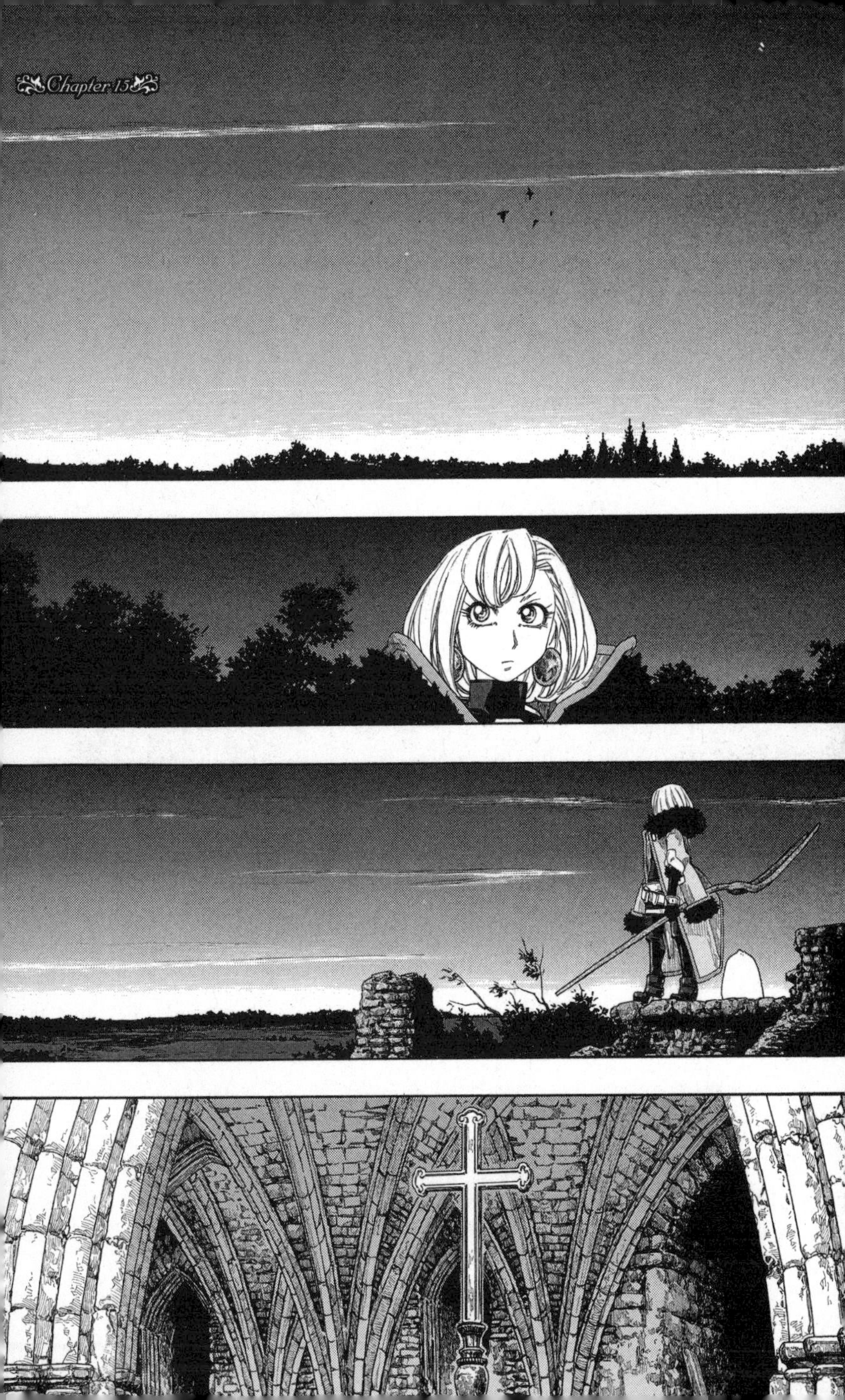
Chapter 15

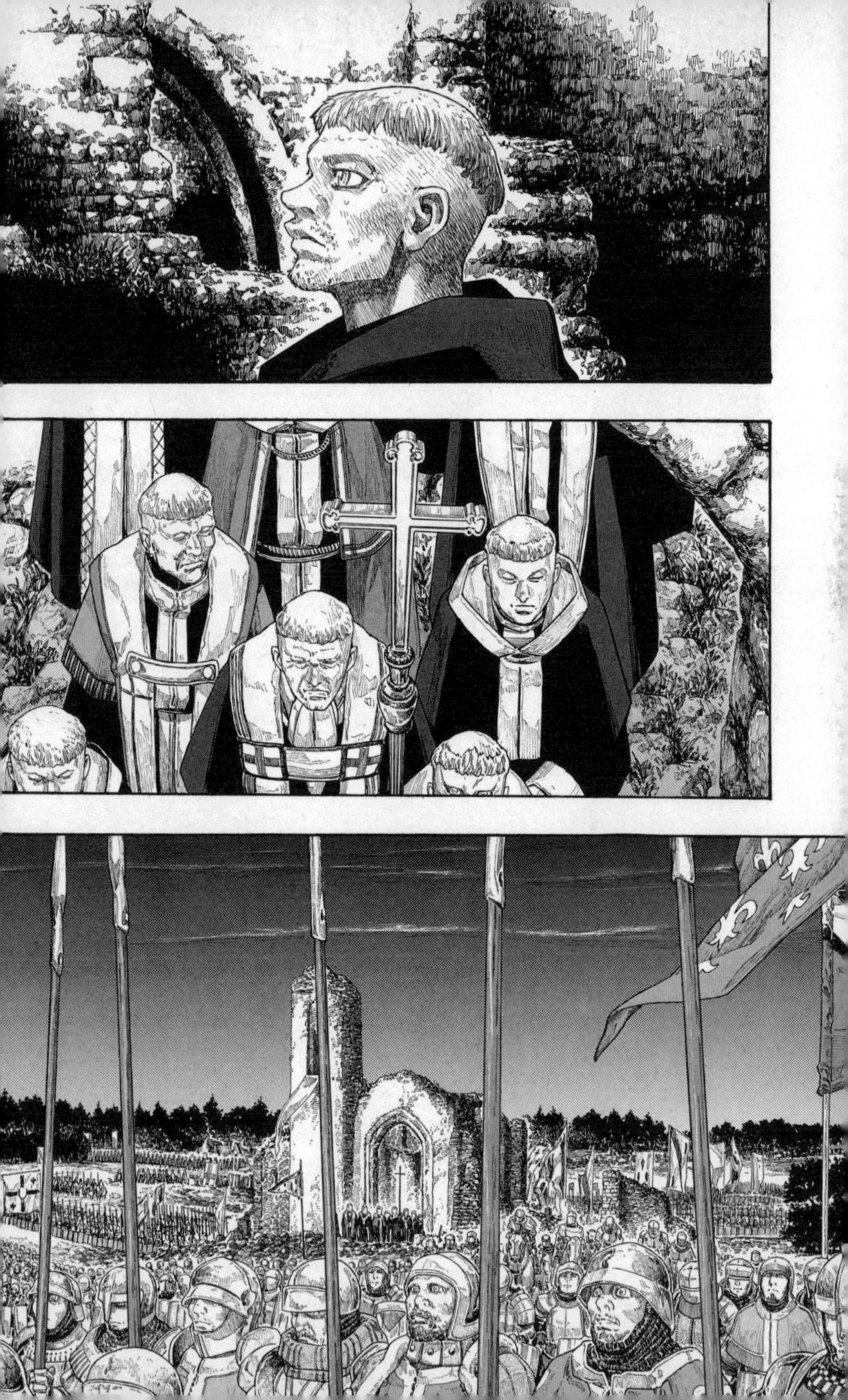

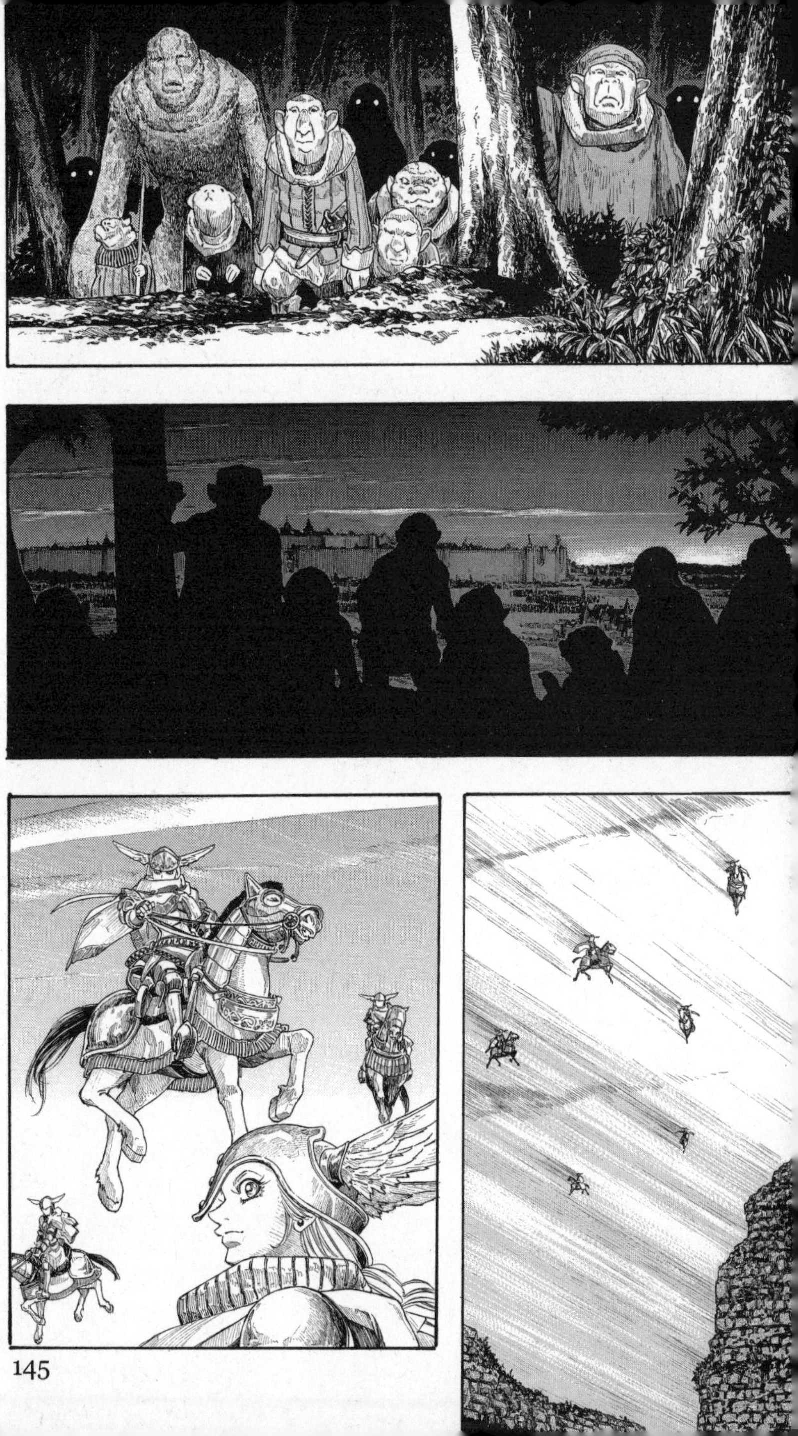

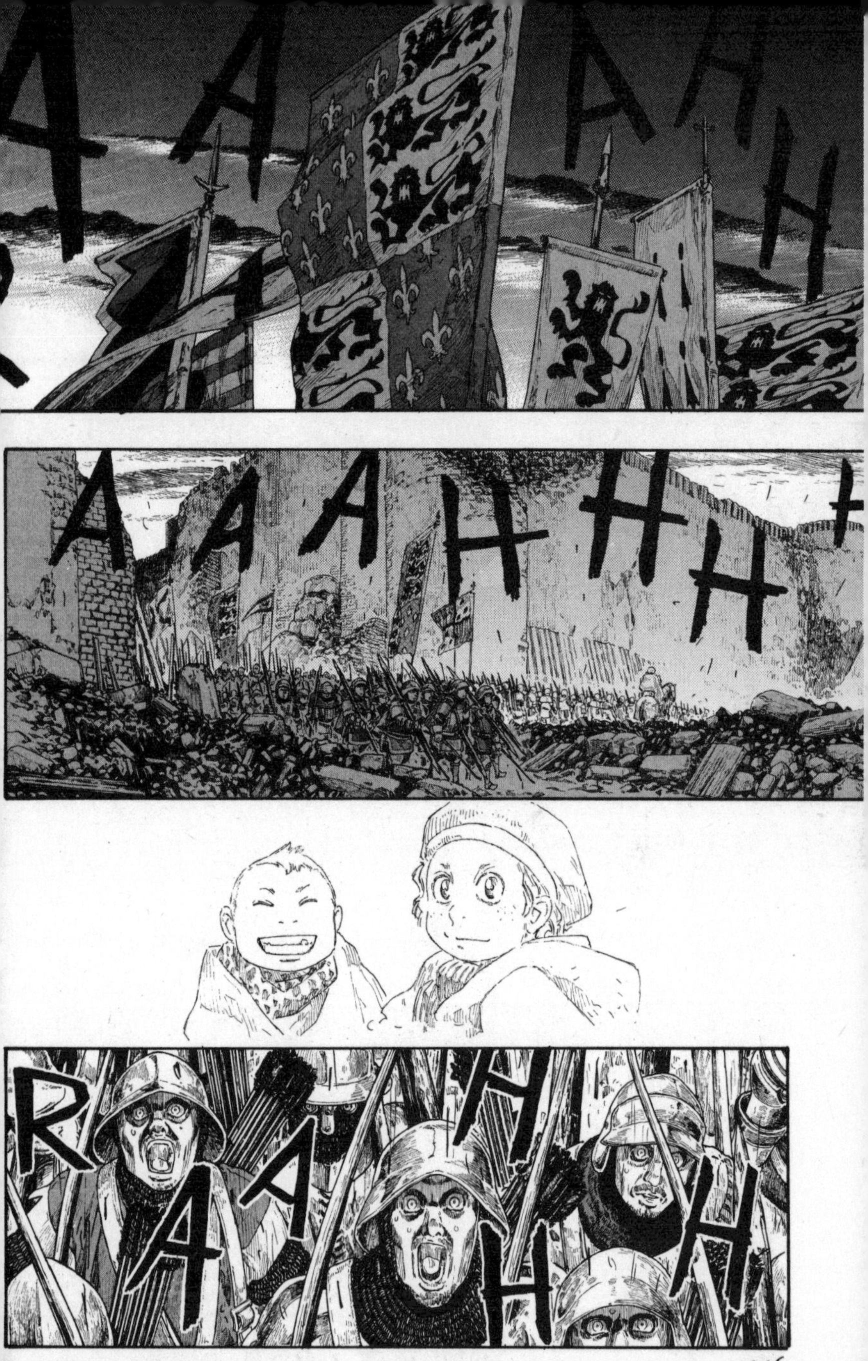
AAAAHH
AAAHHHH
RAAHHHH

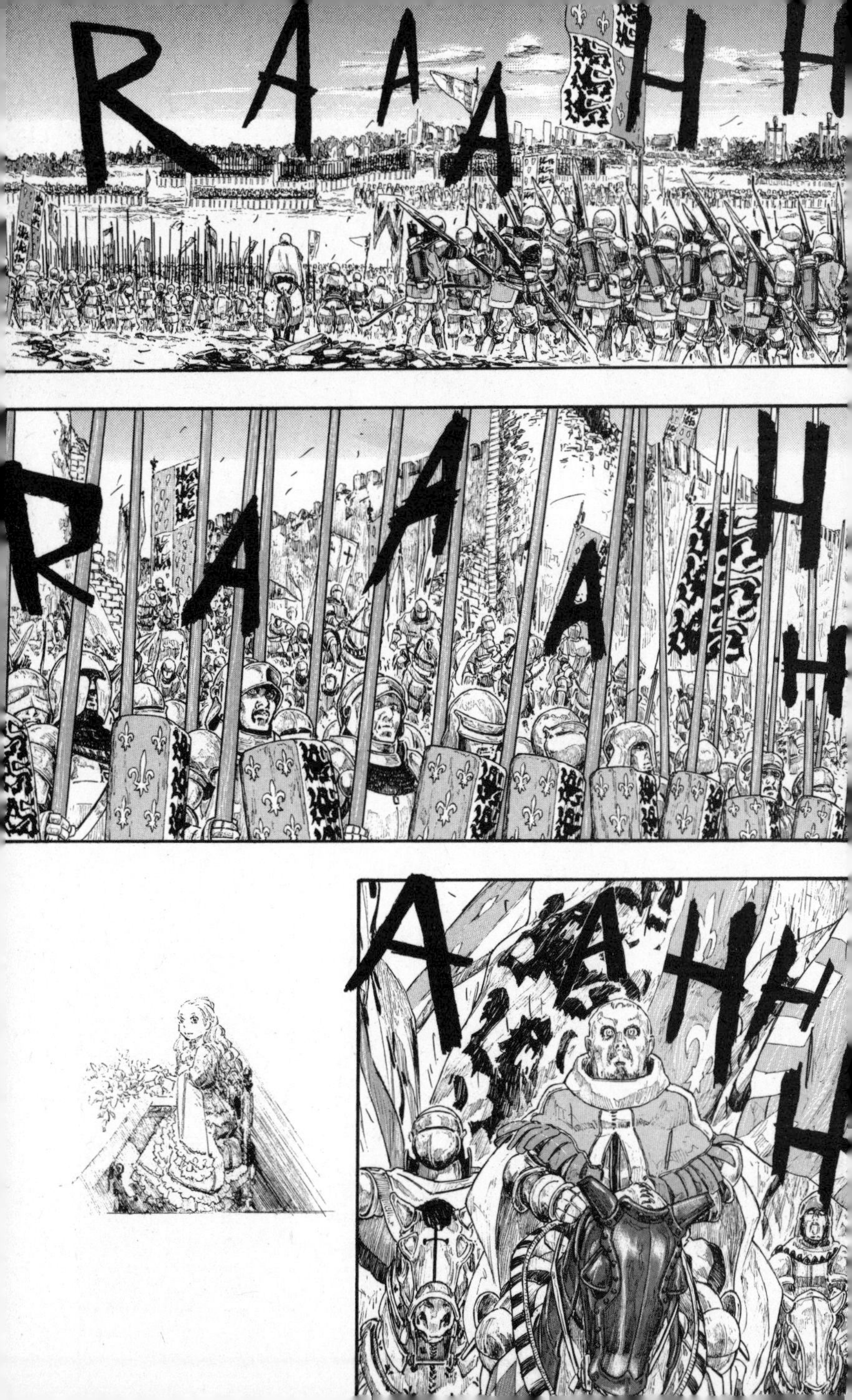
RAAAHH
RAAAHH
AAHHH

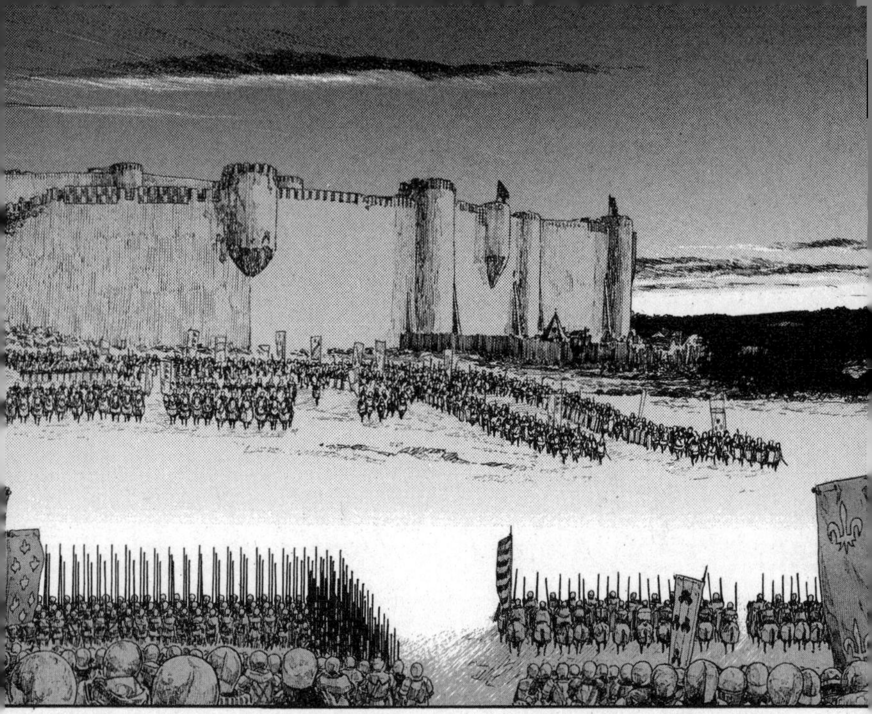
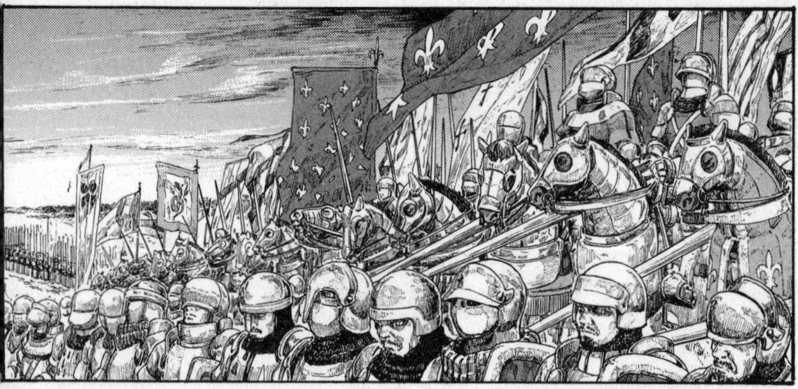
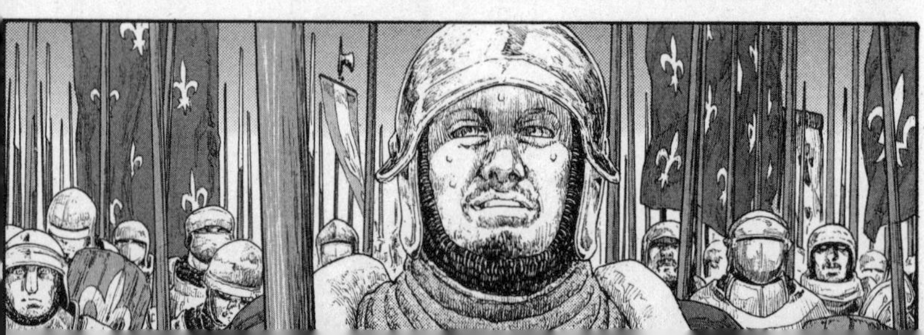

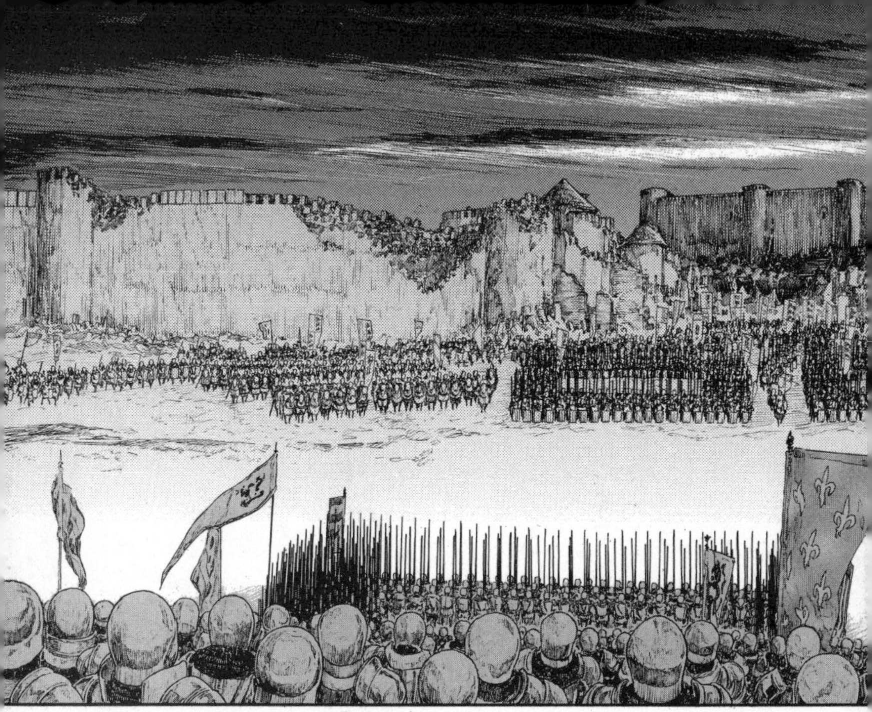

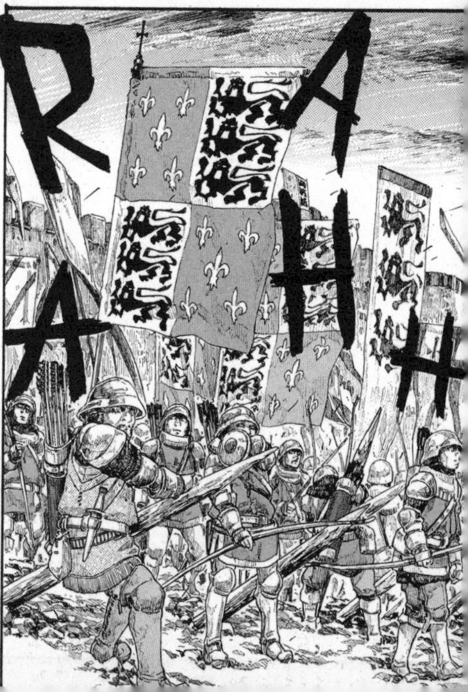
RAAHH

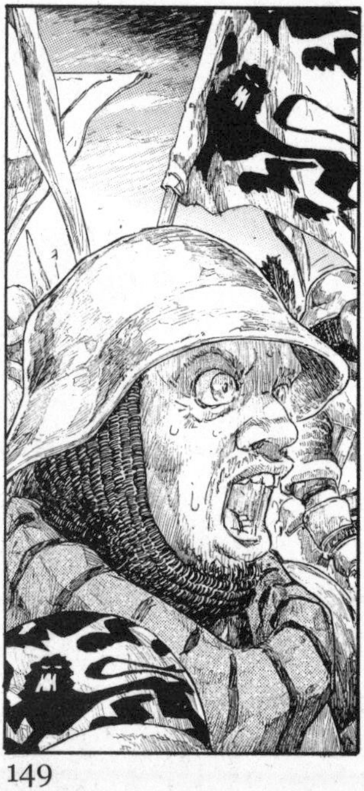

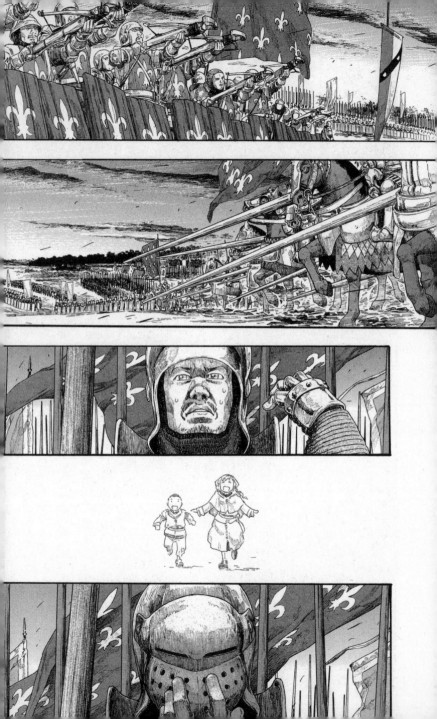

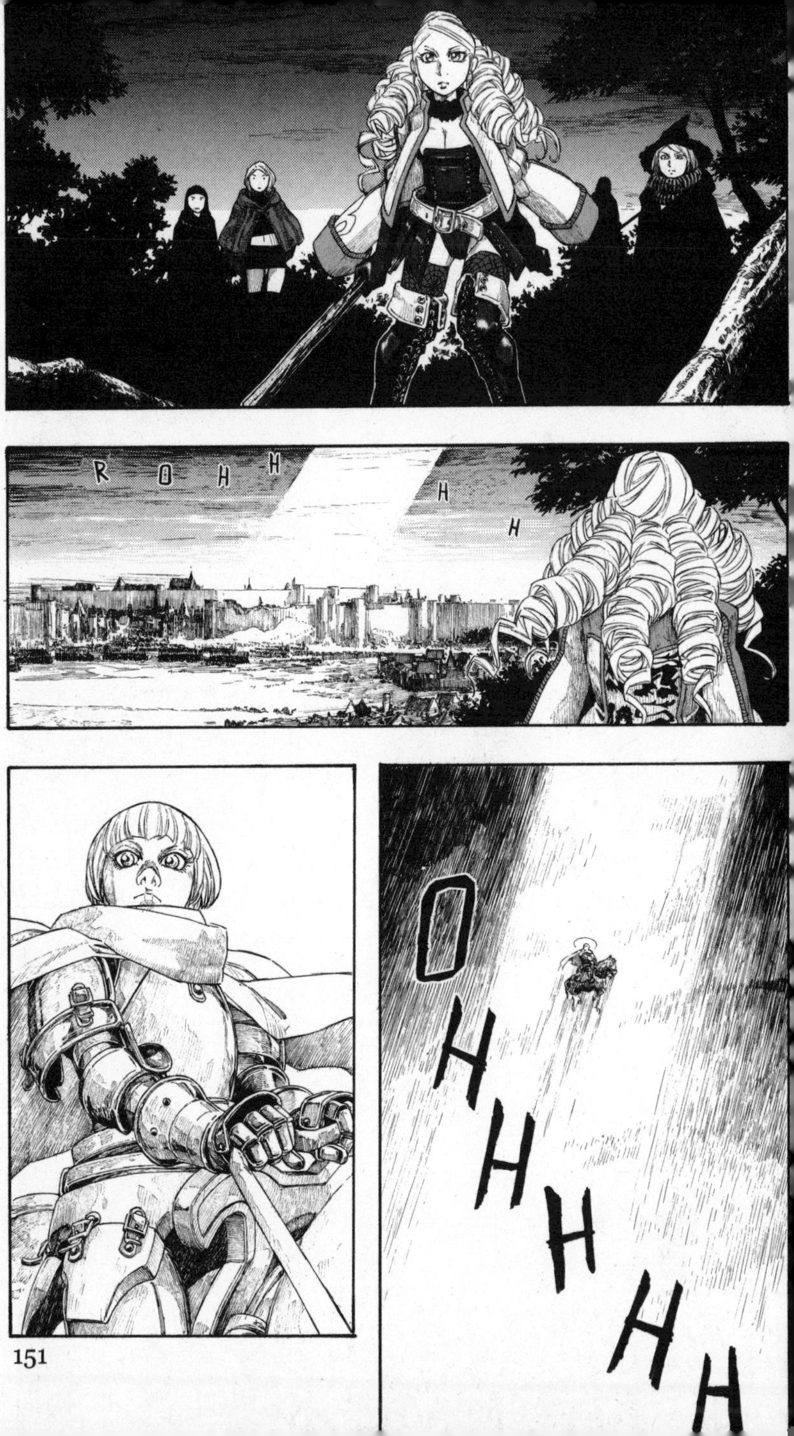
ROHHHH
OHHHHHH

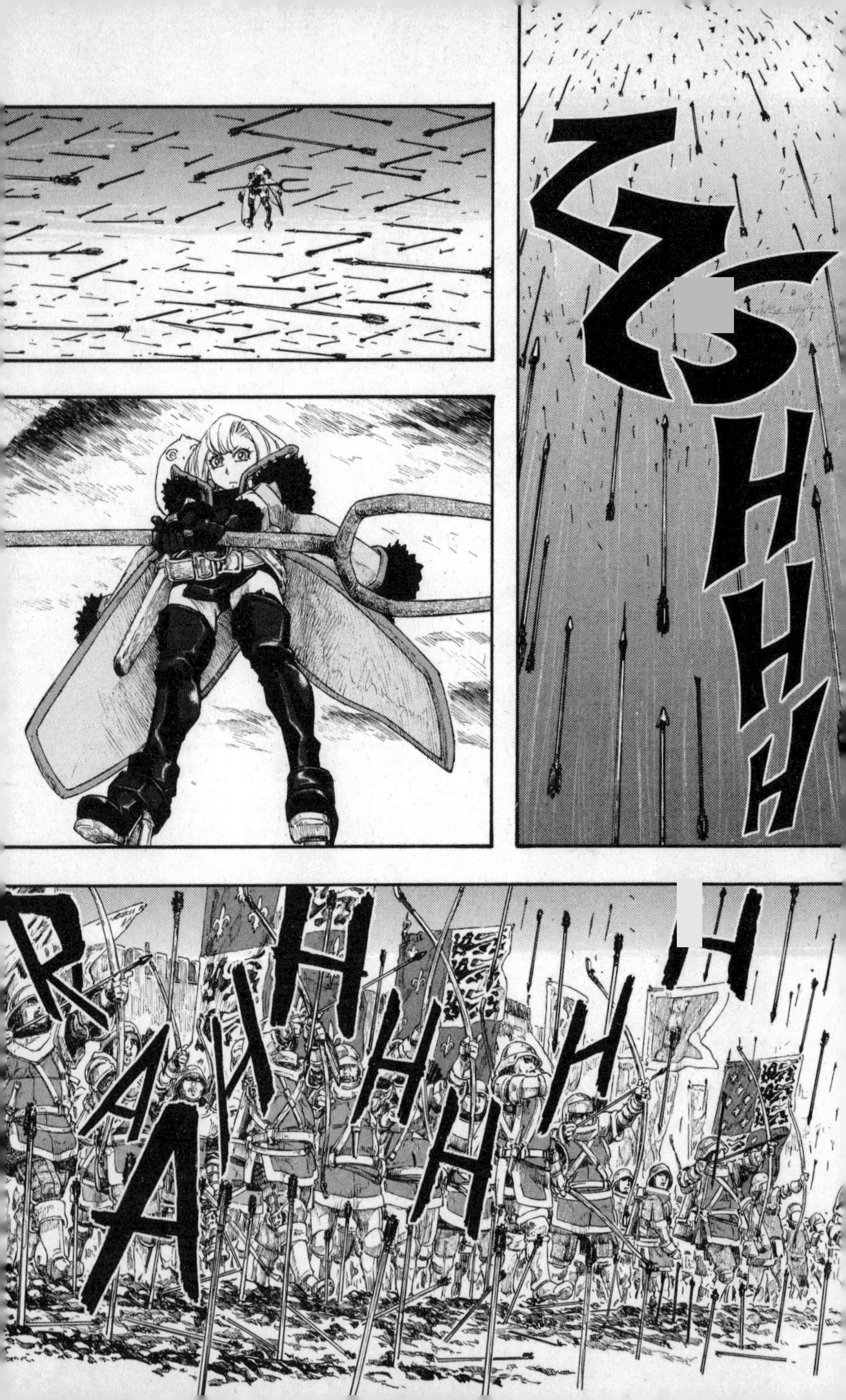
ZZSHHHH
RAAAHHHHHH

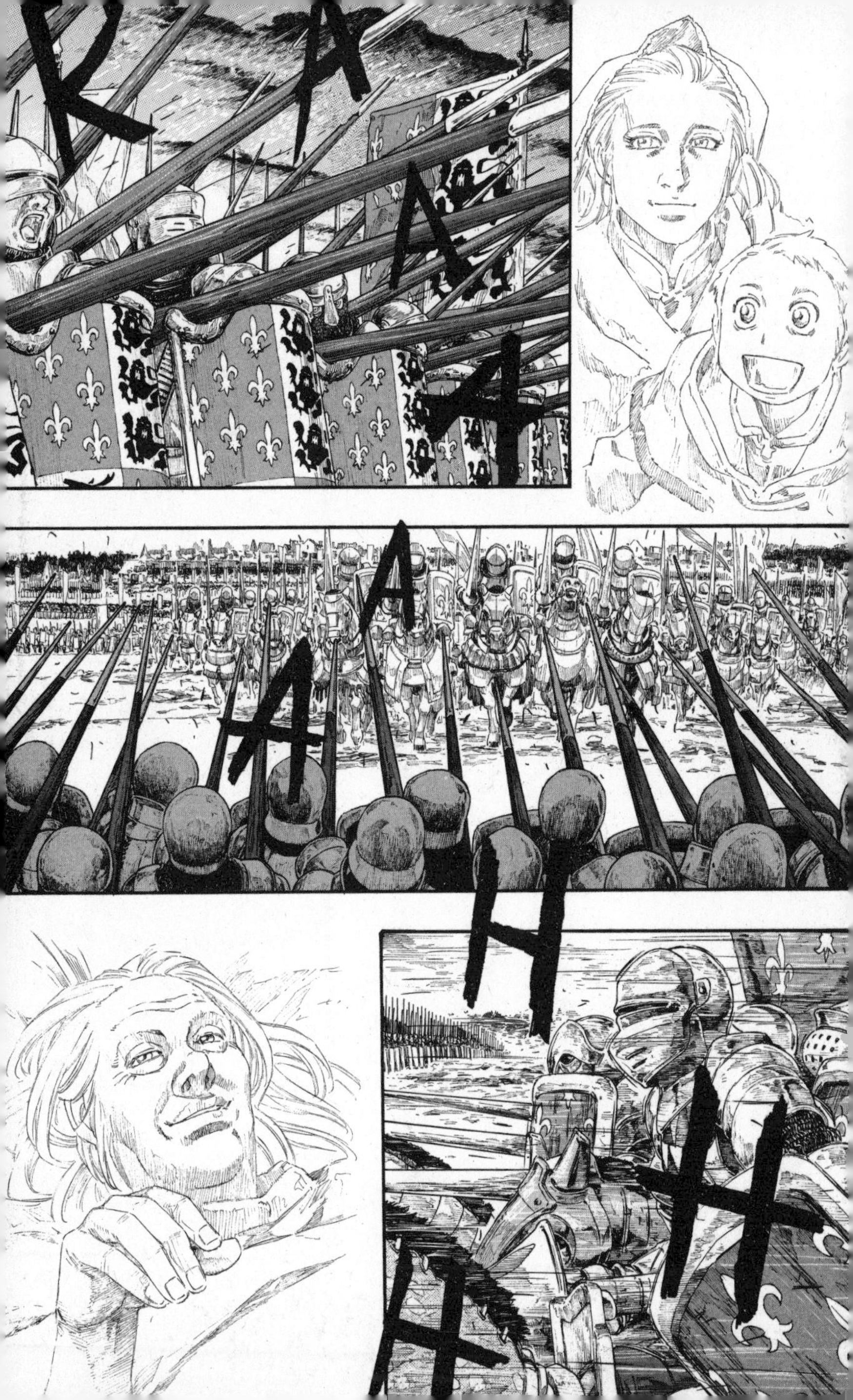
KAAAAAHHHH

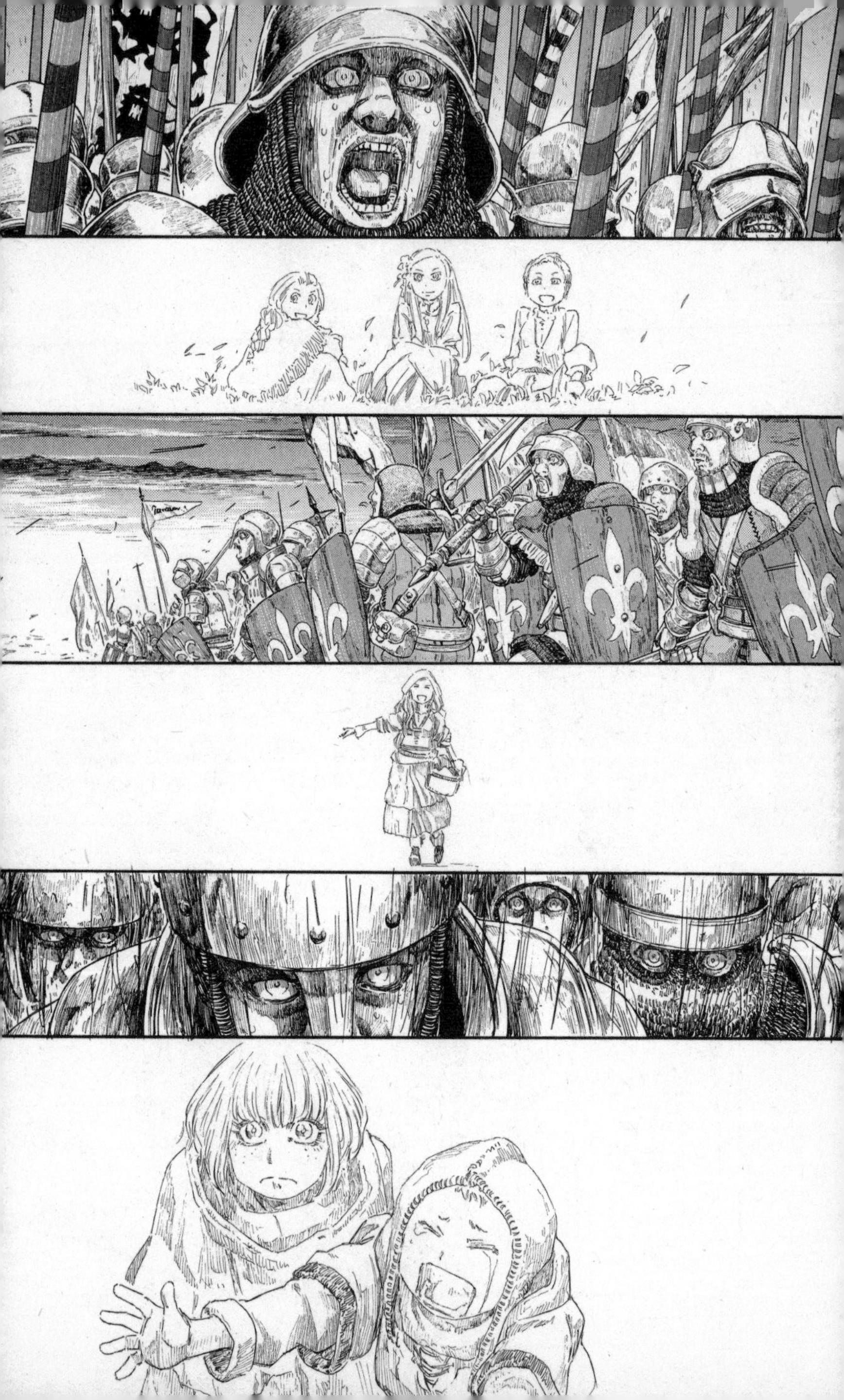

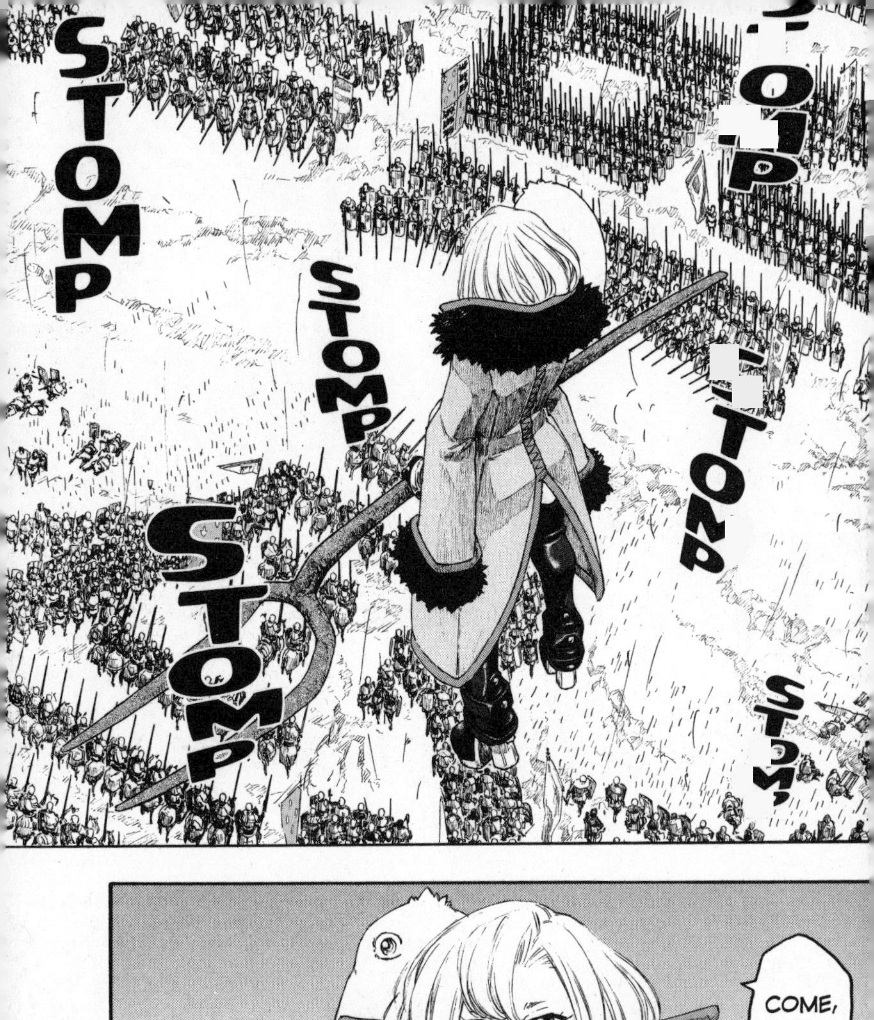
STOMP
STOMP
STOMP
STOMP

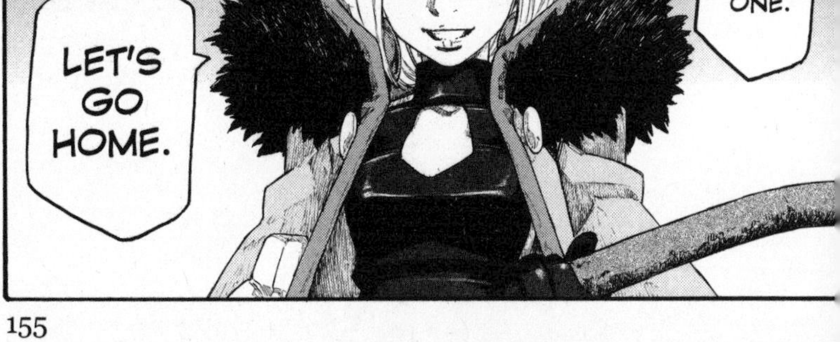
COME, EVERYONE.
LET'S GO HOME.

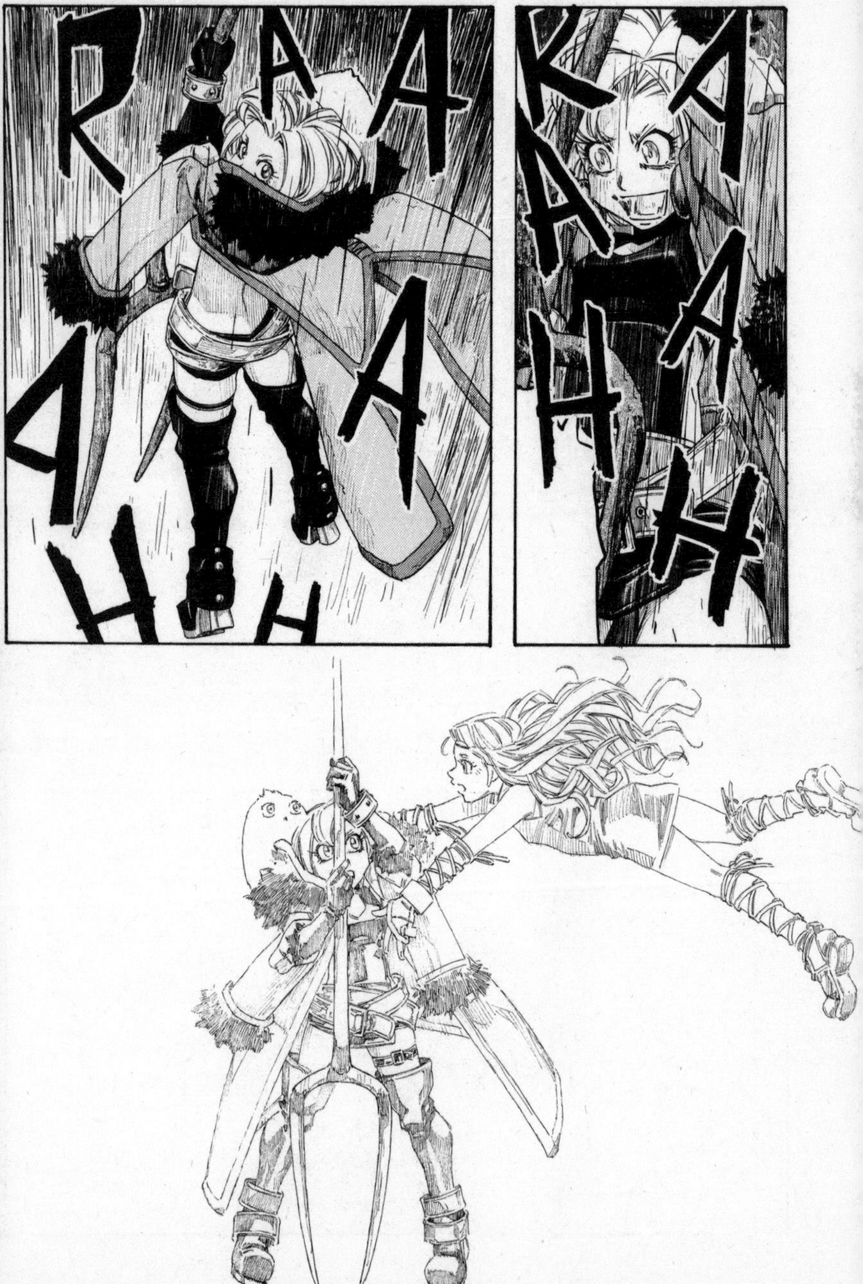
KAAAAHHH
RAAAAHHH

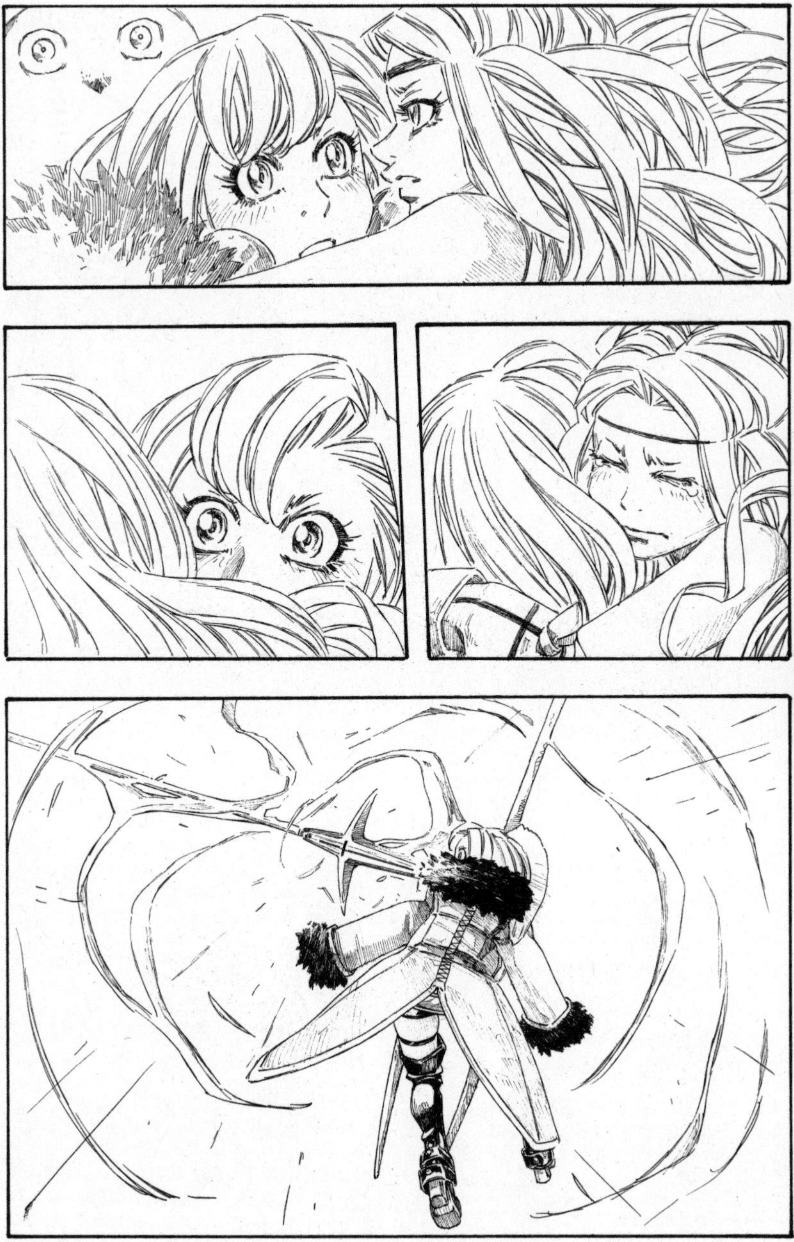

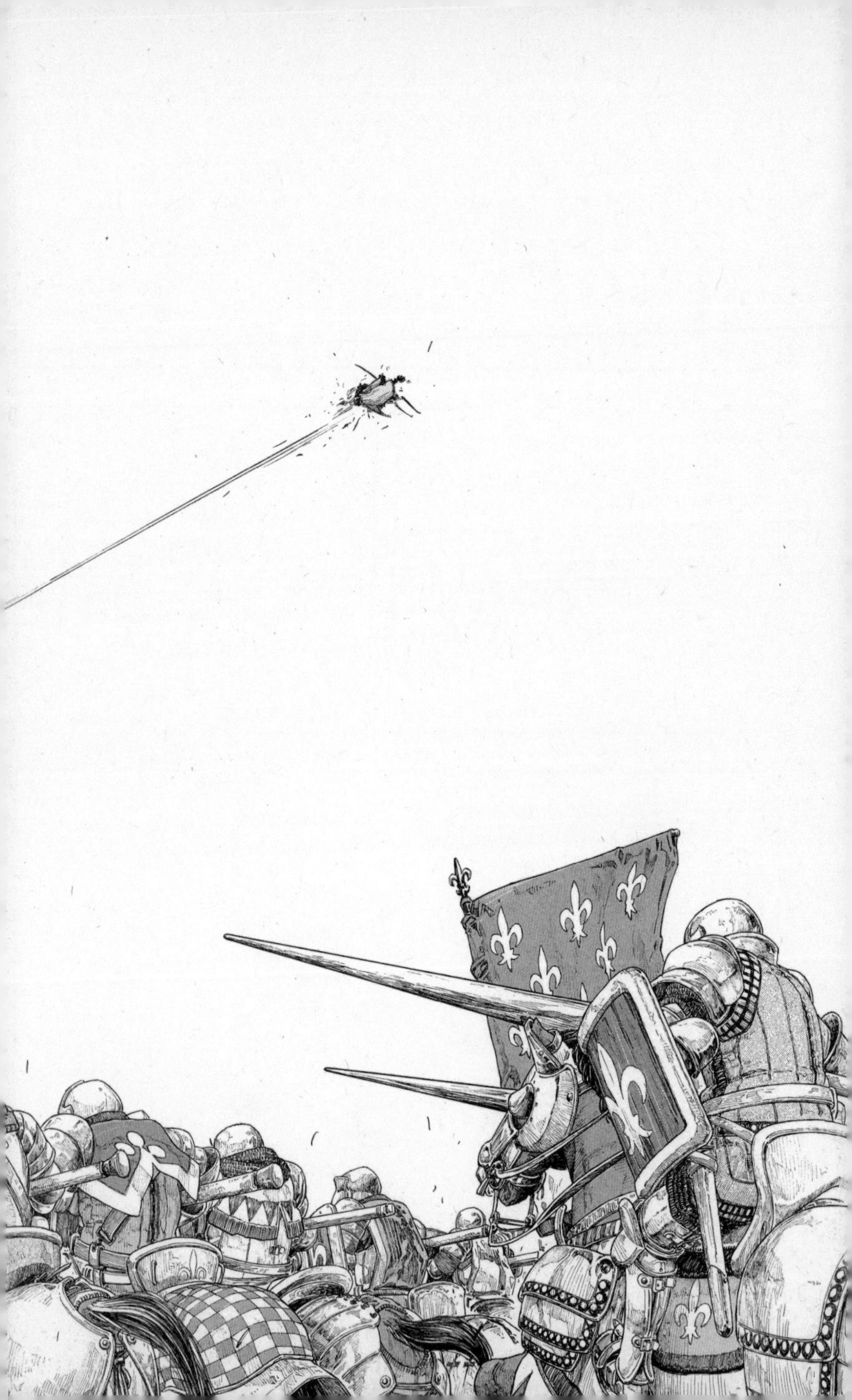

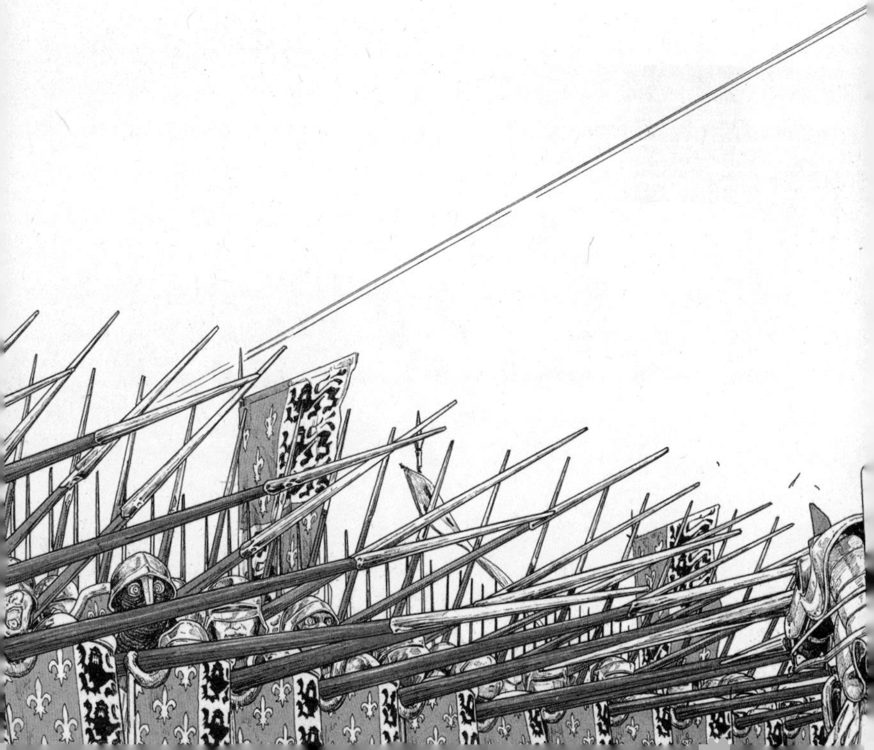

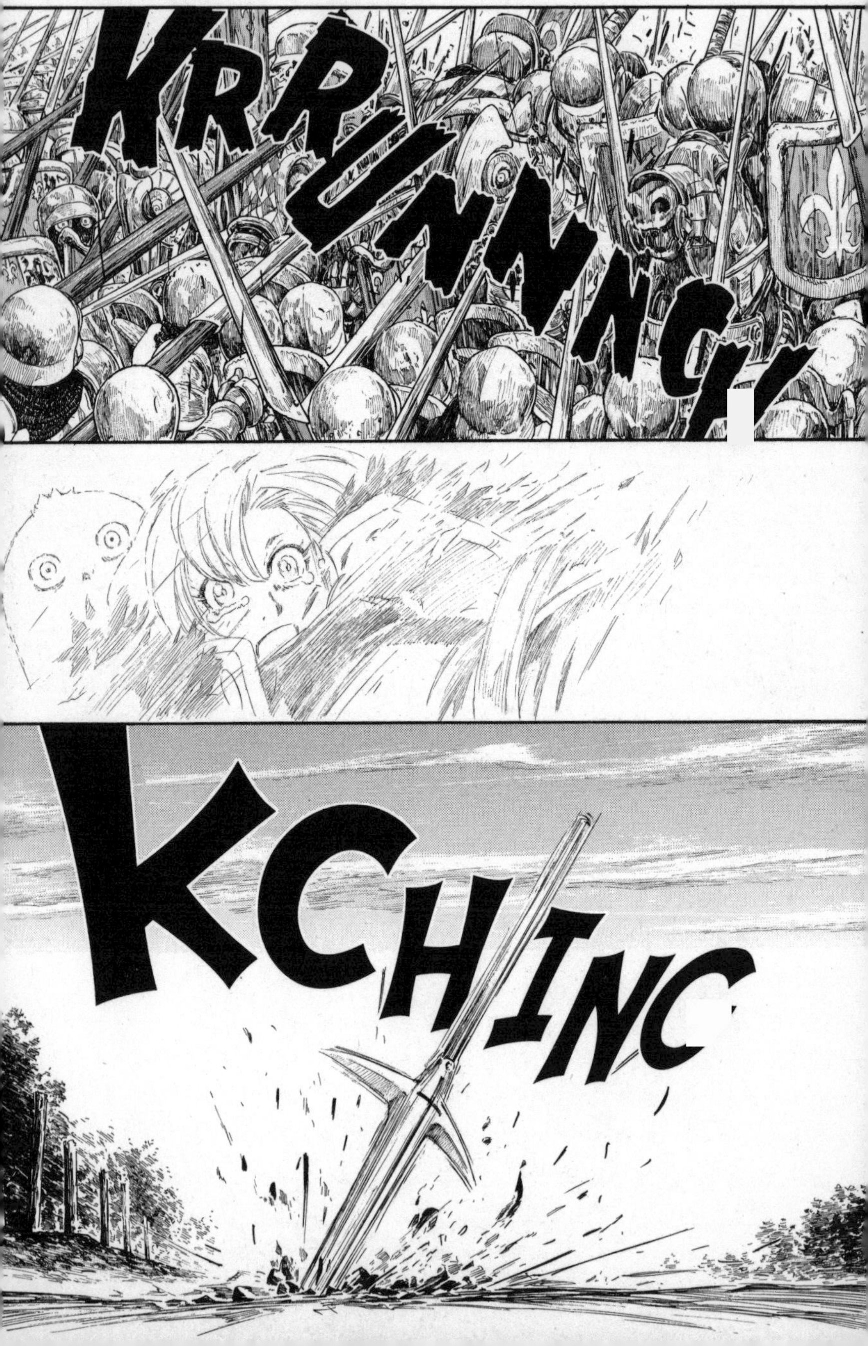
KRRUNNG!!
KCHING

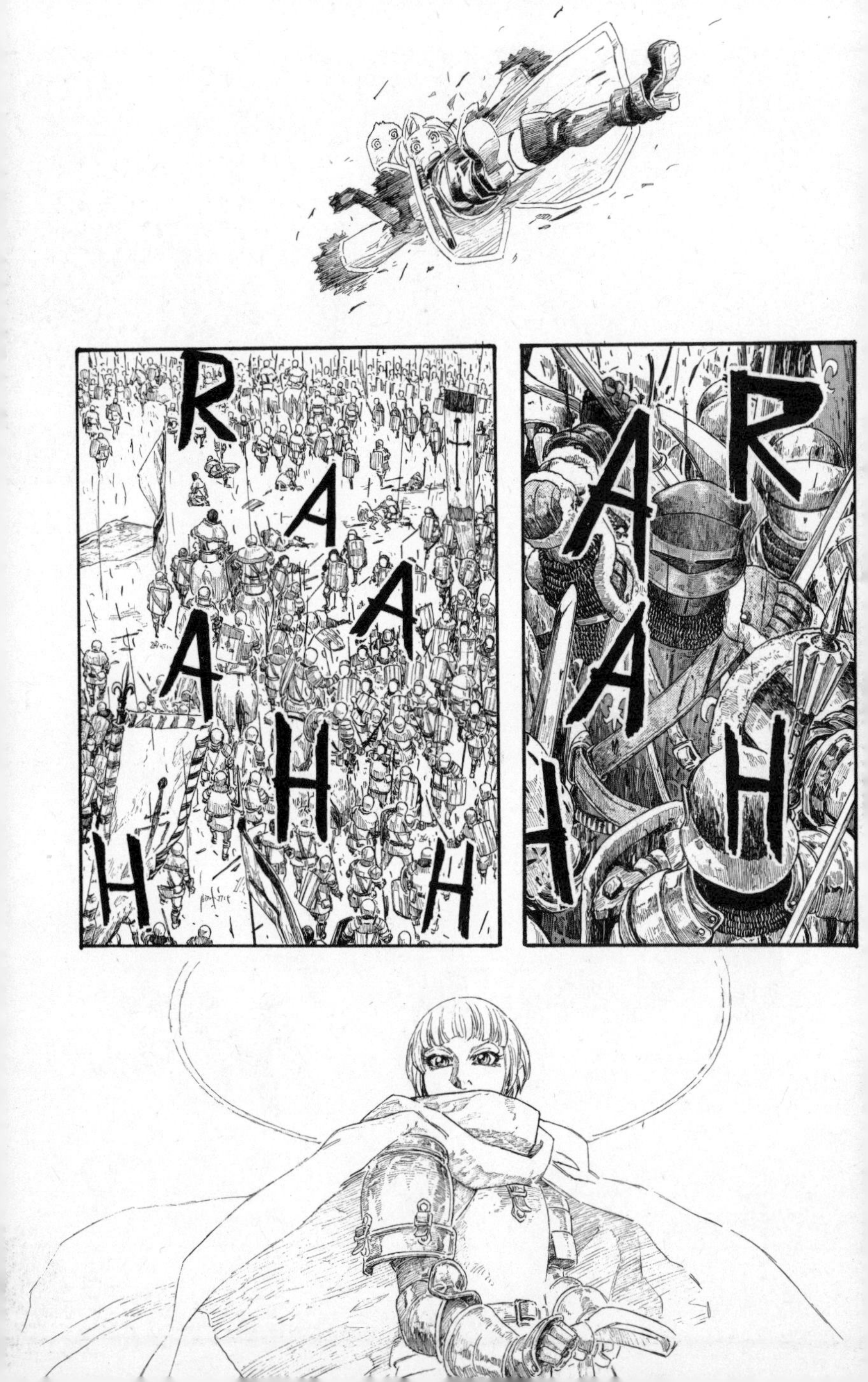
RAAHH
RAAAHHH

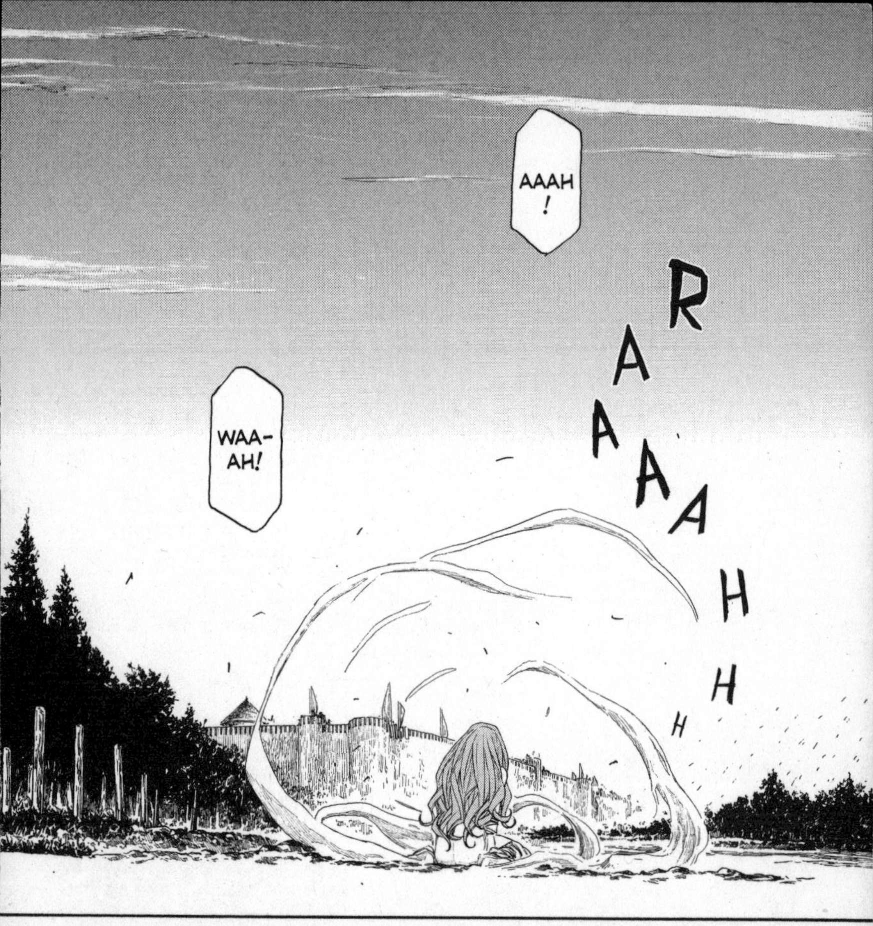
AAAH!
RAAAAAHHH
WAA-AH!

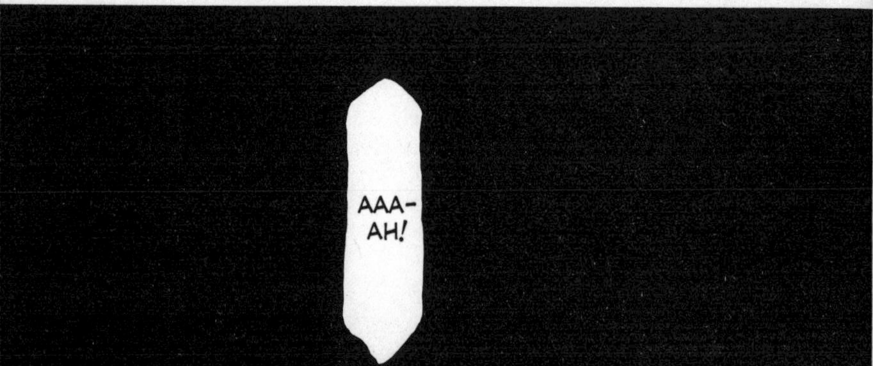
AAA-AH!

Chapter 15 **Rentrons à la maison.**
(Let's go home)

Fin

Hello, I am Ezekiel.

In a scene in Chapter 8, "Virgin Witch and Angel's Servant," the group of mercenaries who attempted to desecrate me were shocked by a stunning vision. Maria and her owls, who were content to sit back and watch my plight unfold, also witnessed this scene.

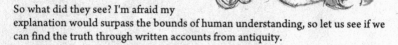

So what did they see? I'm afraid my explanation would surpass the bounds of human understanding, so let us see if we can find the truth through written accounts from antiquity.

Michael gave me my name from the prophet Ezekiel, the namesake of the Book of Ezekiel in the Old Testament. The following passage appears at the beginning of this book:

> And I looked, and, behold, a whirlwind came out of the north, a great cloud, and a fire infolding itself, and a brightness was about it, and out of the midst thereof as it were glowing metal, out of the midst of the fire. Also out of the midst thereof came the likeness of four living creatures. And this was their appearance; they had the likeness of a man. And every one had four faces, and every one had four wings. And their feet were straight feet; and the sole of their feet was like the sole of a calf's foot: and they sparkled like the colour of burnished brass. [...] As for the likeness of the living creatures, their appearance was like burning coals of fire, and like the appearance of lamps: it went up and down among the living creatures; and the fire was bright, and out of the fire went forth lightning. And the living creatures ran and returned as the appearance of a flash of lightning. Now as I beheld the living creatures, behold one wheel upon the earth by the living creatures. [...] And they four had one likeness: and their appearance and their work was as it were a wheel in the middle of a wheel.

The Book of Ezekiel begins abruptly with a description of a vision by Ezekiel the prophet, which ends just as abruptly. There is virtually no lead-in or background, leaving the passage quite mysterious.

Let us put aside the interpretations that "Ezekiel the prophet got a little too excited (ha ha)," or "The worldly church edited the original passage down to this form," and simply examine the text as it is given.

◀1▶ A mighty wind and huge cloud came from the north, surrounded by shining light, and blowing fire.

◀2▶ Something was shining like brass within the fire.

◀3▶ Within that were human-shaped beings that glowed with four wings, four faces, and feet like calves.

◀4▶ Within those beings was a fire like burning coal that also shot lightning.

◀5▶ Beside the beings were wheels, arranged in a way to form wheels within wheels.

In particular, the descriptions in steps one and two seem to match what occurred in the story.

If this is what the mercenaries and Maria saw, then we can find an analogy for this in the last verse of this vision in Ezekiel. In other words:

"This was the appearance of the likeness of the glory of Jehovah."

But what about steps three through five? It is a very mysterious and indecipherable description.

Some claim that this is actually a depiction of an alien or UFO encounter. Apparently, the phrase "wheels within wheels" came to refer to any phenomenon that was mysterious or inscrutable.

Raphael produced a painting called *Ezekiel's Vision.* It is indeed fashioned after the description that appears in the Book of Ezekiel. This is Raphael's interpretation of the scene, and it might prove enlightening to anyone interested.

Pardon me? "What's the point?"
How should I know that?!

At any rate, the one thing we know for certain is that the sight was so astonishing and confounding that everyone present, including me, fell unconscious. Whether it was the glory of the Lord, or the advent of some gigantic spaceship, God only knows.

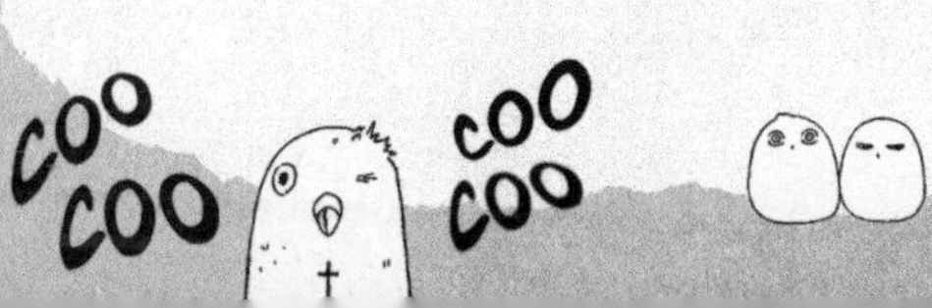
COO
COO
COO
COO

Sorcière de gré, pucelle de force, page 1
French for "Witch by Choice, Maiden by Force." Pucelle means maiden, but La Pucelle (d'Orleans) was also the nickname of Joan of Arc (aka Jeanne d'Arc).

Chevauchée, page 23
A medieval form of "scorched earth" tactics that attempted to do as much damage as possible to enemy territory by riding forth with mounted troops in a lightning strike, burning and pillaging farmland and towns as they went. Though it was considered to be a mercenary's tactic, it was also used quite often by royal forces, and extensively so during the Hundred Years' War, especially by the "Black Prince," Prince Edward of Woodstock. The epithet may have come from his reputation for brutal tactics toward the French during the war.

Chevalier, page 33
The French form of the word "cavalier": a knight.

Beaufort, page 46
Referring to Henry Beaufort, the Bishop of Winchester from 1404 until his death in 1447. Beaufort was an extremely powerful and influential figure within the government of England during this time, and was actually related to the English royalty as a member of the Plantagenet line, making him a target of criticism for holding powerful positions in both church and state.

Arthur de Richemont, page 63
Also known as Arthur III, the Duke of Brittany, a feudal duchy along the northwest coast of modern-day France. He was a notable military figure during the Hundred Years' War who ultimately helped bring the conflict to a close by winning some of the final battles that drove the English from France.

Leviathan, page 95
An enormous sea monster as originally described in the Old Testament. It has been depicted in many ways since, such as a giant sea serpent or a whale (as in Moby-Dick), in countless books, comics, video games, and so on.

Golgotha, page 96
The hill outside of Jerusalem where Jesus was crucified in the Bible.

Preview

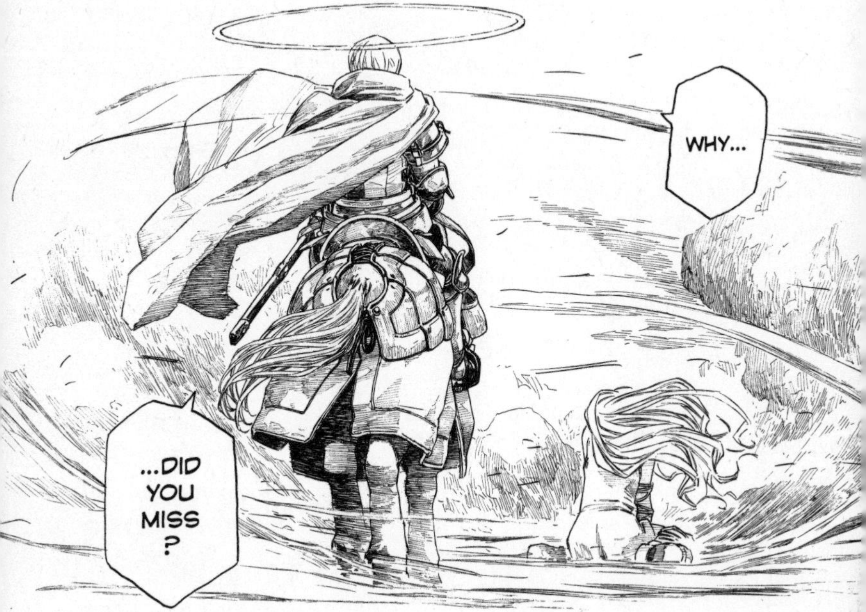
WHY...
...DID YOU MISS?

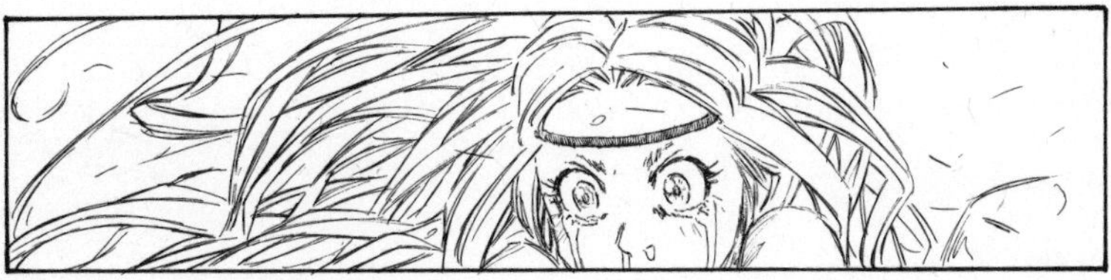

Maria
THE VIRGIN WITCH

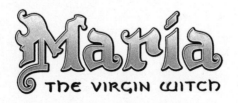

Maria the Virgin Witch volume 2 is a work of fiction. Names, characters, places, and incidents are the products of the author's imagination or are used fictitiously. Any resemblance to actual events, locales, or persons, living or dead, is entirely coincidental.

A Kodansha Comics Trade Paperback Original.

Maria the Virgin Witch volume 2 copyright © 2011 Masayuki Ishikawa
English translation copyright © 2015 Masayuki Ishikawa

All rights reserved.

Published in the United States by Kodansha Comics, an imprint of Kodansha USA Publishing, LLC, New York.

Publication rights for this English edition arranged through Kodansha Ltd., Tokyo.

First published in Japan in 2011 by Kodansha Ltd., Tokyo, as *Jyunketsu no Maria* volume 2.

ISBN 978-1-63236-081-6

Printed in the United States of America.

www.kodanshacomics.com

9 8 7 6 5 4 3 2 1

Translator: Stephen Paul
Lettering: Evan Hayden
Editing: Ajani Oloye